DEBUSSY IN CONTEXT

Exploring the many dimensions of Debussy's historical significance, this volume provides new perspectives on the life and work of a much-loved composer and considers how social and political contexts shape the way we approach and perform his works today. In short, focused chapters building on recent research, contributors chart the influences, relationships, and performances that shaped Debussy's creativity, and the ways he negotiated the complex social and professional networks of music, literature, art, and performance (on and off the stage) in Belle Époque Paris. It probes Debussy's relationship with some of the most influential '-isms' of his time, including his fascination with early music and with the 'exotic', and assesses his status as a pioneer of musical modernism and his continuing popularity with performers and listeners alike.

SIMON TREZISE was Associate Professor in the Music Department, School of Creative Arts at Trinity College Dublin before his retirement in 2021. He is the author of *Debussy: La Mer* (Cambridge University Press) and editor of *The Cambridge Companion to Debussy* and *The Cambridge Companion to French Music*.

COMPOSERS IN CONTEXT

Understanding and appreciation of musical works is greatly enhanced by knowledge of the context within which their composers lived and worked. Each of these volumes focuses on an individual composer, offering lively, accessible and concise essays by leading scholars on the many contexts – professional, political, intellectual, social and cultural – that have a bearing on his or her work. Biographical and musical influences, performance and publishing history and the creative afterlife of each composer's work are also addressed, providing readers with a multifaceted view of how the composers' output and careers were shaped by the world around them.

Titles in the Series
Brahms in Context edited by Natasha Loges and Katy Hamilton
Mozart in Context edited by Simon P. Keefe
The Beatles in Context edited by Kenneth Womack
Richard Strauss in Context edited by Morten Kristiansen and Joseph E. Jones
Stravinsky in Context edited by Graham Griffiths
Mahler in Context edited by Charles Youmans
Liszt in Context edited by Joanne Cormac
Benjamin Britten in Context edited by Vicki P. Stroeher and Justin Vickers
Messiaen in Context edited by Robert Sholl
Puccini in Context edited by Alexandra Wilson
Vaughan Williams in Context edited by Julian Onderdonk and Ceri Owen
Wagner in Context edited by David Trippett
Leonard Bernstein in Context edited by Elizabeth A. Wells
Debussy in Context edited by Simon Trezise

DEBUSSY IN CONTEXT

EDITED BY
SIMON TREZISE
Formerly of Trinity College Dublin

Shaftesbury Road, Cambridge CB2 8EA, United Kingdom

One Liberty Plaza, 20th Floor, New York, NY 10006, USA

477 Williamstown Road, Port Melbourne, VIC 3207, Australia

314–321, 3rd Floor, Plot 3, Splendor Forum, Jasola District Centre, New Delhi – 110025, India

103 Penang Road, #05–06/07, Visioncrest Commercial, Singapore 238467

Cambridge University Press is part of Cambridge University Press & Assessment, a department of the University of Cambridge.

We share the University's mission to contribute to society through the pursuit of education, learning and research at the highest international levels of excellence.

www.cambridge.org
Information on this title: www.cambridge.org/9781108472067
DOI: 10.1017/9781108560986

© Cambridge University Press & Assessment 2024

This publication is in copyright. Subject to statutory exception and to the provisions of relevant collective licensing agreements, no reproduction of any part may take place without the written permission of Cambridge University Press & Assessment.

When citing this work, please include a reference to the DOI 10.1017/9781108560986

First published 2024

A catalogue record for this publication is available from the British Library.

Library of Congress Cataloging-in-Publication Data
NAMES: Trezise, Simon, editor.
TITLE: Debussy in context / edited by Simon Trezise.
DESCRIPTION: [1.] | Cambridge, United Kingdom ; New York, NY : Cambridge University Press, 2024. | Series: Composers in context | Includes bibliographical references and index.
IDENTIFIERS: LCCN 2023057348 | ISBN 9781108472067 (hardback) | ISBN 9781108458955 (paperback) | ISBN 9781108560986 (ebook)
SUBJECTS: LCSH: Debussy, Claude, 1862–1918. | Debussy, Claude, 1862–1918 – Friends and associates. | Debussy, Claude, 1862–1918 – Appreciation. | Music – France – Paris – History and criticism. | Paris (France) – Social life and customs. | Paris (France) – History – 1870–1940.
CLASSIFICATION: LCC ML410.D28 D383 2024 | DDC 780.944/361–dc23/eng/20231226
LC record available at https://lccn.loc.gov/2023057348

ISBN 978-1-108-47206-7 Hardback

Cambridge University Press & Assessment has no responsibility for the persistence or accuracy of URLs for external or third-party internet websites referred to in this publication and does not guarantee that any content on such websites is, or will remain, accurate or appropriate.

In Memoriam
David J. Code (1966–2022)
Reader in Music, School of Culture and Creative Arts,
University of Glasgow

Contents

List of Illustrations *page* x
List of Contributors xi
Preface xiii
Notes on the Text xv
List of Abbreviations xvi

PART I PARIS: CITY, POLITICS, AND SOCIETY

1 Paris, the City 3
   Martin Guerpin

2 Paris and the Nation's Politics 16
   Federico Lazzaro

3 Beyond Paris 25
   Lola San Martín Arbide

4 Feminine Beginnings: Women's Critical Perspectives
   on Debussy (1897–1914) 34
   Christopher Moore

5 Consumption and Leisure 45
   H. Hazel Hahn

PART II THE ARTS

6 Debussy's Impressionism Interrogated 59
   Richard Langham Smith

7 Symbolism 69
   François de Médicis

8 Modernism 79
   Michel Duchesneau

9	*Wagnérisme* Steven Huebner	88
10	*Japonisme*, Collecting, and the Expositions Universelles Matthew Brown	98
11	Cross-Currents in Debussy's Creative World Annegret Fauser	106

PART III PEOPLE AND MILIEU

12	Debussy and the Family in Third-Republic France Kimberly White	117
13	Romantic Relationships Marianne Wheeldon	126
14	Relationships with Poets and Other Literary Figures Caroline Potter	135
15	Publishers Denis Herlin	143
16	Composers with Whom Debussy Was Associated Laura Watson	150
17	Music Education and the Prix de Rome Julia Lu and Kenji Fujimura	159

PART IV MUSICAL LIFE: INFRASTRUCTURE AND EARNING A LIVING

18	The Jobbing Composer-Musician Denis Herlin	169
19	Parisian Opera Institutions: A Framework for Creation Hervé Lacombe	177
20	Société Nationale and Other Institutions Michael Strasser	185
21	Debussy *Noctambule* and Parisian Popular Culture Sarah Gutsche-Miller	193
22	Music Criticism and Related Writing in Paris Michel Duchesneau	201

Contents

PART V THE MUSIC OF DEBUSSY'S TIME

23 Composing for Opera and Theatre outside Established Genres 211
    Hervé Lacombe

24 Ballet and Dance 220
    David J. Code

25 Orchestral Music and Symphonic Traditions 230
    Andrew Deruchie

26 Chamber Music 240
    Matthew Brown

27 Song and Choral Music 248
    David J. Code

28 The Piano 258
    Gurminder Kaur Bhogal

PART VI PERFORMERS, RECEPTION, AND POSTERITY

29 Performers and Performance 271
    Simon Trezise

30 Early Music 281
    Catrina Flint de Médicis

31 Performance Today: Hearing Debussy Anew on Period
    Instruments 291
    Brian Hart

32 Debussy Today 299
    Matthew Brown

Recommendations for Further Reading and Research 311
Index 324

Illustrations

1.1	Poster promoting Les Marionettes Minstrels at the Folies-Bergère (between 1882 and 1888) [Illustrator unknown], Musée Carnavalet, AFF463.	*page* 10
1.2	Poster of the Barnum and Bailey show (Paris, 1901) [Illustrator unknown], Bibliothèque nationale de France, ENT DN-1 (STROBRIDGE2)-ROUL.	13
28.1	Photograph showing Aliquot stringing in a Blüthner grand piano.	265
28.2	Debussy playing Mussorgsky's *Boris Godunov*.	267
32.1	Contrapuntal plan of Debussy, 'Jeux de vagues', *La Mer*, bb. 171–215.	301

Contributors

GURMINDER KAUR BHOGAL, Wellesley College, United States.
MATTHEW BROWN, Eastman School of Music, United States.
DAVID J. CODE, University of Glasgow, Scotland.
ANDREW DERUCHIE, University of Manitoba, Canada.
MICHEL DUCHESNEAU, University of Montreal, Canada.
ANNEGRET FAUSER, University of North Carolina, United States.
CATRINA FLINT DE MÉDICIS, Vanier College, Canada.
KENJI FUJIMURA, Melbourne Conservatorium of Music, Australia.
MARTIN GUERPIN, Paris-Saclay University, RASM-CHCSC, France.
SARAH GUTSCHE-MILLER, University of Toronto, Canada.
HAEJEONG HAZEL HAHN, Seattle University, United States.
BRIAN HART, Northern Illinois University, United States.
DENIS HERLIN, CNRS, France; Royal Northern College of Music, England.
STEVEN HUEBNER, McGill University, Canada.
HERVÉ LACOMBE, University of Rennes 2, France; Institut Universitaire de France.
RICHARD LANGHAM SMITH, Royal College of Music, England.
FEDERICO LAZZARO, University of Fribourg, Switzerland.
JULIA LU, independent scholar, Australia.
FRANÇOIS DE MÉDICIS, University of Montreal, Canada.

CHRISTOPHER MOORE, University of Ottawa, Canada.

CAROLINE POTTER, Royal Birmingham Conservatoire, England.

LOLA SAN MARTÍN ARBIDE, University of Seville, Spain.

MICHAEL STRASSER, Baldwin Wallace University, United States.

SIMON TREZISE, formerly of Trinity College Dublin, Ireland.

LAURA WATSON, Maynooth University, Ireland.

MARIANNE WHEELDON, University of Texas at Austin, United States.

KIMBERLY WHITE, McGill University, Canada.

Preface

Over one hundred years since his death, Debussy's music has lost none of its allure. It continues to communicate with audiences in strikingly different ways, as is demonstrated by his ineffable presence in popular culture; Debussy 'crosses over' easily. Even when his music occurs in 'serious' or mainstream programming, such as his inclusion in the 2023 BBC Proms, it may be as the purveyor of exotic colours or works that evoke the elements. For one concert, 'Ibéria', from the orchestral *Images*, was chosen for 'Impressions of Spain' (that word, 'impression', is so often present), and for the late-night 'Moon and Stars' concert we were offered organ arrangements of the slow movement from the String Quartet and 'Clair de lune'. In 2023, the Los Angeles Philharmonic opened a concert with the *Prélude à l'après-midi d'un faune*, the programme notes for which emphasised the work's sensuous qualities.

The same annotator, Kathy Henkel, also spoke of the work as one of the 'great contributions to modern music', thereby drawing us back to the endlessly fascinating prospect of Debussy as both a popular composer and one of the most radical innovators in the history of music. It is therefore unremarkable, but heartening, that the past few years, galvanised in part by the centenary, have witnessed a rich procession of new publications, including François de Médicis and Steven Huebner (eds.), *Debussy's Resonance* (2018); Gurminder Kaur Bhogal, *Claude Debussy's* Clair de lune (2018); Marie Rolf's translation and revised edition of François Lesure's critical biography (2019); Siglind Bruhn, *Debussy's Instrumental Music in Its Cultural Context* (2019); Teresa Davidian, *Experiencing Debussy: A Listener's Companion* (2019) Alexandra Kieffer, *Debussy's Critics: Sound, Affect, and the Experience of Modernism* (2019); Kiyoshi Tamagawa, *Echoes from the East: The Javanese Gamelan and Its Influence on the Music of Claude Debussy* (2019); François de Médicis, *La maturation artistique de Debussy dans son contexte historique, 1884–1902* (2020); Denis Herlin, *Claude Debussy: Portraits et études* (2021); and David J. Code and Barbara L. Kelly (eds.), *Debussy Studies 2* (in progress). There are also journal articles and the continuing excitement of the *Œuvres complètes*. Furthermore, the early-music movement in performance has started to accustom the world to hearing Debussy with instruments and (occasionally) performing conventions from his time. Even with so much scholarly and practical activity there is still a need for an accessible volume that covers the full gamut of Debussy's life and work without the constraints of a chronological biography. The present volume, drawing on the latest research, sets out to do this, enriching the coverage by positioning Debussy in the world around him, his context.

***

Working with so many distinguished scholars of Debussy and French music has been a joy. I am most grateful to all of them for their enthusiasm and support. I would also like to thank Denis Herlin for kindly checking all thirty-two chapters and the index in addition to his own contributions. Thanks are due to Cambridge University Press and my commissioning editor, Dr Katharine Brett, who has been an invaluable support and source of advice. Abi Sears at the Press has been on hand to provide assistance for the final editing stages and production.

Sadly, David Code's untimely death occurred during the book's preparation for publication. His two chapters were complete at the time and required only a few minor adjustments. In recognition of his remarkable contribution to Debussy scholarship and the world beyond it, this volume is dedicated to his memory.

Notes on the Text

Chapters 8, 19, 22, and 23 were translated from the French by the editor.

Abbreviations

Correspondance   Claude Debussy, *Correspondance (1872–1918)*, ed. François Lesure and Denis Herlin (Paris: Gallimard, 2005)
Debussy Letters   *Debussy Letters*, ed. François Lesure and Roger Nichols, trans. Nichols (Cambridge, MA: Harvard University Press, 1987)
Lesure (Rolf)   François Lesure, *Claude Debussy: A Critical Biography*, rev. and trans. Marie Rolf (Rochester, NY: University of Rochester Press, 2019)
Monsieur Croche   Claude Debussy, *Monsieur Croche et autres écrits*, rev. ed. François Lesure (Paris: Gallimard, 1987)

PART I

Paris: City, Politics, and Society

CHAPTER I

Paris, the City

Martin Guerpin

> Ah! I am fed up with the Eternal City, I feel I have been here for an eternity, and Paris, the people I love, a certain shop in the rue de Rome . . . all this does not seem to exist any more.
> Debussy, letter to Émile Baron, September 1886,
> *Correspondance*, p. 51.

Debussy lived in Paris for most of his life, and apart from summers, which he often spent in seaside resorts such as Houlgate in Normandy, he left the 'City of Light' only with reluctance. Even Rome, the 'Eternal City', bored him. In many ways, Debussy epitomises the new confidence of the city as a centre of culture and good living. His life embraced both its old bohemian neighbourhoods and the new, smart boulevards that had replaced much of the medieval city in the years before the Commune. This chapter explores the City of Light, the city of the Belle Époque, a chrononym that emerged during the 1930s to single out the three decades preceding the First World War, often seen as a golden age.[1] From the point of view of its new town plan, its museums, its transport, and its exhibitions, it describes many aspects of the city that Debussy used, such as the local railway, situated close to the end of his garden, and the adoption of the motor car as a means of transport. Technological advances came raining down in these years; they included typewriters, piano rolls, recordings, new music-printing technology, and much more. This chapter will attempt to describe what it was like to live in this city, both for a struggling bohemian artist like the young Debussy and for the established, bourgeois figure of the later years.

---

[1] Dominique Kalifa, '"Belle Époque": Invention et usages d'un chrononyme', *Revue d'histoire du XIXe siècle* 52 (2016), pp. 119–32.

From the *Quartier de l'Europe* to the *Grands Boulevards*: Debussy and the Modernisation of Paris

The list of Debussy's Parisian addresses reveals that he lived in neighbourhoods marked by modernisation processes.

Until 1887: 13, rue Clapeyron (8th)
September 1888 to September 1890: 27, rue de Berlin (8th)
October to December 1890: 76, boulevard Malesherbes (8th)
January to May 1891: 27, rue de Berlin (8th)
June to 23 July 1891: 42, rue de Londres (8th)
24 July 1894 to December 1898: 10, rue Gustave Doret (17th)
January 1899 to September 1904: 58, rue Cardinet (17th)
October 1904 to September 1905: 10, avenue Alphand (16th)
October 1905 to 1918: 64 and 80, avenue du Bois de Boulogne [avenue Foch] (16th)[2]

Until 1904, Debussy lived in or near the *quartier de l'Europe* (rue Clapeyron, rue de Berlin), the realisation of which (1820–39) was one of the most ambitious transformations made in Paris during the first half of the nineteenth century.[3] That Debussy moved into the 16th arrondissement in 1904, and the following year into a *hôtel particulier* located in the avenue du Bois de Boulogne, shows that he had achieved a bourgeois status, since this neighbourhood was the most expensive in Paris. Beyond this evolution, Debussy's Parisian addresses reveal that he lived in modern parts of Paris and that he could indeed experience the modernisation of the city.

Between 1853 and 1870, Paris underwent the most spectacular renovation plan of its history. In order to reduce the spread of diseases and the criminality rate in a then overcrowded city, and to facilitate communications and interventions by the police and army troops in case of uprisings or revolutions, Napoleon III elevated Baron Georges Eugène Haussmann to *préfet* of the Seine, with the mission to carry out an impressive programme that completely transformed the central districts of the French capital, the plan of which had not changed significantly since medieval times. His new plan was based on the *grande croisée de Paris*, a grand, cross-facilitating east-west and north-south communication. This led to the creation of the rue de Rivoli, the boulevard de Sebastopol, and the boulevard de Strasbourg. In

---

[2] Appendix III, *Correspondance*, p. 2211.
[3] Annie Térade, 'Le "Nouveau quartier de l'Europe" à Paris: Acteurs publics, acteurs privés dans l'aménagement de la capitale (1820–1839)', *Histoire urbaine* 19 (2007), pp. 11–29.

1859, an official parliamentary report could boast that these first renovations works had 'brought air, light and healthiness and procured easier circulation in a labyrinth that was constantly blocked and impenetrable'.[4] A second phase comprised the creation of a network of new boulevards (e.g. boulevards Magenta, Malesherbes, and Debussy's boulevard du Bois de Boulogne, constructed in 1854), which were meant to connect the centre of Paris with the already existing boulevard ring built under Louis XVIII. This programme went hand in hand with the creation of squares, which served both as connecting nodes for the new boulevards and as a way to create more public spaces, such as the place de l'Étoile, the place du Château d'Eau (today place de la République), but also public parks for leisure and hygiene purposes, such as the parc Monceau, the parc des Buttes-Chaumont, and the Bois de Vincennes.

Facilitating communication inside the city was crucial, since in 1860, with the annexation of the suburbs, then composed of eleven communes (Passy, Auteuil, Batignolles, Montmartre, La Chapelle, La Villette, Belleville, Charonne, Bercy, Grenelle, and Vaugirard), Paris doubled in size. It now included all areas circumscribed by the Thiers walls built between 1841 and 1844.[5] Throughout his life, Debussy thus lived in a fortified city and it was not until 1919 that the Thiers wall was progressively demolished and replaced by the ring road we know today as the boulevards des Maréchaux, each segment being named after a First Empire marshal.

The expansion of Paris also raised the question of public transportation. The first tramway service (horse-cars) was created by Haussmann in conjunction with his renovation plan. It was augmented with the Chemin de fer de Petite Ceinture (1852–9) which, in the 1860s, was mainly used by workers. It peaked during the 1900 Exposition Universelle (also known as the 1900 Paris Exposition, a World's Fair), before being progressively abandoned in favour of engineer Fulgence Bienvenüe's Métropolitain, which entered into service during the Exposition.[6]

The plan of the Parisian subway was an underground reproduction of the map of Paris and reflected the importance of modern arts in the French capital,[7] since Hector Guimard's *édicules* made for the entranceways were

---

[4] Quoted in Patrice de Moncan, *Le Paris d'Haussmann* (Paris: Éditions du Mécène, 2002), p. 64.
[5] Nathalie Montel, 'L'Agrandissement de Paris en 1860: Un projet controversé', in Annie Fourcaut and Florence Bourillon (eds.), *Agrandir Paris: 1860–1970* (Paris: Éditions de la Sorbonne, 2012), pp. 99–111.
[6] Claude Berton and Alexandre Ossadzow, *Fulgence Bienvenüe et la construction du métropolitain de Paris* (Paris: Presses de l'école nationale des ponts et chaussées, 1998), p. 83.
[7] Carlos López-Galviz, *Cities, Railways, Modernities: London, Paris, and the Nineteenth Century* (London: Routledge, 2019), pp. 107–79.

heavily influenced by Art Nouveau. Until his death in 1918, Debussy witnessed the birth of ten Métro lines, which transported a total of 467 million people in 1913, the year during which hippomobile tramways and omnibuses were replaced by motorised transportation.[8] No doubt Debussy was interested in these changes, which also aroused the curiosity of Joris-Karl Huysmans, who depicted an omnibus drive in a chapter of his *Croquis parisiens*,[9] one of Debussy's favourite readings during his stay at the Villa Medici.[10]

The 1900 Exposition Universelle was also key to the modernisation of Paris's public transportation system in that it hosted the first Congrès international d'automobilisme. The simultaneous appearance of the subway network and motor cars marked a dramatic evolution and the dawn of a modern era for Paris. In 1900, there were 618 registered private cars in Paris, and most of the owners lived in the 8th, 9th, 16th, and 17th arrondissements,[11] all of which were part of Debussy's daily life. Seven years later, the number of cars had multiplied by ten, in addition to autobuses, which began service in 1906. This development brought important changes in the French capital. From then on, new streets were to be adapted to the circulation of cars while preserving the *cachet* of Parisian urbanity.[12] Pedestrian movement had to be controlled in order to avoid congestion and accidents. Stefan Zweig wrote: 'Paris has become frightening ... the stink of petrol invades the streets, and crossing them is now an adventure.'[13]

The Paris in which Debussy lived was certainly a city marked by spectacular modernisation processes, but what about Debussy's Paris – his own experience of the city? In his correspondence, he does not speak much about the way he gets from one place to another. However, in the 1890s and before his move to the 16th arrondissement, he frequently mentions cafés and brasseries where he meets his friends and takes lunch or dinner. Most of these cafés were located in or next to the *quartier de l'Europe* – for example, the Café Passerelle, in the Saint Lazare railway station; and the Brasserie Mollard (rue Saint Lazare), where he used to meet his close friend Pierre Louÿs (1870–1925). Debussy's frequentation of cafés also served the purpose of artistic discussions and networking. In the late 1880s and 1890s, he regularly met friends and artists

---

[8] RATP, *L'Histoire des transports, des origines à 1948* (Paris: RATP, 2013), p. 6.
[9] Joris-Karl Huysmans, *Croquis parisiens* (Paris: Vaton, 1880).
[10] Debussy, letter to Émile Baron, September 1886, *Correspondance*, p. 52.
[11] Mathieu Flonneau, 'Paris au cœur de la révolution des usages de l'automobile 1884–1908', *Histoire, économie & société* 26 (2007), p. 69.
[12] Eugène Hénard, *Études sur l'architecture et les transformations de Paris* (Paris: H. Champion, 1902–9).
[13] Stefan Zweig, *Journaux 1912–1940* (Paris: Belfond, 1986), p. 37.

at the Brasserie Pousset, then the Parisian hub of the Symbolist group comprising the poet Catulle Mendès, playwright René Peter, painter Paul Robert, fellow composer André Messager, and actor André Antoine, director of the Théâtre Libre. Two other Symbolist gatherings were the 'Mardis de Mallarmé' in the poet's apartment (rue de Rome) and Edmond Bailly's Librairie de l'Art indépendant (rue de la Chaussée d'Antin) close to the *quartier de l'Europe*, where Debussy met writers such as Henri de Régnier, Paul Claudel, and André Gide. At the Librairie, he also often played new music (both popular and art repertoires), together with his fellow composer Erik Satie (1866–1925). The latter was the link between Debussy's two Parises – the modern one, where he lived, and Montmartre, where they met, thanks to their common taste for *café-concerts*. Debussy often went to the Chat Noir[14] and also, at the bottom of the Butte (avenue Trudaine, where Maurice Ravel and Ricardo Viñes often came in the 1890s to play at Emmanuel Chabrier's apartment), L'Âne Rouge and the Auberge du Clou, where he performed with Satie. Debussy's *La plus que lente* (1910) can be heard as a souvenir of *café-concerts*, as well as his 'La Belle au bois dormant' (1890), to a poem by *chansonnier* Vincent Hyspa. One last important location in Debussy's artistic Paris was the salon of Marguerite de Saint-Marceaux (boulevard Malesherbes), where he could meet fellow composers Ravel, Chabrier, Gabriel Fauré, and Reynaldo Hahn, among others. Saint-Marceaux's *hôtel particulier* was close to his apartments before 1904 and later his house in the avenue Foch was directly connected to it via the Arc de Triomphe. This proximity between Debussy's homes up to 1904 and the venues he frequented on a daily basis can be explained by the fact that, until 1900, most Parisians were pedestrians and thus lived in the *quartier* where they worked rather than in the entire city.[15]

From the Music Hall to the Museum: A Capital of Culture and Leisure Entertainment

One other major aspect of the modernisation of the capital that Debussy could observe and experiment with was the arts and entertainment industry.[16] That Napoleon III and Haussmann articulated the renovation of the capital's architecture and urbanism with the development of the arts

---

[14] Steven Moore Whiting, *Satie the Bohemian: From Cabaret to Concert Hall* (New York: Oxford University Press, 1999), p. 79.
[15] Luc Passion, 'Marcher dans Paris au XIXe siècle', in François Caron (ed.), *Paris et ses réseaux: Naissance d'un mode de vie urbain, XIXe–XXe siècles* (Paris: Bibliothèque historique de la Ville de Paris, 1990), pp. 27–43.
[16] Dominique Kalifa, *La Culture de masse en France, 1: 1860–1930* (Paris: La Découverte, 2001), pp. 38–54.

was illustrated by the presence of two theatres: the Nouveau Théâtre-Lyrique (now Théâtre de la Ville) and the Théâtre du Châtelet, at the crossroad of Haussmann's *grande croisée*, which was the new heart of Paris. Another central feature in the plans of Napoleon III and Haussmann to enhance the prestige of the renovated city was the construction of a new building to host the Théâtre national de l'Opéra. Designed by Charles Garnier (1825–98), it was inaugurated in 1875. Debussy was a *habitué*, but used the best of his irony to denigrate both the building and the repertoire: 'for an unsuspecting passer-by, it [the Opéra] still resembles a railway station; when inside, you could take it for a Turkish bath. Peculiar noise continues to be made therein, which people who have paid for it call this music.'[17]

The Paris in which Debussy lived was a capital where theatre had a central place. Since Emperor Napoleon I's 1807 law on the rationalisation of theatrical activities in Paris, only six theatres in addition to the Opéra and the Opéra-Comique were officially recognised (Théâtre-Français, Théâtre de l'Impératrice, Théâtre du Vaudeville, Théâtre des Variétés, Théâtre de la Porte Saint-Martin, and Théâtre de la Gaîté). The creation of any other establishment (for instance, those located on the boulevard du Temple) had to be authorised by the government. This situation spiralled in 1864, when Napoleon III's decree on the liberalisation of theatres triggered a boom in their construction during Debussy's early life, including such theatres as the Bouffes Parisiens (1855), where Debussy discovered Maurice Maeterlinck's *Pelléas et Mélisande* in 1893, and the Bouffes du Nord (1876).[18] Such an environment must certainly have nurtured his ambitions as, in the 1890s, he aspired to create a literary journal and wrote three comedies together with his friend René Peter.[19]

The circus, which had its French golden age during the 1870s and the Belle Époque, was also part of Debussy's daily life in Paris. Paris could then boast five permanent circuses, including the Cirque Molier (1880–1933), which was a five-minute walk from Debussy's *hôtel particulier* in the avenue Foch.[20] Circus shows had a double impact on Debussy. On the one hand, he used them as a reference point in his music criticism, as when he compared the attraction instrumental virtuosity had for audiences to the

---

[17] *Monsieur Croche*, p. 38.
[18] Jean-Claude Yon, *Une histoire du théâtre à Paris: De la Révolution à la Grande Guerre* (Paris: Aubier, 2012).
[19] Edward Lockspeiser, '*Frères en art*: Pièce de théâtre inédite de Debussy', *Revue de musicologie* 56 (1970), p. 166.
[20] Pascal Jacob, *Paris en pistes: Histoire du cirque parisien* (Rennes: Ouest-France, 2013).

fascination exerted by circus acrobats,[21] and Strauss's *Till Eulenspiegel* to a clown act.[22] On the other hand, Debussy also loved clowns, which had a direct impact on his music. 'General Lavine – eccentric' portrays one of the most famous American clowns in Paris, Edward Lavine. The parody of Wagner's *Tristan* in 'Golliwogg's Cake Walk' also stems directly from an act in which a band played tunes from the opera as a comic accompaniment.[23]

In a similar way, Debussy was influenced by the music hall when composing 'Minstrels'. Developed in London, music hall had its Parisian heyday during the Belle Époque, which was marked by a wave of Anglophilia. Debussy participated in this trend, not only in the French vogue of Pre-Raphaelitism and anglicising the titles of five of the pieces from *Children's Corner*, but also by frequenting the Irish and American Bar (rue Royale) and going to music halls.

He witnessed the construction of major French establishments of this type, including the Folies-Bergère (1886), Moulin Rouge (1889), Olympia (1893), and Alhambra (1904). At the Folies-Bergère he saw minstrel acts (Fig. 1.1), which he evoked in 'Minstrels' (*Préludes*, book 1, 1909–1910). Music-hall shows integrated any new type of novelty, artistic or technological, which could have public appeal. This is the reason why, after the first Parisian cinematographic projection organised by the Lumière brothers in the Grand Café (28 December 1895), the *cinématographe* developed as an attraction within music-hall shows. It was not until 1904 that the first cinemas opened in Paris with the Petit Journal (1904), followed by the Théâtre cinématographe Pathé (1906). The success of this new form of popular entertainment was spectacular, for within a year more than a hundred cinemas had blossomed in the capital. Although Debussy did not write specifically about cinema, it was on his mind, since he compared Richard Strauss's rapid succession of musical sequences in *Ein Heldenleben* (1898) to film.[24]

During Debussy's life, Paris hosted three Expositions Universelles – in 1878, 1889, and 1900. They contributed to asserting the cultural and economic influence of France in the world. They helped to transform Paris: the Palais du Trocadéro was built for the 1878 edition, the Eiffel Tower was the landmark of the 1889 edition, and the 1900 Exposition gave Paris the Grand Palais and the Petit Palais. They confirmed Paris's status as

---

[21] *Monsieur Croche*, p. 32.   [22] *Monsieur Croche*, p. 45.
[23] Ann McKinley, 'Debussy and American Minstrelsy', *The Black Perspective in Music* 14 (1986), pp. 249–58.
[24] Claude Debussy, *Monsieur Croche: Antidilettante* (Paris: Librairie Dorbon-Ainé, 1921), p. 94.

Figure 1.1 Poster promoting Les Marionettes Minstrels at the Folies-Bergère (between 1882 and 1888) [Illustrator unknown], Musée Carnavalet, AFF463.

one of the most important cultural centres in the world. For Debussy, attending these exhibitions was not just a matter of leisure and curiosity. His visits to the Exposition Universelle of 1889 had at least two major consequences for his artistic evolution, since it brought Russian and Oriental music to the forefront of his musical imagination (though he had already encountered Russian music when he spent two summers, 1880 and 1881, with Nadezhda von Meck, Tchaikovsky's sponsor). Three concerts were organised – one devoted to popular Russian music, and the two 'Concerts russes' under the direction of Nikolai Rimsky-Korsakov (1844–1908) at the Palais du Trocadéro. The programme featured works by members of The Five, plus Alexander Dargomyjsky, Alexander Glazunov, Mikhail Glinka, and Anatoly Liadov. Four years after these concerts, in 1893, Debussy could tell the journalist Alfred Mortier (1865–1937): 'Chabrier, Mussorgsky, Palestrina, those are the ones I like!'[25] But oriental music was Debussy's most striking discovery during the 1889 Exposition, notably the Javanese gamelan, presented during dance shows in a reconstituted Javanese village. The experience proved formative for Debussy who, five years later, tells Pierre Louÿs, 'Remember Javanese music, which contained every nuance, even those that we cannot name any more, where the tonic and the dominant were only vain ghosts for naughty children.'[26] Pieces such as 'Pagodes' (*Estampes*, 1903) and 'Le Vent dans la plaine' (*Préludes*, book 1, 1910) bear testimony to the influence of Gamelan music on Debussy's stylistic evolution.

The Exposition Universelle of 1900, which was visited by fifty-one million people, also exerted influence on Debussy and other French composers, including Ravel and Maurice Delage. Debussy discovered ragtime and cakewalks – played by John Sousa's American band – two genres from which he borrowed characteristic features in 'Golliwogg's Cake Walk' and *Le petit nègre*. Debussy was also fascinated by the *Danseuses de Delphes* (a Greek sculpture also known as the Acanthus Column), recently discovered by the École française d'Athènes and exhibited in facsimile in the Pavillon de l'archéologie française. Debussy evoked them in his piano preludes (book 1).

Expositions Universelles were only one part of the cultural policy of the Third Republic, which gave priority to the development of museums. The Musée du Louvre (founded in 1793), the topic of one of Debussy's piano pieces ('Souvenir du Louvre', *Images oubliées*, 1894), was profoundly renovated and enlarged after suffering from fire and destruction during the Commune (1871). The Expositions coincided with the development of new museums, which were also places of high interest in Debussy's Paris. He could nurture his passion for the Far East in the two Asian art museums founded during the Belle Époque, in addition to the Musée indochinois,

---

[25] Obituary by Alfred Mortier, quoted in Marcel Dietschy, *A Portrait of Claude Debussy*, ed. and trans. William Ashbrook and Margaret G. Cobb (Oxford: Clarendon Press, 1990), pp. 61–2.
[26] Debussy, letter to Pierre Louÿs, 22 January 1895, *Correspondance*, p. 107.

which opened in 1878 in the Palais du Trocadéro. The first was the Musée Guimet, built in 1889 on the place d'Iéna (16th arrondissement). The second, the Musée Cernuschi, was founded in 1898. More broadly, Debussy witnessed a glut of new museums in Paris, with the inauguration of the Musée Carnavalet (1880), the Musée Gustave Moreau (1897), devoted to one of his favourite painters, and the Musée des arts décoratifs (1905). The opening of the latter was a landmark. Like the World's Fairs, it legitimised the association of art and industry, of artworks and goods.

Technological Advances in Paris: Commodification of the Arts and Artification of Commodities

Debussy's taste for Japonism and Art Nouveau led him to frequent the shops of art dealers such as Siegfried Bing (1838–1905), whose Maison de l'Art Nouveau played a major role in developing functional art and the accessibility of artworks through technological innovations in the fields of lithography and similigravure.[27] Debussy bought prints there, and he attended the sale of Bing's Chinese, Korean, and Japanese collections at the Galerie Durand-Ruel on 5 May 1906.[28]

The trilogy of art, technology, and commerce presided over music printing, which adapted to the emergence of mass culture, epitomised in the rise of the music hall. Publishers like Hachette, Marchetti, and Salabert developed illustrated sheet music in colour, allowing covers to play a similar role to advertisement posters: they used catchy designs and colours, insisted that the songs were already popular successes, and exploited the celebrity of the singers who popularised them.

Reciprocally, posters made by Jules Chéret epitomised the blurring of the frontier between artistic works and commodities, between utilitarian goals and aesthetic ideals, in a way similar to Hector Guimard's *édicules*. Debussy, whose *La Damoiselle élue* was published by Bailly's Librairie de l'art indépendant with an illustration by Nabi painter Maurice Denis (1870–1943), was fond of this type of poster. In 1901, he spent one night 'beholding the posters of the Barnum Circus (then located on the Champ de Mars); at 3:00 am we had only looked at half of them'[29] (Fig. 1.2).

---

[27] Nicholas-Henri Zmelty, 'L'Art et le métier', *Nouvelles de l'estampe* 267 (2022), https://doi.org/10.4000/estampe.2544.

[28] Jean-Michel Nectoux, 'Je veux écrire mon songe musical', in Guy Cogeval (ed.), *Debussy: La musique et les arts* (Paris: Skira Flammarion, 2012), p. 19.

[29] Letter to Paul Robert, November–December 1901, *Correspondance*, p. 628.

1 Paris, the City

Figure 1.2 Poster of the Barnum and Bailey show (Paris, 1901) [Illustrator unknown], Bibliothèque nationale de France, ENT DN-1 (STROBRIDGE2)-ROUL.

Illustrated sheet music was also used to promote recordings at a time when the recording industry was beginning to prosper. In Paris, the recording industry was first dominated by Pathé, which began selling recordings made by American labels such as Columbia, and from 1896 made its own recordings. The Compagnie française du Gramo-phone followed in 1898. Debussy was well aware of the development of the recording industry, since in 1904 he recorded four 78 rpm discs with singer Mary Garden (1874–1967, the first Mélisande) for the Compagnie française du Gramophone. Unfettered by the restricted range of acoustic gramophone recordings, Debussy could also listen to what was then called *musique mécanique* on the reproducing pianos (among other mechanical instruments) commercialised by the Aeolian company from 1885 and popularised in France by the Welte-Mignon reproducing piano (1904). This invention consisted of capturing the pianists' performances on perforated strips. Debussy recorded six piano rolls of this type, containing fourteen of his piano pieces:

WM 2733: *Children's Corner* (complete);
WM 2734: *D'un cahier d'esquisses*;
WM 2735: 'La Soirée dans Grenade' (*Estampes*);
WM 2736: *La plus que lente*;
WM 2738: 'Danseuses de Delphes', 'La Cathédrale engloutie', and 'La Danse de Puck' (*Préludes*, book 1);
WM 2739: 'Le Vent dans la plaine' and 'Minstrels' (*Préludes*, book 1).

That even Debussy's performances were for sale shows how new technologies played a decisive role in blurring and redefining the boundaries between art and commodity.

* * *

Paris was never a subject in Debussy's music, as it was in that of Pierre-Octave Ferroud (*Au parc Monceau*, 1921), Frederick Delius (*Paris: The Song of a Great City*, 1900), and George Gershwin (*An American in Paris*, 1928). However, the city was not just his home; as Walter Benjamin (1892–1940) pointed out, it contributed to shape his artistic culture, perception, and sensorial experience.[30] More than his city, Paris was Debussy's world. As such, he interacted with it, and this interaction undeniably bore fruits in his music.

---

[30] Walter Benjamin, *Paris, capitale du XIXᵉ siècle: Le livre des passages*, trans. Jean Lacoste (Paris: Éditions du Cerf, 1997).

Author's Recommendation
'Golliwogg's Cake Walk', *Children's Corner* (1906–8).

'Golliwogg's Cake Walk' is part of *Children's Corner*, a suite that Debussy composed for his daughter Claude-Emma (Chouchou), born in 1905. The association between cakewalk and childhood may be critically understood as a patronising perspective on African-American music and dance. But thinking that way would also imply that Debussy had only condescension for other music traditions conveyed in *Children's Corner* (piano exercises in 'Gradus ad Parnassum' and Chinese music in 'Serenade for the Doll', for instance). The link between cakewalk and childhood came from the famous circumstances of its first Parisian presentation in 1902, in the pantomime *Les Joyeux Nègres* by Rodolphe Berger, at the Nouveau Cirque. The public was struck by the fact that it starred two children: Rudy and Fredy Walker. Hence Debussy's association between the cakewalk and Golliwogg, a black child doll from Florence Kate Upton's *The Adventures of Two Dutch Dolls and a 'Golliwogg'* (1895). This short piece in ABA' form is also part of a wider French tradition of mocking Wagner and Wagnerism, from Gabriel Fauré and André Messager's quadrille *Souvenirs de Bayreuth* (1888) to front pages of satiric journals such as *L'Assiette au beurre* showing 'Du caporal Lohengrin' in the middle of a circus act (22 April 1905). Similarly, Debussy introduces the main leitmotif from Wagner's *Tristan und Isolde* in the central part of his piece. Such an encounter between high art and cakewalk creates a burlesque effect and desecrates the quasi-religious dimension of Wagner aesthetics.

CHAPTER 2

Paris and the Nation's Politics

Federico Lazzaro

From what can be inferred from the composer's correspondence and writings, Debussy was indifferent to political debate. It is noteworthy that the names of politicians are virtually absent from his letters and that none of the major affairs or terrorist episodes that shook French public opinion are the subject of his public or private writings. There is no mention of the anarchist attack on the Chamber of Deputies by Auguste Vaillant on 9 December 1893, nor of the assassination of the president of the Republic, Sadi Carnot, on 24 June 1894. Debussy never expressed himself on the bellicose and monarchist positions of General Boulanger (who threatened the Republic between 1886 and 1891), nor on the *coup d'état* by Paul Déroulède (23 February 1899). Nor did he mention the assassination of Jean Jaurès on 31 July 1914, who was killed for his pacifist positions at a time when Debussy, by contrast, was very explicit about his own inclination towards anti-German interventionism. François Lesure wrote in this regard that Debussy lived 'a little *hors du monde*' and that 'no real political opinion can be attributed to him';[1] although he was close to pro-Dreyfus circles (including the *Revue blanche*), he also had anti-Dreyfusards as friends (e.g. Pierre Louÿs) and undoubtedly shared a certain ambient anti-Semitism.[2] Debussy's nationalist positions became more and more explicit when he began to take up the pen as a music critic with an anti-German posture that first addressed the musical realm (its first manifestation was within the survey 'L'influence allemande sur la musique française', *Mercure de France*, January 1903) and finally became explicitly political during the First World War (the most famous public stance was 'Enfin, seuls! . . .', *L'Intransigeant*, 11 March 1915).

This chapter highlights a selection of instances where Debussy came into contact with the political. Such contact cannot be reduced to his sole

---

[1] François Lesure, 'Introduction', in *Correspondance*, p. ii.
[2] François Lesure, *Claude Debussy: Biographie critique* (Paris: Fayard, 2003), p. 422.

declarations: although some of the examples given are purely biographical, others relate rather to immediate reactions to his work. The fact that the composer does not seem to have been particularly interested in politics obviously did not isolate him from the effects of certain political events on a personal level. We will consider from this perspective two of the three violent episodes that struck Paris during the composer's life – the Franco-Prussian War and the Commune – in addition to certain fundamental laws adopted during the Third Republic up to 1918. The third major violent episode – the First World War – will be addressed, along with the Dreyfus affair, in connection with Debussy's works.

Indeed, in the process of reconstructing the history of a career, the political events surrounding the public manifestations of a composer (from the performances of their works to the publication of their writings) deserve to be retraced. Even if there is no direct relationship between the composition of the works and history, there is a contextual relationship – one of concordance – at the time of their creation. The context in which a work is first performed can contribute to its success or failure, as well as load it with political meanings. To paraphrase Hans Robert Jauss, when we study musical works from the past, we are dealing with traces of events that took place when the work was listened to by an audience, commented on by critics, and provoked creative reactions in other composers.[3]

The Franco-Prussian War

From the age of six, Debussy had his main address in Paris. It was the end of the Second Empire, the regime established in 1852 by Louis-Napoléon Bonaparte, who proclaimed himself emperor under the name of Napoleon III. The Franco-Prussian War was declared on 19 July 1870, with the aim of strengthening the empire. The result was rather that it was wiped out: following the defeat at Sedan on 4 September, the emperor went into exile and, according to national mythology perpetuated in a famous phrase by Charles de Gaulle, the Republic 'offered itself to the country to repair the disaster'. But while the patriotic and republican forces in the capital were determined to continue the war until victory, the Government of National Defence, led by General Trochu, was leaning towards a rapid peace. Paris, under siege for four months (17 September 1870–26 January 1871, with the

---

[3] Hans Robert Jauss, *Literaturgeschichte als Provokation der Literaturwissenschaft* (Konstanz: Universitätsverlag Konstanz, 1967). A useful timeline paralleling the main political events of the Third Republic and French musical life can be found in Barbara L. Kelly (ed.), *French Music, Culture, and National Identity, 1870–1939* (Rochester, NY: University of Rochester Press, 2008), pp. xii–xix.

armistice being signed on 28 January) suffered the material consequences but did not abandon its positions. Debussy's father, Manuel-Achille, remained in Paris during the war, while the young Achille-Claude spent these troubled times in Cannes with his mother and siblings. It was there that he had his first music lessons.

The Commune

The elections of 8 February 1871 confirmed the republic that had de facto imposed itself in wartime, while increasing the distance between the provinces (monarchist or pacifist republican vote) and Paris (patriotic and revolutionary republican vote). For this 'Republic without republicans'[4] led by Adolphe Thiers, an 'equilibrist of compromise'[5] capable of federating all the pacifist currents around him, peace was well worth the sacrifice of Alsace-Lorraine, which was thus ceded to the Germans (the region became French again in 1919). It was against this government that Paris would rebel on 28 March. An alternative government – the Commune – was created; for some it was inspired by the armed resistance against the invader already experienced in 1792, while for others it offered an alternative, socialist model of society. These two souls of the Commune – the egalitarian Republic and the social Republic – were subsequently crushed by Thiers during the *semaine sanglante* (bloody week, 21–28 May), which resulted in between 7,000 and 15,000 deaths, depending on the sources. Rid of its more leftist components, the Third Republic could finally assert its conservative character (as affirmed by Thiers in his speech of 13 November 1872), defending *order* (i.e. peace, guaranteed by an army of professionals), *property* (defended by a protectionist economy), and *stability* (ensured by a presidential regime, among other things). Each of these elements was established progressively, leading to the constitution of 1875.[6]

Manuel-Achille Debussy had joined the National Guard just before the uprisings that led to the Commune broke out; he was arrested with 40,000 other *communards* and sentenced to four years in prison, but he benefitted from the amnesty of 1873, which allowed the Debussy family to come together again. Achille-Claude did not permanently leave home until twenty years later. These events are not without consequences for Debussy's instruction in music. The composer Charles de Sivry, whom Manuel met at the Satory camp where he was a prisoner, recommended his

---

[4] Jean-Pierre Azéma and Michel Winock, *La Troisième République, 1870–1940*, rev. ed. (Paris: Calmann-Lévy, 1976), p. 68.
[5] Arnaud-Dominique Houte, *Le Triomphe de la République, 1871–1914* (Paris: Seuil, 2014), p. 27.
[6] We summarise here the analysis of Azéma and Winock, *La Troisième République*.

mother, Antoinette-Flore Mauté, as a piano teacher. Seventeen months after the defeat of the Commune, on 22 October 1872, Claude Debussy was admitted to the Conservatoire.

Divorce Act, Trade Union Act

Beyond these traumatic events, Debussy's life was paralleled, and sometimes directly affected, by some of the most important reforms of the Third Republic. From the 1880s onwards, the conservative tendency of the beginning gave way to a centrist, liberal, and secular orientation, complete with some important social measures (especially from 1906 onwards, when the Ministry of Labour was created). These laws embodied the ideals of the Radical Party, founded in 1901; the same year two socialist parties were born, which in 1905 converged in the SFIO (French Section of the Workers' International). The Divorce Act of 27 July 1884, for example, allowed Debussy to marry Emma (divorced from Sigismond Bardac in 1905), while at the same time imposing on him the alimony payable to his ex-wife Lilly Texier, which ate away at his finances. By contrast, another crucial law of the same year – the Waldeck-Rousseau Law of 21 March authorising professional unions – had no impact on Debussy, who never joined a union, whether as a musician or music critic.

Secularism and Public Education

The issue of secularism, which had as its major consequence the separation of Church and State formalised by a series of laws in 1905, intersected with the composer's biography on several occasions. On the very day of his birth, 22 August 1862, Parisian newspapers published and commented on (while denying its authenticity) a dispatch of 19 August concerning a visit by the French ambassador to the Pope in order to 'give His Holiness, in the name of the Emperor, the assurance that the French government, by guaranteeing its integrity, will not allow the invasion of the present pontifical territory'.[7] This defence of the temporal power of the Church, threatened by the arrival of Giuseppe Garibaldi who sought to conquer Rome and annex it to the new Italian state, was one of the pillars on which Napoleon III based his regime, guaranteeing him the support of Catholics. As a consequence,

---

[7] For a commentary on the authenticity of this dispatch, see Adolphe Gaïffe, 'Bulletin du jour', *La Presse* (Paris) (22 August 1862), p. 1. *La Presse* had published the dispatch the previous day, p. 3.

when the French Empire fell in 1870, the Italian army was finally able to seize its future national capital. The Republic would then completely reverse its position. In 1882, the year in which Debussy gave the first public concert of his works (with Marie-Blanche Vasnier) and failed his first Prix de Rome competition, the Jules Ferry Laws of 28 March established the secular character of primary schools, henceforth also compulsory and free (Debussy had not attended any school); the teaching staff would be exclusively non-religious from 1886 onwards (Debussy was by then in Rome as a recipient of the Prix de Rome, finally obtained in 1884).

The separation of Church and State, completed in 1905 (worship was free but in no way subsidised by the State, and diplomatic relations with the Vatican were severed), did not prevent the clergy from interfering with French citizens and their relationship with the arts. In May 1911, the Archbishop of Paris formally forbade Parisian Catholics to attend performances of *Le Martyre de saint Sébastien* by Gabriele D'Annunzio and Debussy because of its mixture of paganism, eroticism, and Christianity, and the fact that the saint was played by a woman, a Jew moreover (Ida Rubinstein).

Responding to the Politics

We have mentioned only a few key moments in the Third Republic that had a more or less direct impact on Debussy's life, yet there are different ways of approaching them, depending on how we consider a composer's career in relation to the political circumstances surrounding it. While politics are rarely reflected in composition (except in occasional pieces), they nonetheless form part of a work when it becomes an event. Curiosity could lead the historian to wonder what was being talked about during the interval at the premiere of an epochal work such as the *Prélude à l'après-midi d'un faune* (22 December 1894), a few days after the creation of the protectorate of Madagascar and the birth of the first French trade union, the CGT (Confédération générale du travail), or to enquire what reactions the abolition of theatrical censorship inspired among the music lovers gathered at the Salle des Agriculteurs for a talk by Louis Laloy on Debussy's work followed by a performance of the first series of *Images* (6 February 1906). One option is to study the press from a broader perspective, and thus to look at Debussy's career in the context of the political debates that animated the Parisian press when it was read on the day of a premiere or carried the reviews of his works. This approach, rather than isolating critical reviews, studies press discourse on music with the aim of situating such discourse (and thus the works commented on therein) in the lives of their readers.[8]

Consider the premiere of *Pelléas et Mélisande* on 30 April 1902. The front page of the daily newspapers – and possibly the principal subject of conversation for most of the audience at the premiere – was the result of the legislative elections of 27 April. The rise of the Nationalist Party was feared but did not happen, and instead the Radical Party emerged victorious from the elections. The fear of a nationalist upsurge was explained by the strengthening of the militarist, anti-Semitic, clerical, and anti-parliamentary (even monarchist) right, reflected in two electoral victories in Paris. The first, in January 1889, saw the triumph of General Boulanger, a populist anti-republican who encouraged military action against Germany to 'avenge' Alsace-Lorraine, and almost led to a *coup d'état* (the first performance of a work by Debussy at the Société nationale de musique – two of the six *Ariettes oubliées* – took place around this time, on 19 February). The second electoral victory of the right in Paris came in the municipal elections of 1900. It occurred shortly after the pardon granted to Captain Alfred Dreyfus by the president of the Republic, Émile Loubet (19 September 1899) as the concluding chapter in a case that had been going on since 1894 and which had divided French public opinion between Dreyfusards (defenders of justice and the law in the face of miscarriages of justice and army corporatism) and anti-Dreyfusards (anti-Semites and revanchists). Debussy had positioned himself in the middle and signed a petition 'for peace' ('*pour l'apaisement*') in January 1899. One can thus see the victory of the radicals on the day of the premiere of *Pelléas* as a definitive affirmation of republican, secular, and pro-Dreyfus France after some fifteen years of risk for the Republic.

Jann Pasler's sociopolitical interpretation of the critical reaction to *Pelléas*, which takes into account some of 'the [enormous] number of extra-musical issues capable of affecting how a critic formulated his message',[9] could be enriched by these considerations: the critics close to the right who were very hard on Debussy's opera were probably ill-disposed towards it on account of their indignation over the electoral results. Moreover, the perception of the gap between *Pelléas* and their expectations could have

---

[8] A plea for the reading of music criticism 'in context' has been made by Katherine Ellis, 'Music Criticism, Speech Acts, and Generic Contracts', in Teresa Cascudo (ed.), *Nineteenth-Century Music Criticism* (Turnhout: Brepols, 2017), pp. 14–19.
[9] Jann Pasler, '*Pelléas* and Power: Forces behind the Reception of Debussy's Opera', *19th-Century Music* 10 (1983), p. 264.

been exacerbated by broader political considerations – an indication, among others, of the fact that the world was moving in a different direction from their values.

First World War

There are also cases where the circumstance of the execution of a work gives it an official, if not political (or politicised), patina. The two works by Debussy played at the Exposition Universelle of 1900 – the String Quartet and *La Damoiselle élue* – may fall into this category. But it was especially during the Great War that the intersection between Debussy's music and political events became greater. Five of the ten compositions completed by Debussy between November 1914 and March 1917 are occasional pieces (*Berceuse héroïque*, *Pièce pour l'œuvre du 'Vêtement du blessé'*, *Élégie*, *Noël des enfants qui n'ont plus de maison*, *Les Soirs illuminés par l'ardeur du charbon*);[10] the others (three of the six sonatas he had planned to write, *En blanc et noir*, and *Douze études* for piano) all had their premiere in a charitable setting.

France and Russia (together with the United Kingdom in the Triple Entente from 1907) entered the war against Germany in early August 1914. Germany invaded Belgium in order to attack France from the north, and Britain joined the war. It is in this context that one can understand the initiative of the British writer Hall Caine to make an art album in honour of the king of Belgium, Albert I, and the Belgian soldiers who died during the German invasion. Debussy, who had taken refuge in Angers on 4 September, the day after the government left Paris for Bordeaux, participated in the album with his *Berceuse héroïque*.

From the very beginning of the war the French president, Raymond Poincaré, called for a 'Sacred Union' of political forces for the defence of the nation. Patriotism or nationalism became commonplace in political as well as artistic life, and not only for ideological reasons.[11] A protectionist decree of 27 September 1914 banned all trade with the enemy, including in music scores. As a result, editions of Beethoven, Mozart, and Schubert, to name but a few, had to be published in France, since the German editions commonly used were now 'Not to be opened during the war' (as stamped

---

[10] For an analysis of the genesis, reception, and programmatic nature of these works, see Marianne Wheeldon, *Debussy's Late Style* (Bloomington, IN: Indiana University Press, 2009).

[11] See Carlo Caballero, 'Patriotism or Nationalism? Fauré and the Great War', *Journal of the American Musicological Society* 52 (1999), pp. 593–625.

on their covers).[12] Debussy was in charge of Chopin's works for Durand's *Édition classique*.

On 21 March 1918, while Paris was under bombardment, the Opéra staged Rameau's *Castor et Pollux*, a sort of musical bomb launched in favour of French tradition. By this time, Debussy could no longer react to the German bombing, either musically (his *Ode à la France* did not go beyond a few sketches) or physically; he did not even have the strength to move down into the cellar to protect himself. He died on 25 March, an eerily musical day in Paris:

> Something strange was heard, the sound of a tam-tam, of a tambourine. It sounded like belly dancing, the fandango, and the Tarasque parade.
> The officers are good people, but most of them can't beat a drum. . . . They had been told, 'Go and sound the bombing alarm. . . .'.
> Never had Paris felt such joy since the war began. . . .
> Listening to the drumbeat, people had completely forgotten about the shells, which, by the way, caused no turmoil. 'Public life continued.'[13]

Author's Recommendation

Berceuse héroïque, 'pour rendre hommage à S. M. le roi Albert 1er de Belgique et à ses soldats' (1914).

The 185 pages of the *King Albert's Book: A Tribute to the Belgian King and People from Representative Men and Women throughout the World* (London: The Daily Telegraph, 1914) included, among letters, poems, short texts, and pictures, a dozen short musical compositions by celebrated composers from those 'civilised countries' that supported Belgium in its 'heroic and ever-memorable' resistance to the German invasion (as stated by Hall Caine in his introduction). The book was intended as a 'tribute of admiration' as well as an offer of 'prayers for the gallant little nation in [her] vast sorrow'. In keeping with this dual purpose, some pieces of music are triumphal marches (Edward Elgar's, for instance, or Ethel Smyth's *The March of the Women*), while others take the form of a prayer or a funeral lament (Pietro Mascagni's *Sunt lacrimae rerum!* or Peter Erasmus Lange-Müller's *Lamentation*).

---

[12] See Rachel Moore, *Performing Propaganda: Musical Life and Culture in Paris during the First World War* (Woodbridge: The Boydell Press, 2018), pp. 173–216.
[13] Anonymous, 'Quelques obus hier sur Paris, puis le silence: "La vie publique continue"', *Le Journal* (Paris) (26 March 1918), p. 1.

Debussy's *Berceuse héroïque* (Heroic Lullaby), as its title suggests, combines these two approaches. Against the background of a funeral march, some bugle signals (echoes of battles) can be heard in the distance (an idea shared with André Messager's *mélodie* 'Pour la patrie'). In the middle of the piece, the theme of the Belgian national anthem, *La Brabançonne*, 'proudly' ('*fièrement*') emerges as a song of encouragement. The orchestral version of the *Berceuse héroïque* was first performed in Paris on 25 October 1915 at a concert that included a work by a German composer for the first time since the beginning of the war: Beethoven's 'Eroica' Symphony.

CHAPTER 3

Beyond Paris

Lola San Martín Arbide

In the course of the fifty-five years of Debussy's lifespan, France was radically rethought.[1] The year of the composer's birth – 1862, during the Second Empire – coincided with the start of Napoleon III's military intervention in Mexico. Napoleon's campaign to establish a monarchy in Mexico failed, and the subsequent defeat inflicted by Prussia led to the proclamation of the Third Republic in 1870, the largest republican regime in Europe at that time. During the composer's lifetime, almost every level of public life at home underwent great changes, and the international relationships of his native country were thoroughly reconfigured. The Second Empire (1852–70) gave way to an anticlerical republic, which greatly increased investment in mandatory free education and was confronted with the challenge of finding concrete and effective ways of articulating mass political participation (i.e. universal suffrage) and fostering spaces for mass culture and massive public demonstrations. Debussy acquired particular notoriety after the operatic premiere of *Pelléas et Mélisande* in 1902. In the wake of his death in 1918, his legacy remained contested: some viewed him as an isolated figure, while others regarded him as a master of the new artistic avenues that he had opened up. For Debussyans like the critic Émile Vuillermoz, the composer had championed the dissemination of the French artistic spirit. Through his participation in the process of recovery and restoration of historical figures from the nation's past, such as Jeanne d'Arc or the medieval poet François Villon, and his references to eighteenth-century French clavecinists, such as Couperin and Rameau, Debussy also

---

[1] This work has received funding from various grants and research projects: the European Union's Horizon 2020 research and innovation programme under the Marie Skłodowska-Curie grant agreement no. 750086; Ramón y Cajal RYC2021-034430-I grant from the Spanish Ministry of Science, Innovation and Universities MCIN/AEI/10.13039/501100011033 and the European Union's NextGenerationEU/PRTR scheme; and the Sound Studies and Music research project funded by the Universidad de Sevilla (Plan Propio de Investigación, Atracción de investigadores con alto potencial, II.5A).

fulfilled the patriotic aim of paying tribute to his native country as the *musicien français* for which he wished to be recognised. The following pages offer a relational study of how Debussy's life and works were connected to the broader web of Parisian and French interactions with the world, with a specific focus on Franco-Russian and Franco-Spanish exchanges.

Beyond Paris, tensions between the city and the regions were at the centre of political, legal, and cultural debates. Efforts to decentralise the country spread across the territory. From 1884 onwards, for instance – coinciding with the year when Debussy won the Prix de Rome with his cantata *L'Enfant prodigue* – all municipalities were given equal powers. But France was still subject to Parisian rhythms, at both material and immaterial levels. In 1891, with trains already running to the centralised time of the capital to simplify travel, the city's clock became that of the entire hexagon and of Algeria. As denounced by some opposing voices, the city's domination over the culture of the country at large was one of the flaws of the young Republic. Maurice Barrès's *Les Déracinés* (*The Rootless*, 1897), for instance, deplored how public instruction disregarded the local and popular cultures of the '*pays*' (country). Indeed, his discourse on the need for the true French people to cultivate their attachment to both their *petit* and *grand pays* – their native province, on the one hand, and France, on the other – attained wide circulation through the collective voice of the Action française, of which Barrès was a member. Together with other right-wing leagues, this nationalist group played a decisive role in defining the cultural politics throughout Debussy's adult life.[2] Decentralisation often meant extending Parisian norms across France, through institutions such as the network of conservatoires established in the main provincial cities. Cultural regionalism was a complementary strategy for the self-affirmation of provincial identity, which took root in other important nodes of French musical life such as Toulouse, Bordeaux, and Lyon.[3]

Nationalist ideas gained support across France from the time of Debussy's youth, undergoing a series of growth spurts triggered by the loss of Alsace-Lorraine in 1871, the anti-Semitic sentiment unleashed by the Dreyfus affair (1894–1906), and, especially in the case of Debussy, the lead-up to the outbreak of the Great War in 1914. Debussy's anti-Germanism was already patent in his various writings for journals such as *La Revue blanche* and *Gil Blas*, although he adopted a more nationalistic agenda in his later criticism,

---

[2] Jane F. Fulcher, *French Cultural Politics and Music: From the Dreyfus Affair to the First World War* (New York: Oxford University Press, 1999).
[3] Katharine Ellis, *French Musical Life: Local Dynamics in the Century to World War II* (New York: Oxford University Press, 2021).

for instance in the musical monthly *S.I.M.* As we shall see, the composer also contributed to the aspirational, if abstract, concept of a unified national identity by turning to the nation's folklore and musical past. At the same time, through its references to Vietnamese theatre, Japanese prints, Russian opera, Scottish tunes, and Spanish songs of Moorish inflection, Debussy's music is proof of the composer's interest in different art forms from across the world – cues that he filtered through his unique creative lens.

In Debussy's France, the quest for a national identity took place against the backdrop of the perceived threat of a dominating foreign force. At the same time, this search for an identity was also at the centre of the colonial plan developed from the 1880s onwards, and of the complementary agenda of reinforcing the country's place within global politics. Germany played a determining role in both instances – first, by becoming the victorious enemy in 1871, and secondly, by not opposing France's global expansion in order to avoid any potential revenge after the Prussian War. At the same time as these events unfolded, France (and its neighbouring countries) was experiencing the powerful wave of *wagnérisme* in the musical sphere, which had started in the 1860s. One may follow Wagner, but, particularly after the early 1890s – as explained by Debussy in his 'Pourquoi j'ai écrit *Pélleas*' – it was necessary to find a manner of reaching beyond him, as expressed in his often-quoted turn of phrase about composing '*après Wagner*' rather than '*d'après Wagner*'.[4] Anti-German sentiment during Debussy's lifetime turned the Leipzig composer, once regarded as the prophet of the music of the future, into an emblem of the enemy. One of the goals of the Société nationale de musique, founded in 1871 shortly after the conclusion of the Franco-Prussian War and of which Debussy became a member in 1893, was to promote the art of national music (*ars gallica*). Debussy's ambivalence towards Wagner became clear in the initial reception of *Pelléas et Mélisande* (1902).[5] Critics would later compare the opera to *Tristan und Isolde*, despite Debussy. In fact, *Pelléas* is highly indebted to Wagner, who is ever-present across Debussy's œuvre.[6] Subsequently, however, critics did not fail to point out the Russian influence on *Pelléas*, especially since Debussy's opera and Mussorgsky's *Boris Godunov* were performed concurrently in 1908.[7]

---

[4] *Monsieur Croche*, p. 63.
[5] Deirdre Donnellon, 'Debussy as Musician and Critic', in Simon Trezise (ed.), *The Cambridge Companion to Debussy* (Cambridge: Cambridge University Press, 2003), p. 46.
[6] Robin Holloway, *Debussy and Wagner* (London: Eulenburg, 1979).
[7] François de Médicis, 'Composing after Wagner: The Music of Bruneau and Debussy, 1890–1902', in François de Médicis and Steven Huebner (eds.), *Debussy's Resonance* (Rochester, NY: University of Rochester Press, 2018), pp. 175–224.

Debussy expanded his compositional techniques by looking beyond the borders of his native France, and thus 're-oriented' Western music.[8] In Western Europe, Paris was one of the nineteenth-century capitals of the Orientalist world, and the city was praised as the chief place of cultural transfer at the time. Home to émigrés from far and wide, the city was attractive to intellectuals and artists for its transnationalism. When it came to specific nations or ethnic groups, however, local audiences, composers, and critics alike often became familiar with stereotypical forms of Otherness. Such exotic constructions were particularly pervasive in countries with imperialist ambitions like France, especially after Napoleon Bonaparte's expedition to Egypt in 1789–1801, and had been locally informed by French romantic poetry, travel writing, painting, etc. In literature, Victor Hugo's *Les Orientales* (1829), Gérard de Nerval's *Voyage en Orient* (1851), and Théophile Gautier's *Constantinople* (1853), to name but a few, are examples of works created by authors who travelled the world, seeking to become prey to the seductions of the picturesque, as was the case, for instance, with Paul Gauguin (1848–1903), whose works so effectively embraced the Orient. Such exoticism codified a Francocentric view of other cultures that the course of history has recurrently confirmed as infused with either fictional, racist, and/ or misogynous accounts of the Other.

In Debussy's time, musical orientalism had also delighted the audiences of Bizet's *Carmen* (1875), Delibes's *Lakmé* (1883), and Saint-Saëns's *Africa* (1891), among many other examples. As a consequence of the popularity of this kind of orientalia, émigré artists thirsty for acceptance and recognition were put in the paradoxical position of auto-exoticism – that is, of having to display their national identity in the precise ways that international and Parisian audiences and commentators would recognise as such. Regional nuances, for example, were often lost for the sake of ethnically hegemonic representations consolidated via the major transnational hubs of the world, such as Paris (an example of this being the identification of Andalusian culture with Spanish heritage at large). The interweaving of international references in Debussy's works must therefore be understood within the wider context of Parisian orientalism and cosmopolitanism.

Material culture played a significant role in this process. Exotic treasures were easy to find in France thanks to those art dealers who guaranteed their flow, and they delighted Debussy. German art dealer Siegfried Bing, for instance, promoted Japanese art and Art Nouveau in the 1870s, and his

---

[8] Roy Howat, *The Art of French Piano Music: Debussy, Ravel, Fauré, Chabrier* (New Haven, CT: Yale University Press, 2009), p. 110.

pavilion at the 1900 Exposition Universelle became a popular success. A little wooden frog figurine originally from Japan, which Debussy named Arkel, became the composer's good luck charm, and his 'Poissons d'or' (*Images*, series 2, 1907) was inspired by a nineteenth-century Japanese lacquer of goldfish, which he kept hung up on the wall.[9] Asian influences – particularly Eastern philosophies, and sounds like the Javanese gamelan that so enchanted Debussy during the 1889 Exposition Universelle – can be heard, for instance, in *Estampes* (1903), in *Images* for piano, series 1 and 2 (1901–7), and in 'Voiles' (*Préludes*, book 1, 1909–10).

The Parisian World's Fairs of 1889 and 1900 were a most important source of foreign and exotic references for Debussy. Although not a 'globetrotter' in the style of Saint-Saëns and other contemporaries, Debussy was a well-travelled man who had much direct knowledge of many of the composers and works that he admired. Having already started to compose *mélodies* in 1879, his first piano pieces were composed in Florence, where he had travelled in 1880 to join the Russian benefactress Nadezhda Filaretovna von Meck at her summer residence. The following year, again with von Meck, Debussy travelled to Moscow. During that Russian stay in his late teens, Debussy discovered the music of Mussorgsky and Tchaikovsky, of whom von Meck was a generous patron. After winning the Prix de Rome for the cantata *L'Enfant prodigue* in 1884, Debussy stayed at the Villa Medici for two years. During the peak of *wagnérisme* – at the precise time when Nietzsche was writing *Nietzsche contra Wagner* – Debussy twice visited Bayreuth, in 1888 and 1889. His foreign trips continued well into the 1900s and 1910s, to destinations such as Vienna, Budapest, Amsterdam, The Hague, and London, as part of tours often motivated by the need to support his family.

Britain was the country that Debussy visited most often. But the musical landscape that left an early and the most indelible mark on his production was that of Russia. Defeat in the Franco-Prussian War had left France wounded and isolated within Europe, and the diplomatic consequences of the conflict had long-lasting ramifications for cultural transfers between France and the rest of the world. The Franco-Russian alliance established in 1891 (which lasted until 1917) ensured that both countries would protect each other and, with the inclusion of Great Britain, led eventually to the Triple Entente of 1907. In the wake of this Franco-Russian pact, artistic exchange between the two powers was encouraged, precisely as a tactic

---

[9] Marie Rolf, 'Oriental and Iberian Resonances in Early Debussy Songs', in de Médicis and Huebner (eds.), *Debussy's Resonance*, pp. 272–98.

intended to legitimise the unlikely alliance between republican France and imperialist Russia. Franco-Russian musical associations immediately began to be established, and Russian music started to figure with increasing frequency in the concert programmes of the Concerts Pasdeloup and the Concerts Lamoureux, for example. The Imperial Academy of Arts in Saint Petersburg began to send its students to France, and in 1900 modern Russian art was included in the Exposition Universelle. Subsequently, Sergei Diaghilev introduced the music of Rimsky-Korsakov, Scriabin, Rachmaninov, and Glazunov at the Paris Opéra through a series of concerts in 1907.

Culturally, the Franco-Russian exchanges of the period had defining consequences. It is hard to underestimate, for example, the enduring legacy of Russian dance across the Western world due to the impact of Russian ballet in France. In this context, ballet, a French invention that was experiencing a period of decline in the West, was modernised in Russia, thanks to the contribution, among others, of Frenchman Marius Petipa, the father of classical ballet, who had moved to Saint Petersburg in 1847. Thus, when Diaghilev brought his Ballets Russes to Paris in 1909, his company was synonymous with the avant-garde and innovation. In the nineteenth century, the Paris Opéra had overtly traded with the sexuality of the *danseuses* by, for instance, allowing male patrons into their warm-up studio – as in the *Foyer de danse* painted by Degas in 1872 – and thus encouraging 'soft prostitution'.[10] By contrast, at Diaghilev's Ballets Russes it was the male body and a renewed concept of athleticism that took centre stage, as when Debussy's *Prélude à l'après-midi d'un faune* (1894) was staged as a ballet at the Opéra in 1912 with Vaslav Nijinsky in the title role.[11] Another important Russian influence on Debussy was Igor Stravinsky, whom he admired for his 'orchestral infallibility', as well as for his original colour and rhythm.[12] The two men had become friends in 1910, the year Stravinsky's *Firebird* was premiered by the Ballets Russes, with *Petrushka* following in 1911. Echoes of the latter can be heard in the ballet *Khamma*, which Debussy started composing in 1911, with Charles Koechlin completing the orchestration in 1913. This work had been commissioned by Canadian dancer Maud Allan and was set in ancient Egypt, a prime locus in the Orientalist tradition described above. It verged on bitonality

---

[10] Marian Smith, 'Dances and Dancers', in David Charlton (ed.), *The Cambridge Companion to Grand Opera* (Cambridge: Cambridge University Press, 2003), p. 106.
[11] Ilyana Karthas, *When Ballet Became French: Modern Ballet and the Cultural Politics of France, 1909–1939* (Montreal: McGill-Queen's University Press, 2015), p. 16.
[12] Robert Orledge, *Debussy and the Theatre* (Cambridge: Cambridge University Press, 2009), p. 146.

and used the combination of C and F♯ major heard in *Petrushka*, which Debussy had also used in *La Mer, Rodrigue et Chimène*, and *Pelléas*. The fact that *Khamma* was set in Egypt and bore a resemblance to Stravinsky exemplifies the overlap between Russia and the Orient in the Western reception, not just of Stravinsky but of Russian art as a whole (another example being Wassily Kandinsky). Diaghilev's Ballets Russes played an important role in this process, offering a self-exoticised image of Russia by, for instance, delving into Stravinsky's neo-primitivism to satisfy the Russophilia of Parisian audiences.

The idea of 'Eastern Europe' as a cultural space both within and beyond the continent had circulated in France since the eighteenth century. Debussy's Paris and France were a hub of cultural power, with self-conferred powers to determine whether foreign countries could enter into or should be excluded from informal cultural alliances. In the realm of music, there were proposals from the likes of Henri Collet and Georges Jean-Aubry to create an aesthetic entente with Spain, Russia, Italy, and Britain that would counterbalance the German dominance over musical taste and its canon and have France as its centre of gravity.[13] Beyond this entente, France also sought to position itself as both *the* protector of Latin heritage against barbaric intrusion and mediator in a global Latinity. Thus it was that in the last third of the nineteenth century the term Latin America was coined and spread worldwide from France, replacing expressions such as South America or Spanish America as part of a wider political and economic strategy to restore presence and power in the wake of Spain's decline in the Atlantic.

In the musical realm, there was of course no need to leave Paris to listen to Spanish music. From the mid-nineteenth century, composers, musicians, and dancers (both Spanish-born and foreign) had generated a true wave of Hispanophilia in France and beyond, as evidenced in Édouard Lalo's 1875 *Symphonie espagnole*, for example. It is important, however, to bear in mind that Hispanomania was only one half of the picture. In the context of the international competition described above, a wave of political and cultural Hispanophobia had also re-emerged, delegitimising Spanish influence. One of the most successful and global operas portraying Spain in the nineteenth century – Bizet's *Carmen* (1875) – highlighted the irrational, unmanageable, and erratic nature of its leading characters, who at the end meet their fatal destiny. Charged with the dual nature of conveying the pleasures of the exotic and the primal state of uncivilised societies – displayed, for example, in

---

[13] Samuel Llano, *Whose Spain? Negotiating Spanish Music in Paris, 1908–1929* (New York: Oxford University Press, 2013), pp. 29–33.

the picturesque, if brutal, spectacle of bullfighting – Spanish-infused music was unavoidable in Debussy's Paris. Works such as Emmanuel Chabrier's *España* (1883) and Maurice Ravel's *Rapsodie espagnole* (1908) are good examples of the wide currency of Spanish-infused French music during that period. Debussy came into direct contact with Spain around 1880, when he crossed the border to visit the northern city of San Sebastián during his trip to Arcachon in the company of Nadezhda von Meck. Spanish composer Manuel de Falla (1876–1946) recalled that the purpose of Debussy's trip to Spain had been to attend a bullfight. In fact, several of his early songs feature bullfighting: 'Madrid, princesse des Espagnes' (1879), 'Séguidille' (1882), and 'Chanson espagnole' (1883), set to texts by Romantic authors such as Alfred de Musset and Théophile Gautier.[14] Some stylistic features of Debussy's music were cemented in this early period, including the exotic effects of chromatic modality, as well as whole-tone and octatonic scales.[15] In *Rodrigue et Chimène*, Debussy's fashionable Hispanicism merged with the *fin de siècle* medieval revival in France. Work for this opera had begun in 1890, with a libretto that Catulle Mendès had written about El Cid, the legendary figure of the Spanish Reconquista in the eleventh century.[16] The opera remained unfinished, however, when the composer turned instead to Maeterlinck's *Pelléas*.

From Glinka to Debussy, many were the composers who devoted works to the sub-Orientalist theme of Alhambrism, reminiscing on the Arab heritage of Spanish cities such as Granada, which Debussy dreamed of visiting and exploring for himself. His 1903 triptych *Estampes* contained his 'La Soirée dans Grenade', which begins with the Cuban rhythm of the habanera that had by then already become a musical signifier of Andalusia and Spain, and which can also be heard in 'Ibéria's' second movement, 'Les Parfums de la nuit' (1905–8) and in 'La Puerta del vino' from the *Préludes*, book 2 (1909–13). Spanish composers such as de Falla and Isaac Albéniz (1860–1909) recognised Debussy's Andalusian pieces as exemplary of the Spanish spirit, and the friendship that bound them – and Catalan pianist Ricardo Viñes (1875–1943) – proved highly productive for Franco-Spanish musical exchanges. Greatly influenced by Debussy were Falla's *Noches en los jardines de España* (1909–16), as well as Albéniz's suite *Iberia* (1905–9). As time went by, the First World War provided a new impetus for the establishment of international cultural institutions promoting further

---

[14] Matthew Brown, *Debussy's 'Ibéria'* (New York: Oxford University Press, 2003), p. 56.
[15] Boyd Pomeroy, 'Debussy's Tonality: A Formal Perspective', in Trezise (ed.), *Cambridge Companion*, p. 156.
[16] See Richard Langham Smith, '*Rodrigue et Chimène*: Genèse, histoire, problèmes d'édition', *Cahiers Debussy* 12–13 (1988–9), pp. 67–81.

artistic exchange. Efforts to create a residence for French artists in Madrid modelled on the Académie française in Rome (Villa Medici), where Debussy had studied in his youth, began in 1916 (resulting in the opening of the Casa de Velázquez in 1928), and the Comité de rapprochement franco-espagnol was founded in 1917.

It is hard to underestimate the role that Debussy played in these international processes of cultural transfer. Not only did the composer come to be regarded as a model for a renewed, modern embodiment of the French spirit, but his works also offered important insights into the questions that composers from abroad were asking themselves in relation to their own musical traditions. Debussy's idea of art was rooted in the pursuit of freedom and pleasure. This quest gave rise to an exercise in transnational cosmopolitanism while at the same time creating such odes to French tradition as the 'Hommage à Rameau' (*Images*, series 1, 1905), *Trois chansons de Charles d'Orléans* (1908), and the *Trois ballades de François Villon* (1910), as well as patriotic pieces such as his *Berceuse héroïque* (1914) and *Ode à la France* (unfinished, 1916–17). The balance Debussy found between modernity and tradition, internationalism and patriotism, together with his defiance of pre-existing rules, made the composer both a unique figure and an inspiring visionary. His works are testament to the rich web of multicultural exchanges that the audacious Debussy triggered and exploited within and beyond Paris.

Author's Recommendation

'Ibéria', *Images* (for orchestra) (1905–8).

Debussy's most cheerful, energetic, and fiery Spanish piece 'Ibéria' is a symphonic triptych from *Images* for orchestra, referred to as series 3 (1905–12), published in 1910 and consisting of the movements 'Par les rues et les chemins' (In the streets and lanes), 'Les Parfums de la nuit' (The fragrances of the night), and 'Le Matin d'un jour de fête' (The morning of a festival day). Debussy made an unprecedented effort to ensure the orchestra would bring the piece to life as vibrantly as possible by annotating the score with more expressive cues than was customary. Yet, to the composer's satisfaction, the unfolding of some of the transitions of the piece sound as if improvised. 'Ibéria' captured the soundscape of Debussy's imagined Spain, featuring the bells, castanets, and tambourines of the streets of Catalonia or Granada, and including sevillana, habanera, and seguidilla rhythms taken from his beloved Spanish folk songs.

CHAPTER 4

Feminine Beginnings: Women's Critical Perspectives on Debussy (1897–1914)

Christopher Moore

Over recent decades historians have come to view the French *fin de siècle* as a period during which gender roles, hitherto largely viewed as immutable, underwent a profound reconceptualisation. As an expression of both discourse and practice, gender reflected and informed anxieties that weighed heavily on *fin de siècle* culture. Masculinity during this period has been conceived in terms of a 'crisis', stemming from a variety of concerns, including the scientific identification of sexual pathologies, widely held perceptions of degeneracy, and concomitant aspirations for moral and physical amelioration across French society. Women's roles were perhaps even more radically reconceived, with the nascent forces of feminism giving rise to a style of 'New Woman' that sought emancipation from the strictures of family and home in a quest to intervene in the wider public sphere.[1] These tendencies reveal various levels of ambivalence about the body, sexuality, and the cultural expressions of desire as they relate to the technological and cultural disruptions of modernity at the turn of the century.

Musicians participated in these rearticulations, and their lives and works were shaped by them. French musical institutions, like the Prix de Rome, which opened itself to female candidates in 1903, were responsive to feminist ambitions and prompted anxieties in musical circles about the emergence of a 'pink peril', ostensibly led by composers such as Juliette Toutain, Hélène Fleury, and Lili and Nadia Boulanger.[2] Musical works, especially those for the stage, while continuing to engage with post-Wagnerian stereotypes of feminine representation (*femme fatale*, *femme-enfant*), also proposed new attitudes about the gendered body, with dancers

---

[1] James F. McMillan, *France and Women, 1789–1914: Gender, Society and Politics* (London: Routledge, 2000).
[2] See Annegret Fauser, '*La Guerre en dentelles*: Women and the *Prix de Rome* in French Cultural Politics', *Journal of the American Musicological Society* 51 (1998), pp. 83–129.

like Isadora Duncan, and later Vaslav Nijinsky, upending traditional conceptions. Evolving social and aesthetic realities compelled some male musicians to express their masculinities in ways that clashed with and challenged normative expectations: Erik Satie's bohemianism, Maurice Ravel's dandyism, and Déodat de Séverac's embrace of *latinité* all expressed gendered identities in the public sphere that were situated on the margins of official culture. These modifications took place at a time when the scientific field was debating the codification of sexual types and behaviours and when artistic outputs dealing with male and female homosexuality were become increasingly prevalent.

Critical writing on the period's most celebrated French composer, Claude Debussy, may also be profitably revisited and re-evaluated with the help of an analytical lens focused on questions of gender. As a gendered subject, Debussy emerges as a man located across various intersectional axes of 'hegemonic' masculinity at the *fin de siècle*. A heterosexual bohemian aiming for (and ultimately achieving) bourgeois respectability through elite cultural standing and marriage, Debussy's dealings with women were nonetheless occasionally viewed as toxic; his 'ferocious appetite for love' at times inspiring the opprobrium of even some of his closest friends and associates.[3] Heterosexual love is a recurring theme across Debussy's output; it forms the very basis of *Pelléas et Mélisande*, and emerges in various ways throughout his *mélodies* (those for Marie-Blanche Vasnier, the *Cinq poèmes de Charles Baudelaire*, the *Chansons de Bilitis*, etc.), piano pieces (*L'Isle joyeuse*), and orchestral works (*Prélude à l'après-midi d'un faune*). Despite the obvious hermeneutic windows that these works provide for gendered analyses, throughout much of the twentieth century Debussy's music and musical reputation were only infrequently described with explicit reference to questions of gender. Prior to the emergence of the so-called new musicology of the 1980s and 1990s, Debussy's overwhelmingly male exegetes took for granted both their own male perspectives and those of their subject. The lack of critical engagement with gender in their accounts, mirrored across the discipline of musicology at large, served to deflect attention away from the ways in which such questions could inform musical composition and performance as well as the ways people could react to them.

An overview of gender and its implications for Debussy's music would far exceed the scope of the current chapter. Rather, as a means of situating Debussy's music within a broader network of concerns and debates about

---

[3] Antoine Goléa, *Claude Debussy, l'homme et son œuvre* (Paris: Pierre Seghers, 1966), p. 22.

gender at the *fin de siècle,* this chapter turns its attention to an examination of women's critical reactions to Debussy's music while the composer was still alive. The primary impetus for this examination stems from the realisation that such accounts are, as is often the case with composers from his period and before, extremely difficult to find. Throughout Debussy's *Correspondance*, for example, only an early career (1881) assessment by Nadezhda von Meck, referring to Debussy's 'charming symphony', stands as a feminine assessment of the composer's work.[4] The ensuing 2,000 pages of his letters, barring any oversights, uniquely concern the musical opinions of men. But this record obscures the more fundamental fact that during this same period the French feminist and feminine presses were in full emergence. Whereas there was little discussion of music in the most 'radical' feminist publications of the period (such as *La Femme et l'avenir, Le Combat féministe* and *La Suffragiste*), music was frequently commented upon in journals and newspapers with moderate feminist editorial positions or in the popular women's press with feminist leanings.[5]

As a means of modestly redressing the enormous gendered imbalance in early Debussy criticism, this chapter focuses on the writings of Cécile Max, Lucie Delarue-Mardrus, and Marguerite Levadé, who wrote articles about music for *La Fronde, Fémina,* and *La Française,* respectively. All three authors wrote about performances of the music of Debussy. Through their activities, these writers may be viewed as exemplars of the 'New Woman', described by historian Mary Louise Roberts as individuals who 'challenged the regulatory norms of gender by living unconventional lives and by doing work outside the home that was coded masculine in French culture'.[6] While we have no record of Debussy's reaction to their articles, he was clearly little impressed with the styles of womanhood that characterised 'New Women' in general. Rather, Debussy's model of acceptable feminine behaviour was informed by the conventions of bourgeois respectability, emphasising feminine discretion and propriety. The composer's bitter interactions with the intrepid Canadian dancer Maud Allan over the ballet *Khamma* may best be understood as resulting from a clash of expectations around such social norms. The misogynist and racist language

---

[4] She is referring to Debussy's unfinished Symphony in B minor, for which only an Allegro exists. See the letter from Nadine de Meck (Nadezhda von Meck) to Debussy, 20 February 1881, *Correspondance*, pp. 11–12.
[5] This categorisation is borrowed from Amanda Harris, 'The Spectacle of Woman as Creator: Representation of Women Composers in the French, German and English Feminist Press, 1880–1930', *Women's History Review* 23 (2014), p. 20.
[6] Mary Louise Roberts, *Disruptive Acts: The New Woman in Fin-de-Siècle France* (Chicago, IL: Chicago University Press, 2002).

that Debussy used to describe Allan in his letters to Jacques Durand strongly suggests that his tolerance for such a socially emancipated and entrepreneurial 'New Woman' was extremely limited.[7]

Engaging with the critical writings of Max, Delarue-Mardrus, and Levadé expands our historical understanding of the deeply gendered field of *fin-de-siècle* music criticism. Significantly, it allows us to see how questions of musical literacy, appreciation, and aesthetics intersected with other fundamental discourses of modernity, most notably feminism. As women signing articles with their own names, female critics sought to carve out authoritative positions in a discursive tradition that had been entirely dominated by men. In their quest to legitimise themselves as critics on a par with their male counterparts, they were often compelled to model their criticism around existing literary conventions with long-standing authority. But not all of this work participated in the buttressing of a hegemonic, masculine model of critical discourse. Rather, critics like Max and Delarue-Mardrus challenged existing conventions both through the content of their written work and through the articulation of new professional identities. Perhaps most significantly, these critics' presence in this critical landscape gave further impetus to ongoing debates about the politics of gender and its impacts on French music and musical life during the years before the First World War.

Cécile Max and *La Fronde*: Discursive Mimicry and Feminist Critique

The daily newspaper *La Fronde*, launched in 1897 by Marguerite Durand, attracted considerable contemporaneous attention in France in large part because it was founded, edited, and written solely by women. The newspaper's subversive approach hinged on the revolutionary notion that women, now working as journalists, could seek and gain access to spaces of power and prestige that had been hitherto reserved for men. Furthermore, *La Fronde* aimed to simultaneously politicise and neutralise gender through literary style: it closely imitated the journalistic conventions of men, thus effecting a radical incursion into a highly gendered space. By copying and emulating the style of masculine journalism, *La Fronde* suggested that women could produce forms of writing that engaged with constructions of reality as opposed to the fantasy spaces of fiction and

---

[7] See Debussy's letters to Jacques Durand, 19 September 1912 and 18 September 1913, *Correspondance*, pp. 1545, 1666.

poetry with which they were more readily associated. This engagement with the 'real' offered a ground upon which a feminist critique could be constructed, one that was far more persuasive and potentially impactful than those couched in genres of fiction.[8]

Cécile Max began writing for *La Fronde* in late 1899 and maintained a regular column there until 1903. In 1901 she succeeded in becoming the only female member of the Association syndicale professionnelle et mutuelle de la critique dramatique et musicale, an entity that sought to defend the moral and intellectual rights of critics while concomitantly attempting to define and circumscribe the nature of professional criticism in general.[9] Nominated by Alfred Bruneau, Hugues Imbert, and Samuel Rousseau, Max gained access to this group, which for decades had largely functioned as an old boys' club.[10] *La Fronde* was quick to highlight her remarkable achievement, pointing to Max's previous 'professional' activities at the newspaper and celebrating her ability to open a door that until then had been 'obstinately closed to women'.[11] Like the other journalists at *La Fronde*, Max's work does not appear revolutionary on the surface, because it so carefully mimics the prevailing discursive styles of *fin de siècle* music criticism. Yet her adhesion to these styles allowed her to more easily insert feminist critique when the opportunity arose.

Take, for instance, Max's review of *Pelléas et Mélisande*, which appeared on 1 May 1902 and thus belonged to the very first wave of articles about the work to appear in large circulation dailies (including *Le Petit Parisien*, *Le Matin*, *Le Journal*, and *Le Petit Journal*).[12] As such, her review would have been largely uninfluenced by the mainstream press or by pro-Debussy critics (like Émile Vuillermoz, Pierre Lalo, and Jean Marnold), whose reviews only appeared at a later date and in more specialised publications.[13] In some ways, her viewpoint resembles that of Henry Gauthier-Villars, published in *Le Matin*, in that it offers a mixed reaction to this new work.[14] But it may also be that Gauthier-Villars's work in general – as the most prominent music critic of the period – constituted the

---

[8] Roberts, *Disruptive Acts*, pp. 90–106.
[9] Isabelle Mayaud, 'Sauver la critique, défendre les critiques. Les stratégies d'un porte-parole: l'Association syndicale professionnelle et mutuelle de la critique dramatique et musicale (France, 1877–1914)', *Sociétés & Représentations* 40 (2015), p. 91.
[10] Mayaud, 'Sauver la critique, défendre les critiques', pp. 79–80.
[11] Anon., 'Candidature féminine', *La Fronde* (29 December 1901), p. 1.
[12] Cécile Max, 'Les Premières', *La Fronde* (1 May 1902), p. 3.
[13] Vuillermoz in the May issue of *La Revue dorée*, Lalo in *Le Temps* (20 May), and Marnold in the June issue of the *Mercure de France*.
[14] Henry Gauthier-Villars, 'Les Premières', *Le Matin* (1 May 1902), p. 4.

very model upon which Max crafted her own publications. Certainly, her review of *Pelléas* functions on similar levels. First, it offers context on both Debussy's career and Maeterlinck's play, placing both within their respective artistic trajectories. Second, it scrutinises the suitability of the play for musical treatment, and acknowledges that Debussy's music periodically endowed the text with 'unexpected importance' that prompted audience members to laugh even during tragic situations. Third, Max establishes her critical authority by highlighting her musical expertise. She understands Debussy's themes as Wagnerian leitmotifs, and informs her readers that she had noted the presence of the themes for Mélisande, Golaud, and Pelléas 'over one hundred times'. She also describes idiosyncrasies of Debussy's harmonic language, citing in particular his 'constant use' of seventh and ninth chords.

This strategy largely conforms to expectations for opera criticism in large circulation dailies from the period, so much so in fact that its content may seem unremarkable. But it is important not to underestimate the prejudice that such writing may have encountered. For example, the writer Jules Renard, who attended the first performance of *Pelléas*, noted that the Opéra-Comique was like a 'huge café where strapless gowns and diamonds and the deaf (who want to give the impression that they can hear) hold their *rendez-vous*'.[15] Max's review operates a disruptive corrective to such misogynist perspectives of the female public. Indeed, she uses her 'professional' review to articulate a feminist critique of opera audiences, upbraiding the men in the public who 'stamped their feet' in indignation at the violent denouement of Golaud's jealousy. In a few lines dripping with irony, she reminds readers that figures like Golaud are not only found in fiction; rather, examples of such spousal violence and revenge were commonplace and largely enabled by France's laws on adultery and marriage. Reforming these laws with the intent of protecting women was a centrepiece of *La Fronde*'s broader editorial line; Max's review implies that the men at the opera would do better to 'stamp their feet' through concrete social action than solely out of dismay at having to witness a sordid spectacle on the theatrical stage.

Lucie Delarue-Mardrus: Massenet versus Debussy

Not all female critics sought out or achieved the type of professional recognition afforded Cécile Max. Take, for example, the poet Lucie Delarue-Mardrus, who replaced Reynaldo Hahn as the primary music

---

[15] Jules Renard, *Journal 1887–1910* (Paris: Gallimard, 1965), p. 760.

critic for *Fémina* in 1911. In her first article for the publication, she employs an ironic tone to state how her work will contrast with those of 'professional' critics:

> I will not propose here what is conventionally referred to as musical criticism. I leave that task to the more competent. I would not know how to write, for example, about the 'beautiful orchestral palette' of some symphony, nor cite themes from memory as critics do. God! How learned they are! We are even more impressed because we do not always understand what they are saying. They often use a form of algebra that puts the intimidated reader in their place.[16]

One recurring aspect of Delarue-Mardrus's criticism (for, despite her remonstrations, criticism it was indeed) was to use Debussy as a technical and aesthetic foil to Massenet, the latter representing something of an ideal type in the critic's appreciation of music. In a remarkable essay entitled 'Massenet, Musician of Women', Delarue-Mardrus praises Massenet's music for offering 'what women wanted to hear'; he universally appeals to their heightened sense of nostalgia and sentimentality. Debussy's music, on the other hand, in his avoidance of melody, offers only 'difficult pleasures and the bitter joy of its false notes'. She astutely, though negatively, likens his craft to 'the modern coldness and dryness that prefers above all the principle of Japanese bonsai trees', a symbol of the contemporary taste for 'paradox, torture, and difficulty'.[17]

Delarue-Mardrus's essentialising of women's taste in this manner is somewhat surprising. For an author often credited with introducing lesbian subjectivities to French poetry, her endorsement of Massenet reveals that at this stage in her career she nonetheless played public lip service to the idea of the 'eternal feminine'.[18] Her article following Massenet's death in 1912 is no exception; it hones in on Debussy once again to make better her point:

> Certainly, the music of Claude Debussy pleases us by its masterly qualities, by its voluntarily restrained lyricism, by its effects created with knowledgeable craftiness, by the prodigality of its sonority, by its consistent distinction. But must we only admit this type of music and all those that resemble it, whether predecessors or successors? This internal violon that we call our nerves, can it only vibrate to that bow?[19]

---

[16] Lucie Delarue-Mardrus, 'Le Papier à musique', *Fémina* (15 November 1911), p. 627.
[17] Delarue-Mardrus, 'Massenet, musicien de la femme', *Fémina* (15 January 1912), p. 34.
[18] Delarue-Mardrus was a member of the circle of Natalie Clifford Barney, who described her at length in Clifford-Barney, *Souvenirs indiscrets* (Paris: Flammarion, 1960), pp. 147–85.
[19] Delarue-Mardrus, 'Massenet et son œuvre', *Fémina* (15 September 1912), p. 510.

4 Women's Critical Perspectives on Debussy 41

Debussy himself was also compelled to write about Massenet's passing in a short article published in *Le Matin*. While not naming Delarue-Mardrus, he equally paints a picture of Massenet as a 'musician of women', but does so in a condescending fashion. Speaking about the composer's popularity with female audiences, he writes: 'Have we ever heard of young dressmakers humming the St Matthew Passion? I don't think so. But everybody knows that they wake up in the morning singing *Manon* or *Werther*.' Although Debussy admits that it must be a 'charming glory' to have been so appreciated, he nonetheless rebukes Massenet's compositional facility, claiming that 'it seems to have sometimes inhibited him from choosing adroitly'.[20] This was not the first time Debussy femininised the work of his colleague, and it suggests that he sought to orientate public reception of his own work in a direction that would discourage recourse to gender in a similar manner.[21]

Certainly, descriptions of Debussy's music in gendered terms were a recurring feature in the feminine and feminist press. In *La Vie heureuse*, which described itself as a 'Revue féminine universelle illustrée', critic Robert L. Ochs reviewed a concert of an unspecified '*Suite*' by Debussy as follows:

> It was soft music, not at all tormented, the exquisite music of a 'minor master' who has accustomed us to more audacity. The hall was full. There were attentive faces, secretively emotional, resting on hands in an attitude of reflection; faces of women that seemed to feel more than us the delicacy of the melodies and to discover behind these notes a hidden sensitivity.[22]

Here, the reception of Debussy veers closely to that of Massenet's dressmakers: it is particularly appropriate to feminine appreciation. But the review may also point to a more fundamental aspect of Debussy reception in that it describes forms of listening in which sentiment and somatic engagement triumph over intellectual understanding.[23] Ochs's inference is

---

[20] Debussy, 'Massenet n'est plus . . . ', *Le Matin* (14 August 1912), in *Monsieur Croche*, pp. 208–9.
[21] Debussy, 'D'Ève à Grisélidis', *La Revue blanche* (1 December 1903), in *Monsieur Croche*, pp. 59–61. See also Steven Huebner, 'Between Massenet and Wagner', in François de Médicis and Steven Huebner (eds.), *Debussy's Resonance* (Rochester, NY: University of Rochester Press, 2018), pp. 225–53.
[22] Robert L. Ochs, 'Les Concerts', *La Vie heureuse* (1 December 1907). Ochs was presumably writing about the first performance of Henri Büsser's orchestration of the *Petite suite* on 3 November 1907 under the direction of Camille Chevillard.
[23] On this changing paradigm and how it was refracted across Debussy criticism during this period, see Alexandra Kieffer, *Debussy's Critics: Sound, Affect, and the Experience of Modernism* (New York: Oxford University Press, 2019).

that women were more likely to feel Debussy's music in this manner; they were more attuned to questions of 'interior emotions' and thus advantageously positioned for the delectation of music, which, in his words, was 'better served by a rare sensibility than a reasoned *intelligence*'.[24]

La Française: Feminist Engagement and the Erasure of Men

The simultaneous growth of both the feminine leisure press and the feminist press during this period prompted an evolution in the way that critics attached to feminist journals wrote about music. In *La Française: Journal du progrès féminin*, a weekly founded by Jane Misme in 1906, coverage of music gradually shifted away from reporting on concerts featuring works by men. By 1910 the emphasis had moved almost entirely to accounts of performances by women, to concerts of the music of female composers, and to articles detailing the roles and contributions of women throughout music history.[25] In *La Française*, Misme, who had previously written for *La Fronde*, clearly abandoned an editorial policy of mimicry for one of even more explicit feminist engagement.

An early review by Marguerite Levadé of Debussy's orchestrated version of 'Le Jet d'eau' from his *Cinq poèmes de Charles Baudelaire* is, as such, a rare example of music criticism on the composer that appeared in the more specialised French feminist press.[26] Debussy's music is here described with considerable favour, despite the fact that the performance was not. Levadé believed that Debussy's 'preciously elegant harmonic research, which perfectly underlines every idea' required 'careful study equal to that which we give to the pages of certain classics'.[27] Put this way, Levadé participates in a certain form of canonisation of the composer, the 'classics' here standing in for a long tradition of masculine endeavour and accomplishment.

It is relatively unsurprising then that such forms of reviewing decreased in *La Française* given its social and political mandate. Levadé's column did not last through to the end of 1907, and the journal's focus gradually centred on musical events, mainly featuring women, that took place in the salon of Mr and Mrs Gabriel Lefeuve, who also began writing regular articles for the paper in 1909. Their contributions, along with that of critic Renée Caillé, represent a new approach to feminist music criticism, characterised during the period 1910–14 by a steadfast desire to highlight and valorise the contributions of women across French musical life.

---

[24] Ochs, 'Les Concerts'. [25] Harris, 'Spectacle of Woman', pp. 28–9.
[26] The work was performed at the Concerts Colonne on 24 February 1907, sung by Hélène Demellier.
[27] 'Musique', *La Française* (3 March 1907).

Conclusion

How did the incursion of women into the masculine space of music criticism affect Debussy? Debussy's ambivalent relationship with criticism is well known; he famously rejected the work of most critics, while being nonetheless keenly aware of their contributions. In 1901 he even began publishing his own criticism, in which the fictitious figure of 'Monsieur Croche' emerges as an imaginary antidote to conventional journalistic criticism in which he had lost all confidence.[28] Writing to critic Louis Laloy in 1906, he further complained: 'You also know – better than I – how much people write about Music; in our present time, when people don't know what to do, nor especially what to say, they try out art criticism!'[29]

This simultaneous expression of deep interest and cynical dismissal suggests that, for Debussy, music criticism was a discursive field that yielded a power from which it was impossible for an artist to escape. Women's participation in this field at the *fin de siècle*, while not visibly altering the composer's views, inevitably modified the rules of the game, the subterranean influence of which it is difficult to measure. To be certain, these perspectives added to the diversity of opinion on the composer and his works, and contributed to the ways in which he and his contemporaries understood and encountered gendered differences in their time. In short, Debussy's music and reputation may be profitably understood within the context of the growing implication of women within the public sphere and concomitant anxieties about their challenge to the hegemonic masculine ordering of French society at the *fin de siècle*.

Author's Recommendation

'Le Jet d'eau', *Cinq poèmes de Charles Baudelaire* (1887–9).

The poem 'Le Jet d'eau', a posthumous addition (1868) to Baudelaire's *Les Fleurs du mal*, was set to music in the late nineteenth century by Maurice Rollinat, Gustave Charpentier, and Claude Debussy, whose version for voice and piano was composed in 1889 and published in 1890 as the third of his *Cinq poèmes de Charles Baudelaire*. The song only began to be regularly performed following its republication by Durand in 1902, first by Victor Debay, and later Camille Fourrier and Jeanne Raunay. Debussy's orchestration of the song, which dates from 1907, while expanding the social

---

[28] See Debussy, 'L'entretien avec M. Croche', *La Revue blanche* (1 July 1901), in *Monsieur Croche*, pp. 45–53.
[29] Letter to Louis Laloy, 10 March 1906, *Correspondance*, p. 945.

contexts in which it could be heard, was harshly critiqued at the time by Émile Vuillermoz for constituting a recycling of earlier material in the face of mounting interest for newly composed works. André Caplet proposed a somewhat lighter version of Debussy's orchestration in 1922. The work represents Debussy's compositional preoccupations of the late 1880s; it shows the influence of Borodin and Mussorgsky in a setting of considerable harmonic complexity that places demands on both performers that would be far beyond the reach of most amateur musicians.

CHAPTER 5

Consumption and Leisure

H. Hazel Hahn

Debussy's Paris was full of consumable, competing attractions that could be entertaining, dazzling, inspiring, disturbing, or overwhelming. Debussy enjoyed a wide variety of popular culture including cabaret and circus. He hated stuffiness, arrogance, hypocrisy, discomfort, and surroundings that were uninspiring, mundane, or worse, crass. His Paris was rife with social, political, economic, and cultural tensions, and saw an extraordinary expansion in visual, print, musical, and consumer culture. Aspects of Haussmann-style urbanism – including the widening of streets and the construction of buildings and street lamps – continued. Transportation options such as carriages, omnibuses, bicycles, and eventually automobiles made all parts of Paris easily accessible. The first line of the Métropolitain opened in 1900 during the World's Fair. This chapter explores Debussy's patterns of consumption and leisure by highlighting their broader contexts in Paris and beyond.

Music Venues and Entertainment

In the 1890s Debussy was very social and a regular at cafés, bistros, bars, taverns, cabarets, music halls, and salons, where he spent time with writers, artists, and musicians.[1] Complex tensions, regarding class, the avant-garde, official culture, and the commercialisation of Bohemia, were pervasive at venues such as Chat Noir. Debussy could take Gabrielle Dupont, his lover until 1898, to cabarets and bars, but not to middle- or upper-class salons and public concerts.[2] Debussy loved the circus, one of the inspirations for *Children's Corner*, *La Boîte à joujoux*, and 'General Lavine – eccentric'.[3]

---

[1] Lesure (Rolf), p. 78.
[2] Robert Orledge, 'Debussy the Man', in Simon Trezise (ed.), *The Cambridge Companion to Debussy* (Cambridge: Cambridge University Press, 2003), p. 23.
[3] Catherine Kautsky, *Debussy's Paris: Piano Portraits of the Belle Époque* (Lanham, MD: Rowman & Littlefield, 2017), pp. 19–22.

Music was consumed at a dizzying variety of venues: public concerts, theatre of all varieties from high art to vaudeville, salons, cabarets, *cafés-concerts*, bars, dance halls, balls, circuses, cafés, restaurants, hotels, department stores, schools, museums, exhibitions, cinemas, sports and leisure venues such as skating rinks and the hippodrome, parks, gardens, other outdoor locations, and events such as parades. The composer Ernest Chausson in 1893 tried to arrange an assistant conducting post for Debussy at the casino in Royan – the kind of work that Debussy despised.[4] The leisure time of the middle and working classes expanded. In the 1890s thousands of men and women bicycled in the Bois de Boulogne each Sunday.[5] Also at the Bois de Boulogne were polo and ice-skating clubs, sites of high-class sociability.[6] A photograph of the skating rink Palais de Glace on the Champs Elysées, converted from a panorama rotunda,[7] shows pairs dancing expertly on ice, presumably to music.

Many of Debussy's compositions were premiered at private salons. In 1882, while he was a Conservatoire student, some of his works were premiered at the salon of the piano manufacturer Flaxland.[8] Later, Debussy was a popular composer at the salon of Princesse Winnaretta Singer de Polignac, an heiress of the Singer Manufacturing Company, the sewing-machine company, whom he met in 1894. Her house on the rue Cortambert included a salon seating 200 and a smaller space for recitals. De Polignac, Marguerite de Saint-Marceaux, and the Countess Greffulhe, all aristocratic *salonnières*, attended the first performance of *Pelléas et Mélisande* on 30 April 1902.[9] Given Debussy's modest social origins and his avoidance of conducting or official commissions, he needed such support of the wealthy.

Performances of 'exotic' music took place not only in music halls but also at the Jardin d'acclimatation, a children's zoo and amusement park established in 1860 in the Bois de Boulogne. In 1877, the first two ethnographic exhibitions were held, of Nubians and Eskimos brought by the

---

[4] Eric Frederick Jensen, *Debussy* (Oxford: Oxford University Press, 2014), p. 56.
[5] Sarah Maris Aloisa Britton Spottiswood Mackin, *A Society Woman on Two Continents* (New York: Transatlantic Publishing Company, 1896), p. 172.
[6] Eleanor Hoyt Brainerd, *In Vanity Fair: A Tale of Frocks and Femininity* (New York: Moffat, Yard and Company, 1906), p. 148.
[7] Karl Baedeker, *Paris and Environs with Routes from London to Paris: Handbook for Travellers* (Leipzig: K. Baedeker, 1898), p. 153.
[8] Jensen, *Debussy*, p. 24.
[9] James Ross, 'Music in the French Salon', in Richard Langham Smith and Caroline Potter (eds.), *French Music since Berlioz* (Abingdon: Routledge, 2016), p. 110.

zoologist Carl Hagenbeck. They were lucrative successes, and from 1877 to 1912 more than thirty ethnographic exhibitions were staged there.[10] The number of visitors in 1878 neared a million.[11] Between 1877 and 1896 there were about thirty ethnographic shows in Paris – at the Jardin d'acclimatation, the Champ de Mars, the Folies-Bergère, and other venues.[12] Similar 'human zoos' were held in other cities, including London, Berlin, New York, Moscow, and Tokyo. The exhibitions were widely publicised through posters, newspapers, magazines, and anthropology journals.

Ethnographic exhibitions, a significant part of the 'exotic' soundscape, were also part of the outdoor soundscape, along with street sellers' cries and barrel organ music, that Debussy mused on.[13] Debussy was surely aware of ethnographic exhibitions. In 1894 a concert, conducted by Colonne at the Palmarium of the Jardin d'acclimatation, was to include Debussy's then unpublished *Marche écossaise*. In 1903 he wrote in *Gil Blas* that the Jardin d'acclimatation was a charming site for a concert, that if one dislikes the music one could look at animals.[14] *Gil Blas* regularly publicised ethnographic exhibitions, including a village of Achantis in 1903.[15] From 1905 he lived a twenty-minute walk from the Jardin d'acclimatation, where he likely went, perhaps with Chouchou; there were outdoor concerts twice a week and plays.

Material Culture, Cuisine, Fashion, and *Objets d'Art*

In 1892 Debussy left his family home and moved with Gabrielle Dupont into a furnished flat at 42 rue de Londres.[16] He recalled later that a wallpaper there, bizarrely enough, depicted President Carnot 'surrounded by little birds!', which made him 'avoid being home'. He remembered a visit there by Mallarmé, who said of the *Prélude à l'après-midi d'un faune*: 'This music prolongs the emotion of my poem and sets its scene

---

[10] Pascal Blanchard, Nicolas Bancel, and Sandrine Lemaire, 'From Scientific Racism to Popular and Colonial Racism in France and the West', in Pascal Blanchard, Nicolas Bancel, and Sandrine Lemaire (eds.), *Human Zoos: Science and Spectacle in the Age of Colonial Empires* (Liverpool: Liverpool University Press, 2008), p. 105.
[11] William H. Schneider, 'The Ethnographic Exhibitions of the Jardin Zoologique d'Acclimatation', in Blanchard, Bancel, and Lemaire (eds.), *Human Zoos*, p. 143.
[12] Isabelle Gaurin, 'Du rapt légitimé de "sujets d'étude vivants": Une démarche de Quatrefages auprès du Ministre de l'Instruction publique (1891)', in Jacques Guillerme (ed.), *Les Collections: Fables et programmes* (Ceyzérieu: Champ Vallon, 1993), p. 80.
[13] Debussy, 'Musique', *Gil Blas* (19 January 1903), p. 2, in *Monsieur Croche*, p. 74.
[14] Debussy, 'Musique', *Gil Blas* (26 January 1903), p. 2, in *Monsieur Croche*, p. 88.
[15] 'Un village Achanti au Jardin d'Acclimatation', *Gil Blas* (5 May 1903), p. 3.
[16] Lesure (Rolf), p. 103.

more vividly than colour could.' Mallarmé was 'draped in a Scotch plaid shawl'.[17]

In 1905 Debussy and Emma Bardac began to rent a townhouse on the avenue du Bois de Boulogne (the widest street in Paris, it became avenue Foch in 1929; its original name was avenue de l'Impératrice), with a garden in one of the most exclusive and expensive areas in the entire world. Their daughter Claude-Emma ('Chouchou') was born in 1905, and Emma's daughter Dolly lived with them for their first six years together.[18] The house was furnished in the Louis XV style. They had a cook, nanny, servants, and an automobile with a chauffeur.[19] In 1908, 46,000 automobiles were in use in France, which places the Debussys in an elite group.[20] The American violinist Arthur Hartmann saw Debussy firing a butler on the spot when he disrupted their silence by whistling in the adjoining room.[21] Debussy then told Hartmann that it was difficult to find good servants, adding: 'This one came but recently and was recommended by a person whom I've always considered a friend, even if a bad musician, but now I know him, *hélas*, to be also *un mauvais collègue*.'[22] Debussy was, unbeknownst to most, continuously in debt, a key source of his melancholia. Had he lived a more modest lifestyle, or written more successful operas, he would have been able to make a living.[23]

Debussy had a refined taste in cuisine. A 'dinner at his house was nothing short of sumptuous', Hartmann noted. He recalled 'a bizarre dinner', revealing Debussy's whimsy, at which 'everything was in red, from the tablecloth and napkins to the champagne'. When Hartmann wanted to invite the Debussys and hire a professional cook, his American wife Marie insisted on treating them at a fashionable restaurant at the Majestic Hotel near the Champs Elysées, where she pre-ordered the meal. The dinner went catastrophically; Debussy bluntly rejected each course. He stared at a half-grapefruit appetiser, asking: 'Mais je voudrais savoir . . . does one *eat that*? Cet animal-là . . . does one, seriously, *eat* it?' When

---

[17] Letter to Georges Jean-Aubry, 25 March 1910, *Correspondance*, p. 1261.
[18] Jensen, *Debussy*, p. 93.
[19] Denis Herlin, 'An Artist High and Low, or Debussy and Money', in Elliott Antokoletz and Marianne Wheeldon (eds.), *Rethinking Debussy* (Oxford: Oxford University Press, 2011), p. 164.
[20] John Heitmann, *The Automobile and American Life* (Jefferson, NC: McFarland, 2018), p. 18.
[21] Arthur Hartmann, *'Claude Debussy as I Knew Him' and Other Writings of Arthur Hartmann*, ed. Samuel Hsu, Sidney Grolnic, and Mark Peters (Rochester, NY: University of Rochester Press, 2003), p. 67.
[22] Hartmann, *'Claude Debussy as I Knew Him'*, p. 67.
[23] See Christophe Charle, 'Debussy in Fin-de-Siècle Paris', in Jane F. Fulcher (ed.), *Debussy and His World* (Princeton, NJ: Princeton University Press, 2001), pp. 271–96.

5 Consumption and Leisure

consommé soup and stuffed chicken followed, Debussy declared: 'What curious people *ces américains*! . . . First that animal of a crrropfrooo, then a soup which ran through water, meals without bread, and bread they take and stuff into the backside of a chicken.' When Hartmann angrily asked him to order his own dinner, he ordered soup, lamb, a half-bottle of red wine, salad, soufflé, and a bottle of champagne.[24] The choice of restaurant was also wrong for Debussy, because he dreaded 'the obligatory evening dress in places called 'Majestical'.[25] Debussy was just as exacting at home. He described his cook as 'a ferocious and frightful master of poisoning'. Even a 'simple tea at the Debussys was as lavish as most dinners'.[26] Debussy held fast to daily rituals of afternoon tea and drinking whisky around ten.[27] He perhaps drank to excess, smoked, and took little exercise.

That Emma was a fashionable woman can be readily discerned in a photograph of her wearing an extraordinary hat entirely covered with feathers. Alongside a vast quantity of images in magazines, advertisements, catalogues, and other print media depicting department store interiors and exteriors were those of fine art. Félix Vallotton, one of the Nabis group, who probably met Debussy in the 1890s as he was a principal artist for *La Revue blanche*, for which Debussy contributed music criticism in 1901, depicted women shopping for fabric assisted by male clerks at the Bon Marché department store in a woodcut in 1893.[28] He also made a triptych of oil paintings in 1898 titled *Le Bon Marché*. One panel depicts goods with fixed prices, a female customer, and a male clerk. Another panel portrays scarves with a 'sale, used' sign, gloves and umbrellas, and female customers. In the central panel is a crowd of largely female customers and displays of jewellery, *objets d'art*, and textiles. These works highlight gendered roles by highlighting women as consumers.

Paris was the undisputed centre of fashion trends followed in Europe, the Americas, and the colonies. Marie-Rosalie (Lilly) Texier, Debussy's first wife, was a model for fashion houses.[29] The designer Charles-Frédéric Worth launched *haute couture* from the 1850s. At the 1900 Exposition Universelle twenty French houses of *haute couture* participated; they played a major role in the French export economy.[30] French fashion drew on

---

[24] Hartmann, '*Claude Debussy as I Knew Him*', pp. 82–6, 106.
[25] Emma Debussy's letter to Marie Hartmann, 2 August 1910, Hartmann, '*Claude Debussy as I Knew Him*', p. 132.
[26] Letter to Hartmann, 23 July 1910, Hartmann, '*Claude Debussy as I Knew Him*', pp. 106, 117.
[27] Raoul Bardac, 'Dans l'intimité de Claude Debussy', *Terres latines* 4 (March 1936), p. 73.
[28] Ashley Saint-James, *Vallotton Graveur* (Lausanne: L'Âge d'Homme, 1986), p. 28.
[29] Jensen, *Debussy*, p. 66.
[30] Gilles Lipovetsky, *The Empire of Fashion: Dressing Modern Democracy*, trans. Catherine Porter (Princeton, NJ: Princeton University Press, 2002), p. 57.

a wide range of foreign sources; a showroom in 1892 showed designs inspired by styles from Russia, the French Empire, Walachia, Greece, and Japan.[31] A famous showcase for fashion was the Grand Prix race at Longchamp in July, which marked the end of the Paris 'season', including the concert season, which began in October or November. The Saturday night before the Grand Prix at the Cirque d'Été was a gala event rivalling the gala at the grand opera.[32] The procession to the Grand Prix along the Champs Elysées was an occasion for self-display, of 'coaches, automobiles, smart traps of all kinds, hired fiacres, high-stepping horses, dapper drivers, exquisitely gowned women, merry-makers of all types'.[33] In Henri Gervex's *Un soir de grand prix au pavillon d'Armenonville* (1905), women in gowns and hats and men in tuxedoes dine at Le Pavillon d'Armenonville on the evening of the Grand Prix. Also present at Longchamps were models wearing the newest fashion designs. Jeanne Paquin, the first prominent French female designer and the chair of the fashion section of the 1900 World's Fair, employed ten models at the Grand Prix or the opera wearing the same outfit.[34] Eleanor Brainerd, an American visitor, observed: 'Every woman with money to spend, spends as much of it as she can spare upon her toilette for this one occasion. She will blossom out gorgeously for Grand Prix, if she goes shabby during the rest of the year.'[35] Designers garnered free publicity at such events, as the media published images of spectators. Images of fashionable women also circulated through fine art. Gervex's painting *Cinq heures chez Paquin* (1906) depicts society women at Paquin's shop, while Jean Béraud's *Sortie des ouvrières de la maison Paquin, rue de la Paix* (1902) shows dressmakers leaving the Paquin shop. In Jean Béraud's *La Pâtisserie Gloppe* (1889) high-class families enjoy desserts.

Debussy was indirectly acquainted with the fashion world through his interactions with the members of Tout Paris at salons and elsewhere. However, he was not known for interest in high fashion or trendy events. The only things he collected were *objets d'art*. During his unhappy stay at the Villa Medici in Rome from 1885 to 1887, he frequented antique shops, acquiring tiny Japanese *objets*.[36] Collecting Asian artefacts became a lifelong passion. Displayed on his large worktable at his house on the avenue du Bois de Boulogne were ceramic or wooden animals and birds from China and

---

[31] Kristin Hoganson, *The Global Production of American Domesticity, 1865–1920* (Berkeley, CA: University of California Press, 2007), p. 67.
[32] Mackin, *Society Woman*, p. 173.   [33] Brainerd, *Vanity Fair*, p. 70.
[34] Holly Price Alford and Anne Stegemeyer, *Who's Who in Fashion* (New York: Fairchild Books, 2014), p. 294.
[35] Brainerd, *Vanity Fair*, p. 68.   [36] Jensen, *Debussy*, p. 30.

5 Consumption and Leisure

Japan, including an 'exquisite Chinese parrot in porcelain'.[37] He always travelled with a 'big wooden toad, a Chinese ornament' named Arkel after the old king in *Pelléas*.[38] Japanese prints were on the walls. Upon returning to Paris from a visit to London to review for *Gil Blas*, he wrote that Normandy, covered with delicate white blossoms, resembled a Japanese[39] woodblock print. He wished that *Pelléas* could have its premiere in Japan.

Debussy seems to have attended exhibitions of Asian objects in the 1880s and 1890s. The dealer Siegfried Bing sent him a private invitation to see his collection on sale in May 1906.[40] He went to shops specialising in Asian products, including tea, which he adored.[41] He also visited the café-restaurant Le Pavillon chinois at the Porte Dauphine, which had been the Chinese pavilion at the 1878 World's Fair.[42] Some of the 'Chinese' objects he admired were made in Europe. Regarding 'the Chinese exhibition at the Pavillon Marsan', in 1910 Debussy declared that 'rarely if ever [had he] seen such beauty and refinement'.[43] The exhibition, organised by the Musée des arts décoratifs, displayed eighteenth-century European furniture, tapestries, bronzes, earthenware, and porcelain with motifs of *chinoiserie* and *japonerie*.[44] Debussy's desire for certain things extended beyond *objets d'arts*. He described this desire to André Poniatowski: 'You have this crazy but inescapable longing, a need almost, for some work of art (a Velázquez, a Satsuma vase or a new kind of tie), and the moment of actual possession is one of joy, of love really. A week later, nothing.'[45]

Travel and Tourism

A vast development in tourism took place in Debussy's lifetime. Today, France is the most visited country in the world; in the nineteenth century, France was one of the most visited countries. Transportation networks through rail, ship, and automobile, and hotels and lodgings for all budgets,

---

[37] Hartmann, '*Claude Debussy as I Knew Him*', p. 48.
[38] Mme Gaston de Tinan, 'Memories of Debussy and His Circle', *Journal of the British Institute of Recorded Sound* 50 (1973), p. 158.
[39] Debussy, 'Musique', *Gil Blas* (1 June 1903), p. 2, in *Monsieur Croche*, p. 184.
[40] Jean-Michel Nectoux, *Harmonie en bleu et or: Debussy, la musique et les arts* (Paris: Fayard, 2012), p. 191.
[41] Nectoux, *Harmonie en bleu et or*, p. 190.
[42] Michel Duchesneau, 'Debussy and Japanese Prints', in François de Médicis and Steven Huebner (eds.), *Debussy's Resonance* (Rochester, NY: University of Rochester Press, 2018), p. 304.
[43] Letter to Jacques Durand, 8 July 1910, *Debussy Letters*, p. 221.
[44] Michel Duchesneau, 'Debussy and Japanese Prints', in de Médicis and Huebner (eds.), *Debussy's Resonance*, p. 304.
[45] Letter to André Poniatowski, dated 'Thursday February 1893 [sic]', *Debussy Letters*, p. 40.

as well as entertainment venues, were all significant aspects of tourism infrastructure. The French automobile industry was the largest in the world. Communication networks through the post, telegraph, and telephone were integral to such developments. The need to coordinate train schedules led to the standardisation of time with Greenwich marking the Mean Time in 1884. The Michelin tire company produced guidebooks for tourism from 1900. In 1919 Michelin would even publish a *Michelin Guide to the Battlefields of the World War* with detailed itineraries for tourists to visit the battlefields. At World's Fairs, travel and tourism were publicised through the temporary exhibition sites replicating monuments and streets of foreign lands and colonies, a vast range of products, the sheer number of foreigners including colonised subjects, and spectacles and entertainment.

Debussy travelled extensively. Perhaps the trips he enjoyed most were some of his earliest ones, when he was a pianist for the Russian widow Nadezhda Philaretovna von Meck and her family. Otherwise, it is rare to find accounts of him thoroughly enjoying a trip, even for a holiday. In the summer of 1880 Debussy joined the von Mecks in Interlaken, Switzerland, then travelled to the south of France, including Nice, and to Genoa, Naples, and Florence. He made his first trip to Russia in July 1881 to join the von Mecks, and travelled with them to Vienna, Trieste, Venice, Florence, and Rome, returning to Paris in December. In September 1882 he travelled with them from Moscow to Vienna, where they stayed two months. These trips significantly enhanced his musical experience and enabled him to encounter different parts of Europe.[46] Debussy went to Bayreuth in the summers of 1888 and 1889 to hear Wagner's *Parsifal*, *Die Meistersinger*, and *Tristan*. In 1893 he spent several days at a château in Luzancy that Chausson was renting for the summer; they and friends worked and undertook river excursions.[47]

European perception of the beach underwent dramatic change from the early eighteenth century – when it was associated with emptiness, foreboding, and death – to a leisure destination by the 1840s. From the 1840s, Trouville in Normandy was already popular with the Parisian bourgeoisie. By the late nineteenth century, the upper-class and bourgeois pattern of taking a long summer vacation was firmly established. Many avant-garde artists vacationed and painted on the Normandy shores. Monet, who had lived in Le Havre since he was a child, painted in Pourville for seven weeks from February 1882 and spent that summer there with his family. Whereas

---

[46] Jensen, *Debussy*, p. 17; Lesure (Rolf), pp. 30–2, 38, 43.
[47] Stephen Walsh, *Debussy: A Painter in Sound* (New York: Alfred A. Knopf, 2018), p. 92.

5 Consumption and Leisure 53

he liked Pourville, an unpretentious small port with only one casino-hotel-restaurant, where he stayed, he disliked Dieppe with its expensive hotel and a café full of 'provincial types'.[48] Vallotton produced paintings like *La Promenade de la mer à Étretat* (1899) and *Quatre baigneurs à Étretat* (1899) during his first family vacation at the fashionable resort of Étretat.[49] At the turn of the century, Trouville, popular with both middle and upper classes from all over Europe, had a casino and a beach promenade, while nearby Deauville, with a race course and luxury villas, was far more exclusive. Dieppe also drew Europeans and some Americans, while Boulogne-sur-Mer, easily accessible from Dover, was popular with the English. Normandy and Brittany were advertised as destinations where Parisian bourgeois families enjoyed picturesque sites and quaint, friendly locals. Ostend in Belgium was very cosmopolitan and offered a 'tennis tournaments, golf tournaments, automobile races, motor-boat races, horse races, children's fêtes, balls, flower festivals, theatre, excursions', and yachting, plus gambling until the government shut it down.[50]

While Debussy avoided crowded resorts, he went away from Paris most summers and often stayed at luxury hotels. For a month in 1901 Debussy and Lilly stayed with Lilly's parents in Bichain in Burgundy, which he enjoyed as the seeming 'opposite end of the earth from Paris'.[51] They repeated the trip the next two summers. Debussy spent many vacations by the sea. He visited the coast of Italy while in Rome.[52] In 1904 he travelled with Emma to the island of Jersey and also Eastbourne. His view of the latter shows that his Anglophilia was limited. While he found Eastbourne 'peaceful and charming', he wrote that 'the sea here moves with a very British regularity' and that 'important and imperialist little bits of English scamper on a well-kept lawn'.[53] They also briefly visited London, which he found 'rather dreary'.[54] Debussy loved the sea, which he 'listened to ... with the passionate respect one owes it'; in composing *La Mer*, he transcribed 'what the sea dictated' to him.[55] He did not always enjoy his later seaside trips with his family. He went away each summer with Emma and Chouchou, except in 1908 and 1909.[56] They were at the Grand Hotel

---

[48] Robert L. Herbert, *Monet on the Normandy Coast: Tourism and Painting, 1867–1886* (New Haven, MA: Yale University Press, 1996), pp. 43–4.
[49] Marina Ducrey, *Vallotton* (Milan: 5 Continents, 2007), p. xiii.
[50] Brainerd, *Vanity Fair*, pp. 119, 121, 138.   [51] Jensen, *Debussy*, p. 72.
[52] Kautsky, *Debussy's Paris*, p. 126.
[53] Letter to Jacques Durand, 26 July 1905, *Correspondance*, pp. 912–3.
[54] Letters to Jacques Durand, 26 July 1905 and to Louis Laloy, 13 September 1905, *Debussy Letters*, pp. 153, 160.
[55] Letter to Pierre Lalo, 25 October 1905, *Correspondance*, pp. 927–8.   [56] Jensen, *Debussy*, p. 94.

du Puy near Dieppe in August 1906. Debussy described the Italian running the hotel as someone who 'brings back the most doubtful food substances [from shops], messes up the fish and the meat, and is patently an assassin'. He found the little beach 'absurd, the hotel the last word in discomfort, and the English the sort who render any *entente cordiale* impossible'.[57] Similarly, in August 1907 he hated Pourville, both his hotel and the town, which he saw as 'an odious place where the people are slightly more ridiculous than elsewhere', from where he wished to 'escape as soon as possible'.[58] In July 1910 he wrote to his publisher Jacques Durand:

> Those around me resolutely refuse to understand that I've never been able to live in a world of real things and real people. That's why I have this imperative need to escape from myself and go off on adventures which seem inexplicable because they figure a man nobody knows; and perhaps he represents the best side of me! After all, an artist is by definition a man accustomed to dreams and living among apparitions . . .
>
> In short, I live surrounded by memories and regrets. Two gloomy companions, but faithful ones – more so than pleasure and happiness![59]

Debussy's desired escape from himself was aided by fantasy, whether fascination with Moorish Spain or Kipling's India in *The Jungle Book*. Debussy read adventure stories, and a picture of Kipling was on a wall in his studio at home.[60]

In September 1916, during the war, the Debussys stayed at the Grand Hotel near Arcachon on the Atlantic coast. Debussy was suffering from rectal cancer. He found the scenery and natural light 'incomparable', although the hotel lacked gas and electricity.[61] He likened the effect of all the pianos at the hotel being played simultaneously to 'St[ravinsky] rewritten by that bloody Hungarian anarchist [presumably Bartók] whose name my memory refuses to retain'.[62] He wrote to Durand that 'the life of a hotel is more difficult for me than ever . . . the walls themselves are hostile to me, not to mention a life in a numbered box'.[63] In 1917 the Debussys spent the summer in Saint-Jean-de-Luz on the Basque coast by the Pyrenees, hoping the mountain air would help Debussy's convalescence.

---

[57] Walsh, *Debussy: A Painter in Sound*, pp. 181–2.
[58] Letter to Victor Segalen, 26 August 1907, *Debussy Letters*, p. 183.
[59] Letter to Jacques Durand, 8 July 1910, *Debussy Letters*, p. 220.
[60] Hartmann, '*Claude Debussy as I Knew Him*', p. 48; Paul Roberts, *Images: The Piano Music of Claude Debussy* (Portland, OR: Amadeus Press, 2001), p. 263.
[61] Lesure (Rolf), p. 330.
[62] Letter to Paul Dukas, 19 September 1916, *Correspondance*, pp. 2027–8.
[63] Letter to Jacques Durand, 12 October 1916, *Correspondance*, p. 2036.

5 Consumption and Leisure

Author's Recommendation
Préludes, book 1 (1909–10) and book 2 (1911–13).

The *Préludes*, two books of twelve piano pieces each, were composed at a relatively fast pace. Debussy placed the title of each piece at the end, suggesting that a performer did not have to know the title until after playing it. He did not indicate if the pieces should be performed in the order of publication or as whole cycles. Technical levels range from medium to difficult, with the last prelude, 'Feux d'artifice', perhaps the most difficult for its pyrotechnical 'fireworks'. The *Préludes* showcase an extraordinary diversity of compositional styles as well as repertoire of emotions, moods, and evocative, poetic imagery. Sources of inspiration include poems ('Le Vent dans la plaine' I no. 3, 'Les Sons et les parfums tournent dans l'air du soir' I no. 4, 'La Fille aux cheveux de lin' I no. 8); fairy tales by Hans Christian Andersen ('Ce qu'a vu le vent d'ouest' I no. 7; 'Ondine' II no. 5); book illustrations by Arthur Rackham ('La Danse de Puck' I no. 11, 'Les Fées sont d'exquises danseuses' II no. 4); a Dickens novel ('Hommage à S. Pickwick Esq. P.P.M.P.C.' II no. 9); a postcard ('La Puerta del vino' II no. 3); a newspaper travelogue ('La Terrasse des audiences du clair de lune' II no. 7); a legend ('La Cathédrale engloutie' I no. 10); Greek sculpture ('Danseuses de Delphes' I no. 1); an *objet d'art* ('Canope' II no. 10); popular entertainment ('Minstrels' I no. 12, 'Général Lavine – eccentric' II no. 6; 'Feux d'artifice' II no. 12); and possibly a wine label ('Les Collines d'Anacapri' I, no. 5).

PART II

The Arts

CHAPTER 6

Debussy's Impressionism Interrogated

Richard Langham Smith

Debussy's youthful companion in Rome, Raymond Bonheur, confirmed that 'painting had an undeniable attraction for Debussy', noting his envy of 'those painters who could retain the freshness of the first sketch' – 'la fraîcheur de l'ébauche' – a phrase much used about the Impressionists but here referring to Debussy's improvisations.[1] Living as he was through a period of immense changes in the visual arts, with a stream of press discourse from the supporters and denigrators of the various artists and movements, Realism, Impressionism, and Symbolism were three primary issues at the time. Parallel with this were advances in photographic reproductions, vastly reducing the cost of hanging artworks on one's wall, albeit in black and white. Among these were the platinotypes of Edward Burne-Jones which decorated Maeterlinck's study in the 1890s.

In one of many articles asking the question 'Debussy est-il un "impressionniste"?', the critic Paul Landormy wrongly claimed that the term had first been applied to Debussy's music. In fact, an article in the *Journal officiel* claimed that the 'music of M. de Maupou seemed to us to belong to the forefront of the modern school whose adherents are comparable to the Impressionist painters; in effect, these musicians become intoxicated with timbres and sounds, just as the Impressionists do with bright colours and vague contours'.[2] The date of 1876 is important, since the term had only come into use two years before in relation to Monet's *Lever du soleil*. Note its pejorative application: this was one of the ways in which the term was interchangeably used against painters who departed from realism and musicians who departed from clear (mainly Germanic) inherited forms.

This first usage at least has a hint of a technical parallel, which was one of the methods of comparison proposed by Étienne Souriau in his *La*

---

[1] 'La Jeunesse de Claude Debussy', *La Revue musicale*, special issue (1 May 1926), pp. 6–8.
[2] Eugène Gautier, 'Impressionnisme', *Journal officiel de la République française* (4 February 1876), p. 1111. All translations are my own.

Correspondance des arts; the others being parallels of subject-matter, *Zeitgeist*, kinship between artists, and a common bond in literature.[3] When Impressionist painting evolved, the perception of *correspondances* deepened in the hands of critics such as Jules Laforgue and Camille Mauclair, who described Debussy's music as 'an impressionism of brush-strokes in sound'.[4]

'Debussy était-il impressionniste ou symboliste?' was a question posed by every hack and by some musicologists who should have known better. Only a few understood that such binary oppositions were too shallow for a composer whose style evolved in so many directions. Such mindless pigeonholing has inhibited study of visual connections with artists closer to the composer's aesthetic. Anyway, what are we talking about: the direct influence of paintings on music or just *correspondances*? I think the latter.

Perhaps Debussy remembered the expression '*impressionnisme vague*' when in 1901 he invented a conversation between himself and his alter ego, M. Croche (in *La Revue blanche*), in which Debussy 'dared to point out that both poets and painters (and I managed to think of a couple of musicians as well) had tried to shake away the dust of tradition and it merely earned them the labels of "Symbolists" or "Impressionists" – convenient as terms of abuse'. M. Croche ironically retorts that such comments are 'only journalists doing their job'.[5] On the other hand, there is a letter from Debussy to Émile Vuillermoz of 25 January 1916 saying how honoured he was to receive a comparison to Monet.

Debussy's ideas on 'music in the open air' can be cited as a *correspondance* with the Impressionists moving their easels from their studios to the open air. Debussy's titling of *La Mer* as 'symphonic sketches' linked to particular times of day – 'de l'aube à midi' – reminds us of his early desire to preserve the 'freshness of the initial sketch' and of the series paintings (different canvasses lined up for different times of day). This was reflected in his advice to Raoul Bardac: 'gather impressions but don't hurry to refine them'[6] – a remark that could have come from any of the Impressionists.

Particularly fertile was the theorisation of divisionism. Paul Signac explained this process and how Camille Pissarro came to reject it, pointing out that Pissarro would be careful to avoid juxtaposing two opposing tints to obtain a vibrancy through their juxtaposition, and would instead use what he called '*passages*', or intermediate colours, to soften such

---

[3] Étienne Souriau, *La Correspondance des arts* (Paris: Flammarion, 1969).
[4] Jules Laforgue, 'L'Art impressionniste', in *Mélanges posthumes* (Paris: Mercure de France, 1919).
[5] 'L'Entretien avec M. Croche', in *Monsieur Croche*, pp. 48–53.
[6] Letter to Raoul Bardac (Rara), 25 June 1906, *Correspondance*, pp. 940–2.

6 Debussy's Impressionism Interrogated 61

juxtapositions. He thus distanced himself from Neo-Impressionism, which was 'based precisely on this contrast'.[7]

It is tempting to compare the juxtaposition of 'opposing tints' of the pointillist techniques of such painters as Georges Seurat and Signac with the vibrant arpeggiations of Debussy, particularly in the piano pieces of the early twentieth century – for example, 'Reflets dans l'eau' from *Images*, series 1, or 'Ce qu'a vu le vent d'ouest', 'Brouillards', and 'Le Vent dans la plaine' from his *Préludes*. Are there not parallels between the surfaces of Neo-Impressionist paintings, where dots or *taches* of opposing colours are combined to create surfaces of modulated vibrancy, and arpeggiated ripples constructed from superimposed chords considered as oppositional within the tonal system – a tritone or a semitone apart, for example? These provide a close parallel of technique with pointillist painting, quite apart from their shared, often watery, subject matter. In 'Reflets dans l'eau' the idea of introducing intermediate added-notes to vary the vibrancy of such pointillist washes of sound could be compared to the '*passages*' Signac had theorised in his 1899 study.

While Louis Laloy suggested such parallels during Debussy's lifetime, Erik Satie amplified these parallels in an unpublished article on Debussy dated 1922, probably intended for *Vanity Fair*. Although a popular rather than an intellectual outlet, his claims are worth quoting as he and Debussy had been close at one time. The mention of 'disengagement from the Wagnerian aesthetic' perhaps stemmed from Satie's reaction *to Pelléas*.

> The aesthetic of Debussy is allied to Symbolism in many of his works and is Impressionist throughout all of them. Pardon me, but aren't I a little to blame? ... I explained to Debussy the need for us French to disengage from the Wagnerian adventure, which didn't have anything to offer our natural aspirations. I remarked that I was in no way anti-Wagnerian, but that we had to have a music of our own – without sauerkraut if possible. Why not make use of the methods of representation shown to us by Claude Monet, Cézanne, Toulouse-Lautrec etc.? Why not transpose these into music? Wouldn't this be a means of expression?[8]

---

[7] Paul Signac, *D'Eugène Delacroix au Néo-Impressionnisme* (Paris: Éditions de La Revue blanche, 1899; repr. Paris: H. Floury, 1911), pp. 66–8. The point about *passages* is discussed in a letter from Pissarro to his son of 20 February 1889. See Camille Pissarro, *Lettres à son fils Lucien* (Paris: Michel, 1950). The flourishing of Debussy's career as a composer coincided with the discourses about Neo-Impressionism rather than with the foundation of the Impressionists in the 1870s.

[8] Erik Satie, *Écrits*, ed. Ornella Volta (Paris: Champ Libre, 1990), p. 69.

The three artists singled out by Satie are perhaps significant in that they represent very different sides of those grouped under the umbrella term 'Impressionism'.

A related question is Debussy's passion for Turner, and here some context can be added to Lockspeiser's and Nectoux's commentaries through his famous remark about his orchestral *Images*: he 'tries to do "something different" and create – in a way – realities that fools call "impressionism", a term as misused as it can be, especially by Art critics' who apply the term to Turner.[9] This showed his awareness of a current '*affaire*' in art criticism, triggered by an English art critic who had published a book on the Impressionists which Pissarro criticised because it cited Turner as a precursor of the movement.[10] Appreciating Turner was a taste reserved for elite connoisseurs, not least because few of his cavasses were exhibited in France, and although there were many reproductions, they were not of those 'pictures of nothing' which depended on colour more than line. No doubt that is why Debussy took time out on his trip to London to see originals.

Supreme in deepening our knowledge of Debussy's connections with the visual arts has surely been the exhibition *Debussy, la musique et les arts*, shown in Paris in 2012. Curated by Jean-Michel Nectoux, its catalogue should be read in tandem with the same author's *Harmonie en bleu et or*. Nectoux's credo is that artworks formed 'the aesthetic landscape to Debussy's musical creations', a view which allows unlimited scope for free-ranging comparisons.[11] It is clear that he profited considerably from the collegiate mix of artists and musicians in his Rome years. Among his co-students were the painter Ernest Redon – a fine amateur musician and brother of Odilon – and Marcel Baschet, whose oil painting of Debussy, dating from 1884–5, was preceded by a crayon sketch, both surviving. Nectoux reproduces a fascinating 'Le Printemps' of 1887, which makes us muse on Debussy's three pieces of this title from the same period.

His time in Rome was also marked by a relatively unexplored aspect of his attraction to the visual arts during the time when he was working on *Diane au bois*, setting a section of an *Acte en vers* by Théodore de Banville concerning Diana's encounter with Endymion. At this time, he became friendly with the Count Guiseppe Primoli, who had an enviable collection

---

[9] *Correspondance*, pp. 1080–1.
[10] Wynford Dewhurst, *Impressionist Painting: Its Genesis and Development* (London: George Newnes, 1904).
[11] See Jean-Michel Nectoux, *Harmonie en bleu et or: Debussy, la musique et les arts* (Paris: Fayard, 2005), p. 10; exhibition catalogue *Debussy, la musique et les arts* (Paris: Skira/Flammarion, Paris, 2012).

of engravings of Watteau paintings, some of which were the inspiration for Verlaine's *Fêtes galantes*.[12] Debussy's admiration for Watteau is documented in a letter of 1914 where he associates *L'Embarquement pour Cythère* with his piano piece *L'Isle joyeuse* of 1903–4, both titles referring to idyllic islands of pleasure.[13] He would no doubt have admired the painter's frequent depiction of musical instruments, which always convey the mood of what is being played, the flute often being associated with seduction, as in *Diane, Faune* and the *Chansons de Bilitis*. Perhaps closest to the theme of *Diane*, where Endymion borrows Silenius's flute – because it has persuaded countless nymphs to lower their undergarments – is Corot's picture *Silène*, depicting Silenius blind drunk with nymphs prancing around. This certainly qualifies as a close 'parallel of subject matter'.

So much for Impressionism, but in general we may ask whether the barrel has run dry for explorations of Debussy's visual associations. Several lines of enquiry have already been inaugurated. The first concerns the artist Henry Lerolle, discussed at length by Nectoux in his 2005 book but further unveiled in the exhibition. He is an artist who cannot be fitted under the sheltering umbrella terms of either Impressionism or Symbolism and was more a social historian, particularly of musical events. Lerolle appreciated music deeply and was among those artists with whom Debussy discussed *correspondances*. Lerolle wrote to Chausson, claiming that Debussy had 'said that there is only one painter that understands music, and that's me'.[14] The period when Debussy was close to Chausson and Lerolle suggests Souriau's 'close kinship' between musicians and artists working together with a sense of 'Frères en art' – a title used by Debussy for a *roman à clef* written around this time.[15]

Another fertile area is the group of artists, scenographers, and book illustrators connected with Maeterlinck at the time of his early plays. The images of Mary Garden in the opera are well known; less so is what Debussy saw when he first encountered Maeterlinck's play – namely, the visual aspect of Lugné-Poe's staging, which was clearly quite unlike the more realistic Opéra-Comique scenography later imposed on Debussy's opera.

[12] See Jacques-Henry Bornecque, *Lumières sur les Fêtes galantes de Paul Verlaine* (Paris: Nizet, 1959).
[13] The title of the painting as 'L'Embarquement *pour* Cythère' is in fact a corruption, since the lovers are clearly departing from the island. See my article '"Le Paradis deux fois perdu": Debussy, Watteau and the *Fête Galante*', in Deborah Mawer (ed.), *Historical Interplay in French Music and Culture, 1860–1960* (London: Taylor & Francis, 2017), pp. 42–3.
[14] Quoted in Jean-Michel Nectoux, 'Degas, Lerolle, Debussy', in Martine Kaufmann, Denis Herlin, and Jean-Michel Nectoux (eds.). *Claude Debussy, Textes* (Paris: Radio France, 1999), p. 69.
[15] See Edward Lockspeiser, '*Frères en art*, pièce de théâtre inédite de Debussy', *Revue de musicologie* 56 (1970), pp. 165–76.

How did that fit in with his highly developed artistic tastes? One wonders whether there was not a considerable rift between his imagined scenario and the sets conjured up by the somewhat old-fashioned scenography of the Opéra-Comique, despite Lucien Jusseaume's expertise in this field.

What Debussy saw on that memorable day in 1893 when literary and visual artists were in his company – Mallarmé and Whistler among them – is difficult to reconstruct: there are no photographs of Lugné-Poe's production of *Pelléas*, although there are images of other Maeterlinck plays staged by his Théâtre de l'œuvre and reviews of the London production.[16] Among preoccupations shared with other plays were blindness; groups of three; lamps of one sort or another (the lighthouses Pelléas and Mélisande contemplate from the clifftop); silence; coincidence; quasi-mediaeval settings; tiled chambers in castles; figures with closed eyes, affliction, pandemics, and famine; wounds, sickness, etc.; and a general sense of spirituality and the mystical often unconnected with religion but (as in *Pelléas*) sometimes with Christian trappings: doves, lambs, and a prie-Dieu.

One of the least-known artists closely connected to Maeterlinck was George Minne (1866–1941), best known as a book illustrator and sculptor. He and Maeterlinck used to walk in silence together and Minne claimed: 'we sometimes communicate so well that it actually seems to me that I produced the Princesse Maleine myself, either with a chisel or a pen'.[17] Maeterlinck wanted to commission murals for his house in Oostacke from Minne, but he was replaced by another artist, Charles Doudelet. Minne was strongly influenced by the late Pre-Raphaelite Edward Burne-Jones, who enjoyed considerable popularity in Belgium. The many connections between Minne and Maeterlinck were celebrated in an exhibition in Ghent in 2011–12.[18] Already, in the artistic hinterland to *Pelléas*, Debussy was far away from the world of Impressionism. Art had moved on even if Impressionist techniques were by no means entirely defunct.

Minne had exhibited in Paris at the first Rose-Croix salon of 1892 (*Les Saintes femmes au tombeau*) and a crayon of two adolescents sheltering among the pines dating from the same period is clearly modelled on

---

[16] See Richard Langham Smith, '"Aimer ainsi": Rekindling the Lamp in *Pelléas*', in Elliott Antokoletz and Marianne Wheeldon (eds.), *Rethinking Debussy* (New York: Oxford University Press, 2011), pp. 76–95.
[17] Franz Hellens, 'Les Dessins de George Minne', *Sélection* (15 July 1921), quoted by Robert Hoozee, 'Belgian Art 1880–1900', in MaryAnne Stevens, *Impressionism to Symbolism: The Belgian Avant-Garde* (London: Royal Academy of Art, 1994), p. 26.
[18] *L'Univers de George Minne et Maurice Maeterlinck* (Brussels: Fonds Mercador, 2011).

6 Debussy's Impressionism Interrogated 65

Burne-Jones's *Love among the Ruins*.[19] In 1894, in Brussels, he illustrated Maeterlinck's *Trois petits drames pour marionettes*, with woodcut *culs-de-lampe*. A copy of this, with a dedication from Maeterlinck to Debussy, has somehow ended up in the Bibliothèque nationale de France.[20] Minne's approach to the *cul-de-lampe* (a 'tailpiece' illustration placed at the end of a section) was rather unusual. As Denis Laoureux points out, his *culs-de-lampe* were never allied to a particular passage in the poem or play, but presented rather tantalising images of the deeper symbolism of the text: 'a sign reduced to an enveloping atmosphere, establishing a link between absence and the consciousness of the self' – a far cry from the unpopulated landscapes that had been a predominant preoccupation of Impressionism.[21]

If 'Light was the goddess to idolise' for the French Impressionists, obscurity underpinned Belgian symbolism.[22] The first production of *Pelléas* the play in Paris was a dark affair, although we know more about it from its London production than from the French critics.[23] Belgian artists, turning their hand to scenography and book illustration, mainly of Maeterlinck, were after all contemporaries of Debussy in the 1890s, whereas the Impressionists and even the Post- and Neo-Impressionists were rather old hat. Other Belgian artists under the spell of Maeterlinck were Auguste Donnay, who illustrated his *Les Aveugles* (The Blind), and Léon Spillaert, who painted lamp-posts on the quay at Ostend as well as 348 illustrations for an edition of the playwright's collected *Théâtre* in 1902–3. Another who was preoccupied with nocturnal paintings was William Degouve de Nuncques, whose mysterious images included an unpopulated painting of the streetlights in the Parc royal in Brussels as well as cyclists on a riverbank with their cycle lamps on. The symbolic associations with lamps are nowhere more poignant than in Geneviève's slowly intoned parting reminder to Pelléas in the beautiful subjunctive of the last line of Act I, scene 2: 'Aie soin d'allumer la lampe dès ce soir, Pelléas'.

Nuncques had shared a studio with Henry de Groux, whom Debussy had met in Paris, expressing admiration for his work. De Groux had done a brass of Debussy, now in the museum of the Bibliothèque-musée de

---

[19] Stevens, *Impressionism to Symbolism*, p. 22. *Love among the Ruins* was exhibited in Paris in 1878 and reproduced as a platinotype during the 1890s.
[20] Maurice Maeterlinck, Alladine et Palomides, Intérieur, *et* La Mort de Tintagiles: *Trois petits drames pour marionnettes* (Brussels: Edmond Demain, 1894). Illustrations by Georges Minne.
[21] Denis Laoureux, 'Les Très Riches Heures de Maurice Maeterlinck', in *L'Univers*, p. 60.
[22] An exception was the group of artists with more allegiance to Impressionism, who worked in Paris. They were of several nationalities and included the Spanish painter Sorolla.
[23] See Langham Smith, 'Aimer ainsi'.

l'Opéra in Paris. Nuncques, who travelled and exhibited widely in France, was also a friend of Debussy's friend and collaborator Maurice Denis, who had designed the sets for Maeterlinck's *Intérieur* (1894–5). The Swiss Carlos Schwabe, who was to illustrate an edition of *Pelléas* the play in 1924, also participated in the designs for d'Indy's *Fervaal* and produced a series of Maeterlinckian images concurrently with his early plays: *Sadness* (1893); *Fate* (1894); *Evening Bells* (1895); *Hymne* and *Mort* (1900). Another who collaborated with Maeterlinck was Jean Delville, whose Wagnerian images of *Parsifal* and *Tristan* were complemented by many 'pictures of silence'. He taught at the Glasgow School of Art for a while. Other Belgian painters of note included Xavier Mellery (*The Hours: Eternity and Death*) and James Ensor, who painted a striking picture entitled *Russian Music*, reminding us of Chausson and Debussy discovering this repertoire together.

It would seem that Debussy's tastes for the cross-currents of European art in the 1890s remained a passion until well into the twentieth century. In an oft-repeated quote of 1911, taken from a letter to Edgard Varèse, Debussy commented 'J'aime presque autant les images que la musique'. But it is the rest of the letter that is the most interesting. He was complaining about the high price of the luxuriously illustrated German art-magazine *Pan,* which had run from 1895 to 1900 and was a leading source in linking the various movements in the visual arts across Europe, from Pre-Raphaelitism, through various Symbolists, to the Secessionists.[24] He complained about the high second-hand prices for this *revue* and wondered whether Varèse (living in Berlin where the *revue* was published) might be able to send him some copies. Although often cited as a vehicle for the dissemination of Art Nouveau, the images ranged much more widely and included realistic illustrations of forests and snowscapes. There were also poems by Maeterlinck illustrated by Charles Doudelet, who had gone on to illustrate an edition of *Pelléas*. A German translation of Rossetti's *Damozel* – Debussy's *La Damoiselle élue* – had a commissioned illustration by a German artist.

French artists who were featured included Puvis de Chavannes, Paul-Albert Besnard, Degas, Lautrec, Félix Vallotton, Gustave Moreau, and Maurice Denis. Foreign artists included Whistler. Beside these were illustrations of forests, landscapes, and empty seascapes not at all in an Art

---

[24] 12 February 1911, *Correspondance*, p. 1389. *Pan* played an important role in the diffusion of Art Nouveau images.

Nouveau style. French writers including Verlaine and Mallarmé were framed with especially commissioned prints. A long article about English illustrators such as William Morris, Rossetti, and Walter Crane would surely have attracted Debussy. As technology advanced, the magazine became notable for its early introduction of *Farbendrücken* (colour illustrations).[25]

One illustrator particularly important for his connections with Maeterlinck was Fernand Khnopff, who had been connected with the Théâtre royal de la Monnaie for some time before the run of *Pelléas* there in 1907 and complemented Ensor's painting *Russian Music* with one entitled *Listening to Schumann*, where the model is looking away, deeply moved. A close friend of Burne-Jones, in 1903 he had designed the costumes for the premiere of Chausson's *Le Roi Arthus* and for Debussy's *Pelléas* he was again involved. Some years later he would illustrate a deluxe edition of *Pelléas* the play.[26] For *Pan*, he illustrated a poem by Mallarmé with an image entitled *Listening to Flowers*.

Writing in 1921, André Caplet, Debussy's close friend, worldwide conductor, and orchestrator of several of his works, compared the up-to-date scenography of the Monnaie to the Salon des refusés in Paris, where such paintings as Manet's *Le Déjeuner sur l'herbe* had found a place after rejection by the Salon des Beaux Arts. As with Satie's reminiscences of the following year, it was perhaps only from the distance of five or so years that the undeniably strong connections between Debussy and the visual arts could begin to be assessed. It is a pity that popular views of him have been all too often restricted to the Impressionist tag, in itself a term which has been reduced to signify many artists whose techniques and preoccupations ill-fitted the original agenda of the movement. Debussy, whose music never stuck in a rut but always moved on with a style and literary associations of its own, was without doubt equally inquisitive about the many strands of development in the visual arts in the 1890s and the new century, already fifty years on from the years of the birth of Impressionism.

---

[25] *Pan* is consultable online via the library of the University of Heidelberg, the city where the later editions of the periodical were published.

[26] See Jacques Detemmerman, 'Le "Wagnérisme français" et la critique belge: *Sigurd* de Reyer, *Gwendoline* de Chabrier et *Le Roi Arthus* de Chausson', *Cahiers du Gram* (2003), pp. 163–83; Denis Herlin, '*Pelléas et Mélisande* à la Monnaie', in Herlin, *Claude Debussy: Portraits et études* (Hildesheim: Olms, 2021), pp. 411–33. The coloured book illustrations are for an edition by the Brussels Société de bibliophiles 'les Cinquante' (1920). For reproduction of these, see Xavier Tricot, *Fernand Khnopff, Catalogue Raisonné of the Prints* (Leuven: Pandora, 2018), p. 205.

Author's Recommendation
Diane au bois (1883–5).

At the time of writing, several of Debussy's shorter vocal pieces remain unpublished. *Diane* is one of several on Hellenic themes from the 1880s and was a precursor of the *Prélude à l'après-midi d'un faune*, both in terms of its text and its music. The text is a section of the play of the same name by Théodore de Banville to whom Debussy was attracted in his youthful years, setting several of his poems, no doubt inspired by Mme Vasnier, his mistress at this time.

Mallarmé's poem *L'Après-midi d'un faune* was itself inspired by Banville's *Acte en vers* (rhymed scene) and there are many musical parallels between Debussy's music for *Diane au bois* and the *Prélude à l'après-midi d'un faune*, most notably the use of the flute (replacing panpipes) as an instrument of seduction with the hunting-horns of Diana's nymphs sounding in the distance – remember Diana was the goddess of both chastity and hunting.

The scene Debussy set depicted Diana and Eros (soprano and tenor). It has enjoyed several performances: first in 1962 on the BBC Third Programme in a version edited and presented by Edward Lockspeiser. In 2012 a performance of the score, expertly orchestrated by Robert Orledge, was given at the Royal College of Music in London, sung by Louise Alder and John McMunn, conducted by Jonathan Darlington.

The single available recording is currently in *Claude Debussy: The Complete Works* from Warner Classics, where it is sung by Natalie Pérez (soprano) and Cyrille Dubois (tenor), accompanied by Jean-Pierre Armengaud (piano).[27] Both *Diane* and another Banville setting, 'Hymnis', will appear in the Debussy *Œuvres complètes* in due course and will hopefully lead to a wider choice of recordings of these important Parnassian settings. *Diane* is not merely interesting in the evolution of Debussy's Hellenistic side, but a fine piece in its own right.

---

[27] CD, Warner Classics 0190295 736750 (2018).

CHAPTER 7

Symbolism

François de Médicis

The critical reception of Debussy was initially associated with the Impressionist aesthetic,[1] until Stefan Jarociński made the case for Debussy's passionate enthusiasm for Symbolist literature and its influence over his creative sensibility.[2] More recently, some scholars have called this into question, either by emphasising the influence of Symbolist writers in theorisations of the Impressionist visual aesthetic, or by pointing to the previously underestimated influence of other intellectual trends on Debussy.

In France, Symbolism developed mainly in literature, more specifically in poetry, as a reaction to Romantic, Parnassian, and Naturalist styles.[3] The most striking features of the movement include an aversion to the grandiose, sentimentality, and materialism, as well as significant distancing from any social agenda. At the same time, Symbolists aimed to musicalise language through the frequent construction of a play of assonances and by renewing the rhythmic cadence of the verse and favouring suggestion and allusion over excessive literal meaning. While writing *Hérodiade* (1864), Stéphane Mallarmé (1842–98) made it his objective to '*paint, not the object, but the effect it produces*', insisting that 'the lines in such a poem mustn't be composed of words; but of intentions, and all the words must fade before the sensation'.[4]

Scholars interested in French literary Symbolism usually consider Charles Baudelaire (1821–67) the most important forerunner, with Paul

I wish to thank Catrina Flint, Rachelle Taylor, and Simon Trezise for their help in translating this text into English.

[1] Ronald L. Byrnside, 'Musical Impressionism: The Early History of the Term', *The Musical Quarterly* 66 (1980), pp. 522–37.
[2] Stefan Jarociński, *Debussy: Impressionism and Symbolism*, trans. Rollo Myers (London: Eulenburg, 1976).
[3] Jean Moréas, 'Le Symbolisme', *Le Figaro: Supplément littéraire* (18 September 1886), pp. 1–2.
[4] Letter to Henri Cazalis, 30 October 1864, in Rosemary Lloyd (ed., trans.), *Selected Letters of Stéphane Mallarmé* (Chicago: University of Chicago Press, 1988), p. 39.

Verlaine (1844–96) and Stéphane Mallarmé as early leading figures. Only in 1886 – long after Baudelaire's death and Verlaine's and Mallarmé's earliest works – was literary Symbolism considered a formal movement. The year 1886 also saw the founding of the journal *Le Symboliste* by Jean Moréas (pseudonym for Ioánnis Papadhiamandopoúlos), Paul Fort, and Gustave Kahn. Supporters of the movement, such as Moréas, René Ghil (pseudonym for René François Ghilbert), Gustave Kahn, Ferdinand Brunetière, and Georges Vanor, struggled to define the nature of the Symbolist phenomenon to better establish their identity and to set themselves apart from other artistic movements. For this, they relied in part on the Baudelairean notion of '*correspondance*', which creates connections between various forms of feeling and sentiment. Generally speaking, Symbolism is rooted in the philosophical dichotomy that opposes things as they appear to humans through the senses (the manifestation, or phenomenon), and the thing in itself (the noumenon) that remains unknowable. Among the main thinkers who nourished Symbolist theorising efforts are Richard Wagner, Arthur Schopenhauer, and the German idealists. For example, Remy de Gourmont's *L'Idéalisme* takes inspiration from Schopenhauer, situating Kant in the same line as Plato, clearly inscribing Symbolism in an idealist perspective.[5]

Between 1882 and 1902, a young Debussy frequented Symbolist circles with worshipful diligence, and with a voracious appetite he drew inspiration from this movement. A biography devoted to this period of the composer's life, written by the eminent specialist Lesure and dating from 1992, is aptly titled 'Claude Debussy avant *Pelléas* ou les Années symbolistes'.[6] Symbolism continued to provide a source of inspiration for Debussy after 1902 but, as we shall see, it would decrease to some extent and blend with a more varied range of literary aesthetics.

Debussy led other musicians in composing works indebted to Verlaine and Mallarmé. And while Baudelaire had inspired many of his elders before him, the future composer of *Pelléas* set himself apart by the significant number of poems from *Les Fleurs du mal* that he set to music. In his early student days at the Conservatoire, Debussy composed a cornucopia of melodies with tireless zeal, his literary taste rapidly leading him to sophisticated, sensitive poets. After showing an early predilection for the Parnassian Théodore de Banville, he quickly discovered Verlaine. Like

---

[5] Remy de Gourmont, *L'Idéalisme* (Paris: Mercure de France, 1893).
[6] This work was later integrated into a monograph of which it constitutes the first part: *Claude Debussy: Biographie critique* (Paris: Fayard, 2003). In English, Lesure (Rolf).

other Symbolists, the latter emerged from the Parnassian aesthetic (in which his *Poèmes saturniens* of 1866 are steeped). There were several points of contact connecting the two literary movements: Banville and Verlaine were both inspired by paintings in the *Fêtes galantes* style as well as figures from the *commedia dell'arte* as portrayed by the eighteenth-century painter Antoine Watteau (1684–1721). Debussy appeared sensitive to this common theme. The art songs (*mélodies*) 'Pierrot', 'Sérénade', and 'Fête galante' are settings of Banville's poems; 'Mandoline', 'Clair de lune', 'Pantomime', 'Fantoches', and 'En sourdine' on poems from the *Fêtes galantes* are Verlaine's. In the 1892 triptych *Fêtes galantes* ('Clair de lune', 'Fantoches', and 'En sourdine'), a much more mature Debussy revisited three of Verlaine's poems that he had already set in his youth.

In 1884, after completing his studies at the Conservatoire, Debussy won the prestigious Prix de Rome. As a result, he spent the years 1885 to 1887 in Italy at the Villa Medici in Rome, at the expense of the French state. The year 1884 also saw him compose 'Apparition', an art song devoid of all academicism and his first foray into Stéphane Mallarmé's world. Later, between January 1885 and around 1887, while dividing his time between Paris and Rome, Debussy composed the *Ariettes oubliées*, a collection of six art songs on poems by Verlaine.[7] This collection marks a turning point in his compositional development; a number of commentators consider it one of the first real manifestations of his personal style. In Rome, Debussy ached for Paris, its cultural life, and his lover Marie-Blanche Vasnier. He wrote to Émile Baron (his book dealer in the French capital) to see if Verlaine had published any new works, to ask him to send Moréas's latest publications (the volume of poems *Les Cantilènes* and a novel written in collaboration with Paul Adam, *Le Thé chez Miranda*), and to order journals that published Symbolists such as *La Vogue* (co-founded in 1886 by Kahn and Léo d'Orfer) and *La Revue indépendante*.[8] In the years between 1880 and 1900, a plethora of short-lived Symbolist journals abounded, generally bearing witness to 'artistic pluralism, aesthetic militancy, and a taste for controversy'.[9] During his time in Rome, Debussy discovered Baudelaire's poetry and writings, and the effect was so deeply felt that it may be discerned in his correspondence, especially in passages devoted to the

---

[7] Lesure, *Claude Debussy*, p. 497.   [8] *Correspondance*, pp. 51–2.
[9] Cédric Segond-Genovesi, 'Du *Mercure* à *La Revue musicale* (1905–1927): Enjeux et étapes d'une filiation', in Myriam Chimènes, Florence Gétreau, and Catherine Massip (eds.), *Henry Prunières (1886–1942): Un musicologue engagé dans la vie musicale de l'entre-deux guerres* (Paris: Société française de musicologie, 2015), p. 359.

composer's evolving aesthetic concerns. Significantly, his *Cinq poèmes de Charles Baudelaire* came into being shortly after his return to Paris.

Debussy's return was shortly followed by another significant event: on 8 January 1888, he joined the Société nationale de musique (or SNM), an important Parisian concert association devoted to the dissemination of new music by French composers. The young musician appeared on one of the programmes for the first time on 2 February 1889, with the premiere of his *Ariettes oubliées*. A musician seventeen years Debussy's senior who has also come down to us for his exceptional gift for communicating a Verlaine sensibility, Gabriel Fauré, was also a member of this society. A few months prior to the *Ariettes* concert, on 28 April 1888, Debussy may well have heard the premiere of this composer's song on a text by Verlaine, 'Clair de lune' Op. 46 No. 2.

Fauré discovered Verlaine a few years after Debussy, in 1886, by way of the poet and dandy Robert de Montesquiou, who was arguably the model for Marcel Proust's Baron de Charlus, a character from his novel sequence *À la recherche du temps perdu*. While Fauré's first work on a text by Verlaine was indeed 'Clair de lune', completed in 1887, Debussy's first attempt with the poet dates from 1882, with 'Fantoches', followed by two different settings of 'Clair de lune', one before and one after Fauré's (in 1882 and 1892). Over a period of seven years, Fauré composed a total of eighteen songs on poems by Verlaine, including two important cycles, *Cinq mélodies 'de Venise'* Op. 58 (1891) and the nine songs of *La Bonne Chanson* Op. 61 (1894). The latter was dedicated to a gifted amateur singer and future wife of Debussy, Emma Bardac (née Moyse), and also Fauré's lover at the time. The senior composer knew Verlaine personally, well enough to visit him at his nursing home in order to discuss a collaborative project, and to sketch a portrait that he later sent to one of his benefactors.[10] Whether or not Debussy met Verlaine in person remains an open question, although young Achille may have found himself in a situation where this may have been possible. Prior to his entry to the Conservatoire, he studied piano privately with Antoinette Mauté de Fleurville, the poet's mother-in-law.[11] Moreover, Debussy was acquainted with Charles de Sivry, the half-brother of Verlaine's wife (Mathilde), but we do not know if the two met while the composer was

---

[10] Gabriel Fauré, *Correspondance suivie de lettres à Madame H.*, ed. Jean-Michel Nectoux (Paris: Fayard, 2015), p. 175.
[11] Lesure (Rolf), pp. 9–11, 78–9.

studying piano with Madame Mauté de Fleurville or after his return from Rome.

Over the course of the nineteenth century, cafés gradually supplanted salons as sites for literary and artistic exchange.[12] By the end of the 1880s and following his return from Rome, this circumstance allowed Debussy to meet Moréas in the Latin Quarter, at the Café Vachette. The two gave themselves over to heated discussions, half serious, half ironic, arguing over Schopenhauer or the second part of Goethe's *Faust*.[13] The musician became an enthusiastic *habitué* of the bibliophile Edmond Bailly and his establishment, the Librairie de l'Art indépendant, a celebrated site for the dissemination of all things Symbolist and occultist, and an important place for the literati to meet and socialise. It was home to the likes of Henri de Régnier, André Gide, Paul Claudel, and Pierre Louÿs. In short, many regulars of Mallarmé's Tuesdays ran into each other at Bailly's place of business. Debussy established a cordial acquaintance there with Régnier (who served a while as his literary counsel), and he maintained a close friendship for some years with Louÿs, with whom he devised several joint projects, of which only the incidental music *Les Chansons de Bilitis* and the three Louÿs settings *Chansons de Bilitis* ever took shape.

It was Bailly who published a luxurious limited edition of the *Cinq poèmes de Charles Baudelaire* in 1890. A number of composers in the generation prior to Debussy had composed *mélodies* on the poet's texts, though sparingly. Some of the more well-known include single art songs by Emmanuel Chabrier ('L'Invitation au voyage') and Ernest Chausson ('L'Albatros'), two by Henri Duparc ('L'Invitation au voyage' and 'La Vie antérieure'), and three by Gabriel Fauré ('Hymne', 'La Rançon', and 'Chant d'automne'). A contemporary of Debussy, Pierre de Bréville had previously set two of Baudelaire's poems, though they were published a long time afterwards ('Harmonie du soir' and 'La Cloche fêlée'). Among Debussy's close friends from his student days, another musician and passionate devotee of poetry and Symbolist literature, Raymond Bonheur, authored 'La Mort des pauvres' and 'Bien loin d'ici'. These two undated songs on Baudelaire poems belong to a short cycle of three that appears to be incomplete. It was from this same generation that the first collections as ambitious as Debussy's five art songs sprang. In 1889, as Debussy was writing 'Harmonie du soir', Gustave Charpentier had already

---

[12] Pamela A. Genova, *Symbolist Journals: A Culture of Correspondence* (Aldershot: Ashgate, 2002), pp. 57–8.
[13] Robert Godet, 'En marge de la marge', *La Revue musicale* 7 (May 1926), pp. 159–60; Letter to Godet, 25 December 1889, *Correspondance*, p. 82.

completed six songs on Baudelaire poems. As a Prix de Rome resident at the Villa Medici, he sang them during his Parisian retreats, in salons and musical get-togethers, years before Hartmann published them in 1895. Following his permanent return to France in June of 1890, Charpentier and Debussy met regularly at the Café Pousset, and in February 1891 Debussy gave him an autographed copy of his own volume of Baudelaire art songs.[14]

Like Debussy and Fauré, Charpentier also took an interest in Verlaine, whose work became the source for four songs in 1890, 1893, and 1894, including 'Les Chevaux de bois' (1893), previously set by Debussy as part of the *Ariettes oubliées*. These works date from some time after Debussy's and Fauré's efforts with Verlaine's poetry, and, without denying their beauty, their vigorous musical strokes push beyond the more muted Symbolist tones. Charpentier later met with success and international fame in 1900 with the premiere of his realist opera *Louise*, shortly before his fellow composer's dreamlike *Pelléas et Mélisande* reached the stage in 1902.

During the same years that these two young Prix de Rome winners were composing their songs, Baudelaire continued to suffer from a scandalous reputation in France. The brouhaha that surrounded a private performance of Debussy's collection captured the attention of Mallarmé, who immediately sought out the composer. The poet had already begun to consider arraying a public reading of his eclogue *L'Après-midi d'un faune* in music, and at the same time, in 1890, he invited Debussy to collaborate with him. So moved was the composer upon reading the poem that he offered copies of the booklet to his friends, including Paul Dukas.[15] The celebrated orchestral tone poem *Prélude à l'après-midi d'un faune* met with enthusiasm when it was premiered at the SNM four years later, after which Mallarmé paid the musician a benevolent tribute in 1897 with the quatrain:

> Sylvain d'haleine première
> Si ta flûte a réussi
> Ouïs toute la lumière
> Qu'y soufflera Debussy[16]

In the meantime, Debussy became a regular at Mallarmé's Tuesday salons – something that has been noted as exceptional, for he was the only musician

---

[14] Appendix V, *Correspondance*, p. 2218.
[15] Simon-Pierre Perret and Marie-Laure Ragot, *Paul Dukas* (Paris: Fayard, 2007), pp. 35–6.
[16] 'O forest god of first breath/If your flute has succeeded/Listen to all the light/That Debussy will blow in there.' See Stéphane Mallarmé and John Buckland Wright, *L'Après-midi d'un Faune: The Translation by Aldous Huxley* (London: Golden Cockerel Press, 1956), front matter.

among the regulars. Debussy attended the poet's funeral in 1898, an eloquent tribute for a somewhat untamed musician, more inclined to avoid public celebrations.

Another Symbolist writer, the Belgian Maurice Maeterlinck (1862–1949), would later inspire Debussy to create a work that solidified his reputation more than any other. This was the opera *Pelléas et Mélisande*, a complete version of which was composed between 1893 and 1895, straddling the genesis of *Faune*. It came after a long search for a libretto that resonated with his aesthetic ideal. An early candidate was Maeterlinck's *La Princesse Maleine*, which struck the cultural milieu like a thunderbolt when it was published in 1889. After initially expressing themselves through poetry, Symbolists appeared keen to widen their reach to the stage, and Maeterlinck's play seemed entirely designed to satisfy their desires. *Le Figaro* published a swift paean of praise on its cover, signed by Octave Mirbeau (guided by Mallarmé), who celebrated a new type of theatre that would surpass even Shakespeare for its beauty(!). Worse luck for Debussy: the rights to musical adaptation slipped away from him, in all likelihood into the hands of Vincent d'Indy, who had acted more quickly to secure them.[17]

Four years later, Debussy was awed to discover *Pelléas et Mélisande*, also by Maeterlinck, which he read from a luxury edition following its publication in 1892. He also saw the single performance given in Paris by the Aurélien-Marie Lugné-Poe company on 17 May 1893 at the Théâtre des Bouffes-Parisiens (a venue normally reserved for lightweight entertainment).[18] Debussy received overtures prior to the staging of his opera version to furnish incidental music for performances of Maeterlinck's play. He refused categorically: his music was far too intimately connected to theatre and speech and ill-suited to that purpose. Fauré was later approached and agreed to write stage music for the play; the orchestral suite that followed has met with considerable acclaim ever since. But Fauré's success sickened Debussy tremendously as he waited for the premiere of his own work.[19] For Fauré, *Pelléas* proved a gateway to a series of works inspired by the Belgian symbolists. After Maeterlinck, Charles van Lerberghe (1861–1907) furnished him with the poetry for two of his late works: *La Chanson d'Ève* Op. 95 (some of which was derived from his music for *Pelléas*) and *Le Jardin clos* Op. 106.

---

[17] Lesure (Rolf), p. 97.
[18] Denis Herlin, '*Pelléas et Mélisande* aux Bouffes-Parisiens', in Herlin, *Claude Debussy: Portraits et études* (Hildesheim: Olms, 2021), p. 392.
[19] Letter to George Hartmann, 9 August 1898, *Correspondance*, pp. 414–15.

It should be mentioned that Debussy himself wrote poems inspired by the Symbolist aesthetic (two of which were published in the *Entretiens politiques et littéraires*). He also set them to music: the published *Proses lyriques* and two of the projected five *Nuits blanches mélodies*, unpublished in the composer's lifetime. The poetry is in free verse and the first set may have been conceived as a trial preparation for setting the poetic prose of *Pelléas et Mélisande*.

Debussy continued to draw inspiration from Symbolist works after 1902, though his tastes broadened to include a variety of literary styles. His particular affection for earlier French poets from the Middle Ages to the seventeenth century should be highlighted here: François Villon (*Trois ballades*), Charles d'Orléans (two of the *Trois chansons de France* and the *Trois chansons de Charles d'Orléans* for a cappella choir), and Tristan L'Hermite (*Le Promenoir des deux amants*).

In 1913, the musical world was shaken by the premiere of Igor Stravinsky's *Le Sacre du printemps*. Having read through the manuscript at the piano with the composer prior to the first performance, Debussy received the work with a mixture of admiration and distress.[20] As though pushed to his limits, he reacted with one of his most daring works, the *Trois poèmes de Stéphane Mallarmé*. Littered with abrupt changes and distant connections, the language of this group of songs testifies to the astonishing development of a style inspired by a Mallarmean poetic, with its daring syntax and sense of ellipsis. Maurice Ravel was also caught up in the cult that surrounded the poet from Valvins. Shortly after the premiere of Debussy's *Faune*, and still in his early twenties, he set the poem 'Sainte' to music in 1896. In a remarkable coincidence, in 1913 Ravel also penned his own collection entitled *Trois poèmes de Stéphane Mallarmé*, of which two poems were also set by Debussy, 'Soupir' and 'Placet futile'. (This resulted in some delicate negotiations over the sharing of rights.) Ravel's work was conceived for voice and small instrumental ensemble, as were Stravinsky's *Three Japanese Lyrics* from the same time period and Schoenberg's *Pierrot lunaire* (a melodramatic collection on poems by the Belgian Symbolist Albert Giraud, translated into German, which Stravinsky had recently heard in Berlin). Ravel's 'Soupir' is dedicated to the Russian composer.

So what might Symbolism entail for a composer's style? As in literature, one could first describe the Symbolist musical style as the rejection of pathos. The aesthetics of Fauré and Debussy reacted, among other things, to Wagnerian excess. Symbolist music does not refrain from tense effects,

---

[20] Louis Laloy, *La Musique retrouvée, 1902–1927* (Paris: Plon, 1928), p. 213.

but avoids emphasising moments of intense emotion with loud and untimely climaxes. As the works of Symbolist composers renewed musical language, they discarded the feverish tension of Wagnerian chromaticism and preferred the variegated colours of a modal style, with an often unpredictable harmonic path capable of capturing the nuances and the course of a thought or a feeling. In vocal music, the sung part offers a stylisation of elocution that is close to spoken language. In other genres, the piano and instrumental ensemble writing radiates with a variety of timbres and fosters a sense of refinement.

A more concentrated, austere style given over to purely instrumental writing marks Debussy's late works (1915–17), with the *En blanc et noir* suite for two pianos, the extended collection of *Études* for piano, and the three chamber sonatas for various instruments. With the First World War and its disruptions to heating fuel supplies, in 1917 Debussy thanked his coal dealer by offering him the manuscript for *Les Soirs illuminés par l'ardeur du charbon* for piano, the title taken from a verse by Baudelaire.

Author's Recommendation
Pelléas et Mélisande, Act III, scenes 2 and 3 (1893–1902).

Two scenes from the third act of *Pelléas et Mélisande* illustrate Debussy's talent for expressing the libretto's Symbolist dimension. In scene 2, Golaud and Pelléas explore the castle's caverns, engulfed in fetid, underground air. Golaud's attitude betrays murderous intentions. In the following scene, as the two emerge into the fresh air above ground, Pelléas is enraptured by pleasurable feelings, which build to ecstasy when he sees Mélisande at the top of the tower.

Scene 3 begins with Pelléas's recitative, followed by rapid figuration in the orchestra that conveys the transformation of the air from its dank underground state to its freely flowing counterpart above ground. From a restrained ambitus, the arabesques expand and become invigorated. The orchestra subsequently illustrates a barrage of sensations that assails Pelléas: feelings of touch, smell, sight, time, and sound. For this, Debussy deploys a stratified style of writing, in which various musical figures emerge from within the various superimposed layers, only to disappear one by one in a process of constant renewal.

The music also conveys both a physical and psychological progression on a broader scale. Following the threat of the caverns, Pelléas experiences an epiphany at the sight of Mélisande atop the tower. A number of musical elements mark this progression – orchestration, registral positioning, and musical scales. In these scenes, Debussy rejects the established forms of traditional opera; he breaks with Romantic rhetoric and its progressions that lead to huge climaxes. Here, the musical progression proceeds in delicate shades, describing a gradual change of colours, accompanying the libretto's psychological and moral evolution in an allusive manner.

CHAPTER 8

Modernism

Michel Duchesneau

When Jean Moréas published his manifesto on Symbolism in *Le Figaro* of 18 September 1886, Debussy was at the Villa Medici (after winning the Prix de Rome). Moréas's text marked the advent of the movement in literature and painting, even though it had already manifested itself in previous years through a number of works.[1] The young composer certainly heard about it; he may have read the manifesto as well. Anyway, a few days later, the figure of the poet had evidently stimulated his curiosity, for at this precise moment Debussy asked the bookseller Émile Baron to send him two works by Moréas, along with the complete works of Shelley and volumes by Paul Verlaine, Albert Jounet, and Charles Morice.[2] Debussy, far from Paris, learnt about the artistic community and its creations through careful perusal of newspapers and magazines. He was thus a reader of *La Revue indépendante*, which at the time would become one of the main organs of Symbolism.[3] Biographical studies of the composer confirm that in the years that followed he frequented avant-garde musical, literary, and fine-arts circles that made Paris one of the focal places of Modernism between 1890 and 1914. How is this cultural world, in which a considerable number of artists circulated around Debussy, articulated and who can we variously associate with one '-ism' or another? The exceptional context of Paris during these two decades undoubtedly contributed to making Debussy a champion of musical Modernism in close association with contemporary artistic trends, because, as Jean-Michel Nectoux points out, 'he participates with all his sensitivity in the literary and artistic movements that surround him, as well as the most lively trends of contemporary taste'.[4] It is therefore

---

[1] A good part of Mallarmé's output dates from before 1886. This is true of *L'Après-midi d'un faune*, which was published in 1876.
[2] Letter to Émile Baron, September 1886, *Correspondance*, p. 51.
[3] See letter to Émile Baron, 6 November 1886, *Correspondance*, p. 53.
[4] Jean-Michel Nectoux, *Harmonie en bleu et or: Debussy, la musique et les arts* (Paris: Fayard, 2005), p. 11.

not surprising that Debussy's music was soon associated with the Symbolist and Impressionist movements.[5] Even if the composer criticised these associations, especially with Impressionism, they bear witness to their influences that the analysis of his work continues to reveal.[6] We can safely say that Debussy would be in contact with many '-isms' (or artistic movements), as he had acquaintances and friends within the artistic world, even if we stick only to the names of Ernest Chausson, Camille Claudel, Maurice Denis, Robert Godet, Henry Lerolle, Pierre Louÿs, Maurice Maeterlinck, Stéphane Mallarmé, Catulle Mendès, Odilon Redon, Henri de Régnier, Erik Satie, Igor Stravinsky, Victor Segalen, and Paul Valéry.

To use the expression coined by François de Médicis, Debussy's 'artistic maturation' took place at the same time as the wind of unparalleled cultural Modernism blew over Paris with great force.[7] Since the early 1880s, Paris had become a place where it was possible to be 'modern'. In the arts, by Modernism we mean a vast movement based on the concept of modernity appealing to the notions of evolution, progress, independence, freedom, and also resistance to certain social and economic change. Modernism in art in the broadest sense will constantly evolve and take many forms. Thus, if Symbolism and Impressionism dominated the Debussyan sphere, many other movements marked the period (1880–1914) and they aroused varied reactions on the composer's part, ranging from the sincerest interest to the most pronounced rejection. To be interested in Modernism in the world of Debussy is therefore to be as interested in Neo-Impressionism, Fauvism, Orphism, Cubism, Naturalism, even in Futurism. Above all, we must not forget Art Nouveau (Modern Style), which is expressed as much in architecture as in sculpture, cabinetmaking, and in the form of decorative objects, and to which Debussy was particularly sensitive (Debussy possessed a magnificent Art Nouveau lamp by the English firm Benson & Co., which he probably bought at the Siegfried Bing gallery, the Maison de l'Art Nouveau, Bing being a great proponent of Art Nouveau).[8] The democratic regime set up with the Third Republic and the economic and cultural liberalism that dominated the political landscape of France at the

---

[5] Léon Bostein, 'Beyond the Illusions of Realism: Painting and Debussy's Break with Tradition', in Jane F. Fulcher (ed.), *Debussy and His World* (Princeton, NJ: Princeton University Press, 2001), p. 142.

[6] Nectoux, *Harmonie en bleu et or*, p. 31; Bostein, 'Beyond the Illusions', p. 143.

[7] See François de Médicis, *La maturation artistique de Debussy dans son contexte historique, 1884–1902* (Turnhout: Brepols, 2020).

[8] See Nectoux, *Harmonie en bleu et or*, pp. 125–7.

time undeniably contributed to the development of these artistic practices, which constantly questioned the precepts of artistic works and the conservative principles that had for so long governed their modes of expression.[9] Freedom of the press, and therefore of expression, is certainly the most convincing evidence of the changes that had occurred. The Parisian artistic effervescence, which is reflected in the presence of a large number of artists, was the ideal breeding ground for limitless creativity, which also involved the expression of the newest ideas. These ideas were relayed by a large number of newspapers and small magazines which, like the movements, would often turn out to be ephemeral and produced by small groups of artists. Debussy was an assiduous reader of several of these journals, including *Revue bleue*, *La Revue indépendante*, *La Revue moderniste*, *Mercure de France*, and *La Revue blanche*. He also took advantage of this effervescent Paris of universal exhibitions, autumn salons, and galleries that he frequented more or less regularly until 1914. A letter to Robert Godet (18 December 1911), for example, reveals that he visited the Salon d'automne in 1911, attracted by an exhibition of Henry de Groux. Close to the Symbolist milieu, Groux was a Belgian artist whom Debussy knew in the 1890s.[10]

Concordances and Discrepancies

The different forms that Modernism takes in literature, in the fine arts, and in the decorative arts unequally influenced the life and work of Debussy. If he refused the epithet of 'Impressionist musician', he had good reason. Aside from the fact that the definition of Impressionist art at the time was vague, it very often seemed to label any work that exhibited characteristics that fell outside the conservative canons of art. Such a mishmash obviously did not suit so fastidious an artist as Debussy. The diversity of expression of artistic modernity that surrounded him is revealed by his literary and visual choices, of which we have traces through the objects he collected, the illustrations in his scores, also his writings, and what he tells us about the arts and crafts in his correspondence.

The Debussyan world took shape between the mid-1880s and 1895, initially indebted to the literary movement of Symbolism, which itself succeeded Parnassianism and in which Pre-Raphaelitism was entangled. English Pre-Raphaelitism was notably driven in France by appreciation of

---

[9] See Christophe Charle, 'Debussy in Fin-de-Siècle Paris', in Fulcher (ed.), *Debussy and His World*, pp. 277–8.
[10] *Correspondance*, p. 1469.

the work of Dante Gabriel Rossetti.[11] We should remember that Debussy's *La Damoiselle élue* is a setting of a poem by the English artist. The catalogue of Debussy's works from these years illustrates this chain of literary currents fairly well: from the Parnassians he took Théodore de Banville (*Diane au bois*, 1880, and a dozen songs, 1880–2) and Leconte de l'Isle (*Les Elfes*, 1881), and from the Symbolists Maurice Maeterlinck (*Pelléas*, 1902) and Stéphane Mallarmé (*L'Après-midi d'un faune*, 1891–4). Mallarmé is closely associated with the Parnassians, because he shares the principles of art for art's sake with them, but he is also linked to the Symbolists, whose development he fostered through his work and influence on young poets.

The fact that Debussy rejected the Impressionist label for his music did not prevent him from having contact with several artists that art historians have associated with the movement, but their influence appears only in subtle ways. Debussy was close to the sculptor Alexandre Charpentier (1856–1909), who had connections with anarchist circles (he frequented the Chat Noir cabaret, just like Debussy) and exhibited at the Salon des XX (considered a high place of the avant-garde) in Brussels in 1893, then at the Salon de la libre esthétique in 1894 with, among others, Maurice Denis, Camille Pissarro, and Paul Signac.[12] Art historians regard the latter two as Neo-Impressionists. It was certainly during the Salon des XX that the two artists met when the Belgian art critic Octave Maus played over Debussy's String Quartet at the avant-garde event.[13] According to Nectoux, Charpentier attracted Debussy with his 'unique and true artistic personality, living in a spirit of total independence from the official world'.[14] From here, following the common thread of Modernism around Debussy leads us through the multiple variations of Modernism where resistance, independence, and freedom – sometimes intuitive, sometimes calculated – are the watchwords.

It was between 1890 and 1900 that the Nabis (meaning 'prophet' in Hebrew), guided by Paul Sérusier, questioned the principles of Impressionism in favour of imagination, subjectivity, and spirituality. Among the main members of the group, which included Pierre Bonnard and Félix Vallotton, Maurice Denis was the principal spokesperson.

---

[11] Gabriel Mourey, a friend of Debussy's, published a work on the Pre-Raphaelites in 1909 that testifies to the knowledge and appreciation of the British movement among the French artistic community: Mourey, *D. G. Rossetti et les préraphaélites anglais* (Paris: Henri Laurens, 1909).

[12] Debussy was sympathetic to anarchist ideas between 1889 and 1892. See Charle, 'Debussy in Fin-de-Siècle Paris', p. 278; and Lesure, *Claude Debussy* (Paris: Klincksieck, 1994), pp. 119–20.

[13] See David J. Code, 'Debussy's String Quartet in the Brussels Salon of "La Libre Esthétique"', *19th-Century Music* 30 (2007), pp. 257–87.

[14] Nectoux, *Harmonie en bleu et or*, p. 128.

8 Modernism

Denis's relationship to music has been widely explored, and in the influential composer Vincent d'Indy he recognised close aesthetic and ideological links.[15] Thanks in part to the mutual acquaintances of the painter Henry Lerolle and composer Ernest Chausson, Denis's affinity to d'Indy did not prevent Debussy from admiring his paintings and decorative work at the time. It was also Denis who provided the illustrations for the score of *La Damoiselle élue* (published 1892). Later, Debussy became very critical of Denis's works, as his correspondence attests. It was the same for many other artists of his time, including the Naturalists Émile Zola and Alfred Bruneau, about whom he wrote to Pierre Louÿs: 'How can you expect people as ugly as Zola and Bruneau to be capable of anything other than striving for the mediocre?'[16] If Debussy intended to grasp a reality in his work, it is obviously a very different reality from that grasped by artistic movements aspiring to paint the modern world in its most realistic light, even if it meant staging its greatest darkness. He wrote to Jacques Durand on the subject of the orchestral *Images* in 1908: 'I'm trying to do "something different" and create – sort of realities – what imbeciles call "impressionism"'.[17] Whether it is Bruneau's music on texts by Zola (*L'Attaque du moulin*, 1893, *Messidor*, 1897) or that of Gustave Charpentier (*La Vie du poète*, 1891, *Louise*, 1900), for Debussy it was about the 'triumph of the brewery'.[18] The composer who is more an aesthete than a political being is bound to be at odds with artists such as Charpentier, Bruneau, and Zola. Debussy preferred to imagine an Orphic project with Victor Segalen from 1907. If the fundamental idea surrounding the myth of Orpheus revolves around the power of music, it is not interpreted in the same way by Debussy and Segalen; they were working on the project of a lyrical drama based on *Orphée-roi* by Guillaume Apollinaire, who published *Le Bestiaire ou Cortège d'Orphée* in 1911. By considering music as the most modern art, because it was abstract, Apollinaire associated Cubist work with the Orphic world during the Salon des indépendants of 1913 where, among others, Francis Picabia and Kandinsky exhibited: 'If Cubism is dead, long live Cubism. The reign of Orpheus begins.'[19] It was in 1905 that the critic Louis Vauxcelles ascribed the title 'Fauves' to a new generation of artists.

---

[15] See Steven Huebner, 'Maurice Denis et Vincent d'Indy: Une fraternité d'esprit', in Sylvain Caron and Michel Duchesneau (eds.), *Musique, art et religion dans l'entre-deux-guerres* (Lyon: Symétrie, 2009), pp. 347–65; Delphine Grivel, *Maurice Denis et la musique* (Lyon: Symétrie, 2001).
[16] Letter to Pierre Louÿs, 9 March 1897, *Correspondance*, p. 347.   [17] *Correspondance*, p. 1080.
[18] Letter to André Poniatowski, February 1893, *Correspondance*, p. 115.
[19] Guillaume Apollinaire, 'Salon des indépendants', *Montjoie!* (29 mars 1913).

Among the exhibitors were Matisse, Derain, and Vlaminck. In 1929, Matisse explained his aesthetic orientation:

> Here are the ideas of that time: construction by coloured surfaces, search for intensity in colour, subject matter is unimportant ... Light is not suppressed, but is expressed by a harmony of intensely coloured surfaces. My painting *La Musique* [1910] was created with a beautiful blue for the sky, the bluest of blues. The surface was coloured to saturation, that is, to the point where the blue, the idea of absolute blue, appeared fully, like the green of the trees and the vibrant vermilion of the bodies. With these three colours I had my luminous harmony, and also purity of colour tone. Above all, the colour was proportionate to the shape. The shape changes according to the reaction of the adjacent areas of colour. Because expression comes from the coloured surface that the spectator grasps in its entirety.[20]

Debussy reacted negatively to the works of the Fauves. About the Salon d'automne in 1908 at which works by Matisse (*Le Jeune marin II*), André Derain (*Baigneuses*), Maurice de Vlaminck (*Voiliers*), Wassily Kandinsky, Marcel Duchamp, and André Lothe were exhibited, he wrote: 'I've been to the Salon d'automne where people, in whom I want to believe without meanness, engage in appalling everyone, and themselves – hopefully – by their painting.'[21]

The pictorial adventures of Fauvism, and obviously Cubism, go beyond Debussy's aesthetic boundaries, but that does not mean he is 'out of the game' – far from it. Nectoux recalls, for example, that at the same time as Matisse (*La Musique, La Danse*, 1910), Klimt, and others 'revived' ancient models, Debussy composed the 'Danseuses de Delphes' (1909–10) and the *Six Épigraphes antiques* (1914).[22]

The Paradox of Modernism[23]

The chain of avant-garde movements accelerated as the twentieth century progressed. Modernism was accompanied by a 'positive conception of time ... extended to the history of art, like a law of progress discovered by the sixteenth century in science and technology'.[24] For many artists, the work of art is now a symbol of an evolving language, also of expression. In

---

[20] Henri Matisse, 'Entretien avec Tériade', *L'Intransigeant* (14 and 22 January 1929), in *Écrits et propos sur l'art*, ed. Dominique Fourcade (Paris: Hermann, 1972), pp. 94–6.
[21] Letter to Jacques Durand, 17 October 1908, *Correspondance*, p. 1119.
[22] Nectoux, *Harmonie en bleu et or*, p. 164.
[23] We take the notion of paradox applied to modernity from Antoine Compagnon, *Cinq paradoxes de la modernité* (Paris: Seuil, 1990).
[24] Compagnon, *Cinq paradoxes*, p. 22.

both cases, paradoxically, it is a question of both letting go of the past and becoming part of a dynamic of opposition to the contemporary world. This modern world is characterised by the rise of the working class, accompanied by a mass economy that only widens the increasingly pronounced gaps in wealth and the rise of a consuming and poorly cultured bourgeoisie. It is therefore not surprising that 'aesthetic modernity is defined primarily by a negative imperative: *antibourgeoise*'.[25]

With Debussy, this situation generates in itself another paradox, because he aspires to an easy and bourgeois life while severely criticising society and especially audiences or even artists who do not grasp the beautiful as he understands it.[26] The paradox is particularly significant in Debussy, whose conception of art makes him resistant to the role that can be attributed to the work at a time when social questions dominate political discourse. Regarding the Bruneau and Zola pairing, he added to what we have mentioned previously: 'with their social concerns and their claim to put life in seventh chords, [these] are only sad moulds, and if indeed they have a vision of life, it is only through the last note of their laundress'.[27] Debussy's reactions to his environment eloquently testify to the tension between Modernism as a motor of novelty from an evolutionary point of view and modernity perceived as the retreat of a certain humanism (dominated by thought, taste, deliberation, freedom) in the face of a mechanised and structured organisation of life with the economy as the main driving force. It is easy to deduce from this that the futurism of Luigi Russolo (*Dynamique d'une automobile*, 1911; *L'Art des bruits*, 1913) had no resonance with the composer.

The artistic currents of the period that we have explored obey a principle of accelerating evolution; regarding the visual arts, it is necessary to take into account the influence of the sciences, which approach the world with new tools, making it possible to grasp its materiality and its mechanisms more acutely. Another paradox inevitably follows: the acceleration of technological innovations as well as artistic innovations reinforced conservative reaction, which in turn favoured the development of a music market, in particular with the advent of the recording, which was built on works that kept listeners in an aesthetic security blanket that did not question their acquired certainties.[28]

---

[25] Compagnon, *Cinq paradoxes*, p. 28.   [26] See Charle, 'Debussy in Fin-de-Siècle Paris', p. 286.
[27] Letter to Pierre Louÿs, 9 March 1907, *Correspondance*, p. 347.
[28] Sylvain Caron, François de Médicis, and Michel Duchesneau (eds.), *Musique et modernité en France, 1900–1945* (Montreal: Presses de l'Université de Montréal, 2006), p.12.

If Debussy resists the work of the avant-garde in the first decade of the twentieth century when he criticises Cubist and Fauvist art, this must be seen as an aesthetic choice that does not stray from the path of modernity. The composer is bathed in this atmosphere of modernities (the plural is important), which act as a driving force for all spheres of activity in Western societies of the time. Debussy takes part in it, as evidenced by the history of art, which includes Debussyism in the long list of movements that made up the Modernism of the twentieth century.

Author's Recommendation
Sonata for flute, viola, and harp (1915).

Originally conceived for flute, oboe, and harp, the work is the second of three 'French' sonatas that Debussy composed during the First World War. Intended for the chromatic harp, which Debussy had discovered in 1903 (the chromatic-harp class was created at the Conservatoire in 1904), the work received its French premiere at a recital hosted by the publisher Durand on 10 December 1916.

In three movements, the fifteen-minute sonata is a stylistic concentrate of Debussy's work. Indeed, he wrote to the conductor Bernardino Molinari in 1915 that 'for many people it will not have the importance of a lyrical drama ... But it seemed to me that it would serve the music better.'[29] He wrote to the dedicatee of the work, Robert Godet, in 1916, that the work 'remembers a very old Claude Debussy – that of the *Nocturnes*'. The modernity of the work is reflected not only in the singularity and remarkable mastery of the instrumentation which, without a doubt, reminds us of the *Nocturnes*, but this modernity is also expressed in the conduct of the voices and the harmonic writing. The first movement (Pastorale) is thus characterised by the flute line, fluid and independent, which is reminiscent of that of the *Prélude à l'après-midi d'un faune*, while polytonal effects tint the initial F major. Although it is certainly in reference to the tradition of the French dance suite that Debussy gives to the central movement (Interlude. Tempo di menuetto) the form of the minuet, its sound world belongs entirely to the work, without any real evocation of the great century. The third movement offers contrast through its liveliness and the strength of the rhythm, made of an accumulation of threes against fours. Arpeggios on the harp and rockets on the flute are indeed reminiscent of 'Fêtes', the second

---

[29] Letter to Bernardino Molinari, 6 October 1915, *Correspondance*, p. 1943.

movement of the *Nocturnes*. There is no fanfare or brilliant brass sound, however, but instead a burst of life, a singular adumbration of a future work, *Le Masque de la mort rouge* (1919) by his friend André Caplet, who was, at the time of Debussy's trio, at the front somewhere in Verdun and playing the piano in the trenches.

CHAPTER 9

Wagnérisme

Steven Huebner

Albert Lavignac (1846–1916) has two principal claims to fame: the first as author of a guidebook for French visitors to Bayreuth called *Le Voyage artistique à Bayreuth* (1897) and the second as a dictation and sight-singing teacher at the Paris Conservatoire, whose pedagogical approach became immortalised in the series *Solfège des solfèges*. In the context of the present volume, we might relate a third claim to the first two: in 1876, he is said to have initiated the fourteen-year-old Debussy into the music of Wagner, surreptitiously, after a class at the Conservatoire, and late into the night. Maurice Emmanuel tells the story, and consonant with his more general account of Debussy's development that accents his rebelliousness *ab ovo*, Emmanuel says that the impromptu lesson began with Lavignac's demonstration of unusual chord progressions.[1] This segued into passages from the overture to *Tannhäuser*. For Achille, they were 'a shock', so new, so fresh. Manifestly, the appeal of Wagner was musical and, as anecdotal as it may be, Emmanuel's account reminds us of a central tenet that often gets forgotten in writing about Wagner's enormous cultural impact in France and elsewhere at the *fin de siècle*. Had Wagner not been possessed of an extraordinary musical imagination in compositional technique and had he not appealed in the first instance to the specifically musical intelligence of composers, performers, and critics, his political, theoretical, and literary influence would surely have been minimal. It was through attraction to the musician that Debussy came to Wagner and upon which his later admiration was founded. After hearing a concert performance of the first act of *Tristan und Isolde* at the Concerts Lamoureux in 1887, Debussy declared it 'definitely the most beautiful thing that I know'.[2] His admiration was lifelong, although over time it became attenuated by different aesthetic values.

---

[1] Maurice Emmanuel, *Pelléas et Mélisande de Claude Debussy: Étude historique et critique, analyse musicale* (Paris: Mellottée, 1926), p. 12.
[2] Letter to Ernest Hébert, 17 March 1887, *Correspondance*, p. 62.

Political Controversy

It seems unlikely that Lavignac's spur-of-the-moment harmony lesson in 1876 was the first time Debussy had heard Wagner's music. Following the infamous failure of *Tannhäuser* at the Opéra in March 1861, for many years the conductor Jules Pasdeloup included Wagner excerpts at orchestral concerts attended by thousands of listeners at the Cirque Napoléon, a large arena that his symphonic events shared with real circuses, equestrian displays, and Turkish wrestling.[3] In 1869, Pasdeloup took over the directorship of the Théâtre-Lyrique and promptly mounted a production of *Rienzi* there that achieved considerable success, though not enough to prevent the bankruptcy of his enterprise.[4] He continued with Wagner performances at his concerts after the defeat of 1870 and the forging of the Third Republic, and eventually faced competitors sharing his taste for *le maître de Bayreuth* in the conductors Edouard Colonne and Charles Lamoureux, who founded their own eponymous concert series.

But the stakes were now different than they had been during the Second Empire. The fabric of Left and Centre politics in the Third Republic was spun from a kind of nationalism attached not to an individual, like a king or an emperor, but rather to the French people as a collective sustained by the principles of the Revolution. As the dominant living German composer – one possessed of an overarching sense of self-importance and often described reductively in terms of his Teutonic characteristics – Wagner became more of an irritant in the post-war environment of redefined nationhood than he had ever been before. His decision in 1873 to publish a tasteless and farcical libretto called *Eine Kapitulation* – part-Offenbach pastiche, part-Aristophanic comedy – that made light of the French dilemma in the war exacerbated the nationalist critique,[5] especially after a condensed form of the libretto was made available in French translation three years later by the travel writer Victor Tissot.[6] *Une capitulation* exercised a tenacious grip on the *revanchard* imagination, while scarcely a complaint was heard about the anti-Semitism in *Das Judenthum in der Musik*, also recently available in

---

[3] See Elisabeth Bernard, 'Jules Pasdeloup et les Concerts Populaires', *Revue de musicologie* 57 (1971), pp. 150–78.
[4] Mark Everist, 'Wagner and Paris: The Case of *Rienzi* (1869)', *19th-Century Music* 41 (2017), pp. 3–30.
[5] Thomas S. Grey, '*Eine Kapitulation*: Aristophanic Operetta as Cultural Warfare in 1870', in Thomas S. Grey (ed.), *Richard Wagner and His World* (Princeton, NJ: Princeton University Press, 2009), pp. 87–122.
[6] Kelly Maynard, 'The Enemy Within: Encountering Wagner in Early Third Republic France', PhD thesis, University of California, Los Angeles (2007), pp. 35–6; Adeline Heck, 'Under the Spell of Wagner: The *Revue Wagnérienne* and Literary Experimentation in the Belle Époque (1878–1893)', PhD thesis, Princeton University (2020).

French as *Le Judaïsme dans la musique* in 1868. Un-nuanced as populist politics often are, the word on the street was that Wagner was a *gallophobe*. Free association extended to the twin threats of Bismarck and Prussian militarism. Through all of this, Pasdeloup's programming of the funeral march from *Götterdämmerung* for the first time on 29 October 1876 drew public demonstrations and much censorious editorialising in the press. The conductor felt driven to declare publicly that he had proven his patriotic mettle with his wartime service. He also stopped programming Wagner for several years.

Even at the tender age of fourteen, Debussy could not have been unaware of the brouhaha surrounding Wagner concert performances in Paris and, like so many others, doubtless puzzled over how to fit together the jagged pieces of aesthetics and patriotism. Wagner excerpts were programmed regularly by Pasdeloup, Colonne, and Lamoureux throughout the 1880s, but any hope of seeing Wagner on local stages was dashed by populist patriotism. As Wagner's works continued their march around Europe and world stages in the 1880s, various projects for a Parisian production ran up against insurmountable opposition.[7] The choice usually fell upon *Lohengrin*, doubtless for its accessibility and generic echoes of the French grand opera tradition, a work whose second act 'could easily be reimagined through the formal lens of Eugène Scribe and his musical collaborators'.[8] A proposal by the baritone and impresario Angelo Neumann to stage *Lohengrin* in 1881 was brazen and futile for one fact alone: he intended to present it in German. A few months later, Opéra-Comique director Léon Carvalho announced his own *Lohengrin* plans, but critics cried foul at the prospect of hearing Wagner at the home of the *genre éminemment national* of *opéra comique*. Carvalho compromised by proposing exceptional matinée presentations of *Lohengrin* so as not to displace evening performances of French repertory. Cancellation of the Wagner followed anyway. Lamoureux managed to see a staging through to performance at a more ephemeral venue called the Éden-Théâtre in May 1887. But now, because of a diplomatic row between France and Germany over the unjustified arrest of a French border official, the anti-Wagner press

---

[7] For a detailed account, see Manuela Schwarz, *Wagner-Rezeption und französische Oper des Fin de siècle: Untersuchungen zu Vincent d'Indy's 'Fervaal'* (Sinzig: Studio, 1999), pp. 8–25; Manuela Schwarz, '"La question de Lohengrin" zwischen 1869 und 1891', in Annegret Fauser and Manuela Schwartz (eds.), *Von Wagner zum Wagnérisme: Musik, Literatur, Kunst, Politik* (Leipzig: Leipziger Universitätsverlag, 1999), pp. 107–36; Maynard, 'The Enemy Within', pp. 41–71.

[8] Thomas Grey, 'Richard Wagner and the Legacy of French Grand Opera', in David Charlton (ed.), *The Cambridge Companion to Grand Opera* (Cambridge: Cambridge University Press, 2003), p. 333.

campaign was more vociferous than usual. Street demonstrations following the night of the premiere, as well as credible threats picked up by the police of more trouble on subsequent evenings, caused Lamoureux to consult government officials and renounce performances for the sake of public order.

It is remarkable, then, that just four years later, in the autumn of 1891, Lamoureux led the triumphant entry of *Lohengrin* onto the stage of the Opéra. Large protests still occurred. 'Les Prussiens à l'Opéra!' screamed one headline.[9] But it became ever more obvious – and this is the position that Debussy surely espoused – that Paris appeared hopelessly retrograde in its continued resistance to Wagner productions, especially the Opéra, seen throughout the nineteenth century as one of the world's leading stages. By the early 1890s, even many provincial stages in France had successfully performed *Lohengrin*. Now, the political will to protect *Lohengrin* at an institution so closely associated with the State was much more pronounced than it had been at the Éden-Théâtre: the symbolic significance of the venue worked as much in favour of Wagner as against him. Traffic around the Palais Garnier was cleared, and the police fully mobilised. After a few performances, the crowds outside the Palais Garnier dispersed. Following the triumph of *Lohengrin*, the Wagner operas all fell into line in the Opéra repertory: *Die Walküre* in 1893, *Tannhäuser* in 1895, and *Die Meistersinger von Nürnberg* in 1897 began the succession.

Elite Practice

Such public trials were not the only face of *wagnérisme* in France at the *fin de siècle*. Elite society embraced the music of the German composer and fostered appreciation of his music.[10] Marguerite Wilson, heiress of a fortune made from the installation of gas in Paris, provided the venue for private salon performances of Wagner in 1876 and 1877, organised by the judge Antoine Lascoux. Private did not necessarily mean intimate: often over a hundred music lovers attended events of what became known in the 1870s and 1880s as *le petit Bayreuth*. Performances there featured a mix of amateur and professional musicians. Although it is not known if Debussy participated, we do know that when he was seventeen his piano teacher Antoine Marmontel set him up for a summer job at Marguerite

---

[9] *L'Intransigeant*, 17 September 1891.
[10] For an overview, see Myriam Chimènes, 'Élites sociales et pratiques wagnériennes', in Fauser and Schwartz (eds.), *Von Wagner zum Wagnérisme*, pp. 155–97.

Wilson's summer estate – the chateau of Chenonceau, no less.[11] Given her Wagnerian tastes, he was almost certainly called upon to accompany Wagner excerpts for her high-society friends. This would not be the only time Debussy worked the upper-class Wagnerian social circuit. In 1893 he accompanied lectures about the *Ring* given by the writer Catulle Mendès to elite Opéra subscribers and complained that Mendès turned it into a cultish event that wrong-headedly suppressed Wagner the musician in favour of Wagner the poet.[12] Less than a year later Debussy was hired by Mme Philippe Escudier, the mother-in-law of his good friend Ernest Chausson, for a series of ten lecture-recitals on Wagner's art for her friends – a lucrative gig. 'It was beautiful', he noted ironically to Chausson, 'No one stirred, not even Mme Rouquairol, who for once didn't babble! As for me, I was worn out! And Wagner is decidedly a very tiring man.'[13]

High-society *wagnérisme* came to include visits to the Bayreuth Festival, where French attendees numbered well over a hundred every year in the 1890s. Lavignac recorded their names in *Le Voyage artistique à Bayreuth*,[14] as well as supplying concise guides to both the town and the operas. The right-wing and anti-Semitic lawyer Émile de Saint-Aubin immortalised this cultural practice by describing his own conversion experience in *Un pèlerinage à Bayreuth*, referring to the town with complete lack of irony as a 'musical Mecca, with its pious atmosphere, its ever-changing population of the curious and the devoted, its sellers of relics, its groups of pedestrians, its harmonious temple and ineffable mysteries that the god reveals'.[15] When the composer Saint-Saëns attended the festival as a journalist for its inaugural edition twelve years earlier, he reported back to his Parisian readers on the blinkers worn by many high-society French Wagner enthusiasts. One well-connected socialite asked Wagner himself to play a chord that she had discovered in the score of *Siegfried*, a harmony 'unprecedented and beyond words'. He replied that it was merely an E minor triad, and that she could play it just as well as he could. 'Oh Master, Master, that chord!' she insisted. After he indulged her, she fell back in her chair and 'unleashed a great cry'.[16] Surely less idolatrous, Debussy himself made the

---

[11] Lesure (Rolf), pp. 26–7. [12] Lesure (Rolf), pp. 108–9.
[13] Letter to Ernest Chausson, 5 February 1894, *Correspondance*, p. 192.
[14] Albert Lavignac, *Le Voyage artistique à Bayreuth* (Paris: Ch. Delagrave, 1897).
[15] Émile de Saint-Aubin, *Un pèlerinage à Bayreuth* (Paris: Albert Savine, 1892), p. 6.
[16] Camille Saint-Saëns, 'Wagner: *L'Anneau du Nibelung* et les représentations de Bayreuth, Août 1876', in Marie-Gabrielle Soret (ed.), *Camille Saint-Saëns: Écrits sur la musique et les musiciens, 1870–1921* (Paris: Vrin, 2012), p. 146.

trip to the festival in 1888 to hear *Die Meistersinger* and *Parsifal*, congratulating himself just a short time later that he had avoided the influence of the second work in *La Damoiselle élue*, recently composed.[17]

During his Paris sojourn for the *Tannhäuser* production in the early 1860s, Wagner had personally navigated several high-society social circles. From the beginning, his work garnered the sort of symbolic capital where the construct of progressive, modern, and challenging art was seen as homologous with the rarefied social milieu in which he travelled (though it is important to remember that not all social elites had a taste for the avant-garde or were dismissive of populist sloganeering). An early touchstone for the avant-garde was Charles Baudelaire's pamphlet *Richard Wagner et* Tannhäuser *à Paris* (1861), in which he argued for music's communicative power and capacity to trigger analogous ideas in different listeners through the operation of synaesthesia. Sounds suggest colours and scents; colours and scents suggest sounds. And together they suggest ideas, a theory of sensory overlap encapsulated in Baudelaire's famous sonnet *Correspondances*: 'Comme de long échos qui de loin se confondent ... Les parfums, les couleurs et les sons se répondent' (Like resonant echoes that blend together from a distance ... Perfumes, colours, and sounds to each other respond). Loosely derived from the concept of *Gesamtkunstwerk* and Wagner's theoretical writings, Baudelaire's *Correspondances* had enormous impact on the subsequent generation of French writers for magnifying the musicality of language, enhancing the role of suggestion within the literary experience and, on a more abstract level, exploring the primordial unity of the world through chains of symbols.

The high-water mark of this strain of Wagnerian influence on French literary modernity occurred in the 1880s well after Baudelaire's death. In Joris-Karl Huysmans's well-known novel *À rebours* (1884), the protagonist Des Esseintes is an isolated aesthete who, translating Baudelairean *correspondances* and *Gesamtkunstwerk* into a luxurious domestic sphere, rides above the bourgeois fray by creating elaborate and expensive synaesthesic experiences in his own house.[18] Here, decadent hermeticism frames artistic experimentation, an essentially Modernist orientation that took hold with several younger writers and for which Wagner's works served as a trigger, if not always a model.

A loosening of French press laws in the early 1880s fostered avant-garde culture for the few by encouraging the establishment of a great many

---

[17] Lesure (Rolf), pp. 75–6.
[18] See Andrès Villar, 'The *Gesamtkunsthaus*: Music in *À rebours*', *Image [&] Narrative* no. 16 (2006), www.imageandnarrative.be/inarchive/house_text_museum/villar.htm.

specialised low-circulation journals, the so-called *petites revues*. One of the beneficiaries was the writer and erstwhile music student Édouard Dujardin, who co-founded the *Revue wagnérienne* in 1885, when he was just a year older than Debussy, and for which he served as editor. In this he was assisted by the Polish expatriate Téodor de Wyzewa, who, as a reader of German, served as its most important informant about Wagnerian theory. In addition to its documentary purpose of recording international news relating to Wagner performances, the *Revue wagnérienne* published a wide range of material: academic studies of Wagner as a cultural phenomenon (Wyzewa's 'Notes sur la peinture wagnérienne et le salon de 1886' and 'La Religion de Richard Wagner et la religion de Léon Tolstoy'; Emile Hennequin's 'L'Esthétique de Wagner et la doctrine spencérienne'); analyses of individual works (Pierre Bonnier, 'Documents de critique expérimentale: Le motif-organe des *Maîtres Chanteurs*'); experimental translations of Wagner libretti; pieces of creative writing inspired by Wagner (Dujardin's 'Amfortas, paraphrase moderne' and Huysmann's 'L'Ouverture de Tannhäuser'); and even reproductions of lithographs (Fantin-Latour, *L'Évocation d'Erda* and Odilon Redon, *Brünnhilde*).[19] Although much of this is of great interest, in accounts of French Modernism the main claim to fame of the *Revue wagnérienne* has centred on Stéphane Mallarmé's contribution of a poem 'Hommage à Wagner', one of seventeen sonnets to pay homage to the composer on its pages, and an extended prose poem/essay entitled 'Richard Wagner, Rêverie d'un poète français', where, as much as Mallarmé was attracted to Wagner's art, the composer appears to function merely as a stepping stone to Mallarmé's own Symbolist literary ideals. Debussy's setting of Mallarmé's poem *Apparition* in 1884, one year before the founding of the *Revue wagnérienne*, was a remarkably avant-garde choice. Three years later the composer offered his friend Paul Dukas a copy of the poet's *L'Après-midi d'un faune* as a gift.[20]

Musical Influence

The hothouse of the *Revue wagnérienne* fostered the germination of French Symbolism by offering a hospitable environment for the cultivation of literary difficulty, multivalence, suggestion, and musicality. But many were

---

[19] Kelly Maynard, 'Strange Bedfellows at the *Revue Wagnérienne*: Wagnerism at the Fin de Siècle', *French Historical Studies* 38 (2015), pp. 633–59.
[20] Lesure (Rolf), p. 73.

unimpressed by the abstruseness of the publication, seeing its contents as more affected and pretentious than insightful. Lamoureux publicly criticised it in 1886 and Saint-Saëns repeatedly lambasted both the lack of musical knowledge of Symbolist Wagnerians and the incomprehensibility of their texts. Yet admiration for Wagner's work among practising musicians remained strong – and this even within the context of a new awareness of a distinctly national musical destiny represented by the founding in 1871 of an influential concert organisation meant to promote new French music called the Société nationale.[21] Although he himself had been represented on the pages of the *Revue wagnérienne*, the painter Henri Fantin-Latour produced an icon of a less literary French Wagnerism in *Autour du piano*, exhibited at the 1885 salon. Informally called 'Les Wagnéristes', the large oil features various critics, patrons, and composers with Wagnerian connections, including Judge Lascoux, gathered around the composer Emmanuel Chabrier seated at a piano. A score placed on the instrument is the luminescent centrepiece of the painting, suggesting a concentration on the art of music itself instead of on broad-ranging aesthetics. That certainly would have been the preference of the composer Vincent d'Indy, who stands to the right in Fantin-Latour's painting. Although he was not insensitive to modern artistic trends, d'Indy's Wagnerism was one that sought to come to terms with Wagner's music in syntactical terms and to historicise it. His account of European music history privileged Gregorian chant and Palestrina, downgraded most of the Baroque, celebrated the Viennese classics including Gluck and Beethoven, and praised both César Franck and Wagner as culminating figures whose legacy offered limitless potential for development. Although d'Indy's immoveable Wagnerism was cutting-edge in the last decade of the nineteenth century, so fast did the barometer of modernity change that it was judged irredeemably conservative in the (post-*Pelléas*) decade before the First World War, even as the right-wing, anti-Semitic Catholic agenda that drove d'Indy's celebration of pre-Baroque music continued to resonate in many quarters.

D'Indy praised Wagner's extension of chromatic harmony and his organic conception of music theatre, from leitmotif to *Gesamtkunstwerk*, and in this he was joined by many other French composers in the years 1880 to 1914. The story of Wagnerian opera in France is one where composers such as d'Indy himself (*Fervaal*, *L'Étranger*), Ernest Chausson (*Le Roi Arthus*) and Albéric Magnard (*Guercœur*, *Bérénice*) adapted the continuous

---

[21] Michael Strasser, 'The Société Nationale and Its Adversaries: The Musical Politics of *L'Invasion germanique* in the 1870s', *19th-Century Music* 24 (2001), pp. 225–51.

textures, prominent orchestra, flexible phrase structures, and recurring musical material to their own individual styles and perceptions of a French sound. Others, such as Saint-Saëns (*Henry VIII*, *Ascanio*) and Jules Massenet (*Esclarmonde*, *Werther*), imagined the French sound as a conflation of more traditional set-piece strategies with Wagnerian principles and explored historical drama as well as adaptations of literary masterpieces. The composer Alfred Bruneau (*Le Rêve*, *L'Attaque du moulin*, *Messidor*) and his sometime librettist Émile Zola embraced Wagnerian musical innovation, but also reconciled it to an aesthetic of realism that was antithetical to what Wagner would have endorsed. Gustave Charpentier's *Louise*, set in working-class Paris, is also in this lineage.

For Debussy, *Louise* was all too trite and only superficially Wagnerian. He characterised the overall tone of it as 'the sentimentality of a Monsieur who returning home at four in the morning develops a soft spot for street sweepers and rag pickers'.[22] The range of aesthetic trends among French musicians who absorbed Wagner's influence, therefore, was wide indeed. And it included *Pelléas et Mélisande*, a Symbolist drama, although Debussy was loath to admit this debt publicly, preferring instead to make the claim that the opera was not written 'in imitation of' ('*d'après*') Wagner, but rather with a view to opening up new terrain 'after' ('*après*') Wagner, a space both more French and filled with more humanity than the mere epigones of the *maître de Bayreuth*.[23]

Author's Recommendation
Cinq poèmes de Charles Baudelaire (1890).

Having recently returned home to Paris in 1887 after his Prix de Rome sojourn, Debussy lost little time in pushing the envelope of current musical syntax for his expressive purposes. He turned to Charles Baudelaire, a challenging poet, rarely set by musicians before that time. It is often said that the *Cinq poèmes de Charles Baudelaire* (1890) – difficult music for both listeners and performers – marked the high water of Wagnerian influence on Debussy's style, but it is more compelling to speak of creative manipulation than of imitation. In the final poem of the cycle, 'La Mort des amants' (The Death of the Lovers), the *Tristan*-like couple synaesthesically extinguishes itself in a single flash of light like a sob ('Nous échangerons un éclair unique,/Comme un long sanglot, tout chargé

---

[22] Letter to Pierre Louÿs, 6 February 1900, *Correspondance*, p. 539.
[23] Debussy, 'Pourquoi j'ai écrit *Pelléas*', in *Monsieur Croche*, pp. 62–4.

9 Wagnérisme

d'adieu'). An angel then reanimates their mirrored souls. Debussy writes syncopated, rising chromatic lines in the *Tristan* manner and sets these off with calm music redolent of the Good Friday episode in *Parsifal*. Yet un-Wagnerian perfect cadences periodically appear, while parallel seventh chords, whole-tone tinges, and sudden changes of harmonic colour also give the piece a more modern sound.

CHAPTER 10

Japonisme, *Collecting*, and the Expositions *Universelles*

Matthew Brown

There can be little doubt that Debussy was swept along by the waves of *japonisme* that washed across France during the late nineteenth and early twentieth centuries. Jacques Durand remembers visiting him in 1904 or early 1905:

> [Debussy's] study was on the ground floor, with spacious bay windows which flooded it with light, and it opened out on to the garden which surrounded the house. The wide table on which he used to work was cluttered with high-class Japanese objects. His favourite was a porcelain toad which he called his fetish and which he took with him when he moved, claiming he could not work unless it was in sight. Many was the time he lamented to me the difficulty of taking his work-table with him on holiday.

Durand added: 'I also remember, in this study, a certain coloured engraving by Hokusai, representing the curl of a giant wave. Debussy was particularly enamoured of this wave. It inspired him while he was composing *La mer*, and he asked us to reproduce it on the cover of the printed score.'[1] As it happened, Debussy's personal collection of Japanese artefacts also included a *koto* and a lacquer panel featuring two 'poissons d'or' that apparently inspired the last of his *Images*, series 2, for piano (1907).[2]

When considering the impact of *japonisme* on Debussy, it is important to remember that the movement began in the 1850s, well before he was born. France had sought diplomatic and trade agreements with Japan as far back as the 1660s, but was thwarted for nearly two hundred years because of the Japanese policy of Sakoku, or self-isolation. Two developments brought matters to a head: Commodore Perry's visits to Japan in 1853 and 1854, and the Crimean War (1854–6), which pitted France and Great

---

[1] Roger Nichols (ed.), *Debussy Remembered* (London: Faber and Faber, 1992), pp. 194–5.
[2] See Roy Howat, 'Debussy and the Orient', in Andrew Gerstle and Anthony Milner (eds.), *Recovering the Orient: Artists, Scholars, Appropriations* (Reading: Harwood, 1994), p. 70.

Britain against Russia.[3] On behalf of France, Baron Gros went to Japan to sign a Treaty of Amity and Commerce between the two countries in 1858. Over the next few decades, Japan rapidly transformed from an agrarian economy into a major industrial power that exported and imported goods to and from the entire globe. It formed political and financial alliances with France, following the latter's defeat in the Franco-Prussian War (1870–1), as well as with Britain and the United States. Those alliances continued until World War I.[4] Japan also had colonial ambitions, and that created tensions with Russia. Japan's victory in the Russo-Japanese War of 1904–5 gave it control of Korea and forced Russia to evacuate southern Manchuria.

A century after being captivated by *chinoiserie*, France succumbed to *japonisme*. The craze began in the 1850s when Marie Bracquemond and Monet first discovered Japanese prints (*estampes*). But the movement blossomed in the 1860s when Louise DeSoye opened La Porte chinoise in Paris in 1862.[5] DeSoye's boutique became a magnet for artists and aesthetes, such as Baudelaire, Edmond and Jules Goncourt, Manet, Fantin-Latour, Degas, Whistler, and Zola. Philippe Burty, another regular at La Porte chinoise, not only popularised the term *japonisme*, but he also founded the Société japonaise du Jinglar de Sèvres in 1867, the same year Japanese *objets d'art* were exhibited at the Exposition Universelle. To satisfy the demand for everything Japanese, Enrico Cernuschi, Théodore Duret, Émile Étienne Guimet, Siegfried Bing, and others toured Japan to acquire materials to sell in Paris. For his part, Bing also published *Le Japon artistique* (1888–91), curated exhibitions of Japanese art (1893), and opened the Maison de l'Art Nouveau (1895). In the meantime, Japanese *objets d'art* featured prominently at the Expositions Universelles of 1878 and 1889. By 1889, however, *japonisme* had entered a third phase: what had started as an elitist conceit in the 1850s and 1860s became a bourgeois fad in the 1870s and 1880s, and a staple of popular culture in the 1890s and 1900s.[6] French aesthetes complained that the tendency for Japan to export items deliberately designed for Westerners vulgarised Japanese art. Japanese officials concurred and decided to display traditional art, often borrowed from ancient temples and shrines, at the Exposition Universelle of 1900.[7]

---

[3] See Meron Medzini, *French Policy in Japan during the Closing Years of the Tokugawa Regime* (Cambridge, MA: Harvard University Press, 1971), p. 9.
[4] See John Albert White, *Transition to Global Rivalry: Alliance Diplomacy and the Quadruple Entente, 1895–1907* (Cambridge: Cambridge University Press, 1995).
[5] For a general overview, see Michael Sullivan, *The Meeting of Eastern and Western Art* (Berkeley: University of California Press, 1989); Elwood Hartman, '*Japonisme* and Nineteenth-Century French Literature', *Comparative Literature Studies* 18 (1981) (East-West Issue), pp. 141–66.
[6] Hartman, '*Japonisme*', p. 146.
[7] See www.tobunken.go.jp/joho/japanese/collection/paris/paris-e.html.

As *japonisme* flourished in Paris, so it inspired every important French painter of the age: first generation Impressionists such as Manet, Degas, Whistler, and Fantin-Latour; *plein air* Impressionists such as Monet and Pissarro; Symbolists such as Redon and Moreau; Post-Impressionists such as Gauguin, Van Gogh, and Toulouse-Lautrec; members of Les Nabis such as Bonnard, Vuillard, and Denis; and even Pointillists such as Seurat and Signac.[8] Although *japonisme* influence on nineteenth-century French authors was less overt, it can still be felt in the writings of Gautier, Baudelaire, the Goncourts, Verlaine, Mallarmé, Huysmans, Loti, Proust, and others.[9] *Japonisme* even cast its shadow over the Parisian stage in works such as d'Hervilly's 'comédie japonaise' *La Belle Saïnara* (1876) and Métra's ballet *Yedda* (1879). And, long before *Madame Butterfly* was performed in French at the Opéra-Comique in 1906, Parisian audiences enjoyed 'Japanese' operas, such as Saint-Saëns's *La Princesse jaune* (1872), Lecocq's *Kosiki* (1876), and Messager's *Madame Chrysanthème* (1893).

What impact did *japonisme* actually have on the work of nineteenth-century French artists? There are several answers to this question. Some responded by including stereotypical Japanese tropes in their own works. Whistler's oil painting *Rose and Silver: The Princess from the Land of Porcelain* (1863–5), for example, shows a European woman wearing a kimono in a Western manner while holding a fan and standing on an oriental rug in front of a Japanese screen beside a large porcelain vase. And, based on the real-life exploits of Count Montesquiou-Fezensac (alias Des Esseintes), Husymans's novel *À rebours* (1884) is equally heavy-handed: allusions to *japonisme* surface

> as architecture – the dining room is like Japanese boxes, a room contained by a room; as *divertissement* – the jewelled tortoise had a Japanese design inlaid on its back, Des Esseintes played perfume compositions from an organ console, an idea coming from Japanese perfume-sniffing parties . . . ; and as criticism – he praised Verlaine for his topsy-turvy sonnets which are turned upside down, like those Japanese fish in coloured earthenware that are stood gills down on their pedestals.[10]

---

[8] See Gerald Needham, 'Japanese Influence on French Painting, 1854–1910', in Gabriel P. Weisberg (ed.), *Japonisme: Japanese Influence on French Art, 1854–1910* (Kent, OH: Kent State University Press, 1975), pp. 115–39; Frank Whitford, *Japanese Prints and Western Painters* (New York: Macmillan, 1977), pp. 96–233.
[9] Hartman, '*Japonisme*', p. 146.
[10] Hartman, '*Japonisme*', p. 159; Joris-Karl Huysmans, *À rebours* (Paris: Bibliothèque Charpentier, 1884), p. 211 / *Against Nature*, trans. Robert Baldick (Harmondsworth: Penguin, 1959), p. 186.

Other artists responded more abstractly by replacing Western techniques, modes of composition, and motifs with those derived from Japan, especially from *estampes*. For example, instead of using Western concepts of perspective, symmetry, and chiaroscuro, they flattened their images and emphasised strong lines, bright colours, and empty spaces; they replaced horizontal forms with vertical images (e.g. scrolls) and polytychs (e.g. screens and fans); and they focused on commonplace subjects, the ephemeral, and the transcendental.[11] These trends are immediately apparent in the prints of Toulouse-Lautrec and Bonnard. But they also shaped the 'vocabulary, similes, syntactical constructions, [and] themes' employed by writers of the period, as well as a penchant for 'short sentences, broken structure, verbless phrases, and colourful nouns'.[12] Some have even linked the development of the short story to the concision of *estampes*, and the principles of variation found in the poems of Maeterlinck to Hokusai's *Thirty-Six Views of Mount Fuji* and Monet's series paintings of Rouen Cathedral.[13]

Ultimately, however, many Western artists appropriated Japanese elements for narcissistic and opportunistic reasons. Few, if any, had any direct knowledge of Japan, few understood the Japanese language, and few translations of Japanese stories were available.[14] Gerald Needham has even suggested that French artists exploited *japonisme*, not because Japanese elements were especially novel but rather because those elements 'corresponded with the effects they had [already] noticed and admired in their own environment'.[15] According to him, 'cut-off compositions and silhouetting occurred in photography; the black outlines adopted by the Pont-Aven artists appeared in the medieval art they admired in the churches in Brittany; and certain daring compositions had been created by French caricaturists of the mid-century'. And, like other forms of exoticism, *japonisme* allowed Western artists to explore topics often regarded as taboo in polite circles: it was more acceptable to paint a Japanese *geisha* than a Parisian prostitute. Furthermore, the vogue for *japonisme* resonated with Baudelaire's image of Modernism and his belief that 'le beau est toujours bizarre'. Baudelaire equated Modernism with city life, the ephemeral, and the seediness of human culture. For him, collecting

---

[11] See Needham, 'Japanese Influence', pp. 116ff.; Hartman, '*Japonisme*', p. 147.
[12] Hartman, '*Japonisme*', p. 150.
[13] Sadakichi Hartmann, *Japanese Art* (Boston, MA: L. C. Page, 1904), pp. 160–3.
[14] See Earl Miner, *The Japanese Tradition in British and American Literature* (Princeton, NJ: Princeton University Press, 1958), p. 45; Hartman, '*Japonisme*', p. 149.
[15] Needham, 'Japanese Influence', p. 116.

japoneries resonated with the *flâneur*'s desire for 'a divertissement': it represented 'the fleeting moment in the eternal continuum, a brief release from a dull and tedious existence'.[16] It even recalled 'the Buddhist concepts that nothing is permanent, and that truth must be grasped in its flight, ideas which appealed to Parnassians, Realists, and Naturalists alike'.[17]

The same concepts appealed to Debussy as well. Growing up in the capital of a major colonial power and a centre for international trade, he was constantly exposed to exotica.[18] His interest in such matters apparently began during his student years. For one thing, he composed a short song 'Rondel chinois' in 1882. For another, he cultivated his interest in Symbolism both by reading a wide range of authors, including Huysmans, and by setting five poems by Verlaine between 1882 and 1883, one by Mallarmé in 1884, and five more by Baudelaire, starting in 1887. In the late 1880s and early 1890s, Debussy even met leading Symbolists at Edmond Bailly's Librairie de l'Art indépendant, Mallarmé's famous *mardis*, and various other venues. He is known, for example, to have discussed Japanese prints with the sculptor Camille Claudel, having met her brother Paul in 1890 through Bailly or Mallarmé. Also notable were Debussy's visits to the Exposition Universelle of 1889, which featured a Javanese gamelan and an Annamite theatre from Vietnam.[19] Over the next decades, he continued to purchase objects for his collection, often spending housekeeping money, much to the chagrin of his partners. Debussy was surely aware that the Exposition Universelle of 1900 featured a concert of Japanese dance music and a Kabuki play entitled *The Geisha and the Samurai*.[20] The former consisted of three dances – *The Lion of Itigo*, *Dance of the Butterfly*, and *Dance of the Parasol* – that were accompanied by three *shamisen* and a *koto*; and the latter featured the celebrated actress, dancer, and musician Sada Yakko.[21] Yakko apparently marketed her own line of kimonos for Western consumers.

Although there is little doubt about Debussy's love of *japoneries* and the work of French artists inspired by *japonisme*, there is no evidence to suggest

---

[16] Hartman, '*Japonisme*', p. 153.
[17] Chaote Lin, 'Chinoiserie and Japonisme in French Literature', PhD thesis, University of Michigan (1966), p. 243.
[18] See Jann Pasler, 'Revisiting Debussy's Relationships with Otherness: Difference, Vibrations, and the Occult', *Music and Letters* 101 (2020), pp. 321–2, 327–30.
[19] See Anik Devriès, 'Les Musiques d'Extrême Orient à l'Exposition Universelle de 1889', *Cahiers Debussy* 1 (1977), pp. 24–37; Annegret Fauser, *Musical Encounters at the 1889 Paris World's Fair* (Rochester, NY: University of Rochester Press, 2005), p. 165; Lesure (Rolf), pp. 82–3.
[20] Edmond Bailly, *Le Pittoresque musical à l'exposition* (Paris: Éditions de l'Humanité nouvelle, 1900), p. 30.
[21] See Julien Tiersot, *Notes d'ethnographie musicale*, 1st ser. (Paris: Fischbacher, 1905), pp. 7–38.

that he had a profound understanding of Japanese music or culture.[22] None of his pieces sounds authentically Japanese, and there are no signs that he intended them to do so. The same can often be said of Debussy's other attempts at exoticism. For example, his song 'Rondel chinois' sounds less like Chinese music and more like 'The Great Gig in the Sky'. And when Debussy's music does sound exotic, it often does so in generic ways. Take, for example, the case of *La Mer*. As mentioned above, the score was apparently inspired by Hokusai's print *Kanagawa oki nami ura* and includes a copy of the print on the front cover of the first edition. The introduction to the first movement does indeed sound exotic, but it seems to recall the opening of 'Pagodes' (*Estampes*, 1903), a work that is widely believed to have been inspired by Javanese gamelan music.[23] As it happens, the Paris Conservatoire's own gamelan had two low gongs tuned to B and F♯, and some types of *gambang* tuned to the notes of the pentatonic or slendro scale (C♯-D♯-E♯-G♯-A♯).[24] The same notes appear at the start of *La Mer*.

This is not to say, however, that Debussy's music never includes Japanese idioms. Robert Waters has suggested that the opening chords of Debussy's piano piece 'Et la lune descend sur le temple qui fut' (*Images*, series 2) resemble those produced on the *shō*, a mouth organ often used in *gagaku*, a traditional form of Japanese music.[25] Although information about Japanese music was available in the West through books and anthologies – for example, F. T. Piggott's *The Music and Musical Instruments of Japan* (London: Batsford, 1893) and Y. Nagai and K. Kobataki's *Japanese Popular Music Series* (Osaka: Miki, 1893) – there is no evidence that Debussy knew either of these sources.[26] However, Debussy may have had the *koto* in mind when composing bars 441–50 of *Jeux* (1912–13): not only does the harp part recreate the *koto*'s distinctive twang, but the piece was written about the same time as Stravinsky's *Three Japanese Lyrics*.[27]

---

[22] Michel Duchesneau, 'Debussy and Japanese Prints', in François de Médicis and Steven Huebner (eds.), *Debussy's Resonance* (Rochester, NY: University of Rochester Press, 2018), pp. 301–25.
[23] See Matthew Brown, *Debussy Redux: The Impact of His Music on Popular Culture* (Bloomington: Indiana University Press, 2012), pp. 140–7.
[24] For details, see Julien Tiersot, *Musiques pittoresques: Promenades musicales à l'Exposition de 1889* (Paris: Fischbacher, 1889), pp. 31–47; Léon Pillaut, 'Le Gamelan javanais', *Le Ménestrel* (3 July 1887), pp. 244–5; Richard Mueller, 'Javanese Influence on Debussy's "Fantaisie" and Beyond', *19th-Century Music* 10 (1986), pp. 157–86.
[25] Robert F. Waters, 'Emulation and Influence: *Japonisme* and Western Music in *fin de siècle* Paris', *Music Review* 55 (1994), p. 224.
[26] Ironically, Heinrich Schenker owned a copy of the latter; see, *Katalog XII, Musik und Theater enthaltend die Bibliothek des Herrn Dr. Heinrich Schenker, Wien* (Vienna: Antiquariat Hinterberger, 1935), p. 14.
[27] See Brown, *Debussy Redux*, pp. 140–3.

While Debussy did not deliberately quote any Japanese music, he certainly captured the spirit of *japonisme* by employing its techniques, modes of composition, and characteristic motifs. In 'Et la lune descend' and 'Poissons d'or' (*Images*, series 2), for example, Debussy avoided traditional functional tonal progressions, symmetrical phrase groups, and clear formal boundaries, and favoured pentatonic and whole-tone patterns, ostinati, pedal tones, and exotic chromatic colorations. In the case of 'Et la lune descend', Pierre Boulez has suggested that Debussy specifically emulated '[Asian] concepts of time and sonority'.[28] On a larger level, Debussy recalled Japanese models in the layout of his scores, both by casting his *Estampes*, *Images*, series 1 (1905), *Images*, series 2, and several sets of songs as triptychs, and by notating the score of his *Images*, series 2, on three rather than two staves, thereby highlighting the linear aspects of the compositions.[29] And he may have been thinking of Japanese prints when he asked Durand to change colours on the title page of his *Estampes* and when he designed his personal monograph.[30]

And yet Carl Dahlhaus has noted that similar devices can be found in every exotic piece written during the nineteenth century.[31] Indeed, just like the Symbolist artists he so admired, Debussy created the aura of *japonisme* by using techniques, modes of composition, and motifs that were already an essential part of his compositional idiom. Though his motivations for doing so may have been based on a genuine love of Japanese *objets d'art*, they were often narcissistic and opportunistic as well. Debussy clearly wanted recognition in artistic circles as an heir to Baudelaire and an advocate of Symbolist aesthetics. *Japonisme* clearly played an integral part of that artistic platform. Moreover, he needed to support his family and was perfectly aware that *japoneries* sold well, especially in the period 1889–1914. Born into poverty, Debussy spent his life trying to enter the bourgeoisie and become part of the musical establishment. His interest in *japonisme* may ultimately reveal more about his inner psyche and social aspirations than about the nature of his music or his understanding of Japanese art.

---

[28] Pierre Boulez, *Orientations*, ed. Jean-Jacques Nattiez, trans. Martin Cooper (London: Faber and Faber, 1986), p. 422.
[29] David J. Code, 'The "Song Triptych": Reflections on a Debussyan Genre', *Scottish Music Review* 3 (2013), pp. 1–40.
[30] *Correspondance*, pp. 769–70; *Debussy Letters*, p. 138.
[31] Carl Dahlhaus, *Nineteenth-Century Music*, trans. J. Bradford Robinson (Berkeley: University of California Press, 1989), p. 306.

Author's Recommendation

'Poissons d'or', *Images*, series 2, for piano (1907).

'Poissons d'or' is one of a string of outstanding piano works that Debussy composed in the opening decade of the twentieth century. The work was first mentioned in July 1903 in a contract he signed with Durand for two sets of six *Images* for piano two hands and piano four hands. After completing the first set of three *Images* for solo piano in 1905, Debussy finished the second set in 1907, concluding it with 'Poissons d'or'. Brilliant and whimsical, the piece is thought to have been inspired by a Japanese lacquered panel owned by Debussy and currently on display at the Musée Debussy in Saint-Germain-en-Laye; this panel features two goldfish swimming in water under a tree. The opening material in F♯ major includes delicate arpeggios intended to represent the shimmering surface of the water and a more angular theme that conveys the darting motion of the two fish. Remarkably, the harmonic orientation of this music recalls 'Le Matelot qui tombe à l'eau' (1882), an early song by Debussy based on a poem by Maurice Bouchor. As it happened, the opening material of 'Poissons d'or' and its progeny return three times later in the piece. It is also interesting to note that Debussy dedicated 'Poissons d'or' to his friend the Spanish pianist Ricardo Viñes. The piece was subsequently recorded by him.

CHAPTER 11

Cross-Currents in Debussy's Creative World
Annegret Fauser

The expansion – both materially and ideologically – of Western traditions constitutes one of the hallmarks of music in *fin de siècle* Paris. Whether by way of the absorption of so-called exotic music that composers encountered at the 1889 and 1900 Paris World's Fairs, or through new developments in the visual arts such as Impressionism and Symbolism, Debussy's creative world was deeply enmeshed in the cultural field of the French capital. Steeped in a post-Enlightenment worldview centred on exploration, accumulation of knowledge, and scientific discovery, no aspect of human experience and its habitats was deemed out of bounds in this path to creative accretion. Like many of his contemporaries, Debussy became fascinated by a wealth of new ideas about the world and the human condition that exploded onto the scene during his lifetime. Mysticism and occultism expanded the horizon within which to understand the mind and its creative potential; archaeological discoveries from Greece and Rome brought alive a past that belied the bland classicism so revered only decades earlier; and a rich smorgasbord of historical research – one that encompassed music and its practice – provided new materials from the foreign worlds of medieval, if not mythical, pasts.

Over the course of Debussy's life, these currents were woven together into the conceptual matrix that sustained his creative world: one that he claimed continually to renew rather than reproduce, yet one that relied on this perspective's cumulative and sustained presence through the years. He wrote in 1910 that moving away from the subjects and approaches of previously successful creations 'is the duty of each artist'.[1] Yet this act of distancing did not mean an abandonment of earlier ideas but, rather, their reconfiguration within new parameters. If Debussy was riveted by Gregorian chant and Palestrinian counterpoint as a young man in the late 1880s, for example, he continued to be enchanted by music from the

---
[1] *Monsieur Croche*, p. 310. All translations in this essay are my own, save where noted.

past throughout the rest of his life. What changed was how these and other interests intersected with his developing compositional preoccupations. In what follows, I focus on three of these currents: Debussy's brief flirtation with occultism and its transformation into a more enduring interest in mysticism, on the one hand, and numerology, on the other; the composer's attraction to antiquity both Roman and Greek, often mediated through decadent poetry by the likes of Stéphane Mallarmé or Pierre Louÿs; and his sustained commitment to a past that could serve as a source not only of inspiration but also of sonic expansion.

Rationalising the Occult

As an ardent patron of the Chat Noir, an artistic cabaret specialising in mystic shadow plays, and of the fashionable bookstore Librairie de l'Art indépendant, well known for its selection of publications on what was then known as the 'occult sciences', Debussy associated closely with a group of Parisians who were in the throes of a quest to expand human consciousness and experience. Already while he was at the Villa Medici in Rome, Debussy had devoured books ordered from Paris that engaged with occult topics, including those of esoteric writers Alber Jhouney and Jules Bois.[2] After his return from Rome in 1887, Bois soon counted among the composer's Montmartre friends. The 'occult sciences' were flourishing in Paris, and Debussy and his circle were fast caught up in their allure.

In 1892, the Symbolist review *Le Saint-Graal* published an announcement stating that at the end of March the experimental theatre Le Théâtre de l'art would present Bois's new 'esoteric drama' *Les Noces de Sathan* (The Wedding of Satan), with music by Debussy. When it was performed, however, the play's incidental music had been composed instead by Henri Quittard.[3] It is unclear why Debussy stepped back from composing the score, even though a letter to the poet cites practical reasons, mainly the haphazard way in which the performing ensemble was going to be put together.[4] Scholars have been quick to assume that Debussy seized on this practical excuse because of the drama's seemingly lurid character.[5] However, nothing he said in the early 1890s supports this interpretation. Rather, this was the time when he was participating actively in esoteric circles, including repeated visits in 1892 to the first salon of the kabbalist

---

[2] Léon Guichard, 'Debussy et les occultistes', *Cahiers Debussy* 7 (1974), p. 11.
[3] Robert Orledge, *Debussy and the Theatre* (Cambridge: Cambridge University Press, 1982), pp. 46–7.
[4] *Correspondance*, p. 105. [5] Lesure (Rolf), pp. 100–1; Orledge, *Debussy and the Theatre*, p. 47.

society Rose+Croix – founded by ardent mystic Joséphin (also known as Sâr) Péladan – that attracted the composer just as it did numerous other Parisians, from the poet Paul Verlaine to his new friend, the composer Erik Satie. An ardent Rosicrucian, Satie wrote three preludes for a performance, on 19 March 1892, of Péladan's *Le Fils des étoiles* that Debussy attended. Indeed, when others might have chafed at Satie's mystic music – as was the case at the first performance of his 'Christian ballet' *Uspud* that same year – Debussy stood up for him.[6] As they exchanged scores, their dedications reveal their shared interest in the mystic and occult. Satie, for instance, wrote in October 1892 on his *Sonneries de la Rose+Croix* (Soundings of the Rose+Cross): 'To the good old chap, Cl.-A. Debussy ... his brother in Christ, Erik Satie'.[7]

Yet while Debussy was often quite outspoken about his other cultural interests, he proved reticent – as Jann Pasler has shown – to comment on his sustained interest in the occult, even though he remained engaged with the changing currents that emerged in this context. These currents included recent esoteric theories about vibrations – in 1893, Debussy actually proposed to Ernest Chausson the founding of a 'Society of Musical Esotericism' – or ideas about sonority channelled through the conversations with, and literature published by, Edmond Bailly, the founder of L'Art indépendant.[8]

This French approach to the esoteric was, however, one cast explicitly as an *ésotérisme occidental* (Occidental esotericism), distancing itself almost polemically from any Eastern mysticism.[9] Part of this strategy of rationalisation was the invocation of numerology as the mathematical expression of natural proportions, the presence of which in art was to ground music, painting, or architecture within the 'universal' laws of the cosmos. Debussy had encountered these ideas through not only his reading but also his acquaintance with the mathematician Charles Henry, who was a regular visitor to the Chat Noir and a prominent numerologist.[10] Whether the Fibonacci series or the golden section, the logic inherent in these proportions could easily be translated into compositional practice, and Debussy was but one of many musicians – including Lili Boulanger, Ricardo Viñes, and

---

[6] Lesure (Rolf), p. 101. [7] Guichard, 'Debussy et les occultistes', p. 11.
[8] Jann Pasler, 'Revisiting Debussy's Relationship with Otherness: Difference, Vibrations, and the Occult', *Music & Letters* 101 (2020), pp. 330–8.
[9] Julian Strube, 'Occultist Identity Formations between Theosophy and Socialism in *fin-de-siècle* France', *Numen* 64 (2017), pp. 589–90.
[10] Roy Howat, *The Art of French Piano Music: Debussy, Ravel, Fauré, Chabrier* (New Haven, CT: Yale University Press, 2009), p. 59.

Eugène Ysaÿe – who turned to them to structure their works.[11] Not only such piano works as *Images* but also songs and symphonic compositions – not least *La Mer* – were organised along principles that Debussy may well have derived from mathematical formulae.[12] Yet, as with his broader interests in occultism, Debussy remained silent on his compositional engagement with numerological principles, a reticence which may well have been a lesson he had learned from what he considered Jean-Philippe Rameau's mistake: to have written down his 'theories before composing his operas ... gave his contemporaries the chance to conclude that there was a complete absence of anything emotional in the music'.[13]

Poetic Antiquities

If Debussy was reluctant publicly to voice his attraction to the 'occult sciences', his compositional engagement with ancient Greece became prominently audible with, and after, the première, in December 1894, of *Prélude à l'après-midi d'un faune*, his musical evocation of Stéphane Mallarmé's famous poem in the form of an 'orchestral eclogue'.[14] Like that of many contemporaries, however, Debussy's musical Greece was an imaginary and eroticised past emerging from modern literature rather than the kind of archaeological reconstruction with which composers such as Maurice Emmanuel and Gabriel Fauré became involved, as when the latter composed the accompaniment to a newly discovered Delphic *Hymn to Apollo* in 1894.[15] Besides Mallarmé, the writer whose antiquity-inspired works most resonated with Debussy was Pierre Louÿs, a friend with whom he collaborated on a variety of projects. Like Debussy, Louÿs was a regular at the L'Art indépendant bookshop, with interests ranging from the occult to the decadent. Some of their joint projects were abandoned early on.[16] One was a ballet titled *Daphnis et Chloé* planned for the Théâtre d'Application in 1895–6. In his letters to the composer, Louÿs connected

---

[11] Bonnie Jo Dopp, 'Numerology and Cryptography in the Music of Lili Boulanger: The Hidden Program in *Clairières dans le ciel*', *The Musical Quarterly* 78 (1994), p. 558.
[12] Roy Howat, *Debussy in Proportion* (Cambridge: Cambridge University Press, 1983); Clive I. Critchett, 'Proportion and the Esoteric: Frederick Delius and His Music', PhD thesis, Royal Northern College of Music (2017), pp. 156–60.
[13] Claude Debussy, 'Jean-Philippe Rameau' (1912), cited in Howat, *Art of French Piano Music*, p. 59.
[14] Debussy's subtitle for *Prélude à l'après-midi d'un faune* was 'Églogue pour orchestre d'après Stéphane Mallarmé'.
[15] On the *Hymn to Apollo*, see Samuel N. Dorf, *Performing Antiquity: Ancient Greek Music and Dance from Paris to Delphi, 1890–1930* (New York: Oxford University Press, 2019), pp. 27–38.
[16] Lesure documents five abandoned Debussy-Louÿs projects: *Œdipe a Colone, Cendrelune, Daphnis et Chloë, Aphrodite*, and *La Saulaie*. Lesure (Rolf), pp. 135–9.

the proposed score with the music of *Prélude à l'après-midi d'un faune* when he suggested not only an 'ardent and naïve' flute solo for Daphnis but also to 'pinch some stuff' from the previous work.[17] Following on its heels, another ballet project centred on the scandalous novel *Aphrodite: Mœurs antiques*, which had taken Paris by storm when it was published in the spring of 1896. Because Debussy expressed interest in a musical adaptation of this 'prodigiously supple' work, Louÿs turned down other composers – a decision he would come to regret.[18]

In 1901, finally, one of their projects came to fruition with the incidental music for two flutes, two harps, and celesta that Debussy composed for a performance – a recitation with *tableaux vivants* – of twelve poems selected from *Les Chansons de Bilitis*, a book of erotically charged poems that Louÿs had cast as translations from ancient Greek.[19] Debussy had already set three of Louÿs's poems as a short song cycle in 1897–8: 'La Flûte de Pan', 'La Chevelure', and 'Le Tombeau des Naiades'. For the incidental music, he created instrumental interludes to avoid competition with the poetic recitations, sticking mainly to 'modal and whole-tone melodies with filigree accompaniment'.[20] Whether or not the audience at the single performance, on 7 February 1901, was 'transported to the great epochs of pure nudity', as an attending journalist claimed, the performance aimed to evoke a Greek past that was as exquisitely archaic as it was titillating.[21] Performed for the élite of Parisian literati, the combination of music, recitation, and *tableaux* created a static rendering of antiquity in which light touches of the exotic ('Les Courtisanes égyptiennes') courted a fantasy of a pastoral world simultaneously contemporary in its embodiment and distant in its imaginary.[22] In 1914, the composer would recycle some of this musical material in his *Six Épigraphes antiques* for piano duet.[23] Just as his orchestral eclogue referenced Mallarmé's poem twenty years earlier, the piano pieces now served as musical evocations of a doubly distant poetic antiquity. In the meantime, ancient Greece fleetingly sounded in the solo flute piece, 'La Flûte de Pan', written in November 1913 as incidental music for Gabriel Mourey's *Psyché* (usually known as *Syrinx*), and it was evoked in two of the composer's piano preludes: 'Danseuses de Delphes' and

---

[17] Letter from Pierre Louÿs to Debussy, c. 14 January 1895, *Correspondance*, p. 303.
[18] Orledge, *Debussy and the Theatre*, pp. 263–4.
[19] Letter to Pierre Louÿs, c. 19 January 1901, *Correspondance*, p. 582.
[20] Orledge, *Debussy and the Theatre*, p. 246.   [21] Lesure (Rolf), p. 170.
[22] Ed. L. [Edouard Lemoine] lists not only the performers and programme of the event but also a cross-section of the audience, 'Les Chansons de Bilitis au Journal', *Le Journal* (8 February 1901).
[23] Marianne Wheeldon, *Debussy's Late Style* (Bloomington: Indiana University Press, 2009), pp. 134–5.

'Canope'.[24] The *Six Épigraphes antiques*, however, formed the end point in Debussy's compositional engagement with ancient Greece.

Debussy's compositional Hellenism – one steeped in the poetics of an eroticised past and a musical idiom drawing on modal auras and the signature sound of the flute – was well in keeping with Parisian practice at the time, as, for example, in Camille Saint-Saëns's opera *Phryné* (1893) and orchestral song *Pallas-Athéné* (1894). And like many of his fellow intellectuals, Debussy routinely evoked Greek tragedy as a model for an uncorrupted artistic progress. As he wrote in 1903, 'Let us then rediscover Tragedy, expanding its primitive musical style with the infinite resources of the modern orchestra and a choir of innumerable voices!'[25] But also like many contemporary musicians and artists – and clearly influenced by the occultist ideas of the time – Debussy's poetic and sonic antiquities embraced more than a Western past. He posited that Javanese dance, for example, might offer as powerful a model as Greek tragedy for artistic renewal and – as he famously and provocatively wrote in 1913 – gamelan music employed a form of counterpoint that made Palestrina's seem like child's play.[26] Indeed, his compositions and abandoned projects evoked not only ancient Greece and Rome – in *Le Martyre de saint Sébastien*, for example (1911) – but also Egypt (*Khamma*, 1911–13) and India (the project for *Siddharta*, 1907–10), among others.

Sounds of Old

While ancient worlds around the globe could serve simultaneously as literary and sonic inspiration and as aesthetic models, Debussy's musical heritage in terms of the Western canon was far more circumscribed, if here, too, in keeping with French *fin-de-siècle* practice. Early music was no longer unfamiliar to the Parisian ears by his time: since the mid-nineteenth century, concerts of early music had sprung up in Paris, with an increasing focus on historical performance practice.[27] The Benedictine monks of Solesmes had brought plainchant into the sonic practice and imagination of French music since they started their performative and editorial revival projects that would culminate, from 1889 onwards, in the *Paléographie*

---

[24] Ibid., p. 134. [25] *Monsieur Croche*, p. 110. [26] *Monsieur Croche*, p. 229.
[27] Katharine Ellis, *Interpreting the Musical Past: Early Music in Nineteenth-Century France* (New York: Oxford University Press, 2005). On historical performance, see Annegret Fauser, *Musical Encounters at the 1889 Paris World's Fair* (Rochester, NY: University of Rochester Press, 2005), pp. 27–42; Jann Pasler, *Composing the Citizen: Music as Public Utility in Third-Republic France* (Berkeley: University of California Press, 2009), pp. 217–29.

musicale.[28] Some of Lully's operas were available in Théodore de Lajarte's series *Les Chefs-d'œuvres classiques de l'opéra français* (1878–83); successive volumes of Henry Expert's *Les Maîtres musiciens de la Renaissance française* started appearing in 1894; and Saint-Saëns and others began the complete edition of Rameau's works in 1895. Debussy was no stranger to editorial projects concerning early music, nor to performances of the repertory. That knowledge of the past was a quality the composer valued can be gleaned, not only from his writings with references to a panoply of musicians from Palestrina to Couperin but also in perhaps unexpected remarks, as when he recommended, in 1906, the Portuguese composer, Francisco de Lacerda, to Albert Carré by emphasising his 'predilection for, and deep knowledge of, the old masters which is rather rare in our time'.[29]

For Debussy, as for his fellow French composers from Vincent d'Indy to Saint-Saëns, the referential substrate of an early-music pantheon mattered in the nationalist reclaiming of a uniquely French tradition in the face of purportedly nefarious German and Italian musical influences. Debussy's attack on Gluck as an ill-famed precursor of Wagner is well known, but he also thoroughly disliked 'that puffed up Florentine' Jean-Baptiste Lully and his impact on French opera.[30] Instead, he found himself in the company of Parisian musicians from Wanda Landowska to Paul Dukas by referring to such emblems of French music as Couperin and Rameau as stand-ins for the routinely evoked qualities of 'a pure French tradition' in their 'clarity of expression' and tightly constructed form.[31] The vocal music of Claude Lejeune and Clément Janequin also received praise in Debussy's writings.[32] This Francophile pantheon rose to prominence in Debussy's music and aesthetics, especially after *Pelléas*, and French classicism would become a compositional touchstone for such later works as his piano *Études* (1915) and chamber sonatas, all of which were written during World War I.[33] This wartime spirit is evident when, in 1915, Debussy reflected on France's musical heritage, turning Rameau's death as the end of its 'pure tradition' and accusing 'a parasitical vegetation' of 'veiling and suffocating the fine branches of our art's genealogical tree'.[34]

It comes as no surprise, then, that Debussy's musical involvement with Rameau would be highly visible. Not only was he the official editor of volume 13 in the complete edition of Rameau's works (*Les Fêtes de Polymnie*, 1908), but he also composed an 'Hommage à Rameau' in his

[28] Katharine Ellis, *The Politics of Plainchant in fin-de-siècle France* (Farnham: Ashgate, 2013).
[29] *Correspondance*, p. 938.   [30] *Correspondance*, p. 1441.   [31] *Monsieur Croche*, p. 91.
[32] *Monsieur Croche*, p. 263.   [33] Wheeldon, *Debussy's Late Style*, pp. 66–70, 96.
[34] *Monsieur Croche*, p. 266.

first series of *Images* (1905), one of only two such works in Debussy's output (the other being the *Hommage à Haydn* of 1909). Other instrumental works such as *Pour le piano* (1901) draw on such eighteenth-century harpsichord movements and dance forms as sarabands and toccatas. Where references are even more pronounced are vocal compositions setting Renaissance poetry and evoking the idiom of French chansons of that period, including the *Trois chansons de Charles d'Orléans* (1898/1908) and the *Trois ballades de François Villon* (1910). In these compositional choices, too, Debussy was in tune with the musical spheres in which he moved: composers as different as Jules Massenet and Erik Satie drew on music of the past to anchor new composition within a distant but definitely French past.

Author's Recommendation
Le Martyre de saint Sébastien, Fragments symphoniques (1911).

One work, in particular, encapsulates the many aspects of Debussy's creative world, from the esoteric to poetic antiquity and early-music practice. In 1911, he composed the incidental music for *Le Martyre de saint Sébastien*, a five-act mystery play by Gabriele d'Annunzio about the martyrdom of the Roman saint. The play, as Marianne Wheeldon summarises it, 'introduced elements of magic, the occult, homoeroticism, and exoticism'.[35] Debussy's music was even more ecumenical in its amalgamation of the exotic and erotic with 'choral and other vocal movements that make free use of styles borrowed from Western sacred-music traditions, such as Gregorian chant and Renaissance polyphony'.[36] This absorption of past and present, local and global, not only in *Le Martyre de saint Sébastien* but also in Debussy's creative output as a whole is, indeed, a hallmark of a musical Modernism, in which no aspect of human experience or of musical expression was deemed out of bounds. The *Fragments symphoniques* were adapted by Debussy and published by Durand in 1912.

---

[35] Marianne Wheeldon, 'Debussy's Legacy: The Controversy over the *Ode à la France*', *Journal of Musicology* 27 (2010), p. 315.
[36] Ralph P. Locke, 'Unacknowledged Exoticism in Debussy: The Incidental Music for *Le Martyre de saint Sébastien* (1911)', *The Musical Quarterly* 90 (2007), p. 372.

PART III

People and Milieu

CHAPTER 12

Debussy and the Family in Third-Republic France
Kimberly White

'Our soul is bequeathed to us by a set of completely unknown people, who, through their descendants, act upon us all too often without our being able to do much about it.'[1] These words, written by Debussy in 1911 to his longtime friend André Caplet, open Marcel Dietschy's 1962 biography of the composer. Dietschy considers how Debussy's family, both immediate and far removed, shaped his upbringing and whether his eventual decision to pursue a professional career in music was a product of, or a reaction to, his family situation. That Debussy himself pondered the weight of family influence is illuminating. As Colin Heywood reminds us, the very idea that childhood shaped one's life was a relatively new concept, put forward notably by Rousseau in his *Confessions* (1781) and later reinforced by the work of Freud in the early twentieth century.[2] These shifts of perception towards childhood accompanied more profound changes in the understanding of the family in France, which became significantly invested with political and social significance in the final decades of the nineteenth century. The family was perceived as essential to the prosperity of the nation, and contemporary visual and written culture reinforced the importance of family and domesticity in the lives of men.[3] This chapter explores Debussy's family, his upbringing, and his role as a family man within the context of the shifting ideological structure of the family in Third-Republic France.

---

[1] Marcel Dietschy, *A Portrait of Claude Debussy*, ed. and trans. William Ashbrook and Margaret G. Cobb (Oxford: Clarendon Press, 1990), p. 1.
[2] Colin Heywood, *Growing Up in France: From the Ancien Régime to the Third Republic* (Cambridge: Cambridge University Press, 2007), p. 3
[3] Temma Balducci, *Gender, Space, and the Gaze in Post-Haussmann Visual Culture: Beyond the Flâneur* (London: Routledge, 2017), p. 160.

The Family in Third-Republic France

Reeling from their defeat in the Franco-Prussian War, followed swiftly by civil war with the Paris Commune, and facing bitter power struggles between monarchists and republicans, politicians in early Third-Republic France nevertheless agreed upon one issue: the central importance of the family in the French nation. France's declining birth rate, falling steadily from the 1850s and exacerbated by the loss of the territory of Alsace-Lorraine, fuelled fears of depopulation, which subsequently influenced domestic and foreign policy. The country's decreasing population served as an explanation in the early 1870s for France's humiliating military losses and later as justification for its colonial exploits. Most important, as Camille Robcis and other historians have pointed out, depopulation became an umbrella term used to cover various social issues plaguing the Third Republic, from secularism to nationalism, republicanism to feminism, and the family emerged as the answer to such questions.[4]

The sentimental cult of the family can be traced to the second half of the eighteenth century. It was intimately bound up with questions of patriotism and morality, with the idea that people could not cherish a remote entity like *la patrie* unless they already cultivated such sentiments for those closest to them.[5] By the final decades of the nineteenth century, the family had become a central preoccupation for all political factions. For republicans, the family was the primary model of social organisation.[6] The health of the family both reflected and contributed to the health of the nation, and for this reason the family required state protection. The family promoted social cohesion and solidarity; it was a secular institution that was, family activists argued, beyond politics and of universal interest to humanity.[7]

Women's roles both within the family and at the workplace remained contentious issues, as feminists and socially liberal republicans clashed with social conservatives and advocates of French repopulation, who feared that increased rights and education for women would result in fewer births. Although by the end of the 1880s women could attend *lycées* (secondary schools) and get a divorce, abortion penalties became stricter and social

---

[4] Camille Robcis, *The Law of Kinship: Anthropology, Psychoanalysis, and the Family in France* (Ithaka, NY: Cornell University Press, 2013), p. 30.
[5] Sarah Maza, *The Myth of the French Bourgeoisie: An Essay on the Social Imaginary, 1750–1850* (Cambridge, MA: Harvard University Press, 2005), pp. 41–68.
[6] Greg M. Thomas, *Impressionist Children: Childhood, Family, and Modern Identity in French Art* (New Haven, CT: Yale University Press, 2010), p. 159.
[7] Robcis, *Law of Kinship*, p. 18.

policies privileged motherhood. In 1874, women's work hours were capped at twelve and the wet-nursing industry became regulated.[8] Lawmakers also sought to put more measures in place to protect children: primary education was made free and compulsory with the Jules Ferry Laws of 1881 and 1882, and an additional series of laws in 1874, 1888, and 1898 sought to divest negligent parents of their parental authority.[9]

Men, too, felt the repercussions of the depopulation fears, as bachelors came under scrutiny for their sexual promiscuity and failure to contribute to the nation through the production of legitimate citizens. Judith Surkis argues that republicans regarded marriage as 'an institution for the social and sexual regulation of men'.[10] Although scholarly discussion about domesticity in nineteenth-century France generally centres on women's experiences, the cultivation of domestic space was also integral to men. Temma Balducci, for example, notes that scholarship in art history has tended to focus on paintings of men meeting in cafés and cabarets (thus embracing Baudelaire's paradigmatic *flâneur*), thereby creating the assumption that such public venues were essential to the identity of men in general and avant-garde artists particularly. However, interior and garden scenes featuring men were in fact far more prevalent. In portraiture, the subject is defined by the objects that surround them: each piece of furniture, its texture, and its placement define the subject's class, profession, family situation, and social connections. Conversely, nineteenth-century men expressed their class, culture, and aspirations through the arrangement of their homes,[11] and etiquette manuals for men outlined their responsibilities and duties in the household.[12]

The perception of childhood shifted in the nineteenth century to promote the psychological, moral, and emotional nurturing of children as the core mission of the nuclear family.[13] In his book *L'Enfance à Paris* (1879), Gabriel-Paul-Othenin d'Haussonville identified the family as the pivotal agent shaping children, claiming that those raised in abusive households were more likely to engage in juvenile delinquency. A stable,

---

[8] Karen Offen, *Debating the Woman Question in the French Third Republic, 1870–1920* (Cambridge: Cambridge University Press, 2018), p. 105.
[9] Dorit Geva, *Conscription, Pronatalism, and Decline of Familial Sovereignty in the Early Third Republic* (Cambridge: Cambridge University Press, 2013), pp. 55–6.
[10] Judith Surkis, *Sexing the Citizen: Morality and Masculinity in France, 1870–1920* (Ithaca, NY: Cornell University Press, 2006), p. 5.
[11] Hannu Salmi, *Nineteenth-Century Europe: A Cultural History* (Cambridge: Polity, 2008), pp. 73–7.
[12] Louise d'Alq, *Le Maître et la maîtresse de maison* (Paris: Bureau de Causeries Familières, 1882), pp. 7–8.
[13] Thomas, *Impressionist Children*, p. xxi.

more affectionate home, conversely, could provide children with more opportunities to become productive members of society. Writings about child-rearing equally shifted to encourage closer and more affectionate relationships between fathers and their children. Gustave Droz's successful book *Monsieur, madame et bébé*, first published in 1866 and in more than one hundred subsequent editions by 1882, suggested that the daily routines of family life were a source of pleasure for bourgeois men.[14] Impressionist painting conveyed new models of childhood and the family through depictions of family relations in intimate settings. Edgar Degas (1834–1917) created touching portraits of fathers at home with their children, most notably with his painting *Henri Rouart et sa fille Hélène* (c. 1871–7).[15] Fatherhood was presented as not only an important component of the lives of adult men but also essential for the nation.[16] Larousse's dictionary of 1872 reminded fathers that by teaching their children respect and cultivating their affection they were contributing to the important work of forming the nation's citizens.[17]

Debussy's Family

Debussy's parents came from working-class backgrounds and struggled to find stable employment. After seven years in the marines, Manuel-Achille Debussy (de Bussy, 1836–1910) married Victorine Manoury (1836–1915) and, around the time of Debussy's birth, the couple ran a porcelain shop in Saint-Germain-en-Laye. They left their business in 1864 when it began to fail and, after several interim moves, the family settled in Paris in 1867. Manuel worked initially as a travelling salesman in household goods and later at a printing and lithography shop. In keeping with the household organisation of most nineteenth-century working-class families in France, Victorine contributed to the household finances as well, working as a seamstress. With the outbreak of the Franco-Prussian War, Manuel lost his job as a printer. He eventually took a position with the National Guard and fought as a communard.

The early years of the Third Republic were pivotal for the Debussy family. In May 1871, the Paris Commune was crushed by Adolphe Thiers's government. As General MacMahon's troops penetrated the capital on 22 May, Manuel, only recently promoted to the rank of captain of the Second Company of the Thirteenth Federate Battalion in the National

---

[14] Balducci, *Gender, Space, and the Gaze*, p. 178.   [15] Thomas, *Impressionist Children*, p. 171.
[16] Heywood, *Growing Up in France*, p. 146.   [17] Thomas, *Impressionist Children*, p. 159.

12 Debussy and the Family in Third-Republic France

Guard, was taken prisoner at the bastion de la Muette and later imprisoned at the Satory camp. Manuel was sentenced to four years in prison, leaving Victorine solely responsible for their four children: Achille-Claude, born in 1862, his sister Adèle (1863–1952), and two younger brothers, Emmanuel (1867–1937) and Alfred (1870–1937). A fifth sibling, Eugène-Octave, was born in 1873 but did not survive his fourth year. Instability remained endemic for Debussy and his siblings; Victorine moved the family to a small two-room attic apartment at 59 bis rue Pigalle, and in 1874 they moved again to a two-room apartment at 13 rue Clapeyron. Victorine eventually managed to get her husband's sentence reduced. Manuel was released from prison, but was subsequently deprived of his civic and family rights.[18]

The turbulent events during these years exacerbated the Debussy family's already precarious economic situation and left deep marks on the young Achille-Claude, only nine years old when his father was imprisoned. Yet these years also marked a beginning for Debussy. He began taking piano lessons in 1871 while in Cannes, safely tucked away from the conflicts, and entered the Paris Conservatoire in October 1872. Debussy had not received any formal education prior to the Conservatoire, besides that provided at home by his mother. The Jules Ferry Laws, which instituted free, secular education for all children aged six to thirteen, would not be enacted until the early 1880s. Debussy's piano teacher, Antoine Marmontel, remarked that the boy was somewhat behind in theory and basic principles, but he studied hard.[19] Although several of his colleagues came from well-off families, such as Paul Vidal and Ernest Chausson, Debussy was not the only student from the working classes. In the first half of the century, many of the piano students were from modest middle-class families, with parents working as civil servants, in the military, or as musicians themselves.[20] The Conservatoire admitted students by audition and provided education free of charge. Families, such as Debussy's, who would otherwise be unable to afford private tuition, therefore had an opportunity to provide their children with training that would in turn increase their chances of securing a position as a professional musician.

---

[18] Marcel Dietschy, 'The Family and Childhood of Debussy', *The Musical Quarterly* 46 (July 1960), pp. 301–14.
[19] Léon Vallas, 'Achille Debussy, jugé par ses professeurs du Conservatoire', *Revue de musicologie* 34 (1952), p. 48.
[20] Frédéric de La Grandville, *Une histoire du piano au Conservatoire de musique de Paris, 1795–1850* (Paris: L'Harmattan, 2014), pp. 114–16.

Although the Conservatoire provided Debussy with the necessary training in addition to a network of contacts in musical circles, making one's living exclusively as a composer was challenging. For composers at the *fin de siècle*, there were various pathways to having one's music heard and appreciated: writing music that appealed to popular audiences, receiving official commissions, or finding support among the highly influential members of *le monde*. Debussy's artistic aesthetics and principles positioned him as an innovator, which essentially precluded him from using the first two means of achieving success; instead, he had to find support from the leisured class of the fashionable quarters in Paris.[21] Although Debussy's humble family origins did not grant him access to *le monde*, he eventually found both support and acceptance among this influential community. As he gained recognition, he sought to demonstrate the social markers of distinction. These included not only physical displays of wealth – property, belongings, fine clothing – but also adherence to social structures, such as marriage and family.

Debussy, the Family Man

Debussy married Lilly Texier in 1899. The spectre of his impoverished childhood still loomed, influencing, among other aspects, Debussy's spending habits, which inevitably led to marital conflict. In an often-cited anecdote, Lilly would wait anxiously for her husband's return from his piano lessons to buy food for the evening's dinner, while Debussy tarried and spent his wages instead on antiques.[22] Financial issues pervaded Debussy's life; however, in this case, disagreements about money were only part of a larger problem. It was not a happy marriage. In a letter to Lilly in 1904, Debussy justified his ineptitude as a husband by repeating the commonly held assumption that a true artist was incapable of conforming to the strictures of domesticity: 'an artist is, in short, a dreadful domestic man and perhaps also a deplorable husband? Besides, when the question is turned around, a perfect husband is often a pitiful artist ... It's a vicious circle.'[23] While he insists that he honestly thought he could make her happy by devoting his life to her, he subsequently alludes in the same letter to feeling alienated by Lilly and frequently provoked to angry outbursts. As

---

[21] Christophe Charle, 'Debussy in Fin-de-Siècle Paris', in Jane F. Fulcher (ed.), *Debussy and His World* (Princeton, NY: Princeton University Press, 2001), p. 280.

[22] Robert Orledge, 'Debussy the Man', in Simon Trezise (ed.), *Cambridge Companion to Debussy* (Cambridge: Cambridge University Press, 2003), p. 11.

[23] Letter, Tuesday, 19 July 1904, *Correspondance*, pp. 853–4.

12 Debussy and the Family in Third-Republic France

much as Debussy might have sought to uphold societal expectations regarding marriage, he was unable to conform to the quotidian demands, at least towards his first wife. When it became clear that Lilly and Debussy could not have a child together (Lilly was pregnant in 1900, but either suffered a miscarriage or terminated the pregnancy) – an essential ingredient for the nineteenth-century definition of a family – he most likely gave up entirely on the relationship.[24]

With the success of *Pelléas* in 1902, followed closely by the Legion of Honour in 1903, perhaps Debussy also felt that he needed a wife and family more suited to his rising social status.[25] This he found in Emma Bardac, born Emma-Léa Moyse. Well known in society, married to the banker Sigismond Bardac, Emma moved comfortably in musical circles: she had enjoyed a close relationship in the 1890s with Gabriel Fauré, who dedicated several *mélodies* to her.[26] In the short term, Debussy's decision to begin a new life with Emma was catastrophic, as it necessitated disrupting several social conventions regarding the family. Although it was once again possible to obtain a divorce in France, it tested the limits of social acceptance, made worse because Debussy left his first wife for a wealthier woman (the match was perceived as being motivated solely to achieve upward social mobility). More immediately, though, was the effect of Debussy's abandonment of Lilly, who attempted suicide by shooting herself with a revolver. For women at the turn of the twentieth century, abandonment by a husband was socially and financially devastating. Debussy lost the support of many friends and acquaintances as they shifted their allegiance to Lilly.

In the long term, the marriage with Emma provided Debussy with the necessary elements of a bourgeois lifestyle: a family and a stable home. The composer thus finally had the lifestyle that he had never experienced as a child, but one that he could offer to his daughter. Their child, Claude-Emma (Chouchou), was born in 1905, the same year they moved into a private home on the avenue du Bois de Boulogne. Debussy demonstrated genuine affection for Chouchou and wrote works as a testament to his love for her, such as *Children's Corner* (1908) and *La Boîte à joujoux* (1913). Like other bourgeois men, Debussy took pride in his home, which Emma furnished elegantly, even extravagantly.

Debussy's sumptuous lifestyle, however desirable after experiencing a childhood of want, was unsustainable, and he was plagued by financial

---

[24] Orledge, 'Debussy the Man', p. 21; Lesure (Rolf), p. 165.   [25] Lesure (Rolf), p. 285.
[26] Lesure (Rolf), p. 213.

problems until he died.[27] His second marriage was similarly afflicted with problems, but, at fifty years of age, he resigned himself to remaining in the relationship. In the final years of his life, Debussy reflected on the pressures he felt in his position as the head of the household. In a letter to his publisher Durand in 1913, Debussy wrote:

> Struggling alone is nothing! But struggling within the family becomes hideous! Add to that the domestic demands of past luxury that no one understands has now become impossible to sustain.
> I for one fight only in the name of what may be a mistaken point of honour.[28]

The fundamental incompatibility of family life and an artistic career which Debussy had identified years prior was still unresolved. For Mary Garden, the composer was simply too self-absorbed. As she wrote in her autobiography: 'I honestly don't know if Debussy ever loved anybody really. He loved his music – and perhaps himself. I think he was wrapped up in his genius.'[29] Despite his ardent desire to make up for everything he did not have as a child, Debussy struggled to reconcile the quotidian demands of his family with his professional aspirations at a time when men were increasingly expected to participate in – and enjoy – family life. Whether his struggles emanated from his artistic aspirations or his self-centred character, Debussy's personal and professional choices were undoubtedly shaped by the circumstances of his upbringing and the increasing importance accorded to the family in French society during his lifetime.

Author's Recommendation

Noël des enfants qui n'ont plus de maison (1915); arrangement for two-part children's chorus and piano (1916).

Noël des enfants qui n'ont plus de maison is Debussy's final song, for which he also wrote the text. The patriotic lament documents the impact of the First World War on France's most vulnerable population: children. They have lost their homes, their schools have been burned, their fathers are fighting in the war, and their mothers are already dead. Debussy likely had

---

[27] Denis Herlin, 'An Artist High and Low, or Debussy and Money', in Elliott Antokoletz and Marianne Wheeldon (eds.), *Rethinking Debussy* (New York: Oxford University Press, 2011), p. 164.
[28] *Correspondance*, p. 1641.
[29] Mary Garden and Louis Biancolli, *Mary Garden's Story* (New York: Simon and Schuster, 1951), p. 80.

not forgotten the misery he endured during the last war: he was just a child during the Franco-Prussian War, and in the civil war that erupted afterwards his father fought as a communard and was imprisoned. *Noël des enfants* adopts the breathless voice of a child, at once pleading and vengeful, over an agitated motif in the piano. Originally scored for voice and piano, Debussy arranged the song for children's choir in 1916.

CHAPTER 13

Romantic Relationships
Marianne Wheeldon

Debussy's relationships with women cannot be considered in isolation from the realities of class and social mobility in *fin-de-siècle* Paris. In terms of social origin, Debussy hailed from the working class. His parents briefly entered the ranks of the *petite bourgeoisie* when they owned a small pottery shop in Saint-Germain-en-Laye (1861–4). After selling the business, they moved to Paris and thereafter their various employments (and unemployment) placed them in the working class. In terms of social position, Debussy's status was more nebulous. Money mattered, as did the way it was earned, but this income had to be complemented by 'a certain degree of refinement, for belonging to the bourgeoisie was preeminently the art of being "correct"'.[1] Herein lay the possibilities of social ascension for a composer such as Debussy. On the one hand, his conservatoire training, Prix de Rome prize, and prodigious talent meant that he possessed the requisite degree of cultivation that made him welcome in bourgeois drawing rooms. On the other hand, the art of being 'correct' often eluded him, especially in his relationships with women. This chapter considers Debussy's romantic relationships from the perspective of bourgeois marriage conventions and class mobility. Through matrimony, Debussy attempted on several occasions to marry upwardly, ultimately succeeding in 1908 with his marriage to Emma Bardac.

1880–1887: Marie Vasnier

Debussy's seven-year affair with Marie Vasnier illustrates the latitudes and limits of bourgeois marriage conventions – in this instance, the unwritten

---

[1] Richard Holt, 'Social History and Bourgeois Culture in Nineteenth-Century France: A Review Article', *Comparative Studies in Society and History* 27 (1985), p. 715.

rules governing the arranged marriage. In the nineteenth century, at all levels of society, 'arranged marriages were an accepted family strategy for amalgamating wealth'.[2] One marker of the arranged marriage was its tolerance towards adultery. For men and women seeking romantic love in a marriage of convenience, these conflicting interests were often resolved 'by keeping the familial and political alliances that came with arranged marriage, while allowing both men and women to pursue love in a series of extramarital affairs'.[3] It is likely that Henri Vasnier had extramarital affairs and equally likely that he was aware of the relationship between his wife and the eighteen-year-old Debussy. Given the hours Debussy spent with the Vasnier family, it would be hard to believe otherwise. He was welcomed into their home, where he was provided with a piano and a small room in which to work. Between 1880 and 1884, he went 'many afternoons and almost every evening to study, compose, and to accompany Mme Vasnier'. During the summers, Debussy visited the family daily at Ville d'Avray, where they rented a villa for the season.[4] By keeping the affair close to home, Vasnier perhaps hoped to monitor Debussy's infatuation with his wife and ensure that it remained within the bounds of propriety.

It was the preservation of proprieties that undoubtedly led Henri Vasnier to put an end to the liaison. By 1885, Debussy's youthful infatuation had turned into something serious and he began to demand more from his relationship with Marie. Repeated entreaties to meet her without Henri's knowledge changed the tenor of their affair. As Debussy pushed the limits of 'acceptable' adultery, Marie began to pull away from the relationship. Debussy confided to Gustave Popelin that '*her last letter . . . scarcely concealed all the trouble that my presence there would make for her, telling me that it would be very imprudent for us to see each other*'.[5] By the end of 1885, Henri, who had been corresponding regularly with Debussy during his sojourn at the Villa Medici, stopped writing altogether. When Debussy returned from Rome in March 1887, his affair with Marie was waning and, by the end of the year, it was over.

---

[2] Patricia Mainardi, *Husbands, Wives, and Lovers: Marriage and Its Discontents in Nineteenth-Century France* (New Haven, CT: Yale University Press, 2003), p. 5.
[3] Michèle Plott, 'The Rules of the Game: Respectability, Sexuality, and the *Femme Mondaine* in Late-Nineteenth-Century Paris', *French Historical Studies* 25 (2002), p. 556.
[4] Margaret G. Cobb and Richard Miller, 'Claude Debussy to Claudius and Gustave Popelin: Nine Unpublished Letters', *19th-Century Music* 13 (1989), p. 40.
[5] Lesure (Rolf), p. 63.

1893–1894: Thérèse Roger and Gabrielle Dupont

Debussy's next romantic entanglement came to the attention of his friends when he announced his engagement to Thérèse Roger in February 1894.[6] Thérèse was twenty-seven years old, an accomplished pianist and soprano, and from a good bourgeois family. If Debussy's affair with Marie disclosed the unwritten rules of the arranged marriage, his engagement to Thérèse revealed the expectations of the companionate marriage. Although bourgeois marriage conventions were slowly moving away from the arranged marriage common at the beginning of the nineteenth century towards the notion of the companionate marriage by the century's end, there was still a strong culture of at least trying 'to reconcile strategic marriage with love and happiness'.[7] Thus it was incumbent on the Roger family (widowed mother and son) to use the traditional two-month engagement period to scrutinise the background of the prospective son-in-law and to ascertain what precisely he could bring to the union.[8]

Both Debussy's finances and his lifestyle were major impediments to his marriage with Thérèse – a fact of which he was keenly aware. In a letter to Henry Lerolle (25 February 1894), Debussy mentions both problems:

> I have told Madame Roger everything about my situation, and I would like her daughter to retain all *her material independence*!
> As for me, I will always be able to manage. . . .
> Moreover, I am *completely free*, my last girlfriend having left me one morning in February – in order to improve her situation.[9]

Debussy certainly did not tell Madame Roger everything. While he may have been forthcoming about his meagre income, it is doubtful that he provided an accurate account of his debts. Moreover, despite his claims to the contrary, Debussy was not 'completely free' – his working-class girlfriend Gaby Dupont was still living with him, as she had been since 1892.

Debussy's first attempt to marry into the bourgeoisie came the closest to succeeding: the marriage was planned for 16 April 1894 and an apartment was rented for the couple on the rue Vaneau.[10] Given bourgeois marriage conventions and the details of Debussy's life, it is surprising that the relationship progressed as far as it did. Three weeks after the

---

[6] Letter to Henry Lerolle, c. 24 February 1894, *Correspondance*, pp. 196–8.
[7] Michelle Perrot, 'Roles and Characters', in Michelle Perrot (ed.), *A History of Private Life: From the Fires of Revolution to the Great War*, trans. Arthur Goldhammer (Cambridge, MA: Harvard University Press, 1990), p. 186.
[8] Anne Martin-Fugier, 'Bourgeois Rituals', in Perrot (ed.), *A History of Private Life*, pp. 312–13.
[9] *Correspondance*, p. 197.   [10] *Correspondance*, p. 196 n. 2 and p. 197 n. 2.

announcement of the engagement, however, others intervened. Ernest Chausson received an anonymous letter, urging him to prevent the marriage. Madame Roger, as well as several friends of the composer, were also recipients of anonymous letters.[11] Whether these letters revealed the extent of Debussy's debts or his cohabitation with Gaby, either circumstance was sufficient to put an end to the marriage.

1895–1896: Catherine Stevens and Gabrielle Dupont

Debussy apparently learnt little from the debacle of his engagement with Thérèse. The pattern he had established in this last relationship – cohabiting with a woman from the working class while pursuing another from the bourgeoisie – would persist for the next eight years. Gaby continued to earn a living and manage their household, while Debussy continued to court women from the bourgeoisie. Debussy's attempts to inhabit different social worlds – each with their own rules of conduct – perhaps explains his clumsiness when traversing between the two. In bohemian circles, 'multiple affairs were the rule, and infidelity was a principle'. Beneath the surface, bourgeois circles were no different, but whereas bohemia was a 'communal and public life' that 'shared everything, including women', bourgeois private life was closed, discreet, and valued the appearance of propriety above all.[12]

It was a dual existence that Debussy's next love, Catherine Stevens, observed in him: 'Among great artists, even bohemians (as he was in this epoch) he was always deep down bourgeois.' Catherine was the daughter of Alfred Stevens, a Belgian painter who reached the height of his success in the 1860s. According to Catherine's notes, Debussy began visiting her home in 1891 in the company of her brothers and 'by the end of 1895, beginning of 1896, came to the house two or three times a week'.[13] Debussy's increased visits to Catherine, however, coincided with her family's reversal of fortunes. Undeterred, Debussy continued to pursue Catherine and proposed to her in 1896. While Catherine refused, she recalled the situation as follows: '[Debussy] demonstrated such a *disinterested* love for me during the worst moment of crisis that my family experienced – he, to whom one attributed such feelings of cupidity.'[14]

---

[11] *Correspondance*, p. 199 n. 4 and p. 201 n. 1.   [12] Perrot, 'Roles and Characters', p. 251.
[13] Centre de Documentation Claude Debussy, DOSS 04.49 Stevens (famille).
[14] René Peter, 'Debussy et l'amour', *Comœdia* (4 July 1942), p. 4.

Catherine's argument for Debussy's 'disinterested love' was based on his continued courtship despite her family's financial crisis. But this does not cohere with the value judgments of the bourgeoisie. 'Neither [wealth nor profession] sufficed to create class distinction. ... For there were manual laborers who were rich, just as there were bourgeois who were poor. Wealth, consequently, was not determinative of class.'[15] In this light, Catherine was *bourgeoise* regardless of her family's financial downfall, her status being secure due to her upbringing, the social circles she inhabited, and the way she conducted her life. Had Debussy's proposal been accepted, his marriage to Catherine would have certainly lifted him into the bourgeoisie.

1897–1899: Alice Peter and Gabrielle Dupont

Debussy continued to live with Gaby, who remained with him from 1892 to 1898, despite his proposals to Thérèse in 1894 and Catherine in 1896. Gaby was to endure yet another affair. On 9 February 1897, the composer wrote to Pierre Louÿs: 'Gaby with the piercing eyes found a letter in my pocket that left no doubt as to the advanced state of a love affair containing all the romance necessary to touch even the most hardened heart.'[16] Denis Herlin speculates that this letter was from Alice Peter, who was involved with Debussy from the beginning of 1897 to June 1899.[17] Née Alice Loewenstein, she married Maurice Abraham Meyer Van Ysen, with whom she had a son. This first marriage of nine years (1882–91) was followed by a second to Michel Peter in 1894, although the couple separated shortly thereafter in either 1896 or 1897. As Herlin observes, the date of Alice's separation from her second husband roughly coincides with her liaison with Debussy.[18]

Alice was no ingénue and it appears that she was an active participant in the affair. Her brother-in-law, René Peter, described her as playing along in the relationship, prolonging it as long as Debussy was willing, flattered to be the muse of the 'great man of tomorrow'.[19] From Alice's perspective, this was not a relationship moving towards matrimony. Debussy, in a letter

---

[15] Michel Lallement, 'Social Trajectory and Sociological Theory: Edmond Goblot, the Bourgeoisie, and Social Distinction', *Social Epistemology* 30 (2016), p. 703.
[16] *Correspondance*, p. 342.
[17] Denis Herlin, 'Un cercle amical franco-belge de Debussy: Les Dansaert, les Loewenstein et les Peter', in Herlin, *Claude Debussy: Portraits et études* (Hildesheim: Olms, 2021), p. 140.
[18] Herlin, 'Un cercle amical', p. 140. [19] Peter, 'Debussy et l'amour', p. 4.

to his editor Georges Hartmann (14 July 1898), appears to have thought otherwise:

> My life is decorated with complications of a sentimental nature, turning it into the most troubled, the most complicated thing I know. I would need a lot of money to leap over or even destroy the barriers erected by law to separate those who want personal happiness; and as I have barely enough money not to die of hunger, I am powerless and witness the ruin of all my beautiful and tender dreams.[20]

Debussy's letter is significant for its acknowledgement of 'barriers', specifically the social barriers that prevented his marriage to Alice (and previously to Thérèse or Catherine). His comments admit both his desire and his inability to surmount these obstacles in his relationship with Alice.

1899: Lilly Texier and Alice Peter

Debussy's courtship of Lilly represents something of an anomaly in his romantic life. For the first time, he fervently pursued marriage with a working-class woman, on this occasion with a bourgeois woman remaining in the background. What contributed to this volte-face in Debussy's romantic endeavours? Perhaps after three failed attempts to marry upwardly, Debussy gave up on the notion of marrying into the bourgeoisie. Moreover, at the end of 1898, Gaby left him.[21] After an eight-year relationship, six of them living together, Gaby's departure was a major loss. These two situations – the hopelessness of his relationship with Alice, the departure of Gaby – left Debussy largely alone at the beginning of 1899. Enter Lilly Texier, who appeared in Debussy's life at a moment when he was perhaps rethinking his matrimonial strategies.

For the first time, Debussy's correspondence to a lover has survived, shedding light on his courtship of Lilly. Between April and July 1899, he wrote numerous love letters to her, first once a week and then on an almost daily basis. These letters not only show Debussy at his most ardent, but they also reveal the fault-lines that were beginning to emerge in this relationship. June was a tumultuous month, with many of the issues that had plagued Debussy's previous relationships returning to trouble his pursuit of Lilly. On 15 June 1899, Debussy's correspondence refers to yet another anonymous letter, one that apprised Lilly of his debts.[22] Two days later, after Lilly

---

[20] *Correspondance*, p. 411.
[21] Letter to Georges Hartmann, 1 January 1899, *Correspondance*, p. 446.
[22] *Correspondance*, p. 499.

threatened to leave him, Debussy defended his love for her, their future together, and, in the process, admitted to infidelity: 'while you can truly say that you've been cheated on once, why doesn't your feminine intuition tell you that you can trust me, without dreading any kind of betrayal!'[23]

Debussy managed to allay Lilly's fears, because she moved in with him in July 1899. However, this was not the end of their problems: Lilly discovered a letter in Debussy's pocket from Alice (just as Gaby had two years earlier).[24] Debussy's correspondence reveals the repercussions: he describes how Lilly's 'resolution to leave was implacable'; he apologises for acting with a 'shameful frivolity'; and he begs forgiveness '*for the last time*'.[25] Once again, Debussy managed to retrieve the situation, and the couple married on 19 October 1899. It may have been Debussy's original intention to establish Lilly in the position formerly occupied by Gaby. But by threatening to leave him on two occasions, Lilly succeeded in extracting a promise of matrimony – something that had eluded Gaby for six years.

1903–1904: Emma Bardac and Lilly Debussy

Debussy's affair with the married Emma Bardac replicates certain features of his previous relationships. The Bardacs' union (like the Vasniers') was arranged and followed the conventions of the bourgeois marriage of convenience – Sigismond Bardac condoned his wife's affairs while he pursued his own in return. Debussy's involvement with Emma also recalls his relationship with Thérèse. Just as Debussy became engaged to Thérèse while living with Gaby, he became involved with Emma while married to Lilly, in each case forsaking his long-term relationship with a working-class woman in an effort to marry a bourgeois woman. Ten years later, however, the stakes were much higher: whereas in 1894, Debussy, Thérèse, and Gaby were all single, in 1904 the parties involved were all married. And ten years later, Debussy's actions and their consequences were more extreme. After his abandonment of his wife to 'elope' with Emma, Lilly attempted suicide by shooting herself in the stomach. The public scandal that followed led to Debussy's social ostracism, almost all of his colleagues severing contact with him. While 'discreet adultery – known to one's friends but not to the public' – was acceptable,[26] abandoning one's wife, who had no means of support and who then tried to commit suicide, was not.

---

[23] *Correspondance*, p. 501. Translated in Lesure (Rolf), p. 159.
[24] Herlin, 'Un cercle amical', p. 141.   [25] *Correspondance*, p. 513.
[26] Plott, 'Rules of the Game', p. 553.

Yet Debussy ultimately joined the ranks of the bourgeoisie, divorcing Lilly in 1905 and marrying Emma in 1908. What changed in the intervening years that allowed him to marry upwardly? For one, his official recognition as a composer began to transcend his family's social origins: 'the older one was, the more important was one's own social position rather than that of one's parents. Consequently, lower-class children who married quite late had more chance of attracting a middle-class spouse.'[27] At the age of forty-two, with a successful opera and the Legion of Honour to his name, Debussy could begin to rise above his humble origins. But his professional success was still insufficient to enter the ranks of the bourgeoisie. Writing in 1925, Edmond Goblot notes, 'the principal difficulty of becoming bourgeois is that one cannot become it alone. Everybody belongs to a family before belonging to a class.'[28] Since Debussy's class mobility was restricted by his family background, he had to attach himself to another whose bourgeois credentials were unassailable. His relationship and marriage to Emma ultimately allowed Debussy 'to leap over or even destroy the barriers' separating him from the bourgeoisie.

Throughout his adult life, Debussy's desire for the trappings of bourgeois life was a major determinant in his romantic relationships. From the 1890s on, he cohabited with or married a working-class woman (Gabrielle Dupont, Lilly Texier) while simultaneously pursuing marriage with a bourgeois woman (Thérèse Roger, Catherine Stevens, Alice Peter, Emma Bardac). It was a strategy that paid off in 1904, albeit with dubious results: while Debussy finally gained admittance to the bourgeoisie, it came at the price of a public scandal that any member of this social class would be at pains to avoid.

Author's Recommendation
Recueil Vasnier (c. 1880–4).

There are several instances of Debussy combining courtship with composition, especially in the genre of the *mélodie*. Examples occur early in his career with the twenty-nine songs inspired by, composed for, and performed with Marie Vasnier during their seven-year affair (1880–7). Two decades later there was another outpouring of *mélodies*, this time

---

[27] Bart van de Putte, Michel Oris, and Koen Matthijs, 'Marrying Out of the Lower Classes in Nineteenth-Century Belgium', *Continuity and Change* 24 (2009), p. 428.
[28] Edmond Goblot, *La Barrière et le niveau: Étude sociologique sur la bourgeoisie française moderne* (Paris: Félix Alcan, 1925), p. 7.

coinciding with Debussy's affair with Emma Bardac (1903). Other relationships – with Thérèse Roger, Catherine Stevens, and Alice Peter – also inspired *mélodies* for the women Debussy loved. In each case, these songs functioned as more than mere gifts: destined for bourgeois women, they were implicated in the composer's repeated attempts at social ascension, providing him with moments of musical intimacy with the women he was hoping to marry.

The *Recueil Vasnier* offers one such example – a collection of thirteen *mélodies* presented to Marie Vasnier shortly before the composer departed for his two-year sojourn at the Villa Medici in Rome (1885). Copied by hand and never intended for publication, the songs contained in this manuscript were a private and deeply personal offering to Madame Vasnier, a testament to their musical and romantic relationship. Characterised by their high vocal range and virtuosic technique, these *mélodies* had been composed to showcase Marie Vasnier's agile coloratura voice and were only ever meant to be performed by her, accompanied by the composer at the piano.

CHAPTER 14

Relationships with Poets and Other Literary Figures

Caroline Potter

The composer Paul Dukas, one of few people who were long-term friends of Debussy's, said in 1926: 'The strongest influence that Debussy came under was that of writers, not composers.'[1] Writers were also prominent in his friendship circles, and this chapter will outline the importance of these circles to Debussy's musical development. So many French composers have been influenced by artists of all types, at least as much as by their musical peers. The formative years of composers as different as Erik Satie and Pierre Boulez were marked by significant meetings with non-musician artists; Satie's early years spent as a café pianist in Montmartre brought him into contact with humourists, writers, journalists, and eccentrics of every stripe, while Boulez's time as music director of Jean-Louis Barrault and Madeleine Renaud's theatre company took him around the world and gave him his first conducting experience.

Debussy was no exception to this. Perhaps surprisingly for someone so personally reserved, his face-to-face encounters with writers were at least as important to him as the time he spent reading their books. But as a collaborator, he was far better at discussing projects than actually completing them, as Robert Orledge's *Debussy and the Theatre* makes abundantly clear; Debussy's list of projected theatrical works is considerably longer than his list of achievements in this sphere. His personal connections with writers started with the odd coincidence that Debussy's first piano teacher was Paul Verlaine's mother-in-law, Antoinette Mauté de Fleurville; her daughter, Mathilde, and the poet lived under her roof when the nine-year-old Debussy studied with her. Did the child ever encounter the poet whose verses he would so memorably set to music several years later?

Mauté de Fleurville's son by her first marriage, the composer and musical director Charles de Sivry (1848–1900), met Debussy's father,

---

[1] Robert Brussel, 'Claude Debussy et Paul Dukas', *Revue musicale* 7 (1926), p. 101.

Manuel, when both were imprisoned after the defeat of the Commune in May 1871.[2] Sivry – who, perhaps unexpectedly, trained as an accountant before turning to music – was a member of the Hydropathes group (no doubt so called because they preferred stronger beverages to water), who originally met at locations on Paris's Left Bank, but from 1881 their regular haunt was the Chat Noir in Montmartre. This area, then on the northern fringes of Paris and not subjected to its drink taxes, is inextricably associated with late nineteenth- and early twentieth-century bohemian and artistic culture. Other Hydropathes included Paul Bourget (1852–1935); Charles Cros (1842–88), who in 1877 invented the *paléophone*, an early sound-recording device; and the humourist and editor of the *Chat Noir* journal Alphonse Allais (1854–1905).

Debussy first met members of this circle in the 1880s, when he occasionally accompanied singers at the Chat Noir. A more regular musical collaborator at that cabaret was Satie, who met Debussy in this period and remained friends with him until the *succès de scandale* of the ballet *Parade* (1917) soured their relationship. Debussy set Cros's poem 'L'Archet' in 1881, and also met Bourget and made musical settings of seven poems from his collection *Les Aveux*.[3] Many Hydropathes were preoccupied with the occult and alchemy as well as the arts; Sivry joined Cros in alchemical experiments, for instance. But this interest existed alongside more light-hearted pursuits, as the Chat Noir was also famous for its cabaret performers, whose witty and satirical performances formed such an important aspect of the Montmartre environment. Vincent Hyspa (1865–1938) was a comic singer and poet who frequently worked with Satie in Montmartre cabarets. Author of the lyrics of several Satie cabaret songs, such as 'Tendrement' and 'Chez le docteur', he also wrote the picturesque text of Debussy's 'La Belle au bois dormant' (1890).

The pseudo-medieval décor of the Chat Noir represented in physical form another common interest of many of its regulars. For them, there was not the gulf one might assume between the café-concert environment and the cathedral; as Roger Shattuck put it, 'In those days ... it was a conveniently short distance from esoteric religions to cabaret gaiety.'[4] This was a space where creativity sprang from a confluence of diverse

---

[2] See Marcel Dietschy and Edward Lockspeiser, 'The Family and Childhood of Debussy', *The Musical Quarterly* 46 (1960), p. 312.

[3] Arthur B. Wenk, *Claude Debussy and the Poets* (Berkeley, CA: University of California Press, 1976), p. 2.

[4] Roger Shattuck, *The Banquet Years: The Origins of the Avant-Garde in France, 1885 to World War I*, rev. ed. (London: Jonathan Cape, 1969), p. 120.

14 Poets and Other Literary Figures

interests – satire and esotericism, popular culture and recondite ideas, the ancient and the avant-garde. The medieval revival of the *fin de siècle* prompted the rediscovery of François Villon (1431–63), the poet of the late Middle Ages whose work speaks of the streets of Paris and its marginalised inhabitants. This poetic encounter did not bear fruit for Debussy until the early twentieth century, when he composed *Trois ballades de François Villon* (1910), collapsing the distance between Villon's vivid portrayals of his contemporaries and Debussy's own era. Towards the end of his life, Debussy tapped into the enthusiasm for Villon as a national figure in his *Ode à la France* (1916).[5] Others in the Montmartre orbit whose paths crossed with Debussy included the mathematician Charles Henry (1859–1926) and the authors Villiers de l'Isle-Adam (1838–89) and Jules Bois (1868–1943).[6]

Another Paris location that was a central meeting point for Debussy and other artists was the bookshop run by Edmond Bailly, L'Art indépendant, which opened in 1889. Far more than just a shop, L'Art indépendant was also a salon and publisher of both literature and music. Its focus was on esotericism and religion in its broadest sense: Bailly 'published a journal, *La Haute Science*, and an important library of major sources', including key texts of Eastern and ancient religions.[7] Surely Debussy also appreciated that he had common ground with Bailly, who was a trained musician.[8] Bailly's taste for luxury editions chimed well with Debussy's desires: Debussy's *Cinq poèmes de Charles Baudelaire* was first published in an edition of 150 in 1890, and three years later Bailly printed the vocal score of *La Damoiselle élue* with a decorative cover by Maurice Denis. Bailly was, in Robert Orledge's words, 'largely responsible for the vogue for esotericism and the occult at the time': it was at L'Art indépendant that Satie and Debussy may have first met, and definitely where they encountered the author and eccentric Rosicrucian mystic Joséphin Péladan (1858–1918).[9] Other regulars at the bookshop included Debussy's friends Henri de Régnier, Pierre Louÿs, and Jean de Tinan,[10] as well as Stéphane

---

[5] See Marianne Wheeldon, 'Debussy's Legacy: The Controversy over the *Ode à la France*', *Journal of Musicology* 27 (2010), pp. 304–41.

[6] For details on Debussy's contacts with Henry, see Roy Howat, *Debussy in Proportion* (Cambridge: Cambridge University Press, 1983), pp. 164–7.

[7] Jann Pasler, 'Revisiting Debussy's Relationships with Otherness: Difference, Vibrations, and the Occult', *Music and Letters* 101 (May 2020), p. 332.

[8] See Denis Herlin, 'À la librairie de l'Art indépendant: L'univers symboliste de Debussy', in Herlin, *Claude Debussy: Portraits et études* (Hildesheim: Olms, 2021), pp. 16–47.

[9] Robert Orledge, '"To Boldly Go": Erik Satie's "Simple Little Prelude" of 1894 Sets Out on an Esoteric Astral Journey towards "The Heroic Gate of Heaven"', *Musical Times* 160 (2019), p. 56. See also Robert Orledge, *Satie the Composer* (Cambridge: Cambridge University Press, 1990), pp. 40–1.

[10] Pasler, 'Revisiting Debussy's Relationships', p. 332.

Mallarmé, who was later to welcome Debussy to the gatherings at his home and to become inextricably linked with the composer through the orchestral *Prélude à l'après-midi d'un faune* (1892–4).

There are multiple connections between the Librairie de l'Art indépendant regulars and the Montmartre cabaret scene. Péladan, who styled himself 'Sâr' Péladan, was linked to the Chat Noir as editorial secretary of the house journal, when he was not writing mystical plays or organising Rosicrucian-themed events. Debussy was involved in projected operatic or theatrical collaborations with many of these writers. For example, in 1892 he considered composing incidental music for Jules Bois's *Les Noces de Sathan* (1890),[11] but while his friend Satie wrote his *Prélude de la porte héroïque du ciel* for Bois's play of the same title, Debussy's work was never started.

All these authors contributed to the dark, intense *fin-de-siècle* atmosphere in Paris; following Baudelaire and Edgar Allan Poe (1809–49), Joris-Karl Huysmans (1848–1907) wrote *À rebours* (1884), a novel with strong musical subthemes and a standard-bearer for the Symbolist and Decadent movements. While the black dinner of the protagonist, Des Esseintes, is the most celebrated scene in the book, the description of his liqueur organ, with each individual timbre associated with a particular tipple, is equally memorable. Debussy's good friend, the poet Gabriel Mourey (1865–1943), knew Huysmans well, and the multiple interrelationships between people in Debussy's circle are illustrated by Mourey's translations of Poe, first published in 1889 with a preface by Péladan. Mourey is another figure who met Debussy at L'Art indépendant.

Dark Gothic subject matter of the Baudelaire and Poe variety was also favoured by authors outside France. The Italian author Gabriele D'Annunzio (1863–1938) collaborated with Debussy when he wrote the text for *Le Martyre de saint Sébastien* (1911), but his prime period as a writer was the 1880s and 1890s, when he was strongly influenced by the French *fin-de-siècle* Symbolist and Decadent movements. In particular, his novel *Il piacere* (1889) has a good deal in common with *À rebours*, and for D'Annunzio life imitated art: he modelled the decoration of his own home after the descriptions of Baron des Esseintes's home in Huysmans's novel.[12]

---

[11] See Orledge, 'To Boldly Go', p. 57; Robert Orledge, *Debussy and the Theatre* (Cambridge: Cambridge University Press, 1982).

[12] William Corwin, 'Joris-Karl Huysmans Art Critic', in *The Brooklyn Rail* (2020) https://brooklynrail.org/2020/02/artseen/Joris-Karl-Huysmans-Art-Critic.

14 Poets and Other Literary Figures

Poe never visited France, but he had a surprisingly big impact on nineteenth- and early twentieth-century French culture. This can almost entirely be ascribed to Baudelaire's translations. Baudelaire first purchased works by Poe in London in 1851, and subsequently translated Poe writings, including his two sets of *Histoires extraordinaires*.[13] Poe's vivid imagination, ghost stories, and predilection for dark fantasy Gothic atmosphere captured the French imagination; Baudelaire saw him as a kindred spirit, as later did Debussy. Fragile Poe heroines, such as Lady Madeline in *The Fall of the House of Usher*, had an obvious appeal for the composer of *Pelléas et Mélisande*; the contemporary vogue for the *femme fragile* resonated strongly with Debussy.

Poe's poem *The Raven* heralded the *fin-de-siècle* preoccupation with darkness and decadence. Mallarmé's translation of this poem, *Le Corbeau*, illustrated by Manet, was published in 1875, and he echoed Baudelaire's sentiments towards Poe, referring to him as 'the purest among the spirits ... made of stars, made of lightning'.[14] Poe's own analysis of *The Raven* was published as *The Philosophy of Composition*, and Baudelaire's commentary on the text (translated as *La Genèse d'un poème* and published in 1864) was especially influential in France, an impact that stretched well beyond the literary sphere. Later, Ravel provocatively described Poe to a US newspaper as 'very French'; further, 'On at least three different published occasions, Ravel testified that "my teacher in composition was Edgar Allan Poe, because of his analysis of his wonderful poem 'The Raven'. Poe taught me that true art is a perfect balance between pure intellect and emotion."'[15] This balance was bound to appeal to Ravel; it appears that French artists discovered in Poe whatever they wanted to find.

Debussy worked on two Poe operas, *La Chute de la maison Usher* and *Le Diable dans le beffroi*, for many years after the premiere of *Pelléas et Mélisande*, though he completed neither and *Usher* survives only in fragmentary form (*Le Diable* hardly at all). In a letter to Paul Dukas (himself no stranger to incomplete projects) written in 1916, Debussy wrote of *Usher*, 'Destiny should allow me to finish it';[16] sadly, destiny did not.

Another author Debussy met at L'Art indépendant was the Belgian-born Pierre Louÿs (né Louis; 1870–1925), though his work is situated in the

---

[13] Anne Garrait-Bourrier, 'Poe Translated by Baudelaire: The Reconstruction of an Identity', *CLCWeb: Comparative Literature and Culture* 4 (2002), p. 4.
[14] Cited in Andrea Goulet, 'France', in Kevin J. Hayes (ed.), *Edgar Allan Poe in Context* (Cambridge: Cambridge University Press, 2013), p. 44.
[15] Interview with André Révész for the Madrid newspaper ABC (1 May 1924), in Arbie Orenstein (ed.), *A Ravel Reader: Correspondence, Articles, Interviews* (Mineola, NY: Dover, 2003), p. 433.
[16] Letter, 10 August 1916, *Correspondance*, p. 2016.

exotic and erotic sphere rather than Péladan-type esoteric weirdness. His novel *Aphrodite: Mœurs antiques* (1896), an account of a courtesan's life in Alexandria, was hugely successful during his lifetime. Debussy, who can only have dreamed of such success for his own work, had exclusive rights to compose an opera based on Aphrodite, though like so many of his theatrical projects, this came to nothing. Debussy was a close friend of Louÿs until, like so many of Debussy's associates, he withdrew from the composer after he left his wife for Emma Bardac. But Debussy's attraction to Louÿs's *Chansons de Bilitis* (1894), a set of 143 prose poems, lasted longer than their friendship. Louÿs claimed the poems were translations from the ancient Greek; however, while he borrowed some passages from writers including Sappho, Louÿs was the true author. Debussy made settings of three of them for voice and piano in 1897–8, following this with interludes for a reading of twelve of the poems, performed once in his lifetime in 1901. Debussy's scoring of these interludes for two flutes, two harps, and celesta responded to contemporary perceptions of ancient Greek music. Later, in 1914, he reused this musical material in *Six Épigraphes antiques* for two pianos, whose titles recall Louÿs's collection though no textual content is present.

Debussy was always eager to escape the tedium of everyday life, if only in his imagination. Eastern and ancient religious texts that he discovered at L'Art indépendant gave him contact with completely different worlds and thoughts: Bailly published 'the Hindu Bhagavad-Gita, translated from Sanskrit; the Tao Te Ching of Lao Tzu, translated from Chinese; translations of the divination of Chaldo-Assyrians and the Ethiopian Apocrypha; the ancient Egyptian Tarot; and secondary literature on esoteric Buddhism and neo-spiritualism'.[17] Victor Segalen (1878–1919), whom Debussy met in 1906, further enhanced his knowledge of Asian and Pacific countries. Segalen, whose cousin was the composer Jean Cras, was a writer and naval doctor who travelled extensively and spoke Chinese fluently.[18] His interests encompassed non-Western music at a time when this was highly unusual, and his article 'Voix mortes: Musique maori' (Dead voices: Maori music), published under the pseudonym Max Anély in *Le Mercure musical* in 1907, is dedicated to Debussy. Like so many other writers with whom Debussy was acquainted, Segalen was keen to collaborate with the composer, and in 1906 he proposed a drama, *Siddartha*, on the life of the Buddha. However, Debussy wrote to him on 26 August 1907 that he could not conceive 'music which could penetrate this abyss! ... I don't mean it's impossible – simply

---

[17] Pasler, 'Revisiting Debussy's Relationships with Otherness', p. 332.
[18] Segalen was also close to Huysmans towards the end of his life.

I'm afraid of it.'[19] Having no luck with this idea, Segalen moved on to a new topic, the Orpheus legend, inspired by Gustave Moreau's paintings.[20] But this project would similarly prove fruitless. Segalen left for China in April 1909, and while Debussy continued to correspond with him, there was to be no further discussion of possible musical projects.

While Mallarmé's work made a significant impact on and beyond poetry in the twentieth century, in his lifetime his weekly salon held in his flat at 89 rue de Rome was an important meeting place for artists. These meetings took place on Tuesdays from the mid-1880s until the end of Mallarmé's life in 1898. By 1890, Debussy was a regular attender at these gatherings; a complete list of *mardistes* would be a Who's Who of Parisian intellectual life, including both French and visiting foreign artists. The literary crowd included Verlaine, Gide, Valéry, Rilke, Oscar Wilde, W. B. Yeats, and, among visual artists, Renoir, Degas, Redon, Whistler, Monet, and Rodin. (One of Debussy's more intriguing projects that never came to fruition was an 1896 projected ballet collaboration with Louÿs on the *Daphnis et Chloé* legend.[21]) Debussy met Verlaine at Mallarmé's salon, though 'Debussy's relationship with Verlaine never included the personal intimacy of his friendship with Louÿs or the immediate contact with the philosophy of Symbolism that he encountered in the *mardis chez Mallarmé*'.[22] But while the salon was certainly a meeting place, for Mallarmé it was primarily a space to work on his own ideas. Rosemary Lloyd makes the important point that:

> While several Mardistes have argued that they were not merely devoted to listening to Mallarmé speak, and that he did encourage the participation of others in his meditations on art, society, and life more generally, it remains the case, as his letters reveal, that he was above all interested in exploring his own mind and intellectual and emotional responses.[23]

There is an interesting parallel here with Debussy. His connections with writers resulted in important friendships and collaborations, whether or not these projects were ultimately successful. But perhaps the most vital aspect of these relationships was that they enabled Debussy to test and develop his ideas in dialogue, and ultimately to find his own creative voice as a composer.

---

[19] Annie Joly-Segalen, *Segalen et Debussy* (Monaco: Éditions du Rocher, 1962), p. 66.
[20] Ibid., p. 13.   [21] Wenk, *Claude Debussy and the Poets*, p. 283   [22] Ibid., p. 130.
[23] Rosemary Lloyd, *Mallarmé: The Poet and His Circle* (Ithaca, NY: Cornell University Press, 1999), p. 179.

Author's Recommendation
Trois poèmes de Stéphane Mallarmé (1913).

Debussy first set a Mallarmé poem to music in 1894: this was 'Apparition', which is dedicated to Madame Vasnier. The first complete volume of Mallarmé's poetry was published in 1913, and in that year, quite independently, Debussy and Ravel chose three of his poems. Debussy's 'Soupir', 'Placet futile', and 'Éventail' for voice and piano are pared-back settings whose simplicity paradoxically gets to the heart of Mallarmé's famously recondite verse, and the first two make an interesting comparison with Ravel's contemporaneous settings for a larger ensemble. They are musically a world away from Debussy's imaginative, languorous orchestral evocation of Mallarmé's faun.

CHAPTER 15

Publishers

Denis Herlin

Although losing more and more ground to German firms in the 1880s, the large French music publishing houses, such as Hartmann, Heugel, Choudens, and Durand, played a predominant role in French musical life by distributing all kinds of music, from the most popular to the most learned, as well as numerous adaptations and transcriptions, for example when an opera or a work was a huge success. Apart from those publishing houses that dominated the French market, the Parisian market was teeming with small publishers. Before being supported by Georges Hartmann in 1894, the young Debussy tried to have his works published by all sorts of publishers, from the most prestigious such as Durand or Choudens to the least known such as Paul Dupont.

With the exception of the *mélodie* 'Nuit d'étoiles', Debussy's first work to be published by Bulla in 1882, the publication of the cantata *L'Enfant prodigue*, with which he won the Prix de Rome in 1884, really marked his entry into the world of music publishing. Thanks to the recommendation of his composition teacher at the Conservatoire, Ernest Guiraud, Durand-Schoenewerk agreed to publish his work in October 1884, as Jacques Durand recalls:

> My father, delighted with Debussy's success, told him, through Guiraud, that he would gladly publish *L'Enfant prodigue*.[1] This is how the author entered the publishing house of the place de la Madeleine: I see him, arriving in his father's office, with his score under his arm and accompanied by this good Guiraud. I don't know who, the teacher or the student, was more moved and joyful.[2]

This publishing house could have quickly become his exclusive publisher, especially since Jacques Durand, the son of Auguste Durand, one of the founders of the house, met the young musician at the Conservatoire, as the

---

[1] Contract, *Correspondance*, p. 17.
[2] Jacques Durand, *Quelques souvenirs d'un éditeur de musique* (Paris: Durand, 1924), p. 31.

latter records in his memoir. After having published the *Petite suite* for piano four hands (1890), *Deux arabesques* (1891), and three songs including 'Mandoline' (1890), the Durand publishing house also entrusted him between 1889 and 1891 with the transcription for piano four hands or two pianos of four works by Saint-Saëns (*Caprice pour piano sur les airs de ballet d'Alceste de Glück, Introduction et rondo capriccioso* Op. 28, the *Airs de ballet d'Étienne Marcel*, and the Symphony No. 2 in A minor Op. 55), as well as the overture to Wagner's *Der fliegende Holländer*, an opera for which Durand acquired the French rights, and Schumann's *Six études en forme de canon pour piano ou orgue à pédales* Op. 56.[3] This work did not delight him, as he confided to his friend Robert Godet in October 1889: 'Come on Wednesday, from 2 a.m.; I am busy until then with an arrangement of *Étienne-Marcel* (former city councillor) by the "so musical" Saint-Saëns. It's hard! Daily bread!'[4] Debussy ceased his relations with Durand Editions at the time of the publication of the String Quartet (1894). In a letter to Chausson in October 1893, he does not hide his bitterness at having sold it 'to the barbarians of the place de la Madeleine [the head office of the house Durand], 250 fl.!', and adds that Auguste and Jacques Durand had 'the cynicism to confess that they did not give [him] a sum proportionate to the work that "*œuvre*" represents'.[5]

But Durand was not the only publisher Debussy solicited after his return from Rome in March 1887. Having no doubt been refused the publication of several *mélodies*, he obtained from the widow Girod the publication of several such works: the six *Ariettes* (1888), 'Fleur des blés' (1891), and 'Beau soir' (1891). On the other hand, Debussy decided to publish the *Cinq poèmes de Ch. Baudelaire* (1890) on his own account and by subscription, no doubt because of the complexity of the music, which baffled the publishers, but also in order to have an edition that corresponded to his bibliophilic tastes: large format (37 x 28.5 cm); imitation parchment cover; titled in blue, gold, and brown; large margins; spaced engraving; blank pages introduced so that each song begins on a *belle page* (French printer's term for blank sheets introduced in such a way that, as here, each *mélodie* begins on the recto side of a new sheet).

If one draws up a chronological table of publications of Debussy's works, the years 1889, 1890, and 1891 are particularly rich. In addition to the works sold to Durand and the widow Girod already mentioned, the young

---

[3] Contracts, *Correspondance*, pp. 69, 89–90, 98–101. Debussy arranged Raff's *Humoresque* for the Hamelle publishing house.
[4] *Correspondance*, p. 79.   [5] *Correspondance*, pp. 165–6, 168–9.

musician also came into contact with Choudens, probably through the intermediary of the writer Catulle Mendès,[6] and in April 1890 gave him the rights to a large-scale work, the *Fantaisie* for piano and orchestra, which was never published during his lifetime, but of which the second and third proofs with the Choudens plate number (A.C. 8430) have been preserved.[7] He also entrusted him with several works for piano (*Marche écossaise* for piano four hands, *Rêverie, Ballade slave, Tarentelle styrienne*),[8] all published in 1891, as well as the *Suite bergamasque*, which was not published until 1905 by Fromont.[9] Curiously, a few months later, in August 1891, Debussy offered Hamelle, the publisher of many of Fauré's works, two of the piano pieces already given to Choudens (*Rêverie* and *Mazurka*) and *Trois mélodies de Paul Verlaine*, which the publisher did not publish until June 1901.[10] This carelessness can be attributed to the young musician's need for money and corresponds to the moment when the grant he had received for four years (from 1885 to 1888) from the Prix de Rome ceased. Finally, in 1892, he sold a *Nocturne* for piano to a small publisher, Paul Dupont.

Shortly before he ended his relationship with Durand, Debussy considered entrusting his new works to Edmond Bailly, whose Librairie de l'Art indépendant, founded in 1890, published young authors, notably André Gide, Paul Claudel, Pierre Louÿs, Henri de Régnier, etc. From its creation, the musician regularly visited this Symbolist bookshop on the rue de la Chaussée d'Antin, where he found a place that was conducive to his intellectual development. From 1893 onwards, Bailly began publishing music, starting with the song-piano reduction of Debussy's *La Damoiselle élue*. This publication is decorated with a splendid colour lithograph by the painter Maurice Denis and the stylised monogram of the composer, an interweaving of the capital letters of his two first names (Claude-Achille) and his surname. Opposite the title page is a list of works to be published by Bailly: *Prélude, interludes et paraphrase finale pour l'après-midi d'un faune* and the *Premier cahier de Proses lyriques*. However, neither of these works was to be published by the Librairie de l'Art indépendant. It was Chausson's Concert for Violin, Piano, and String Quartet Op. 21 that was to be the second in the series, which Bailly soon abandoned due to financial difficulties. Although the publishing

---

[6] Lesure (Rolf), p. 86.
[7] Contract, *Correspondance*, pp. 87–8; Denis Herlin, *Collection musicale François Lang* (Paris: Klincksieck, 1993), p. 53.
[8] Contract, *Correspondance*, pp. 94, 978.
[9] Contract, 21 February 1891, and letter to Mme Fromont, 21 April 1905, *Correspondance*, pp. 97, 903–4.
[10] Contract, *Correspondance*, pp. 101–2.

venture with Bailly satisfied Debussy's aesthetic requirements, he was aware that Bailly's publishing house was permanently on the verge of bankruptcy and that it could not guarantee a proper distribution of his works.

After the break with Durand and the defection of Bailly, Debussy met Georges Hartmann, probably at the end of 1893 or beginning of 1894. The son of a Bavarian umbrella merchant and representative of Schott in Paris, he had a reputation for supporting young French musicians, notably Georges Bizet, Saint-Saëns, César Franck, and above all Jules Massenet, almost all of whose operatic works he published, before Heugel bought out his collection after the liquidation of his publishing house for debt in 1891. However, he continued his musical activity using the name Eugène Fromont.[11] He sponsored Debussy's entry into the SACEM (Société des auteurs, compositeurs et éditeurs de musique) with André Messager in 1895 and wrote in October of the same year to Victor Souchon, the director of this establishment:

> My dear friend, in chatting so pleasantly with you this morning, I totally forgot to ask you to register me as editor of Debussy's *Prélude de l'après-midi d'un faune*, which Colonne is playing on Sunday at the Concerts du Châtelet, the former Concert National! ! ! I will try to launch this young author (Debussy, not Colonne!) and take all his works from him, on deposit only with Fromont.[12]

Having sensed Debussy's talent, he set about convincing Albert Carré and André Messager to stage *Pelléas et Mélisande* at the Opéra-Comique, which he did in 1898. From 1895 to 1901 Hartmann published Debussy's major works under the name Fromont, of which Hartmann retained ownership (there was, however, no contract between Hartmann and Debussy): *Proses lyriques* (1895), *Prélude à l'après-midi d'un faune* (1895), *Chansons de Bilitis* (1899), *Nocturnes* (1900), and *Pour le piano* (1901).[13] In addition, he endeavoured to buy back from Choudens all the works Debussy had given him. According to Lesure, Hartmann assured Debussy an annual income of 6,000 francs.[14] After the premiere of *Prélude à l'après-midi d'un faune* in December 1894 and the completion of a first version of *Pelléas et Mélisande* in August 1895, Debussy went through a period of doubt, which is reflected

---

[11] See Anik Devriès and François Lesure, *Dictionnaire des éditeurs de musique français* (Genève: Minkoff, 1988), pp. ii, 212.
[12] *Correspondance*, p. 297 n. 2.
[13] See Denis Herlin, 'An Artist High and Low, or Debussy and Money', in Elliott Antokoletz and Marianne Wheeldon (eds.), *Rethinking Debussy* (New York: Oxford University Press), pp. 171–2.
[14] François Lesure, *Claude Debussy: Biographie critique* (Paris: Fayard, 2002), p. 468.

in several of the eighty letters addressed to Hartmann between May 1895 and April 1900,[15] for example the one dated 31 December 1897:

> I can find a way of escaping extreme sadness at the end of this dreary year, a year in which I did almost nothing of what I wanted to do, and in making up my mind to send you my best wishes, I think of all the happiness that I have forfeited by not being able to live up to my expectations. ... However, you must know, once and for all, the true value I put in your friendship; please believe that in my worst moments it is a great comfort to be able to rely on it.[16]

After Hartmann's death on 22 April 1900, Debussy confided to Pierre Louÿs that 'he had been a providential person for me, and he played this part with a good grace and a good smile, quite rare among art philanthropists'.[17] As testimony of his immense gratitude to Hartmann, he dedicated two major scores to him: the three *Nocturnes* for orchestra (1901) and *Pelléas et Mélisande* (1902).

Following Hartmann's death, General Albert Bourjat, his executor, had to claim part of the advances made to Debussy. Unfortunately, there is no evidence to show how the negotiations between Debussy, Bourjat, and Fromont went exactly. Anyway, Fromont published *Pour le piano* (1901), which had been given to Hartmann; the *Suite bergamasque* (1905); and the first collection of *Fêtes galantes* (1903), three songs on poems by Verlaine. At the same time, following Debussy's success with *Pelléas et Mélisande* from April 1902 onwards, Fromont continued to expand his catalogue by buying the *Ariettes* from Girod (which Debussy revised for the occasion) and publishing them under the title *Ariettes oubliées* (1903) with a dedication to Mary Garden, the creator of the role of Mélisande. Fromont also reissued early piano works, much to Debussy's displeasure, as he told him in April 1905:

> You are wrong to publish the *Rêverie* ... It was an unimportant thing done in a hurry to do Hartmann a favour, in two words: it is bad! As for the transfer of *Pour le piano*, I will only do it on condition that I no longer hear about the *Mazurka*. I really have no taste for this kind of piece, especially at the moment.[18]

The transfer of *Pelléas et Mélisande* to Durand in March 1905, to which Debussy retained the rights, put an end to Debussy's relationship with Fromont.

---

[15] Only five letters from Hartmann to Debussy, written between September 1899 and April 1900, survive.
[16] *Correspondance*, p. 380.   [17] *Correspondance*, p. 557.   [18] *Correspondance*, pp. 904.

The success of *Pelléas et Mélisande* at the Opéra-Comique in 1902 gave Debussy the opportunity to approach the publisher Durand. In June 1902 they began to reissue the *Cinq poèmes de Ch. Baudelaire*, which the composer had published on his own account in 1890, and in October 1902 the song and piano version of *La Damoiselle élue*, which Edmond Bailly had published in 1893.[19] But it was above all the publication of *Estampes* in October 1903 that marked the renewal of relations between Jacques Durand and Debussy. This was followed in 1904 by a series of publications such as the *Trois chansons de France*; the second collection of *Fêtes galantes*; two pieces for piano, *L'Isle joyeuse* and *Masques*; *Danses sacrée et profane* for chromatic harp and string orchestra; and the signing of the contract for *La Mer*.[20] The links between Debussy and Durand were strengthened definitively in 1905, with the transfer of the rights to *Pelléas et Mélisande* on 31 March, which he was obliged to give up in order to pay for his divorce from Lilly Debussy, and with an exclusivity contract signed on 17 July, which included an arrangement whereby the Durand publishing house 'undertook to pay Madame [Lilly] Debussy, in the hands of her solicitor, and in the name of Monsieur Debussy, a monthly life annuity of four hundred francs'.[21] From that moment on, the two men became increasingly close friends, as Jacques Durand recalls:

> Debussy used to see me almost every day, either when he came to the publishing house or when I went to his house. We had a constant exchange of ideas ... If we couldn't see each other, correspondence worked. So I have ... some of the most interesting, even captivating letters. Debussy, on arriving at the office, always began by lighting his cigarette; then there were long and pleasant talks on art in general, and music in particular. He would often sit down at the piano, either to play me the manuscripts he brought me, or to sketch a fragment of the work in progress. I have already described his admirable mastery of touch. ... In his private life, Debussy was charming, playful, full of abandon. He was a great reader, had his own views on all things, and a very fine sense of the character of men. As soon as he found himself in society, he became concentrated, fearing to give himself up to anyone, preferring to follow his chimera than a general conversation. At heart, he was a tender man with a great passion. He was stingy with his friendship, but he was willing to count me among the few privileged ones; I am very proud of this.[22]

---

[19] *Correspondance*, p. 659.   [20] *Correspondance*, pp. 764, 842–3, 851–2, 856–7, 878.
[21] Denis Herlin, 'Debussy et l'argent', in Herlin, *Claude Debussy: Portraits et études* (Hildesheim: Olms, 2021), pp. 176–7.
[22] Durand, *Quelques souvenirs*, pp. 122–3, 125.

Of this important correspondence, both friendly and professional, three hundred and forty letters have survived, most of them written between 1902 and 1917. Although it is regrettable that only three letters from Durand to Debussy have been preserved, the fact remains that of Debussy's 2,581 published letters, the correspondence with his publishers Hartmann and Debussy predominates, accounting for almost a fifth of the epistolary exchanges. This correspondence reveals both the daily life of a composer and the portrait of an era. The question of money is intertwined with the sincere friendship between them, as Debussy was unable to get out of an increasing spiral of debts from 1910, a few years after his marriage to Emma Bardac. At the time of his death, the deficit in Debussy's account amounted to a hefty 66,235 francs. This was due to the payment for *Le Diable dans le beffroi*, an opera based on a libretto by Poe which Debussy did not compose and for which Durand paid the princely sum of 24,000 francs. The second and main reason is the monthly pension paid to Lilly Debussy-Texier. As a note in Durand's hand states:

> There was never any difference between the manuscripts given and the pension paid. The manuscripts were always paid in full in cash. We even added payments for works in progress and for manuscripts that were never handed over (*Le Diable dans le beffroi*). Hence an overdraft formed by the pension.[23]

Nevertheless, Debussy showed his gratitude to the Durands by dedicating *Printemps* (1904) to Jacques' father, Auguste, *La Mer* to Jacques himself in 1905, and *Jeux* to his wife in 1913.

Author's Recommendation

Nocturnes (1899).

The *Nocturnes*, dedicated to Georges Hartmann, turn symphonic writing on its head. If the *Prélude à l'après-midi d'un faune* introduced flexibility into orchestral music, the *Nocturnes* play with sound masses and spatialisation, especially in 'Nuages', where the sound masses increase or decrease, like the march of the clouds in the sky, or in the middle part of 'Fêtes', where the distant fanfare comes closer and closer, as if it were marching before our eyes and ears. As for 'Sirènes', this piece, which Debussy revised several times, marks the attempt to use the voice as an orchestral timbre.

---

[23] Paris, Durand Archives.

CHAPTER 16

Composers with Whom Debussy Was Associated
Laura Watson

Debussy was associated with various French composers, whose work stylistically spanned nineteenth-century tradition to the twentieth-century avant-garde. This chapter explores his connections with Ernest Guiraud, Ernest Chausson, Camille Saint-Saëns, Gabriel Fauré, Paul Dukas, and Erik Satie. It assesses key issues in each setting. Various relationships are represented here: the student-teacher archetype, less formalised mentorship, peer friendships, the more distant collegial relationship, and sometimes adversarial exchanges. Debussy and these composers engaged with each other in multiple ways: dynamics shifted such that the student became the teacher; a distant figure became a colleague; a peer became a critic. Studying these relationships casts new light on Debussy and the other parties.

Ernest Guiraud (1837–1892)

Debussy's composition teacher at the Paris Conservatoire was born in New Orleans, Louisiana, to French parents: a piano-virtuoso mother and a father who had won the Prix de Rome. Jean-Baptiste Guiraud pursued conducting opportunities at the Théâtre d'Orléans, a venue which proved a formative influence on his son. The young Ernest probably attended its US premieres of French operas by Auber, Halévy, and others. Here, at the age of fifteen, he witnessed the performance of his first opera, *David*. Emigrating to Paris in 1854, he assisted Berlioz with rehearsals for *L'Enfance du Christ* and enrolled at the Conservatoire. Prix de Rome success followed in 1859. Nowadays, he is mostly remembered for contributing recitatives to Bizet's *Carmen* (1875) and completing Offenbach's *Les Contes d'Hoffmann* (1881).

16 Composers with Whom Debussy Was Associated

He was a respected composer in the 1870s and 1880s. His *Suite d'orchestre* (1872) broke the German stranglehold on the Concerts populaires.[1] The *Suite* and symphonic poem *Chasse fantastique* (1887) count among his few recorded works. His final opera, the unfinished *Frédégonde*, was completed and orchestrated by Saint-Saëns and Dukas for performance in 1895. Unlike its predecessors, *Frédégonde* is Wagnerian. An expansive five-act work, this legend-inspired music drama even calls for a soprano to perform the role of Brunhilda. Guiraud's new-found interest in Wagner developed in proximity to his association with Debussy.

Guiraud started teaching composition at his alma mater in 1880; Debussy joined the class the same year and won the Prix de Rome in 1884. His Wagnerism initially confounded his teacher, who expressed mixed views of his experiences at Bayreuth in 1876 and 1882.[2] Around 1889, Guiraud began *Frédégonde*.[3] It was hardly unusual for a French composer to submit to Wagner's influence then, but Guiraud's conversion was more profound. By 1890 he had evidently concluded that Wagner was central to the history of musical style. This realignment of values must partly be attributed to Debussy, with whom he regularly discussed Wagner. The shift in mindset first became apparent when Guiraud's *Traité pratique d'instrumentation* appeared in 1890. This orchestration manual gives insights into what Debussy (and others) learned from Guiraud in the early 1880s and implies that the novice-teacher dynamic bent so that the professor became receptive to learning from his student.

The *Traité* features ninety notated examples. Most draw on classical tradition and the *grand opéra* Guiraud discovered at the Théâtre d'Orléans (e.g. Auber's *Le Domino noir*, Halévy's *La Reine de Chypre* and *La Juive*). Wagner appears too, though, and is prominent in the appendix. This comprises eight excerpts illustrating 'the principal transformations [of the orchestra] accomplished in a space of nearly three hundred years': it commences with a passage from Monteverdi's *Orfeo*, then cites Lully's *Psyché*, Rameau's *Acanthe et Céphise* Overture, Mozart's 'Paris' Symphony No. 31, Beethoven's Symphony No. 9, Rossini's *William Tell* Overture, Berlioz's *Carnaval romain*, and, finally, *Götterdämmerung* Act III.[4] What is remarkable here is not so much the inclusion of Wagner but the context. Only a few years earlier Guiraud had been startled by Debussy's argument

---

[1] Daniel O. Weilbaecher, 'Ernest Guiraud: A Biography and Catalogue of Works', DMA thesis, Louisiana State University (1990), p. 61.
[2] Ibid., pp. 82–4   [3] Ibid., p. 113.
[4] Ernest Guiraud, *Traité pratique d'instrumentation* (Paris: A. Durand & fils, 1890), p. 191.

that Wagner's innovations were rooted in classical tradition.[5] By 1890, however, he was persuaded of it, structuring his appendix to position Wagner as a natural step in and the apex of the evolution of European music. That a new appreciation of Wagner ran deeper than orchestration is evidenced in the trajectory of Guiraud's opera career, which concluded with *Frédégonde*. The *Traité*, reprinted often over the next forty years, became a core text for Conservatoire students. Ironically, within a few years of its publication, Debussy was rethinking Wagnerism.

Ernest Chausson (1855–1899)

Debussy's Wagnerism weakened as his friendship with Chausson deepened. Debussy fondly regarded this composer 'like a big older brother in whom one has complete confidence'.[6] Seven years his senior, Chausson played the role of responsible elder sibling in a few ways: he sourced accompaniment jobs to assist Debussy financially and invited him to network at gatherings of artists, writers, and musicians. If Debussy then was a young rebel who rejected tradition and association with groups of composers, Chausson usually fulfilled social expectations and upheld norms of the Parisian music world. Having studied with Franck, he was part of the loyal *bande à Franck*. Elected secretary of the Société nationale de musique in 1886, he became further aligned with Franck (the new president) and Wagnerians such as d'Indy. Chausson admired Debussy's independence but remained committed to the musical establishment and sought opportunities for composers (himself included) to establish new voices within that framework.

The friendship was also defined by a shared concern with *déwagnérisation*. Chausson, who had once idolised the Bayreuth composer, articulated this goal in 1886, when he began the opera *Le Roi Arthus*.[7] Correspondence between him and Debussy years later shows it was a slow process. In 1893 Debussy advised: 'I would like to see you lose your preoccupation with "hidden depths"; ... we have been led into that by the same old R. Wagner'.[8] Chausson responded that the third act of his opera was 'becoming clear and de-Wagnerised'.[9] What was once an open,

---

[5] Weilbaecher, 'Ernest Guiraud', p. 114.
[6] Jean Pierre Barricelli and Leo Weinstein, *Ernest Chausson: The Composer's Life and Works* (Norman, OK: University of Oklahoma Press, 1955), p. 64.
[7] Mark Seto, 'Ernest Chausson's *Viviane*, "Déwagnérisation", and the Problem of Descriptive Music', *19th-Century Music* 41 (2017), p. 49.
[8] Letter to Chausson, 23 October 1893, *Correspondance*, p. 167.
[9] Letter from Chausson to Debussy, 12 November 1893, *Correspondance*, p. 174.

supportive relationship deteriorated by 1894, though. A letter from Debussy laments tensions between them: 'I find the exile from your friendship very long.'[10] Further hurt by Chausson's remarks on his String Quartet, he retaliated: 'You do not let yourself go enough . . . you enervate yourself in useless struggles.'[11]

Before this difference of opinion, they had pursued similar 'de-Wagnerised' or post-Wagnerian paths. Debussy began *Pelléas et Mélisande* in 1893, the same year Chausson reported his breakthrough with *Le Roi Arthus*. They were mutually enthusiastic about Symbolist writers. Chausson's *mélodies* included settings of Maeterlinck's *Serres chaudes* (1893–6), which Debussy praised as 'little dramas'.[12] Their compositional timeline parallels that of *Pelléas* drafts. Further reflecting shared sensitivities, in September 1893 Debussy sought his friend's opinion on a completed *Pelléas* scene.[13] Meanwhile, the vocal writing of Chausson's opera preserved 'the natural inflections of [French] speech'[14] (as *Pelléas* does); it also resembles *Pelléas* with orchestral writing that sometimes 'speaks more clearly than texted music'.[15] Posthumously premiered in 1903, *Le Roi Arthus* has had few revivals. Still, its development in the late 1880s and early 1890s marks its composer as a progressive, even though he operated within the more traditional parameters of his musical world.

Camille Saint-Saëns (1835–1921)

Two other Société nationale stalwarts in Debussy's milieu were Saint-Saëns and Fauré. Tensions with Saint-Saëns dated to 1886 when he denounced Debussy's musical explorations of 'the bizarre, the incomprehensible, the unplayable'.[16] Their conflict escalated in the early 1900s, with Debussy using his platform as a critic to respond, occasionally with personal taunts: 'Is there no one who likes Saint-Saëns enough to tell him that he's written enough music and would be better employed in his lately acquired vocation of explorer?'[17] In 1911, a survey of French composers on text and music prompted a response from Saint-Saëns which reads as an attack on *Pelléas et Mélisande*. French prose, he claimed, was 'anti-musical': its 'light

---

[10] Letter to Chausson, 5 February 1894, *Correspondance*, p. 192.
[11] Letter to Chausson, 5 February 1894, *Correspondance*, p. 193.
[12] Barricelli and Weinstein, *Ernest Chausson*, p. 122.
[13] Letter to Chausson, 3 September 1893, *Correspondance*, p. 156.
[14] Barricelli and Weinstein, *Ernest Chausson*, p. 198. [15] Seto, 'Ernest Chausson's *Viviane*', p. 51.
[16] Brian Rees, *Camille Saint-Saëns: A Life* (London: Faber and Faber, 2012), p. 13
[17] Robert Orledge, *Debussy and the Theatre* (Cambridge: Cambridge University Press, 2009), p. 287.

stresses ... frequent hiatuses ... and series of weak syllables deprive it of the rhythm and sonority which music requires'. Thus, its musical use was 'a regression and a heresy. The success of some recent works cannot modify my opinion.'[18]

Four years later, he condemned *En blanc et noir* as an 'atrocity' and campaigned to bar Debussy from the Institut de France. Saint-Saëns's violent rhetoric likened his colleague to a wartime enemy.[19] His disingenuous accusation minimised their shared values. Like Saint-Saëns, Debussy was preoccupied with French sensibility, with Rameau central to his historical imagination.[20] Both men had contributed to the Rameau *Œuvres complètes*, with Debussy preparing a new edition of *Les Fêtes de Polymnie* (1908). He acknowledged Saint-Saëns as important too, but whereas he associated Rameau with the contemporary renewal of French style, he felt Saint-Saëns had little to offer. In *Gil Blas* he lamented that his colleague had 'lost the respect of all those young people who counted ardently on him to open new paths, to satisfy their longing for freedom'.[21] In the 1860s, though, Saint-Saëns had introduced the progressive ideas of Schumann, Liszt, and Wagner to students such as Fauré.

Gabriel Fauré (1845–1924)

Fauré's friendship with his former teacher may have precluded closeness with Debussy. Another personal complication was his affair with singer Emma Bardac before she met and married Debussy. Divergent musical goals and professional trajectories contributed to a 'cautiously polite' relationship.[22] Although they shared an affinity for renewal and sincerity, Fauré strove to refine and perfect melodic and harmonic expression.[23] Debussy, as Dukas put it, *extended* harmonic principles beyond familiar recognition.[24]

---

[18] Peter Low, 'French Words and Music a Century Ago: Composers' Responses to a 1911 Survey', *Fontes Artis Musicae* 52 (2005), pp. 166–7.
[19] Glenn Watkins, *Proof through the Night: Music and the Great War* (Berkeley, CA: University of California Press, 2003), p. 92.
[20] Anya Suschitzky, 'Debussy's Rameau: French Music and Its Others', *The Musical Quarterly* 86 (2002), pp. 398–448.
[21] Rees, *Camille Saint-Saëns*, p. 15.
[22] Graham Johnson, *Gabriel Fauré: The Songs and Their Poets* (Abingdon: Routledge, 2016), p. 244.
[23] Carlo Caballero, *Fauré and French Musical Aesthetics* (Cambridge: Cambridge University Press, 2001), p. 147.
[24] Laura Watson, *Paul Dukas: Composer and Critic* (Woodbridge: Boydell and Brewer, 2019), p. 148.

16 Composers with Whom Debussy Was Associated

Fauré and Debussy also differed in attitudes towards education and leadership. Fauré directed the Paris Conservatoire from 1905 to 1920. Debussy, in contrast, told an interviewer in 1911: 'Don't believe . . . that I want to position myself as the head of a school or reformer!'[25] Fauré's appointment intrinsically rendered him such an authority figure. *Le Figaro* declared him a 'fine example' for students.[26] *Le Ménestrel* detailed his nine main curricular reforms.[27] Enshrining the study of the past as integral to a creative education, Fauré made the music history class mandatory for composition and harmony students. Despite Debussy's aversion to associating with any 'school', from 1909 he became directly, albeit peripherally, involved when appointed to the Conservatoire's Conseil supérieur. In this post he composed competition pieces and served on juries. Whereas Fauré systematically reconsidered Conservatoire pedagogies, Debussy was content to focus on how the clarinettists performed his *Rapsodie*.[28]

Paul Dukas (1865–1935)

Dukas was another alumnus who welcomed Fauré's overhaul. Three years younger than Debussy, he had experienced a similar, almost ritualistic Conservatoire training: teachers who disapproved of Wagner, composition studies with Guiraud, and several (albeit unsuccessful) attempts to win the Prix de Rome. Dukas and Debussy, lifelong friends since the 1880s, paralleled each other in their professional lives too: both composed, critiqued, and edited. Apart from their early Wagnerian phases, neither subscribed to artistic or institutional dogma; they cherished their independence instead. Each composed landmark symphonic poems in the 1890s (*Prélude à l'après-midi d'un faune*, 1894, and *L'Apprenti sorcier*, 1897), produced operatic adaptations of Maeterlinck in the early 1900s (*Pelléas et Mélisande*, 1902, and *Ariane et Barbe-Bleue*, 1907), and participated in a commemorative Haydn commission (1910). They both collaborated with the Ballets Russes (*Jeux*, 1913, and *La Péri*, 1912), although a dispute with Diaghilev saw Dukas's *Péri* staged in Natasha Trouhanova's Concerts de danse instead. Apart from ballet, where Dukas conceptualised an original synthesis of music, dance, and drama for his 'poème dansé', Debussy tended to lead Dukas by a few years. Dukas was open to learning

---

[25] Georges Delaquys, 'La Pensée d'un grand musicien: M. Claude Debussy nous confie ses projets et nous dit ses espoirs', *Excelsior* 18 (January 1911), p. 7.
[26] André Nède, 'Le Nouveau Directeur du Conservatoire', *Le Figaro* (14 June 1905), p. 4.
[27] Arthur Pougin, 'Les Réformes au Conservatoire', *Le Ménestrel* (1 October 1905), p. 316.
[28] Eric Frederick Jensen, *Debussy* (New York: Oxford University Press, 2014), pp. 88–9.

from his innovations. In addition to quoting the 'Mélisande' motif when the 1902 protagonist appears in *Ariane*, he adopted a similar approach to vocal writing, often using subtle accompanied recitative to convey the impression of natural conversation between characters.[29]

Nonetheless, Dukas remained an independent artist with a distinct sense of purpose. His critical career was pivotal to this. Whereas Debussy arrived at *La Revue blanche* in 1901 an established composer, Dukas was hired as a *Revue hebdomadaire* columnist in 1892, five years before he made an impact with *L'Apprenti sorcier* and his Symphony in C.[30] His substantive reviews and topical essays testify to an authoritative understanding of historical and contemporary European musical thought. Unlike Debussy, who had little interest in educating, Dukas made it his mission to synthesise and transmit knowledge in ways that empowered others. For lay audiences, he explained and contextualised music. In the same articles he urged fellow composers to prize originality and sincerity. Critics who barely grasped but objected to new ideas were schooled in their errors (notably, in his *Pelléas* review). Later, Dukas instructed formally, teaching orchestration at the Paris Conservatoire (1909–14), then composition at the École normale and the Conservatoire (from 1926 and 1928 respectively, until his death). He encouraged the 'individual creative character of each student' while also developing their repertoire knowledge and 'taste'.[31] This pedagogical approach reflected Dukas's artistic philosophy: his internalisation and critique of tradition provided fertile ground for cultivating an independent new voice.

Erik Satie (1866–1925)

Debussy knew Satie for almost as long as he had known Dukas, but Orledge's evaluations of the Debussy–Satie personal and professional relationship reveal a different dynamic.[32] Satie's unconventional career left him on the peripheries of concert life and dependent on figures such

---

[29] Laura Watson, 'Fifty Shades of Bluebeard? Dukas's *Ariane et Barbe-Bleue* in the Twenty-First Century', *Twentieth-Century Music* 15 (2018), pp. 399–438.
[30] Laura Watson, 'Dukas, Critical Conversations, and Intellectual Legacies', in Helen Julia Minors and Laura Watson (eds.), *Paul Dukas: Legacies of a French Musician* (Abingdon: Routledge, 2019), pp. 17–37.
[31] Christopher Brent Murray, 'The Dukas Composition Class at the Paris Conservatoire', in Minors and Watson (eds.), *Paul Dukas*, p. 115.
[32] Robert Orledge, *Satie the Composer* (Cambridge: Cambridge University Press, 1990); Orledge, 'Debussy and Satie', in Richard Langham Smith (ed.), *Debussy Studies* (Cambridge: Cambridge University Press, 1997), pp. 154–78.

as Debussy for networking. When recognition arrived in 1911, he sensed his friend's jealousy.[33] In 1917 they stopped speaking and only reconciled at Debussy's deathbed. That dispute casts Debussy in a new light – painting him as a member of the old guard instead of the iconoclast that emerges when he is compared to Guiraud, Chausson, Fauré, Saint-Saëns, and even Dukas. Recalling how Debussy once regarded Chausson like a big brother, Orledge characterises Debussy and Satie as 'artistic brothers' but with the former assuming a dominant, quasi-paternalistic role.[34] Satie's *Parade*, however, prompted him to withdraw support. His disapproval of the work began at rehearsals, to Satie's deep irritation. 'Tiresome teasing, and repeated over and over. Really! Quite unbearable', the *Parade* composer complained to Emma Debussy.[35]

Nor did Debussy reconsider his position after the 18 May 1917 premiere, which featured on the first Ballets Russes wartime programme. The audience proved hostile too, with *Parade*'s gunshots and sirens jolting them back to a reality from which they had sought reprieve.[36] Sound effects were only part of the provocation: Cocteau's scenario, animated by Satie's burlesque score and Picasso's cubist production, essentially transformed the theatre into a circus. Wheeldon contrasts *Parade*'s reception with the enthusiasm weeks earlier for Debussy's Violin Sonata, a work which accorded with the 'new cultural conservativism' of wartime Paris.[37] Its 'pure' style was opposed to *Parade*'s experimentalism. Satie's score presented radical sonorities that reflected the work's collaborative nature, embracing the dissonance of music and extra-musical noise. His assertion that 'painters ... taught me the most about music' is born out in blocks of sound that suggest cubism's structural influence.[38] This visual aesthetic contributed to his boundary-breaking inter-art practice, which eventually encompassed cinema (his music for *Entr'acte*, 1924).

By 1922, Satie viewed his conflict with Debussy as having signalled the beginning of a deeper artistic divergence. 'And to think that if he were still alive, we would today be the worst of enemies. ... We were no longer on the same road.'[39] Unlike other composers with whom Debussy had been associated, Satie was an avant-gardist who drove a post-1918 generation in radical new directions.

---

[33] Orledge, *Satie the Composer*, p. 59 [34] Orledge, *Satie the Composer*, p. 40.
[35] Lesure (Rolf), p. 333. [36] See Pierre Lalo, 'La Musique', *Le Temps* (28 May 1917), p. 3.
[37] Marianne Wheeldon, *Debussy's Late Style* (Bloomington, IN: Indiana University Press, 2009), p. 10.
[38] Simon Shaw-Miller, '"The Only Musician with Eyes": Erik Satie and Visual Art', in Caroline Potter (ed.), *Erik Satie: Music, Art, Literature* (Aldershot: Ashgate, 2016), pp. 92, 107.
[39] Orledge, *Satie the Composer*, p. 67.

Author's Recommendation
Jeux: Poème dansé (1913).

Debussy's 'danced poem' subtitle for *Jeux* (Games) is likely inspired by Dukas's original use of this term (related to the symphonic poem) to conceptualise his 1912 ballet *La Péri*. Appropriate to its subtitle, Debussy's work is imbued with an ever-shifting sense of movement, created through an episodic form which, in turn, as Jann Pasler observes, is rendered coherent by the composer's attention to rhythmic detail as an organising structure. *Jeux* doubled as a vehicle for Ballets Russes star Vaslav Nijinsky. The scenario about tennis 'games' between three players culminates in a 'triple kiss'. Its erotic charge is underscored by the music's timbral sensuality.

CHAPTER 17

Music Education and the Prix de Rome

Julia Lu and Kenji Fujimura

In the *Dictionnaire des professions* published in Paris in 1880, the entry on 'musicians' marvelled that 'in no other era has the art of music been more respected and lucrative than today'.[1] The cult of the virtuosi, as epitomised by the likes of Chopin and Liszt, and the extraordinary popularity of operatic heavyweights from Meyerbeer to Verdi, had no doubt catapulted music into the echelon of desirable occupations and seduced generations of young hopefuls to seek the path to Parnassus.

The allure was perhaps doubly attractive for those from humble economic backgrounds such as the Debussys, although in Achille's case his early encounters with music were nothing short of serendipitous. In 1870, Achille's aunt Clémentine paid for his first piano lessons while the young boy sought refuge with her in Cannes during the Franco-Prussian War. Although lessons lapsed after his return to Paris the following year, it was not long before fate intervened once again and Achille was introduced to his second piano teacher and socialite Antoinette Mauté de Fleurville, thanks to an unlikely connection made by his father while a Communard prisoner. Recognising the young boy's talent and offering to teach him for free, Mauté insisted that 'he must become a musician'.[2]

To become a musician, of course, required years of practice and training. Just how accessible was music education in France? What opportunities were available to aspiring musicians during their formative years? It is no secret that Debussy struggled with the education system he experienced, often on the brink of being expelled while a student at the Paris Conservatoire. Yet was this symptomatic of a failing system or reflective of a unique personal temperament? Was his experience the norm or the exception? To answer these questions, we must trace the common path trodden by many pupils of

---

[1] Édouard Charton (ed.), *Dictionnaire des professions, ou Guide pour le choix d'un État*, 3rd ed. (Paris: Hachette, 1880), p. 367.
[2] Louis Laloy, *Claude Debussy* (Paris: Les Bibliophiles fantaisistes, 1909), p. 11.

music, illuminate the opportunities and challenges along the way, and compare the varied responses to that rite of passage.

A Head Start in Life: Rudimentary Music Lessons

Much like today, rudimentary music lessons in Debussy's time were mostly offered in the form of private or small-group tuition by individual teachers. Advertisements for music lessons can be found in many magazines of the day, and teachers with a prestigious pedigree, such as those from the Paris Conservatoire, were highly regarded and sought after.[3] Additionally, lessons that were comprehensive, well structured, and based on reputable method books were deemed highly desirable. For example, in one advertisement by a Mademoiselle Dupré, solfège and piano methods by Édouard Batiste, Henri Valiquet, Félix Cazot, Antoine Marmontel, and Camille Stamaty were painstakingly listed as being a part of the curriculum.[4] In another announcement, the celebrated pianist and composer Wilhelm Krüger was said to be offering a 'complete music education course' comprising solfège, piano, elementary and practical harmony, and accompaniment – taught by no fewer than five different teachers at Krüger's residence.[5]

As can be expected, music education was an activity reserved for the more affluent, since the cost of a lesson could equal that of a day's wage for the working class. For example, in 1870 the lesson fee for the pianist-composer Georges Pfeiffer, a partner in the piano firm Pleyel, Wolff & Cie and a well-known musician in the Parisian circle, was 20 francs per month for four piano lessons and 15 francs per month for eight solfège lessons.[6] A total of 35 francs a month was no small outlay in the second half of the nineteenth century, particularly for families of limited means. The costs were even higher if one considers the expenses of purchasing or renting an instrument and the ongoing costs of acquiring sheet music. To put it in context, the average income for a male worker in 1871 was 4.99 francs a day and the average cost of living for a single person from the working class was between 70 and 100 francs per month.[7] Since living

---

[3] See, for example, the 'annoncement' regarding Mademoiselle Anaïs Roulle in *Le Ménestrel* 40 (8 November 1874), p. 391.
[4] *Le Ménestrel* 36 (25 April 1869), p. 167. [5] *La France musicale* 33 (31 October 1869), p. 348.
[6] *Le Ménestrel* 37 (8 October 1870), p. 360.
[7] Emile Chevallier, *Les Salaires au XIXe Siècle* (Paris: Librairie nouvelle de droit et de jurisprudence, 1887), p. 42; Gabriel-Paul-Othenin d'Haussonville, *La Vie et les salaires à Paris* (Paris: Imprimerie de A. Quantin, 1883), p. 24.

costs would increase with every child in the family, music tuition would have been an unnecessary luxury for many of the working class.

Fortunately for Debussy, Madame Mauté taught him piano free of charge – a blessing given his impoverished background.[8] By comparison, many of Debussy's friends and contemporaries enjoyed more favourable circumstances that helped to support their musical studies. For example, Gabriel Pierné (1863–1937), Xavier Leroux (1863–1919), Augustin Savard (1861–1942), and Edmond Missa (1861–1910) came from musical families, where their earliest music instruction was from their own parents.[9] Others such as Paul Dukas (1865–1935), Ernest Chausson (1855–99), and Georges Hüe (1858–1948) issued from affluent households where music education would have been an indispensable element of good upbringing.

While early advantage in music education did not guarantee career success as a musician, it could nevertheless tip the scales in favour of those who had access to the best teachers and networks. In 1872, at the age of ten, Debussy was admitted into the Paris Conservatoire under the guidance of Madame Mauté. This was to be a life-changing moment for the son of a poor shopkeeper, even if it would be many years before Debussy would make his mark on the world.

Cachet de Distinction: The Paris Conservatoire

For any student with serious intent of pursuing music as a career, the Paris Conservatoire was naturally the top school of choice. Long regarded as the premier music institution in France, the Conservatoire was not only known for having the best teachers, it also attracted the best students. Such was its appeal that applicants had been known to fake their age in order to gain admission, and musicians falsely claimed affiliation with the institution in order to advance their careers.[10]

Given the prestige of the Conservatoire, one would perhaps expect a fairly high rejection rate for admissions. However, in 1872, the year when Debussy was admitted, 38 per cent of all applicants were accepted. This figure stood even higher a decade earlier, at an astonishing 55 per cent. It was not until the end of the nineteenth century that the admission rate

---

[8] Eric Frederick Jensen, *Debussy* (New York: Oxford University Press, 2014), pp. 7–8.
[9] Julia Lu, 'The Prix de Rome Competition: Success, Failure, or Prophet?', Master of Music dissertation, University of Melbourne (2002), pp. 125–7.
[10] Constant Pierre, 'Le Conservatoire national de musique', *La Revue musicale* 3 (15 July 1903), pp. 314–15.

dropped to about 20 per cent, as the number of applicants increased exponentially.[11]

To be accepted into the Conservatoire, applicants had to be between nine and twenty-two years of age.[12] It was customary for students to audition for entry into the instrumental or voice class of a particular teacher, and to complete fundamental subjects such as solfège and aural harmony before applying for admission into more advanced classes such as written harmony and composition.[13] As the curriculum was wholly devoted to music education, instructions in literacy and numeracy were expected to be sought elsewhere. For those from poor families, such as Debussy, it meant that these were sometimes entirely absent.

The length of time a student spent studying at the Conservatoire was dependent upon their progress. As tuition at the Conservatoire was free for all students, only those who showed the most promise were permitted to continue their studies. This was enforced through a rigorous *concours* system, which became an obsession for both students and teachers alike. Not being admitted to compete due to an insufficient standard, or performing worse in a competition compared to that of the previous year, could spell the end of a candidate's time at the Conservatoire.[14]

In many ways, Debussy's progression through the Conservatoire was rather typical. Admitted as a ten-year-old, he spent the next twelve years honing his musical craft. Others, including Pierné, Georges Bizet, and Jules Massenet, followed a similar path, entering the Conservatoire at a young age and crowning their studies a decade or so later by winning the Prix de Rome. But it can be said that they were the luckier ones. For those who lived in the provinces and with limited financial means, the prospect of studying at the Conservatoire depended not just on gaining admission but also on being able to afford the high costs of living in the nation's capital. Gustave Charpentier (1860–1956), for example, had to work at a spinning mill until the age of eighteen, when fortunes reversed and benefactors made possible his studies in Lille and Paris.[15]

What was perhaps more unusual about Debussy's experience at the Conservatoire was his clear disdain for the place and the strained relationships he had with his teachers and fellow students. He often portrayed the institution as hidebound and conservative, a place 'where the dust of bad

---

[11] Constant Pierre, *Le Conservatoire national de musique et de déclamation* (Paris: Imprimerie nationale, 1900), pp. 874–5.
[12] There were occasional exceptions; see ibid., p. 258. [13] Ibid., p. 874. [14] Ibid., p. 259.
[15] Françoise Andrieux, *Gustave Charpentier: Lettres inédites à ses parents* (Paris: Presses universitaires de France, 1984), pp. 11–14.

traditions sticks to one's fingers'.[16] Yet his experience was a far cry from those of many Conservatoire graduates, who recalled their alma mater with much fondness. Massenet, for example, was so attached to the Conservatoire that he undertook a daring escapade from the country where his father was recovering from illness and travelled back to Paris alone, at the mere age of fourteen: 'I escaped ... and started for Paris without a sou or even a change of clothes. For Paris, the city with every artistic attraction, where I should see again my dear Conservatoire, my masters ... for the memory of them was still with me.'[17]

A Worldly Education: The Prix de Rome

In a music education system dominated by *concours* and prizes, the most coveted of them all was no doubt the Prix de Rome for composition. Awarded annually by the Institut de France since 1803, it offered winners a generous four-year scholarship valued at approximately 3,500 francs per annum.[18] Laureates typically spent the first two years living at the Villa Medici in Rome, the third year travelling throughout Germany and Austria, and the fourth year back in France.

For students of composition, the rewards of the Prix de Rome must have seemed irresistible. Not only did winning the prize promise accolade and recognition, in practical terms it also allowed laureates to buy time by avoiding conscription and to further hone their craft.[19] After all, imagine a young, aspiring composer nearing the end of their Conservatoire musical training. They are at once hopeful and fearful of their future. What will they do once they have left the safe harbour of the Conservatoire? How will they make their name known to the public? Will they ever come close to experiencing the fame enjoyed by their *maîtres*? Winning the Prix de Rome provided temporary financial security while laureates sought to find their compositional voice and establish their name. Unsurprisingly, many regarded winning the prize as a matter of 'life and death' for their careers.[20]

Unlike studies at the Conservatoire, what the Prix de Rome offered was a kind of real-world education, where laureates broadened their horizons

---

[16] Denis Herlin, 'An Artist High and Low, or Debussy and Money', in Elliott Antokoletz and Marianne Wheeldon (eds.), *Rethinking Debussy* (New York: Oxford University Press, 2011), p. 150.
[17] Jules Massenet, *My Recollections*, trans. H. Villiers Barnett (Boston, MA: Small, Maynard & Company, 1919), p. 15.
[18] *Académie des Beaux-Arts: Statuts et règlements* (Paris: Firmin Didot, 1873), pp. 148–50.
[19] Charles Gounod, *Autobiographical Reminiscences*, trans. W. Hely Hutchinson (New York: Da Capo, 1970), p. 41.
[20] Gounod, *Autobiographical Reminiscences*, pp. 44–5.

through travelling and self-education. It was often the first time a young artist had travelled abroad independently, leaving behind the support network of families and friends. The life of a laureate was a curious assortment of travel adventures, high-society engagements, juvenile amusements, and youthful *ennui*. As can be seen in Pierné's letters to his parents, the marvels of witnessing the extraordinary foreign lands and artworks filled his head with inspiration.[21] The endless invitations to socialise with locals, visitors, and expats in Rome offered great opportunities for meeting the affluent and the influential. By contrast, life with fellow Prix de Rome laureates at the Villa was never short of mischief and buffoonery, as one would expect from young men in their late teens and twenties. Then there were the moments of quiet solitude, or as Pierné described, 'My God it's a great place to compose!'[22]

Critics of the Prix de Rome have often questioned the purpose of sending composers to Rome, since Paris was widely regarded as the musical capital of Europe. However, the tenet of the Prix de Rome had always been about the benefits of a worldly education. As Camille Saint-Saëns said to departing Prix de Rome laureates in 1901:

> You are happy to leave school; but, believe me, your studies have not finished: they are only just beginning. You will learn the 'grand' education, one that each must one day give oneself. Like a bee which tastes all the flowers for making its honey, you will study all the styles, make your choice, and the materials that you collect along the way will help to build your own style.[23]

Unsurprisingly, the value of the Prix de Rome 'education' depended a great deal on personal temperament and circumstance. It is no secret that both Debussy and Hector Berlioz detested their Rome sojourn, not least because of the inevitable separation from their beloveds. For an introvert like Debussy, communal living at the Villa Medici must have also seemed unsettling, particularly if one did not make friends with ease. However, for most Prix de Rome laureates, their Rome sojourn was one of happy memories. In his *Souvenirs*, Charles Gounod recalled his 'grief at quitting the Academy [Villa Medici]', where he spent 'two happy years'.[24] Similarly, Georges Bizet noted how much he 'loved' Rome and how he had 'never

---

[21] Gabriel Pierné, *Correspondance romaine*, ed. Cyril Bongers (Lyon: Symétrie, 2005), p. 29.
[22] Pierné, *Correspondance romaine*, p. 51.
[23] Camille Saint-Saëns, 'Discours', in Marie-Gabrielle Soret (ed.), *Camille Saint-Saëns: Écrits sur la musique et les musiciens, 1870–1921* (Paris: Vrin, 2012), p. 563.
[24] Gounod, *Autobiographical Reminiscences*, p. 95.

cried so much' upon leaving the city.[25] Pierné, who arrived in Rome two years before Debussy, described 'choking back tears' during his last supper at the Villa: 'How I felt that the most beautiful years of my life were over! I thought about the life that awaited me in Paris, the lessons, the worries, etc. Adieu tranquillity, sweet liberty, I will never find you again.'[26]

It can be said that the story of a *grand prix de Rome* is a coming-of-age story. A story of transition – from child to man, from pupil to artist. The worldly learnings gained through the travels, occurring at a time when young artists were learning to think for themselves, offered a once-in-a-lifetime education surpassed by few other opportunities.

'Teachers Open the Door, but You Must Enter by Yourself'

In assessing the merit of an education system, it is easy to be swayed by the testimonies of its most famous graduates, particularly if the recollections are steeped in sarcastic undertones that make highly entertaining reading. However, as any educator would attest, there is no one-size-fits-all solution to imparting knowledge and cultivating talent. Just as every teacher instructs differently, every student also learns differently. Temperament, talent, and work ethic can all play a part in shaping the success of a student. Hence, given the same environment, one student may thrive while another may fail miserably.

To complicate matters further, the historical discourse of artists tends to favour the rebel, embracing misfits and mavericks as signs of true genius. How often has it been said that Debussy had sacrificed his visions in order to comply with the strictures of the Conservatoire and the Prix de Rome?[27] Yet, for all the fame that he achieved later in life, we should be under no illusion that at the time of studying at the Conservatoire and competing for the Prix de Rome Debussy was all but a student who had yet to develop a distinct compositional voice. While hindsight is a wonderful gift, few at the time – Debussy himself included – could have anticipated the illustrious career he was to later enjoy.

To understand the value of the available music education in France, it would be more useful to frame Debussy's experiences in terms of opportunities. A more fitting question to ask would be whether the poor boy from Saint-Germain-en-Laye might have ever attained his accomplishments

---

[25] *Lettres de Georges Bizet* (Paris: Calmann-Lévy, 1907), pp. 265–6.
[26] Pierné, *Correspondance romaine*, pp. 358–9.
[27] See, for example, John R. Clevenger, 'Debussy's Paris Conservatoire Training', in Jane F. Fulcher (ed.), *Debussy and His World* (Princeton, NJ: Princeton University Press, 2001), p. 299.

without the teachings, networks, and cachet of distinction offered by the Paris Conservatoire and the Prix de Rome. Indeed, would the same doors or opportunities ever have opened to him if he had never attended the Conservatoire? How might the Parisian music circle have reacted to his eccentricities and experiments without the prestigious pedigree he enjoyed? It is hard to imagine how the history of French music might have unfolded if Debussy had never received the education he had. But one thing is certain, the Paris Conservatoire and the Prix de Rome fostered generations of successful musicians – a profound impact that should not be underestimated.

Authors' Recommendation
Fantaisie, for piano and orchestra (1889–90).

As a condition of receiving the Prix de Rome, laureates were required to submit a composition to the Institut de France each year to show productivity and progress. Debussy diligently complied for the first three years, but he never submitted his work for the final year – a *Fantaisie* for piano and orchestra. Written in three movements, the *Fantaisie* shows Debussy maturing as a composer, with unmistakable signs of his signature orchestral colour, poetic harmonies, and exotic influences throughout. Although cast in a concerto-like form, the title *Fantaisie* suggests a deliberate distinction from the piano concertos of the time. In Debussy's work the piano and orchestra play more complementary than antagonistic roles, and the use of two principal themes throughout gives the work a cyclical unity. These qualities perhaps make Vincent d'Indy's *Symphonie sur un chant montagnard* (1886) its closest relation, both in style and form. The 1890 premiere of the work was withdrawn by Debussy after the conductor, the same d'Indy, revealed his intention to perform only the first movement. Debussy made a number of revisions of the work in subsequent years, but it remained unperformed and unpublished until after his death. Its premiere was in 1919.

PART IV

Musical Life: Infrastructure and Earning a Living

CHAPTER 18

The Jobbing Composer-Musician
Denis Herlin

Unless one had a personal fortune like Ernest Chausson, it was difficult for composers at the end of the nineteenth century to live solely from their profession. Most of the time they supplemented their income through a position at the Paris Conservatoire or in a musical institution, such as the Paris Opéra, or making a living as a performer. However, Debussy throughout his life did not fall into any of these categories. The comparison with four composers who won the Prix de Rome in Debussy's lifetime is very enlightening in this respect. Georges Marty (1860–1908), winner of the Prix de Rome in 1882, on his return from the Villa Medici became conductor of singing at the Opéra, then at the Opéra-Comique, before becoming co-conductor with Paul Taffanel of the Société des concerts du Conservatoire from 1903. Parallel to his conducting activities, he taught ensemble music at the Paris Conservatoire from 1892 and harmony from 1904. Gabriel Pierné (1863–1937), who received the Prix de Rome the same year as Marty, succeeded César Franck as organist of the Parisian church of Sainte-Clotilde before becoming assistant conductor at the Concerts Colonne from 1903, then taking over the direction of the orchestra in 1910 following Édouard Colonne's death. Paul Vidal (1863–1931), who won the Prix de Rome in 1883 a year before Debussy, obtained the post of conductor at the Opéra and was a professor at the Paris Conservatoire – first, of music theory in 1894, then of accompaniment in 1896, and finally of composition in 1910 – before being appointed director of the Opéra-Comique from 1914 to 1919. As for Xavier Leroux (1863–1919), winner of the Prix de Rome in 1885, he became professor of harmony at the Paris Conservatoire in 1896.

On his return from Rome in March 1887, Debussy was struck by his fellow musicians' busyness and business-like attitudes:

> Vidal, very busy, painfully granting me the favour of having lunch with him! Leroux granting me an audience in the street between two appointments!

Pierné! this one I don't even dare to approach. Finally, all these people treat Paris as a conquered city! and we must see how flexible they are, how they have lost those beautiful indignations of yesteryear!'[1]

Returning to Debussy's more official career, one can only mention that in February 1909 he agreed to be part of the Conseil supérieur d'enseignement at the Paris Conservatoire (now under the direction of Gabriel Fauré), replacing Ernest Reyer,[2] and that from that date he served as a member of the jury for several competitions at the Conservatoire. But what seems to be a refusal to assume an official post does not arise from a point of principle, personal or political: unlike Maurice Ravel, Debussy unhesitatingly accepted the Legion of Honour in January 1903. In July 1914, he planned to apply for membership of the Académie des beaux-arts, only the outbreak of the First World War forestalled this. Despite the financial constraints that the lack of an official position would generate throughout his life, we must see in it his desire to remain free in his work as a composer, even if in absolute terms he would have liked to be freed from material constraints, as he confided to Roger-Ducasse in November 1907: 'an artist should not expect his bread from his work, but on the contrary, from a patron, a prince of state, who would provide him with everything he needed. The last interesting artistic manifestation was Wagner. The day Ludwig II found him, he was able to devote himself entirely to his ideas.'[3]

Aware of his talent and his profound originality, Debussy made some interesting points about his profession as a composer to a *New York Times* journalist who came to interview him:

> There are days and weeks and often months that no ideas come to me. No matter how much I try I cannot produce work that I am satisfied with. They say some composers can write, regularly, so much music a day – I admit I cannot comprehend it.[4]

Debussy indeed went through periods of great self-doubt, for example from 1895 to 1899 after completing a first draft of *Pelléas et Mélisande*, or after 1915 when he was suffering from the cancer that would end his life:

---

[1] Letter to Ernest Hébert, 17 March 1887, *Correspondance*, p. 61.
[2] Letter to Gabriel Fauré, 14 February 1909, *Correspondance*, p. 1154.
[3] Jean Roger-Ducasse, *Lettres à son ami André Lambinet* (Sprimont: Mardaga, 2001), pp. 44–5.
[4] David Grayson, 'Claude Debussy Addresses the English-Speaking World: Two Interviews, an Article, and *The Blessed Damozel*', *Cahiers Debussy* 16 (1992), p. 26.

18 The Jobbing Composer-Musician

What has happened since – I almost dare not think about it! but, I am still sick and the catalogue of my works has not increased much! . . . I absolutely have to find a way out of it; to shake this kind of fog that seems to clog my brain, otherwise I will wander off into the other world.[5]

Before becoming a recognised and influential composer after the premiere of *Pelléas et Mélisande* in April 1902, Debussy supported himself in various ways. During the 1880s, from 1883 to the end of 1884, he worked as accompanist for the La Concordia choir directed by Henriette Fuchs. From 1885 to 1888 he received an annual pension of about 2,500 francs (once maintenance costs had been deducted) following the award of the Prix de Rome. The end of this source of income corresponds precisely with the moment Debussy tried to find other ways of earning a living. Between March and October 1889 he produced, for the publisher Durand, piano-duet versions of Wagner's overture to *Der fliegende Holländer*, Robert Schumann's *Studien in kanonischer Form* (published as *Six études en forme de canon pour piano ou orgue à pédales*), and four works by Camille Saint-Saëns. He was not the only young composer to do such transcriptions for piano duet or piano four-hands. For example, Fauré transcribed for Durand six works by Saint-Saëns between 1877 and 1881, including *La Suite algérienne* Op. 60. Likewise, Guiraud, Debussy's composition teacher at the Paris Conservatoire, produced a piano-duet version of the four symphonic poems by Saint-Saëns in September 1883. While it is not known how much Fauré and Guiraud were paid for those works, it is known that Debussy was paid 100 francs for each arrangement, except for the Symphony No. 2 of Saint-Saëns, for which he received 250 francs. Unenthusiastic about this kind of work, which he gradually abandoned in 1890 and 1891, he endeavoured to sell to the publishers Durand, Choudens, and Hamelle several of his compositions – mainly songs, including for example 'Mandoline', or piano pieces, such as the *Deux arabesques* – for which he obtained between 100 and 200 francs.[6] He felt a certain bitterness when he sold his String Quartet to Durand for just 250 francs in October 1893, which was the same amount he had received for the transcription of Saint-Saëns's symphony. Yet in 1911 he would look nostalgically back on this period of his life – 'the period in which I was writing my String Quartet, a period which did not bring me much gold but which was

---

[5] Letter to Jacques Durand, 12 September 1917, *Correspondance*, pp. 2148–9.
[6] Denis Herlin, 'An Artist High and Low, or Debussy and Money', in Elliott Antokoletz and Marianne Wheeldon (eds.), *Rethinking Debussy* (New York: Oxford University Press, 2011), pp. 169, 171.

nonetheless a truly golden age!'.[7] The meeting with the publisher Georges Hartmann, who granted him an annual annuity of 6,000 francs, put an end to the disposal of his works in this way.[8] However, after the outbreak of the First World War he agreed to edit the complete works of Chopin and four volumes of Bach's chamber music as part of the new classical edition that Durand was launching to replace the German editions. For this work he was paid 1,000 francs for the four Bach volumes and 1,500 francs for five of the twelve Chopin volumes.

Despite the support of this publisher and a rather modest lifestyle, it is clear that until the performances of *Pelléas et Mélisande* at the Opéra-Comique in 1902, Debussy experienced a very precarious financial situation in the 1890s. Although there is a lack of tangible evidence, several of the composer's friends, such as René Peter, Pierre Louÿs, as well as members of the Loewenstein family, seem to have helped him financially. When Debussy got to know Chausson and his brother-in-law, the painter Henry Lerolle, more intimately from April 1893, they found various ways to support him. For example, Chausson and Lerolle organised a series of ten Wagnerian sessions between February and March 1894 at the home of their mother-in-law, Madame Philippe Escudier. He accompanied himself in acts from *Parsifal* and *Tristan und Isolde*, and received for each performance the generous sum of 1,000 francs.[9] In addition, Chausson suggested he let it be known that he was looking for students.[10] But Debussy did not seem very inclined to give lessons, as in November 1896 he wrote to his publisher Hartmann, asking to be excused for not having come to the agreed appointment: 'My only student! (Let's salute! ...) changed the time of his lesson by coming this morning without warning.'[11] The list of his only known students comprises just three names: Michèle Worms de Romilly in piano and singing, and Raoul Bardac and Nicolas Coronio in composition.[12] Finally, Debussy's dependence on Chausson was curtailed when he found Debussy a position as second conductor at the casino of Royan.[13] There is no doubt that despite the moral and material support of several friends, he contracted debts before his marriage to Lilly Texier in

---

[7] Letter to Jacques Durand, after 15 March 1911, *Correspondance*, p. 1401.
[8] François Lesure, *Claude Debussy: Biographie critique* (Paris: Fayard, 2002), p. 468.
[9] Due to the break-up of the engagement with Thérèse Roger in mid-March 1894, the sessions were interrupted after the fifth.
[10] Letter from Ernest Chausson to Debussy, 26 October 1893, *Correspondance*, p. 171.
[11] Letter to Georges Hartmann, after 11 November 1896, *Correspondance*, p. 332.
[12] *Correspondance*, pp. 2240–1, 2248, 2294.
[13] Letters to Chausson and from Chausson to Debussy, 1 and 5 January 1894, *Correspondance*, pp. 184–5.

1899, the amount of which remains difficult to assess. Should we believe what he confided to Pierre Louÿs in June 1899: 'Excuse me if I take advantage of this letter to ask you for the service of lending me fifty francs – I am in the blackest mire, not to mention my 300,000 francs of debts.'[14] If it turned out that the figure put forward is accurate, Debussy's indebtedness would represent a gigantic sum for the time.

What is more, Debussy was not a composer in the Saint-Saëns mould. It was only exceptionally that he performed in the 1890s as a pianist, as for example in May 1893 when he played excerpts from Wagner's *Das Rheingold* on two pianos with Raoul Pugno at a conference organised by Catulle Mendès.[15] And if he accompanied a singer in 1894 in songs by Edvard Grieg, played the *Capriccio espagnol* of Nikolai Rimsky-Korsakov arranged for piano duet with René Chansarel, or took the piano part in Guillaume Lekeu's Piano Quartet in February 1896 and January 1897, he did so only in order to render service to the Société nationale de musique, of which he was a member. Apart from these examples and a few private concerts, he only exceptionally performed the works of other composers in public. However, from 1908 he agreed to perform in public as a conductor, and more rarely as a pianist – a 'small revolution', as he wrote to his publisher Jacques Durand in 1907.[16] This change of attitude was mainly dictated by financial needs that continued to grow following his second marriage, to Emma Bardac, and a radical change of lifestyle: between 1903 and 1907 he went from a modest two-room apartment to a mansion on the avenue du Bois de Boulogne (now avenue Foch). Most of these concerts took place abroad, in England, Austria–Hungary, Russia, Italy, Belgium, and the Netherlands. Debussy negotiated large fees (5,000 francs per concert) comparable to those of the most fashionable artists, such as the Polish pianist Ignacy Jan Paderewski. On several occasions, Debussy brought the competition into play – for example, in 1913, between Alexandre Ziloti and Serge Koussevitzky with a view to organising a tour of Russia. Ziloti, the first to contact Debussy, backed down in favour of Koussevitzky, his competitor, who had much greater financial means thanks to his wife's income. When he agreed to accompany the singer Ninon Vallin-Pardo in Paris in March 1914, at the Salle Gaveau, and to play some of her works for piano, he asked for the sum of 1,000 francs and commented that 'it is still poorly paid!'.[17] Finally, his activity as a critic and

[14] Letter to Pierre Louÿs, 18 June 1899, *Correspondance*, p. 497.
[15] Letter to Chausson, 7 May 1893, *Correspondance*, pp. 126–7.
[16] Letter to Durand, 17 July 1907, *Correspondance*, p. 1015.
[17] Letter to Durand, 15 July 1913, *Correspondance*, p. 1642.

conductor was too sporadic for him to be able to guarantee a regular income. The resumption of a regular column in *S.I.M.* in 1912, after nine years of silence, is surely linked to the remuneration of 500 francs per article offered by Émile Vuillermoz, editor-in-chief of the periodical.[18]

After the success of *Pelléas*, Debussy's main financial support came from Durand, his official publisher from 1902, then exclusively from 1905. On his death, Debussy owed him the sum of 66,235 francs. Despite a relatively stable debt from 1907 to 1910, Debussy having given up part of his composer's copyright to repay some it, it continued to grow thereafter to reach this figure on his death. This debt is initially traceable back to the payment for *Le Diable dans le beffroi*, a one-act opera on a text by Edgar Allan Poe, for which Durand paid the sum of 24,000 francs without having seen a single note. The second reason – and the main one – comes from the monthly payment (400 francs) of a pension to Lilly Debussy-Texier, his first wife, following his divorce in 1905. As a note in Durand's hand states:

> The difference between the manuscripts transferred and the pension paid has never been made up. Manuscripts have always been paid for in full in cash. They even added payments on work in progress and on manuscripts that were never submitted (*Le Diable dans le beffroi*). So the pension was responsible for much of the debt.[19]

Should we deduce from this that Debussy was a poorly paid composer? Although he did not like discussions about money, he was able to skilfully negotiate the transfer of his works. Paid little before 1904 for his piano compositions (100 francs each), he received 500 francs for a piano piece between 1904 and 1908 (*Masques, L'Isle joyeuse, Children's Corner*), reaching 1,000 francs for each of the *Préludes* of the second book and *Études* from 1912.[20] By way of comparison, Durand offered Ravel 1,000 francs in April 1910 for the collection of five pieces for piano four hands *Ma mère l'Oye*, then a year later, in April 1911, 1,300 francs for the *Valses nobles et sentimentales*. As for Fauré, he generally received 1,000 francs, whether for a barcarolle or a nocturne – an amount identical to that received by Debussy from 1912. On the other hand, in April 1912 Saint-Saëns was offered 2,000 francs for his collection of *Six études pour la main gauche* Op. 135, which was two-thirds less than what Debussy received three years later for his *Études*.

---

[18] See Daniel Gregory Mason, *Music in My Time and Other Reminiscences* (New York: The Macmillan Company, 1938), p. 256.
[19] Paris, Durand Archives.   [20] Herlin, 'An Artist High and Low', p. 169.

18 The Jobbing Composer-Musician

Apart from the transfers of works of all kinds to Durand, *Pelléas et Mélisande* – whose success during Debussy's lifetime, whether on the stage of the Opéra-Comique (107 performances), in the provinces (Lyon, Nice, etc.), or abroad (Belgium, Germany, United Kingdom, Italy, Switzerland, Austria–Hungary, United States) was considerable – represents one of Debussy's main sources of income. In addition, there were the proceeds from *Le Martyre de saint Sébastien*, the choreographies of the *Prélude à l'après-midi d'un faune* and *Jeux* by Vaslav Nijinsky, and the *Nocturnes* and *Children's Corner* by Loie Fuller, not to mention the stage performances abroad (England, United States, Germany, Italy) of the new orchestration of *L'Enfant prodigue*, the cantata with which he won the Prix de Rome in 1884. Nevertheless, for Debussy to be assured of a sufficient income in relation to his new lifestyle, he would have had to compose other operas. The two dramas he tried to create on texts by Poe after *Pelléas* – *Le Diable dans le beffroi* and *La Chute de la maison Usher* – ended in failure. He quickly abandoned the former, while he tried in vain to complete the latter in 1916, leaving only a third of the work completed.

The spiral of debts weighed heavily from the 1910s, as Debussy confided to Durand in July 1913:

> Struggling alone is nothing! But struggling within the family becomes hideous! Add to that the domestic demands of past luxury that no one understands has now become impossible to sustain. . . . It may be my fault, because I only have energy intellectually; in everyday life I stumble at the slightest small stone, which another would send for a walk with an easy kick![21]

This increasingly difficult financial situation led him to perform in public, as we have seen – even though he was, by most accounts, a mediocre conductor – and also to accept – despite his reluctance – commissioned works, such as that of the dancer Maud Allan, who asked him to compose *Khamma*, a ballet based on a scenario of her own creation. The many hassles caused by this Canadian artist distracted him from the work, the orchestration of which he did not complete (it is mostly by Charles Koechlin). A few months later, he was asked by Gabriele D'Annunzio to write music for *Le Martyre de saint-Sébastien*, a theatrical work by the Italian poet with choreography by the Russian dancer Ida Rubinstein. When he received D'Annunzio's letter in Vienna on 30 November 1910,

---

[21] Letter to Durand, 15 July 1913, *Correspondance*, pp. 1641–2.

he was hardly in favour of the proposal, fearing that he would 'appear to have a thing for dancers'. But the charm of D'Annunzio and the friendly pressure exerted by Gabriel Astruc and Rubinstein on Emma Debussy overcame his reluctance.[22] In addition, the contract signed on 9 December 1911 states that 'in a feeling of high convenience and artistic respect'[23] the sum of 20,000 francs is acquired by him, even if he does not meet the deadlines. Similarly, the ballet *Jeux* would not have seen the light of day in 1912–13 without Diaghilev's insistence and finance. Let us add that the proposals of Maud Allan, D'Annunzio, and Diaghilev freed him from the impasse in which he found himself with his opera *La Chute de la maison Usher*, while still allowing him to write theatrical works. Without these well-paid contracts and financial pressure on the composer, perhaps we would not have had these major orchestral works.

Reading Debussy's correspondence might suggest that he was a poorly paid composer who was always short of money. If in the first years of his career he had a difficult time of it, he became, thanks to *Pelléas et Mélisande*, a famous musician enjoying a comfortable income. A change of lifestyle linked to his remarriage and a difficult divorce, plus the absence of other operas in his catalogue, explain the spiral of indebtedness that kept increasing right up to the end of his life, a spiral aggravated by the outbreak of the First World War.

Author's Recommendation
Le Martyre de saint Sébastien, 1911.

Composed in a very short time and partly orchestrated by André Caplet, *Le Martyre de saint Sébastien* does not occupy the place it deserves within Debussy's orchestral and vocal works. D'Annunzio's oversized text overshadows masterful pages exhibiting a refined orchestration that anticipates *Jeux*. Removing the text and thus performing the musical numbers on their own proves problematic, for the various sequences are intimately linked to the unfolding of the theatrical action. Aware of this pitfall, Désiré-Émile Inghelbrecht, Leonard Bernstein, and later Pierre Boulez persevered with the original text in a radically condensed or paraphrased form, thereby contributing to the rediscovery of this neglected work.

---

[22] *Correspondance*, p. 1344.
[23] Letter from Gabriel Astruc to Emma Debussy, 9 December 1910, Correspondance, pp. 1357–8.

CHAPTER 19

Parisian Opera Institutions: A Framework for Creation

Hervé Lacombe

Cultural and Institutional Context

In the nineteenth century, French musical activity was mostly structured around opera; it is hard for us to imagine the extraordinary influence it exerted over composers, the press, and consumers of music and performance. It was everywhere, not just in the theatres dedicated to it, but also in concerts and salons, resulting in a truly operatic culture.[1] Piano music, as demonstrated by Liszt, was deeply indebted to opera through reductions, transcriptions, fantasies, variations, and potpourris of all sorts. Vocal models also affected the performance and composition of instrumental melodies by many composers. In hypercentralised France, the heart of this world was Paris in the handful of theatres devoted to opera, which produced most of the original works. The French operatic system functioned with a centre and periphery: there was a producer (the capital) and a multitude of receivers (the provincial towns).

The Napoleonic decrees of 1806 and 1807 affected theatrical life for a long time. French opera was heavily compartmentalised by institution with 'privileges' tied to specific genres:

- At the Opéra (Royal, Imperial, or National Academy of Music, according to political regime), it was the grand genre, entirely sung, which became *grand opéra* at the end of the 1820s.
- At the Opéra-Comique, the genre was *opéra-comique* (it is not comic opera!), with alternating spoken dialogue and sung musical numbers.
- At the Théâtre-Italien, Italian repertoire prevailed.

In the 1850s, operetta, a generic term indicating different forms of light opera with spoken dialogue, was born under the joint initiatives of Hervé

---

[1] For further information, see Hervé Lacombe, 'Une culture lyrique nationale dans un espace international', in Lacombe (ed.), *Histoire de l'opéra français*, vol. 2: *Du Consulat aux débuts de la IIIe République* (Paris: Fayard, 2020), pp. 1163–7.

at the Théâtre des Folies-Concertantes (subsequently called Folies-Nouvelles) and Jacques Offenbach at the Théâtre des Bouffes-Parisiens.

Two years after the birth of Debussy, a decree of 6 January 1864 freed theatres from these constraints, thereby finally putting an end to the system of privileges. This decree proclaimed the free operation of theatres, subject only to a preliminary declaration, and in theory gave them the freedom to embrace all genres. It was the very popular operetta that most benefitted from this liberalisation of the theatres. In fact, even after the decree of 1864 the Opéra and Opéra-Comique continued to be supported and managed by the State through the appointment of directors, grants, and *cahiers des charges* (which controlled their artistic forces and their genres); this perpetuated their historical repertoire and thus the identities of the two theatres. Moreover, censorship continued to exert a controlling influence over all theatres until 1906.[2] Debussy did not escape it: at the end of the dress rehearsal of *Pelléas et Mélisande* on 28 April 1902, he was asked to make some modest cuts to his score.[3]

In the Parisian operatic landscape of the nineteenth century, a special place must be accorded to the Théâtre-Lyrique, which, under the Second Empire, allowed composers such as Gounod and Bizet to express themselves relatively freely, without surrendering to the official genres of *grand opéra* and *opéra-comique*. This theatre, which gave a place to young composers and permitted the birth of a new, more poetic operatic aesthetic, also revived old works, notably by Gluck and Mozart, and welcomed unfamiliar repertoire, including Weber's operatic works.

Debussy began his musical studies at the Paris Conservatoire shortly after a series of events that transformed the Parisian musical landscape: the Franco-Prussian War of 1870 signalled the end of the Second Empire and led to the establishment of the Third Republic, the only political regime that the composer of *Pelléas* would know in his adult life. The founding of the Société nationale de musique in February 1871 galvanised French creativity, especially in the field of chamber music, and allowed musicians outside the operatic career path to find fulfilment. Daniel François Esprit Auber's death at that very moment, in May 1871, symbolised the end of the old operatic regime (he had been the creator of grand opera with *La Muette de Portici* and the master of *opéra-comique* for several decades). It also marked the end of a conservative spirit at the Conservatoire, where Auber

---

[2] Odile Krakovitch, *Hugo censuré: La liberté au théâtre au XIXe siècle* (Paris: Calmann-Lévy, 1985).
[3] David Grayson, 'Avant-propos', in *Œuvres complètes de Claude Debussy*, ser. VI, vol. 2: *Pelléas et Mélisande*, vocal score, ed. Grayson (Paris: Durand, 2010), p. xiv.

had been the director; Ambroise Thomas was his successor. In the 1870s and 1880s, around the time Debussy completed his studies and won first prize in the Prix de Rome (1884), the organisation of the Parisian operatic world continued to change. The new freedom of theatres and the war of 1870 dealt a fatal blow to the Théâtre-Italien, which closed in September 1878. Despite a few attempts to bring it back in the 1880s, it never remained for long. The new realist (verismo) music of Leoncavallo, Mascagni, and Puccini was introduced to Paris in French and at the Opéra-Comique, which a few years before would have been unthinkable. The Théâtre-Lyrique closed its doors during the siege of Paris and was burnt down during the Commune of 1871. Like the Théâtre-Italien, it was never resurrected from the ashes. What remained were the operetta theatres, which rapidly multiplied, and the two great institutions, already more than a century old, the Opéra and the Opéra-Comique, to which it is necessary to add a few often short-lived initiatives to present opera in other theatres. Thus, the two Isola brothers, Émile and Vincent, directed the Théâtre-Lyrique de la Gaîté in the square des Arts-et-Métiers between 1908 and 1913. Aesthetically, French resistance to Wagner faded away as his work gained new admirers. The 1880s and 1890s witnessed his success on stage and also his increasing influence on French composers. Despite its desire to represent French *art lyrique*, the Opéra was getting set to become the temple of Wagnerism: between 1908 and 1914, Wagner would represent more than a quarter of the productions staged at the Garnier![4] Finally, to give the whole picture, it is important to recall that two theatres on the borders of France welcomed French composers – namely, the Théâtre royal de la Monnaie in Brussels, where Vincent d'Indy's *Fervaal* was premiered in 1897, and the Monte Carlo Opéra, which hosted several Massenet productions.

Debussy and the Operatic Establishment

Forces of revival and administrative change took a long time to profoundly alter French customs and 'musical thought'. The elitist and intimate concept of art that Debussy developed, not least by spending time with poets like Mallarmé, placed it a priori outside the sphere of opera as practised in France. In 1892, he attributed a speculative, abstruse, and dream-like quality to his music and, at the same time, defined his 'great ambition': 'to do theatre

---

[4] Mathias Auclair, 'Verdi, Wagner et l'opéra de Paris (1847–2013)', in Jean-François Candoni, Hervé Lacombe, Timothée Picard, and Giovanna Sparacello (eds.), *Verdi/Wagner: Images croisées, 1813–2013* (Rennes: Presses universitaires de Rennes, 2018), p. 184.

all by myself.[5] This ideal, paradoxical theatre, which is defined outside society and against the taste of his contemporaries, did not fit with any operatic institution of the period. The avant-garde theatres were better suited to this 'theatre of mine alone'. It should be remembered that the houses where spoken dramatic repertoire was presented often used incidental music, especially the Théâtre Antoine and Théâtre de l' Œuvre. However, this was not opera. It was at the Théâtre de l'Œuvre that Debussy attended the original production of a play by Maurice Maeterlinck (*Pelléas et Mélisande*), directed by Lugné-Poe, on 17 May 1893. If the production of his opera based on this play was originally envisaged in this theatre in 1895, it was not until 1910 that an avant-garde hall surfaced that based its programming on the combination of theatre, opera, and ballet: Jacques Rouché, future director of the Paris Opéra, assumed the directorship of the Théâtre des Arts (boulevard des Batignolles) and combined contemporary and early music. This was too late for Debussy. In the interim, after several years of uncertainty, Debussy had found asylum at the Opéra-Comique, which in many ways was not the obvious destination for *Pelléas*.

Rather like the Prix de Rome, establishment operatic institutions were in Debussy's mind hindrances to the imagination of the authentic artist. His stance was very similar to that of Berlioz (a totally atypical composer in nineteenth-century France), whose dramatic genius was nevertheless denied by Debussy.[6] The constant need for new ideas and renewal that must preoccupy the independent creator is challenged by the demand for continuity and convention, security and success, which shaped the opera houses. For example, Saint-Saëns's *Les Barbares*, premiered at the Opéra in 1901, retained certain characteristics of *grand opéra* instead of inventing a new form. The lyrical conception holding sway at the Opéra, which Saint-Saëns did not challenge, was founded firstly upon the distribution of tasks that are brought together in traditional opera (viz. the work of the librettist, the music of the composer, and the singers' interpretation); second, upon the theatrical response to a vast range of dramaturgical conventions; and third, upon the complicity between composer and audience according to a broad range of expectations (Debussy, for his part, aimed to achieve an ideal, not satisfy the audience). Hence this regret expressed by Debussy's alter ego Monsieur Croche: 'Why this obsessive need to write operas and fall from Louis Gallet to Victorien Sardou, spreading the detestable misconception that one must "do theatre", which will never be compatible with

---

[5] Letter to André Poniatowski, 5 October 1892, *Correspondance*, p. 111.
[6] *Monsieur Croche*, pp. 169–70.

"making music"?'[7] Debussy not only rejected opera as it existed at the Opéra and the Opéra-Comique; by opposing institutions and their repertoire, and writing music criticism, he reinforced his own position. In other words, the 'errors' of musicians that he condemned helped him to better define and affirm his own operatic work.

The opera institutions, with their troupes and repertoire, their *emplois* and staging codes, perpetuated a dramaturgy, an art of singing and performance generally, which undermined originality. Debussy sought 'truth' uncontaminated by convention; he pursued a dream that was opposed to realism and everyday life; and ranging throughout his work was a quest for the inexpressible, the ideal of the Symbolists (who spurned the commonplace and ordinary). The notion of *emploi* is crucial to understanding nineteenth-century opera. It indicates a type of character linked to particular dramatic skills, to a vocal profile, and potentially a physiognomy. A role is often based on an artist who has established their mark, character, voice, style, and physique in a series of roles of a similar character. For example, let us consider the roles associated with Dugazon and Martin, dating from the end of the eighteenth century, which continued to flourish in French opera until around 1900. Louise-Rosalie Dugazon (1755–1821) had performed many of Grétry's and Dalayrac's roles. Nicolas-Jean-Blaise Martin (1768–1837) established himself through his exceptional tessitura and as a comic actor. The recruitment of artists according to their established roles (the *emplois*) contributed greatly to the maintenance of the theatrical repertoire. Conversely, new works (libretto and scores) drew heavily on pre-existent roles. Even if the system of roles reconfigured itself in the course of the century and gradually disintegrated, it still influenced a considerable part of operatic life. On this level, too, Debussy breaks with tradition. If Pelléas is still often associated with Martin's baritone Fach, it is in an effort to specify its range, not the role itself.

Situation at the Opéra

After the Orsini bombing on 14 January 1858 in front of the Salle Le Peletier, which had been home to the Opéra since 1821, Napoleon III decided to build a new theatre. Charles Garnier won the architecture competition and built what rapidly became one of the symbols of the French capital. However, the Emperor never experienced this 'palace', the true apotheosis of the eclectic style of the Second Empire, as its official

---

[7] *Monsieur Croche*, p. 57.

opening only took place in 1875. The new Republic had no difficulty in making it one of the flagship landmarks of Parisian social and artistic life. The epitome of prestige under the preceding regimes, the Opéra continues to be a place associated with grandeur, luxury, and national reputation, both in the field of opera and dance. But the institution became sclerotic and lost its international leadership of previous decades when the *grand opéra* genre, represented by Auber, Halévy, and Meyerbeer, caught Europe's attention and attracted the likes of Rossini, Donizetti, Verdi, and Wagner. Productions had less resonance and, above all, the genre became obsolete. Its often historical themes, dramaturgy, and musical form had difficulty adapting to the advanced language, the new aesthetic trends, and especially Wagnerian music drama, which emerged as the new dominant ideal. Even so, directors' specifications (*cahiers des charges*) never stopped recalling these demands for luxury and grandeur. It was not until 1891 that *grand opéra*'s endless formulas were abandoned and the performance of all operatic forms was authorised, with the exception of genres reserved for the Opéra-Comique. With the ordinances of 1893, the Opéra could finally, in theory at least, perform most types of work.[8] However, some practices were long-standing and the legacy of *grand opéra* was still present in the image of the Opéra. It is understandable that at the beginning of the 1890s the young Debussy, pressurised by Catulle Mendès, had tried to write *Rodrigue et Chimène* in a bid to bring him closer to attaining recognition, which was also a good way to earn money as a composer;[9] but it is equally understandable that he failed to bring this opera to completion. The conventional versification, traditional theme, pursuit of exotic colour (long awaited and responding to a form of realism) defined an aesthetic space at the antipodes of the operatic ideal that Debussy was increasingly drawn to. The question of libretto reveals another obstacle to the creative freedom of the musician: the profession of the librettist is based on *savoir-faire*, the conventions and the literary themes associated with institutions and genres. Born in 1841, Mendès was a nineteenth-century man. He wrote for Émile Pessard, Emmanuel Chabrier, and André Messager; he went on to collaborate with Reynaldo Hahn, Jules Massenet, Camille Erlanger, and others. Turning away from a collaboration with a professional librettist is a way to free oneself from this predefined operatic universe.

---

[8] See Frédérique Patureau, *Le Palais Garnier dans la société parisienne, 1875–1914* (Liège: Mardaga, 1991).
[9] Lesure (Rolf), pp. 87–8.

Pathway towards the Opéra-Comique

After fire destroyed the second Salle Favart on 25 May 1887, the Opéra-Comique was accommodated on the place du Châtelet in the hall that we today call the Théâtre de la Ville (15 October 1887–30 June 1898) and for a few weeks at the Théâtre du Château-d'Eau (26 October–30 November 1898), before taking its place in the third Salle Favart, inaugurated on 7 December 1898, where it is still active.[10] It was at the Opéra-Comique that French opera reinvented itself and where French composers presented the most distinguished works of the new Republic, including, among others, *Carmen* in 1875, *Les Contes d'Hoffmann* in 1881, *Lakmé* in 1883, *Manon* in 1884, *Louise* in 1900, and *Pelléas* in 1902. The years 1870–80 witnessed a rise in the importance of the generation of Léo Delibes (1836–91), Georges Bizet (1838–75), and Jules Massenet (1842–1912). Gustave Charpentier (1860–1956) and Debussy (born two years later) belong to the next generation. This generational change corresponds to an extraordinary moment in the history of the Opéra-Comique: the disappearance of the genre which had been its *raison d'être*. *Carmen* is still an *opéra-comique*, in structure if not in subject matter (tragedy and the representation of death are very rare at the Opéra-Comique[11]), with spoken scenes; *Manon* uses speech, but it is continuously accompanied by music. The next step was the elimination of speech. If the old works continued to be performed with spoken scenes, the new ones would be able to free themselves from them. Gounod's *Roméo et Juliette*, which had been premiered at the Théâtre-Lyrique in 1867, was the first entirely sung work to be presented on the stage of the Opéra-Comique (20 January 1873). After this initiative from the director Camille du Locle, the new director Léon Carvalho (1876–87, 1891–7) obtained the right to stage entirely sung works. A work such as *Pelléas* would have been unimaginable at the Opéra-Comique before these developments. Albert Carré (1852–1938), who succeeded Carvalho in 1898,[12] brought a new spirit that the former director, born in 1825, could not embody. Playwright and librettist, director, manager, advocate for young

---

[10] Nicole Wild, *Dictionnaire des théâtres parisiens, 1807–1914* (Lyon: Symétrie, 2012), p. 332.
[11] Hervé Lacombe, 'La Fin de l'opéra-comique', in Lacombe (ed.), *Histoire de l'opéra français*, vol. 2: *Du Consulat aux débuts de la IIIe République* (Paris: Fayard, 2020), pp. 1160–1.
[12] Michela Niccolai, 'Albert Carré directeur de l'Opéra-Comique à la Comédie-Française (1898–1915)', in Sabine Chaouche, Denis Herlin, and Solveig Serre (eds.), *L'Opéra de Paris, la Comédie-Française et l'Opéra-Comique: Approches comparées, 1669–2010* (Paris: École nationale des chartes, 2012), pp. 347–66; see also Philippe Blay, '"Un théâtre français, tout à fait français" ou un débat fin-de-siècle sur l'Opéra-Comique', *Revue de musicologie* 87 (2001), pp. 105–44; Philippe Blay, 'Albert Carré et la rénovation de l'Opéra-Comique', *Revue musicale de Suisse romande* 57 (March 2004), pp. 42–59.

composers and the new generation, Carré joined forces with the expertise of his friend André Messager (1853–1929) as director of music. A variety of conditions had to be met to facilitate the premiere of *Pelléas* at the Opéra-Comique. These contingencies as they pertained to Debussy's opera bear witness to an important aspect of the world of Parisian opera theatres, which included networks of knowledgeable and influential people, in this case Georges Hartmann (1843–1900), Debussy's first publisher, who was also the librettist of *Madame Chrysanthème*, Messager's *comédie lyrique*, premiered at the Opéra-Comique in 1893. Hartmann worked to raise Messager's awareness of Debussy's score.

Author's Recommendation
Rodrigue et Chimène (1890–3).

The idea of making El Cid an operatic character is not new. Bizet left an unfinished manuscript on this subject and Massenet wrote an eponymous work in 1885. Catulle Mendès, who had a libretto on the same subject on his shelf since at least 1878, persuaded Debussy to compose the music. The libretto is conventional, inscribed in a historical fresco, carried by a heroic figure, mixed with local colour and choruses. According to Paul Dukas, to whom Debussy played his opera, it was 'perfectly worthless!'. Debussy set to work in 1890, conscious of struggling against himself, but knowing that he had the means to be institutionally recognised and earn money. On 8 August 1893, he obtained permission to compose *Pelléas*. *Rodrigue et Chimène* would never be completed.

One could say that with this project Debussy tried to forge a lyrical space between Wagner, French grand opera, and his own style. With *Pelléas*, he managed to create a work without genre, freed from conventions, which, thanks to Maeterlinck's play, liberated him from any 'libretto dramaturgy'. On another level, the opposition between love and duty, which structures the earlier work and inscribes in it a traditional character and plot design, was going to be replaced in *Pelléas* by two more abstract or Symbolist oppositions: one that confronts light with darkness, the other life with death. This transition from one work to another allowed Debussy to escape from a moral vision of the world in favour of a drama of a metaphysical order. On the other hand, by writing as much as he did of *Rodrigue*, he could experiment with a way of appropriating leitmotif technique. He could also write ample and intense scenes while developing his harmonic style and making characters sing in different situations and atmospheres.

CHAPTER 20

Société Nationale and Other Institutions

Michael Strasser

In the years around 1900, Paris was home to three major, well-established orchestras, each of which had its loyal patrons. Concerts took place on Sunday afternoons, except during Easter week, when they were moved to Good Friday and took on a more solemn character. While there were some differences in programming philosophy, concerts of all three ensembles generally featured an eclectic mix of music of different genres and from different eras. They might contain as many as eight to ten different works, and concerts might last as long as three hours. The concert season lasted from mid-October until late March and each orchestra presented around twenty-four concerts during the season.

While Beethoven, Mendelssohn, Schumann, and other classic composers appeared frequently on programmes, there was a great deal of both contemporary and 'ancient' music, and one might hear a work by Bach, Handel, or Gluck next to a Wagner excerpt or a new work by a French, Russian, or German composer. The leading singers of the day were often featured, and extended excerpts from operas and other dramatic works were regularly included in programmes, as were art songs.

Other orchestras occasionally emerged, offering concerts on Sunday afternoons or, alternatively, on Thursday evenings, always seeking to establish themselves as viable alternatives to the more famous ensembles. Some of these attained a certain level of success over a season or two before fading from the scene.

Anyone who remembered the state of Parisian musical life during the Second Empire would have marvelled at all this activity and especially at the presence of so much French music on programmes. In 1862, the year of Debussy's birth, there was one important orchestral concert organisation in Paris, the venerable Société des concerts du Conservatoire. Founded in 1828, it had become a fixture on the Parisian musical scene and was counted among the elite institutions of the city's musical life. Entry to its Sunday afternoon concerts was limited by the small size of the hall on the rue du

Conservatoire, and tickets were available only by subscription. Devoted in its early years to presenting the relatively new and unknown symphonies of Beethoven to Parisian listeners, the organisation had 'evolved into a museum', a sanctuary for high art and higher prestige where very few new works were introduced. Works by Beethoven, Haydn, Mendelssohn, and Mozart comprised over 90 per cent of the repertoire performed at Conservatoire concerts between 1828 and 1870.[1] Music by French composers was notably absent from its programmes.

Although there were various attempts to establish other concert organisations in Paris during the Second Empire, some of which featured works by young French composers, none were able to provide a viable addition to the city's musical life until 1863, when Jules Pasdeloup launched his Concerts populaires, which were performed in the Cirque Napoléon, renamed the Cirque d'Hiver after the fall of the Empire. The large seating capacity of this venue enabled Pasdeloup to offer tickets at much-reduced prices, and his formula of accepted masterpieces and low ticket prices enabled him to tap a previously unmined vein. The large and enthusiastic crowds of lower- and middle-class listeners who attended his concerts demonstrated that there was a much greater interest in concert music than anyone had heretofore imagined, and that if tickets were affordable, a vast new audience was eager to be introduced to such music. Unfortunately, he offered few opportunities for his listeners to hear works by young French composers, and as the decade came to a close, the prospects for wide acceptance of French concert music remained bleak.

The twin tragedies of the Franco-Prussian War and the Commune uprising shocked the nation and led to much soul-searching. There was widespread agreement that the perceived decadence of French society during the Second Empire had led directly to its recent humiliations, and there was no small amount of criticism of French musical life. One writer later remembered that in the months following the defeat, 'one was almost ashamed to go to the theatre strictly for amusement', adding that Parisians were smitten with the desire for personal and national regeneration, and that there was a taste for art that would instruct as well as entertain.[2] This attitude contributed much to the great expansion of Parisian concert life that occurred in the decades following *l'année terrible*.

---

[1] Jeffrey Cooper, *The Rise of Instrumental Music and Concert Series in Paris, 1828–1871* (Ann Arbor, MI: UMI Research Press, 1983), p. 36–7.

[2] Francisque Sarcey, *Souvenirs d'âge mûr* (Paris: Paul Ollendorff, 1892), p. 96.

And, for the first time, Parisian listeners were eager to hear compositions by French composers.

It was at this moment, in late 1871, that Camille Saint-Saëns, Romain Bussine, and several other French composers founded the Société nationale de musique (SN) to encourage the composition and performance of new French music. The founders were certainly motivated by patriotic sentiments, but like Ernest Renan, Hippolyte Taine, and other thinkers who insisted that the road to national recovery lay in emulating the most admirable characteristics of France's conqueror, the Société's founders looked to German masters from Beethoven to Wagner to light their way, convinced that the 'pure' music emanating from across the Rhine was that of a strong and vital society. They viewed their advocacy of such music, and the incorporation of both its ideals and its techniques into their own style, as nothing less than a moral imperative, essential to the regeneration of French culture and society. They conceived of their new organisation as a forum for the presentation of 'serious' music written by French composers and, thus, a tool that would aid in the rebirth of the nation. While some critics viewed the SN as a welcome addition to the French musical landscape, others considered it as nothing more than a nest of Wagnerians, describing its members as musical revolutionaries and arsonists bent on destroying the traditions of French music.[3]

Over the next forty-four years (operations were suspended in 1914 and did not resume until November 1917), the SN presented approximately ten Saturday evening concerts per season. Most of these can be best described as 'chamber' concerts, held in the intimate confines of the old Salle Pleyel on the rue Rochechouart and sometimes, after 1900, in the somewhat larger Salle Érard. The programmes consisted of a wide variety of music: chamber works, pieces for solo instrument, transcriptions of orchestral works for one or two pianos, songs, and choral pieces. These works were often performed by the composer and various other SN members, but concerts also featured appearances by some of the leading figures of Parisian musical life. Beginning in 1873, the SN offered an average of two orchestral concerts each season. One usually took place in the Salle Érard or, later, the Salle Gaveau, and another, featuring a smaller ensemble, was given at the Salle Pleyel. Depending on the location, these concerts featured an orchestra of from forty-five to sixty-five musicians.

---

[3] Michael Strasser, 'The Société Nationale and Its Adversaries: The Musical Politics of *L'Invasion germanique* in the 1870s', *19th-Century Music* 24 (2001), pp. 225–51.

Audiences at SN concerts consisted of members, invited guests, and journalists. These were private affairs, and tickets were generally not sold to the general public. Based on the number of programmes ordered for the 1880–1 season, it appears that chamber concerts drew, at most, around two hundred listeners, and orchestral concerts perhaps as many as four or five hundred.[4]

During the early 1880s, a group of young composers, devoted followers of César Franck and among the most enthusiastic of the French Wagnerians, began to exert ever more control over the organisation, and in 1886 both Saint-Saëns and Bussine resigned their leadership positions. Franck was elected as the new president, but it was his most fervent disciple, Vincent d'Indy, who exercised actual control over the next quarter century.

Debussy joined the SN in January 1888, undoubtedly attracted by its reputation as the home of some of the most advanced composers on the French musical scene, as the Franckist/Wagnerians certainly were at that time. (Debussy had already exhibited an interest in Franck's teaching by enrolling in his organ class at the Paris Conservatoire, which many former students remembered as a de facto composition class.[5])

Over the next quarter century, Debussy's name appeared on twenty-six SN programmes, beginning in February 1889, when two of his *Ariettes* were performed. Several of his songs and works for piano received their first performances at SN concerts, including *Pour le piano*, *Estampes*, *L'Isle joyeuse*, and the *Trois poèmes de Stéphane Mallarmé*. His String Quartet was probably written specifically for the SN.[6] Premiered on 29 December 1893, it was subsequently performed on four other occasions before 1914, when the onset of the First World War led the SN to suspend its activities. *La Damoiselle élue* was introduced at an SN orchestral concert on 8 April 1893, and the *Prélude à l'après-midi d'un faune* was premiered on 22 December 1894 (unusually, the concert was a joint venture between the SN and the concert series conducted by Eugène Harcourt; thus, it was attended by subscribers to Harcourt's series as well as the usual SN members and invited guests).

---

[4] See Michael Strasser, 'Ars Gallica: The Société Nationale de Musique and Its Role in French Musical Life, 1871–1891', PhD thesis, University of Illinois (1997), pp. 205–9.
[5] Ibid., p. 462.
[6] For information on the quartet's composition, see Michel Strasser, 'Grieg, the Société Nationale, and the Origins of Debussy's String Quartet', in Barbara L. Kelly and Kerry Murphy (eds.), *Berlioz and Debussy: Sources, Contexts, and Legacies* (Aldershot: Ashgate, 2007), pp. 103–15.

Although the administrative records for the SN grow increasingly patchy after d'Indy assumed control, there is evidence that Debussy played an active role in it for many years. He was elected to the administrative committee (responsible for examining and approving works that had been submitted for performance, setting policies, etc.) on two different occasions: 1893 and 1902; and he remained a member after Maurice Ravel and Charles Koechlin quit in 1909 to form a rival organisation, the Société musicale indépendante. When Gabriel Fauré proposed in early 1917 to reunite the two organisations in the spirit of patriotic brotherhood, Debussy expressed doubt about the prospects for success. After both Ravel and Koechlin forcefully rejected these overtures, Fauré sought instead to revive an 'enlarged' SN, and Debussy was named once again as a member of the committee. Unfortunately, he did not live long enough to contribute in any meaningful way to the post-war direction of the SN.[7]

The SN clearly played an important role in Debussy's development. It provided him and many other aspiring composers with the support and encouragement of like-minded colleagues, and it served as a welcoming venue for some of his first masterpieces. But, with very rare exceptions, SN concerts were not open to the general public, and as important as the organisation was to the development of French music, it had limited direct impact on public taste.

In fact, most new orchestral works by French composers were premiered not at SN concerts but at those of the various orchestral societies that flourished in Paris after 1870. The Concerts du Conservatoire and Pasdeloup's Concerts populaires were joined in 1873 by a new concert series, conducted by Édouard Colonne, which, after its first season, found a home in the spacious Théâtre du Châtelet. Throughout the 1870s, Colonne placed a new emphasis on the works of living French composers and featured those of the greatest French Romantic, Hector Berlioz. Pasdeloup also included a vastly increased number of French works on his post-war programmes, and between them these two conductors performed works by over fifty French composers during the 1870s. Even the staid, tradition-bound Concerts du Conservatoire opened its portals, ever so slightly, to modern French music.[8]

Unfortunately, this happy situation was not sustained into the last two decades of the century. Both Pasdeloup and Colonne continued to

---

[7] Michel Duchesneau, *L'Avant-garde musicale à Paris de 1871 à 1939* (Sprimont: Mardaga, 1997), pp. 47–8.
[8] Strasser, '*Ars Gallica*', pp. 210–76.

programme French music, but there were fewer compositions by new composers and an increasing reliance on works by well-established figures who had come of age during the 1850s and 1860s: Saint-Saëns, Franck, Massenet, Lalo, Chabrier, etc.

Of even greater impact was the public's sudden and growing fascination with Wagner's music. The new-found fervour for the German composer's works stood in stark contrast to the hostile reception with which they had been greeted in the previous decade, when the memories of France's humiliations were still fresh. And it was fuelled by the appearance of yet another new concert society in 1881, the Concerts Lamoureux. The orchestra, established and conducted by Charles Lamoureux, soon gained renown for its precision and musicianship, rivalling that of the Concerts du Conservatoire, which was then considered one of the world's finest ensembles. Lamoureux was also credited with establishing a new code of audience conduct at his concerts. 'Frequently, if he heard the slightest noise, the slightest murmur, he did not hesitate to stop his orchestra, sit down, and once absolute silence had returned, start the work over.'[9] Although Lamoureux performed a great deal of modern French music as well as works by the classical masters, the music of Wagner was always featured, with multiple excerpts or even entire acts from his operas dominating the programmes. Of the 212 concerts presented by Lamoureux in the 1880s, only twenty-nine did not feature at least one work by the German master.[10]

The increased competition from Colonne and Lamoureux finally forced Pasdeloup from the scene in the mid-1880s, and from then until the First World War Parisian concert life was dominated by Colonne, Lamoureux, and the Concerts du Conservatoire. Over the years, Colonne's devotion to Berlioz came to define his organisation. Between 1875 and 1914 he presented *La Damnation de Faust* an astounding 175 times – an average of almost five times per season – and he also regularly programmed *L'Enfance du Christ* and the Requiem. Lamoureux, of course, was most closely associated with the music of Wagner, and his emphasis on audience discipline gave his concerts a reputation of pious solemnity, which certain critics naturally associated with the philosophical pretensions of Wagner's most fervent admirers. In fact, the differences in the programming philosophies of these two organisations was merely one of degree. Both Berlioz

---

[9] Gustave Doret, 'Charles Lamoureux et Edouard Colonne', in Doret, *Musique et musiciens* (Paris: Fischbacher, 1915), p. 124.
[10] Strasser, '*Ars Gallica*', p. 517.

and Wagner figured prominently on the programmes of each. And the Concerts du Conservatoire, with their continued devotion to the classics, retained their status as the most tradition-bound, conservative, and exclusive of the three, even though they were by then regularly programming works by Saint-Saëns and Franck, an occasional orchestral work by Wagner, and, rarely, a composition by a younger French composer.

As the century drew to a close, there were increasing complaints that, as was the case during the Second Empire, the younger generation of composers was being denied the opportunity to make their works known to the public. Between them, Colonne and Lamoureux, during the period 1891–1903, programmed works by some forty-five French composers who were born after 1850, but most of these took the form of short symphonic poems; 'scènes lyriques' or similar works for soloists, chorus, and orchestra; instrumental or vocal excerpts from operas; *melodies*; and the like. Seventeen of these composers appeared on only one programme, and very few received more than a handful of performances. D'Indy received the most performances during these years, with twenty-two by Colonne and twenty-five by Lamoureux. Works by Gustave Charpentier were heard twenty-four times at the Concerts Colonne, but only five times at the Concerts Lamoureux.

The concerns about orchestral concert programming finally reached the floor of the Assemblée nationale, which provided substantial subsidies to all the major musical institutions in the capital. The result was a rule instituted by the ministère des Beaux-Arts in 1904 that required both Colonne and Camille Chevillard (Lamoureux's successor) to programme a minimum of three hours of new French music each season or risk losing their subventions. The conductors were not at all happy about this new diktat and for several years thereafter went to substantial lengths to circumvent its requirements.[11] But in spite of their passive resistance to the government's mandates, both Colonne and Chevillard continued to perform works by contemporary French composers on a regular basis.

Debussy's orchestral music certainly did not suffer from a lack of exposure. The *Prélude à l'après-midi d'un faune* had been heard at the Concerts Colonne on 13 October 1895, less than a year after it was premiered by the SN, and the first two *Nocturnes* were performed by Lamoureux's orchestra on 9 December 1900. (The complete work was heard for the first time on 27 October 1901.) During the years 1895–1902,

---

[11] Brian Hart, 'The Symphony and National Identity in Early Twentieth-Century France', in Barbara L. Kelly (ed.), *French Music, Culture, and National Identity, 1870–1939* (Rochester, NY: University of Rochester Press, 2008), pp. 140–3.

Debussy's music received a total of nine performances by these two ensembles.

After the première of *Pelléas et Mélisande* in 1902, interest in Debussy's orchestral music grew rapidly; between 1903 and 1914, his various orchestral compositions were performed an astounding seventy-five times by the three major orchestral societies. *Faune* was by far his most popular work and was performed thirty-one times by the three major orchestras over that span. The more substantial and difficult *Nocturnes* and *La Mer* were heard less often, and there were only two pre-war performances of *Jeux* and a single hearing of the complete *Images*. Perhaps the greatest testament to Debussy's growing stature during this time is the fact that his works were heard nine times at the Concerts du Conservatoire between 1905 and 1914 – an acknowledgment and confirmation of his position as the leading French composer of his generation.

Author's Recommendation
Prélude à l'après-midi d'un faune (1894).

Debussy's *Prélude à l'après-midi d'un faune* was inspired by Stéphane Mallarmé's Symbolist poem. There is some indication that the composer's original conception included several movements which were to serve as incidental music for a dramatic reading of the poem, but in the end the *Prélude* stands alone. Scored for a small orchestra of three flutes, two oboes, two clarinets, four horns, two harps, and strings, the work was premiered at an SN orchestral concert on 22 December 1894, given in partnership with the Concerts d'Harcourt and thus open to the public. By all accounts, Debussy's work was enthusiastically received by the audience, but initial critical reaction was decidedly mixed. Over the remainder of Debussy's life, the *Prélude* was by far the most frequently performed of his orchestral works. In 1910, Debussy recalled that when he had played his new work for Mallarmé, the poet remained silent for some time before remarking that 'this music prolongs the emotion of my poem and evokes the setting more passionately than colour could'.

CHAPTER 21

Debussy Noctambule *and Parisian Popular Culture*

Sarah Gutsche-Miller

For anyone wanting a night out on the town, late nineteenth-century Paris was paradise. Referred to nostalgically as the Belle Époque, the period has become synonymous with the burgeoning popular entertainment industry that gave rise to its moniker. As contemporary tourist guidebooks promised, one could partake in the city's bustling street life and lively cafés, revel in its raucous balls and unruly dance halls, be dazzled by the latest music-hall acts and dreamy romantic comedies, and delight in any number of spectacular theatrical extravaganzas. It was an exciting time to be in Paris, and a fun one.

The rise of French popular culture aligned almost exactly with Debussy's lifetime, his childhood coinciding with the deregulation of French theatres and subsequent opening-up of a free market for theatrical production. By the time Debussy completed his studies, the entertainment industry was flourishing. Alongside the ever-fashionable boulevard theatres arose a dizzying array of new venues that presented a seemingly endless succession of novelties and marvels, setting trends and creating the buzz that gave Paris its reputation as the nightlife capital of Europe.

Debussy was a night owl, well acquainted with Parisian nightlife. He could happily while away his evenings in cafés and cabarets, he enjoyed operetta and the latest music-hall entertainments, and he relished band concerts and the circus. Like many of his contemporaries, besides seeking amusing diversions in these eclectic and adrenaline-charged establishments, he was also inspired by the whimsical fantasies and sensual delights they offered. Echoes of this world can be found in many of his works, from cakewalks and clowns in the *Préludes* and *Children's Corner* or recollections of Pierrot in *Fêtes galantes* and *Suite bergamasque* to music-hall ballets in *La Boîte à joujoux* and *Jeux*. His encounters with popular trends also had a more ineffable impact: as with contemporary visual artists from Toulouse-Lautrec to Picasso, path-breaking artistic developments in popular entertainment introduced Debussy to creative possibilities not seen or heard in state establishments and encouraged unconventional approaches to musical composition.

This chapter provides a glimpse into the Parisian popular entertainments that Debussy would have known. I begin my tour with an overview of the various boulevard theatres that he visited, then move to what was on offer at the most famous *café-concerts*, music halls, variety theatres, and circuses. I end in Montmartre for a look at the bohemian world of balls, cafés, and cabarets.

Les Grands Boulevards

At the heart of Paris's entertainment industry were the majestic spectacle theatres that graced the city's *grands boulevards*: the Théâtre des Variétés, the Théâtre de la Porte Saint-Martin, the Théâtre de la Gaîté, the Théâtre des Nouveautés, and the Théâtre des Folies-Dramatiques, along with smaller but equally beloved institutions such as the Théâtre des Bouffes-Parisiens (historically an operetta theatre, but it is also where Debussy saw Maeterlinck's *Pelléas et Mélisande* in 1893). Long-established destinations of the middle and upper classes, the boulevard theatres remained trendy throughout the late nineteenth and early twentieth centuries, appealing to a broad but still upscale audience that wanted pleasant, predictable entertainment. The theatres themselves were impressive. Although not as grand as the Opéra, the Variétés, Gaîté, and Porte Saint-Martin boasted luxurious surroundings and sumptuous décor. Their shows, too, were lavish. Costumes and stage sets tended towards awe-inspiring opulence, and productions often included ballets, crowd scenes, or other eye-catching tableaux. In content, however, the spectacle theatres afforded little that was new. At the *fin de siècle*, repertoire consisted primarily of reprises of the elaborate *féeries*, operettas, comedies, and dramas 'à grand spectacle' popular in the mid-century, such as *La Dame de Monsoreau* and *Le Bossu*, both of which Debussy saw at the Porte Saint-Martin in the 1890s. They were both new productions of earlier successes.

What most often brought Debussy to the boulevard theatres was his predilection for operetta. Operetta and comic opera remained popular genres throughout the *fin de siècle*. Not only did established theatres such as the Gaîté, Bouffes-Parisiens, and Théâtre des Variétés continue to stage older repertoire – Debussy particularly appreciated Offenbach and Hervé – several theatres also staged new operettas. Claude Terrasse's *Le Sire de Vergy*, for example, which Debussy declared had marked a renaissance for the genre, was premiered at the Théâtre des Variétés.[1] Debussy, who sought novelty, also favoured productions in smaller theatres, *café-concerts*, and music halls, where generic conventions were more often dispensed with. The Nouveau-Théâtre, a new theatre that adjoined the Casino de Paris music hall, regularly premiered original comedies, operettas, pantomimes, and ballets by young authors and composers, as did high-end *café-concerts* such as the Eldorado and the Alcazar, and fashionable music halls such as the Folies-Bergère and the Olympia.

Spectacles Variés

Debussy's penchant for novelties was best met by the city's *café-concerts*, music halls, variety theatres, and circuses. Of these, *café-concerts* were the most prevalent. With over two hundred establishments operating in Paris alone, they were a staple of *fin-de-siècle* popular entertainment.[2] Descendants of the *café chantant* and working-class cafés, Belle Époque *café-concerts* offered patrons a laid-back ambience for an evening of drinks and entertainment. They were especially famous for their singers, including the legendary Yvette Guilbert and Mistinguette, and the now lesser-known Paul Delmet, a singer favoured by Debussy, who sang at the Ambassadeurs, Scala, Éden-Concert, and Chat Noir. As the century waned, *café-concerts* increasingly came to resemble music halls, then the most popular form of entertainment with their evening-length mixed programmes of circus acts, singers, dancers, and theatrical numbers. Many *café-concerts* turned to presenting evenings of variety acts and, as mentioned above, the larger, more ambitious venues such as the Alcazar, Eldorado, and Parisiana began staging operettas, pantomimes, ballets, and eventually revues. By the early 1900s, many *café-concerts* were virtually indistinguishable from the many music halls that sprang up across Paris in the last years of the nineteenth century.

The music hall at the forefront of Parisian entertainment trends was the Folies-Bergère. Inaugurated in the early 1870s, the Folies-Bergère was the oldest and most famous music hall in the city. Situated steps away from the Grands Boulevards (and until 1911 around the corner from the Conservatoire), the Folies-Bergère provided a world of fantasy, novelty,

---

[1] Debussy's review of Terrasse's *Le Sire de Vergy* in April 1903 is enlightening regarding his views on Offenbach. *Monsieur Croche*, pp. 158–9.
[2] François Caradec and Alain Weill, *Le Café-concert* (Paris: Fayard, 2007); André Sallée and Philippe Chauveau, *Music-hall et café-concert* (Paris: Bordas, 1985); Elizabeth Pillet, 'Café-concerts et cabarets', *Romantisme* 75 (1992), pp. 43–50.

and variety unmatched by any other venue. It had the financial means to hire the most sought-after stars and stage the most enticing entertainments: internationally renowned acrobats, athletes, and clowns; glamorous singers and dancers; and titillating theatrical numbers, including pantomimes, ballets, and revues. The hall itself was comfortable, inviting, and opulently decorated, and it attracted an upscale audience.

Debussy spent many a night at the famous hall. It was at the Folies-Bergère that he became familiar with Loie Fuller, whose diaphanous performances of movement and light are said to have inspired 'Voiles', much as they inspired numerous Symbolist artists and writers. Debussy and Fuller planned a collaboration, but the project fell through.[3] The clown Foottit performed there, as did Émilienne d'Alençon, Cléo de Mérode, and Liane de Pougy, all mentioned in Debussy's letters.[4] It was also at the Folies-Bergère that Debussy most likely developed a lifelong interest in ballet. In a review of a music-hall ballet that he saw at the London Empire in 1903 'as a reward for having been so well behaved during [Wagner's] Ring', he proposed what his ideal ballet aesthetic would be in Symbolist terms that foreshadowed his own approach to ballet writing.[5] Although he ultimately shied away from composing a music-hall ballet with Pierre Louÿs for the Olympia in 1897, he did accept – though never completed – two commissions for ballets slated to be performed in English music halls.[6] The ballets he did compose, including *Jeux* for the Ballets Russes, all suggest a familiarity with popular forms of the genre. *La Boîte à joujoux* recalls several music-hall toy ballets; *Jeux* followed a trend for contemporary ballets that broke with narrative conventions; and the unfinished *Khamma* was in keeping with the sensuous exoticism then in fashion.[7]

Debussy could indulge his penchant for variety theatre at several other establishments as well. Parisian audiences had an insatiable appetite for novelty and variety, and many venues cashed in on this predilection. Along

---

[3] Robert Orledge, *Debussy and the Theatre* (Cambridge: Cambridge University Press, 1982), pp. 157–9.
[4] Pierre Louÿs involved Debussy in a project to write a ballet, *Daphnis et Chloé*, to be performed by d'Alençon, Mérode, and Labounskaya. On Fuller and Debussy, see Catherine Kautsky, *Debussy's Paris: Piano Portraits of the Belle Époque* (New York: Rowan & Littlefield, 2017), pp. 35–6.
[5] Debussy, 'Musique: Impressions sur la Tétralogie à Londres', *Gil Blas* (1 June 1903), p. 3, in *Monsieur Croche*, p. 183. In 1909, Debussy compared Ballets Russes costumes unfavourably to those of the Folies-Bergère. Orledge, *Debussy and the Theatre*, p. 151.
[6] Orledge, *Debussy and the Theatre*, pp. 186–205. For Louÿs's letters about his prospective music-hall ballet, see *Correspondance*, p. 372.
[7] On Debussy and the Ballets Russes and on *La Boîte à joujoux*, see Orledge, *Debussy and the Theatre*, pp. 149–76, 177–85. On music-hall ballet, see Sarah Gutsche-Miller, *Parisian Music-Hall Ballet, 1871–1913* (Rochester, NY: University of Rochester Press, 2015).

with the Olympia and Casino de Paris music halls, inaugurated in the wake of the Folies-Bergère's success, theatres such as the Théâtre Marigny, Éden-Théâtre, and Nouveau-Théâtre turned to presenting evenings of mixed programmes, showcasing circus acts and song-and-dance performances along with more conventional theatrical numbers such as pantomimes, comedies, ballets, and operettas. Debussy discovered the American clown General La Vine – immortalised as 'General Lavine – eccentric' in *Préludes*, book 2 – not at a circus but at the Théâtre Marigny.[8] The reverse was also true. Several circuses staged pantomimes and ballets alongside circus acts, or incorporated comic sketches and acrobatic acts into pantomimes and revues.[9] It was in a pantomime at the highly fashionable Nouveau Cirque, for instance, that Debussy first saw his favourite clowns, the duo Foottit et Chocolat; it is also where he might have seen Mr and Mrs Elks dance the cakewalk, whose syncopated music Debussy became enamoured with after hearing Sousa's band perform cakewalks at the 1900 Exposition Universelle in Paris.[10] Star attractions made the rounds of the variety-theatre circuit and popular trends reached far and wide. Debussy could also have seen Foottit et Chocolat perform their improvisatory slapstick sketches at the Folies-Bergère or, individually, at other circuses around the city, and the cakewalk craze permeated all aspects of Parisian life – from performances by the Elks at music halls and circuses to amateur public competitions and private soirées. Debussy eventually met Foottit et Chocolat at the popular American Bar Reynolds. Debussy also frequented Chez Thommen on the Left Bank and Chez Pousset in the ninth arrondissement, which attracted artists and writers such as Catulle Mendès, Villiers de l'Isle-Adam, Gabriel Mourey, Charles de Sivry, and Adolphe Willette; the Café Vachette in the Latin quarter, where Debussy probably became acquainted with Jean Moréas and other Symbolists; and the upscale Café Weber in the eighth arrondissement, a meeting place of the artistic and literary elite, where Debussy met Marcel Proust.[11]

---

[8] Paul Roberts, *Images: The Piano Music of Claude Debussy* (Portland, OR: Amadeus Press, 1996), pp. 201–27.
[9] *Guide des plaisirs à Paris* (Paris: Édition photographique, 1899).
[10] Dominique Jando, 'Foottit et Chocolat', www.circopedia.org/Foottit_et_Chocolat; Davinia Caddy, 'Parisian Cake Walks', *19th-Century Music* 30 (Spring 2007), pp. 288–317; James Deaville, 'Debussy's Cakewalk: Race, Modernism and Music in Early Twentieth-Century Paris', *Revue musicale OICRM* 2 (2014), pp. 20–39.
[11] Lesure (Rolf), pp. 78–80, 141–2; Edward Lockspeiser, *Debussy: His Life and Mind*, 2nd ed., vol. 1 (London: Cassell, 1966), pp. 135–41. See also references to cafés in *Correspondance*, pp. 82, 92, 183, 209, 337.

La Bohème Montmartroise

Up the hill from the fashionable boulevards with their music halls and circuses stood another mecca of pleasures: Montmartre. Historically a working-class neighbourhood and established outpost of the bohemian avant-garde and revolutionary politics, Montmartre in the last decades of the nineteenth century became a destination for those seeking escapist frivolity. The area quickly grew famous for its many cafés, dance halls, *café-concerts*, and cabarets, which attracted increasingly large and diverse crowds. Yet Montmartre did not lose its unconventional spirit, and its entertainments differed markedly from those of the boulevards: the cabarets were edgier, and the cafés, dance halls, and *café-concerts* coarser and rowdier than those of the gentrified boulevards, with several Montmartre establishments trading on a reputation for debauched and sensational entertainments. Famous venues included the Moulin Rouge, home of the famous 'naturalist quadrille' of high-kicking dancers, along with the Moulin de la Galette and the Élysée Montmartre, the raucous dance halls vividly depicted by Toulouse-Lautrec and Willette.

Equally rowdy, but appealing to a more intellectual crowd, were Montmartre's many cabarets, including the legendary Chat Noir, Auberge du Clou, Cabaret des Quat'z'Arts, Mirliton, and Lapin Agile. Cabarets – also known as *cabarets artistiques* – were a specialty of Montmartre, popular with artists, writers, intellectuals, and young radicals, as well as with wealthy gentlemen curious to partake in this irreverent subculture. Like *café-concerts*, cabarets offered a relaxed and permissive atmosphere for drinks and entertainment. However, the audience of the cabaret differed in one important respect: patrons were often also participants, performing songs or improvising stories and sketches for each other. The Chat Noir, for instance, often served as a testing ground for artists, writers, and musicians to experiment, to parody high art and its academic conventions, and to have a laugh. The tone of these shows was alternately witty, ironic, satiric, or macabre, often with political or social overtones, and performances almost always defied conventions.[12]

Debussy, a frequent visitor to many Montmartre establishments, including cafés, dance halls, and *café-concerts*, was especially fond of the cabaret, first attending soirées at the Chat Noir, and later frequenting the Auberge du Clou. The Chat Noir he knew was the second establishment of

---

[12] Michela Niccolai, '"Aux Muses et à la joie": Le Chat Noir entre musique et mise en scène', in Phillip Dennis Cate (ed.), *Autour du Chat Noir: Arts et plaisirs à Montmartre, 1880–1910* (Paris: Flammarion, 2012), p. 58.

that name, a more spacious venue that had a small stage but which retained its original quirky carnivalesque *décor* and boisterous ambiance. The Chat Noir presented artistic soirées of cabaret fare such as humorous or caustic dramatic sketches, poetry, and songs; however, it also inaugurated a new attraction: elaborate shadow-puppet shows created and performed by the cabaret's members.[13] The shadow-puppet plays spread the Chat Noir's fame far and wide, and prompted several other cabarets to install their own shadow theatres. The Auberge du Clou, for instance, initially a rustic tavern, was transformed into a *cabaret artistique* in the wake of the Chat Noir's success, with similar amusements for a similarly convivial group of artists and writers, including several who defected from the increasingly commercial Chat Noir.[14] Debussy grew to prefer the Auberge du Clou, spending many evenings there in the company of fellow artists and musicians including Erik Satie.[15]

Conclusion

By 1900, Paris boasted the highest concentration in Europe of cafés, *café-concerts*, dance halls, costume balls, music halls, cabarets, theatres, circuses, puppet shows, skating rinks, travelling carnivals, outdoor band concerts, fairs, festivals, and parades. Debussy did not need to go to great lengths to seek out new delights: popular entertainment was hard to miss. Illustrated placards announcing headline attractions lined the exterior walls of theatres and music halls, and advertisement posters – such as the one for Barnum and Bailey's circus that Debussy admired at 3 a.m. – decorated the many Morris columns that adorned the cityscape.[16] He could also keep abreast of the latest novelties through reviews and theatre listings in the daily press; or he could simply stroll along the city streets. Debussy's musical development was shaped by this fertile environment. Open to novelty, he absorbed all artistic, musical, and literary trends, including those of the popular world. Some are evoked or alluded to in his music; others opened his mind to new ways of conceptualising musical structure and sound; still others he simply enjoyed.

---

[13] Phillip Dennis Cate, 'Autour du Chat Noir', in Cate (ed.), *Autour du Chat Noir*, pp. 28–9.
[14] Raphaël Gérard, 'Montmartre', in Delphine Christophe, Georgina Letourmy, and Béatrice de Andia (eds.), *Paris et ses cafés* (Paris: Action artistique de la Ville de Paris, 2004), p. 74.
[15] Steven Whiting, *Satie the Bohemian: From Cabaret to Concert Hall* (Oxford: Oxford University Press, 1999), pp. 110–13.
[16] Letter to Paul Robert, end of November–beginning of December, *Correspondance*, p. 628.

Author's Recommendation

Khamma: Légende dansée (1911–13 premiered 1924 in a concert version).

Commissioned by the popular music-hall dancer Maud Allan (1873–1956) as a vehicle for her sensuous exotic performances, *Khamma* exemplifies the melodramatic erotic exoticism popular with French audiences from performances of Diaghilev's Ballets Russes. The score, which closely parallels the scenario, evokes the fantastical yet sinister world of a young Egyptian woman who, as a sacrifice to save her people, ecstatically dances herself to death in the temple of the sun god Amun-Ra. Debussy's music features the full range of his compositional language – whole tone, chromatic, octatonic, modal, and non-syntactical diatonic harmonies; juxtapositions of binary and ternary rhythms; and distinctive melodic gestures – while revealing deep harmonic, melodic, and rhythmic affinities with Stravinsky's recent ballets *Firebird* (1910) and *Petrushka* (1911).

CHAPTER 22

Music Criticism and Related Writing in Paris
Michel Duchesneau

'In the writings of Claude Debussy, there is such insight (disguised as paradox), and such a true love of his art!'[1] This is how the composer Charles Koechlin spoke about Debussy's music criticism in 1927. Debussy's writings left their mark on the imagination of his contemporaries, not least because they contain aspects of his thought and 'through his elliptical style, raise and sometimes resolve problems of musical aesthetics'.[2] Many French composers of the late nineteenth and early twentieth centuries took up writing to air their views on their art and that of others. In Debussy's case, this writing is fragmented, principally divided into three main collections intended for journals. But if Debussy's writings half open the door to a musical world that seems both mysterious and deeply modern, we only get, as Lesure rightly points out, what the composer was willing to vouchsafe us.[3] For Debussy, writing was definitely a way to contribute to the artistic and musical life of his time, because the press was the main media outlet. Writing was also a way to earn money – surely a key factor for the extravagant composer. Debussy displays a caustic spirit in his writings, which are as much general reviews and reflections on music as music criticism. Debussy certainly took the music criticism of his contemporaries seriously, but only rarely found it helpful to his cause. About the premiere of two of his *Nocturnes* ('Nuages' and 'Fêtes') on 9 December 1900 by the Concerts Lamoureux, Debussy wrote to Dukas in February 1901: 'May I say that from the latent silence of your pen, which is usually more sonorous, rises a persuasive force due to an almost unique kind of virtual collaboration. But possession of an intelligence at the service of an

---

[1] Charles Koechlin, 'Les Compositeurs et la critique musicale', in Koechlin, *Écrits*, vol. 2: *Musique et société*, ed. Michel Duchesneau (Collines de Wavre: Mardaga, 2009), p. 177.
[2] Ibid., p. 179. Regarding Debussy's aesthetic approach in his writings, see François de Médicis, 'La Musique en plein air et l'idéal esthétique de Claude Debussy', in Michel Duchesneau, Valérie Dufour, and Marie-Hélène Benoit-Otis (eds.), *Écrits de compositeurs: Une autorité en questions* (Paris: Vrin, 2013), pp. 165–85.
[3] François Lesure, *Claude Debussy* (Paris: Kincksieck, 1994), p. 204.

infinite understanding is a luxury familiar to you.'[4] Very soon after, it was Debussy's turn to try to express himself on music, combining intelligence and understanding.

La Revue Blanche

Journals, often short-lived, proliferated in France's rich literary and artistic environment. Debussy agreed to write for *La Revue blanche*, starting March 1901. He succeeded André Corneau (1857–?), author, theatre and music critic. Corneau had succeeded the well-known critic Willy (Henry Gauthier-Villars, 1859–1931), who had upset the editors by belittling Zola, an unforgivable misdemeanour during the Dreyfus affair, since Zola was a supporter of the unjustly imprisoned Jewish officer. The journal was founded in 1891 by the Natanson brothers. Alexandre was the editor-in-chief, and Thadée and Louis-Alfred were members of the editorial board. It was an avant-garde literary journal that supported left-wing ideological ideals. Identified as openly Dreyfusard, it was considered by conservatives to have virtually anarchist tendencies. Copiously illustrated, notably by Pierre Bonnard, Édouard Villard, Félix Vallotton, Maurice Denis, and Toulouse-Lautrec, it was closely associated with the Nabis movement. Debussy was certainly very pleased with the journal's iconography.

The relationship between Debussy and the Natansons dated back to a dinner at Pierre Louÿs's in May 1894. During the soirée, Debussy met Léon Blum, executive editor of *La Revue blanche* at that time. Given her active role in the journal, it was probably Thadée Natanson's wife, Misia Natanson (née Godebska), a piano student of Fauré's and considered an important patron of musicians, painters and writers, who suggested that Debussy should replace Corneau. Debussy's contribution was short-lived, as he ceased writing for it in December 1901. He wrote to Félix Fénéon, one of the main architects of the journal, explaining the exhaustion he was feeling due to the preparation of *Pelléas*: 'It is with deep regret that I leave *La Revue blanche*, not because of the minor position I held there, but for the precious sympathy it represented for me.'[5]

Its editorial freedom allowed Debussy to write without restrictions. Fénéon, considered an anarchist, was at the heart of the operation of the journal during Debussy's brief tenure. The journal's anarchist values surely appealed to the composer, who saw it as a symbol of resistance to the institutions he criticised in his articles, especially the Paris Conservatoire. In the same vein, he criticised

---

[4] *Correspondance*, p. 585. [5] *Correspondance*, p. 628.

composers considered conservative, including Saint-Saëns and even Massenet. Furthermore, the journal was affiliated to an artistic world Debussy wanted to embrace: Mallarmé and Verlaine published in the journal; Denis illustrated the first edition of *La Damoiselle élue*, published by the Librairie de l'Art indépendant. In addition to these intellectual and artistic appeals was the need for financial gain. *La Revue blanche*'s proposal came at just the right moment, when Debussy was typically short of money.[6] In his article on Debussy and money, Denis Herlin estimates that the composer received around 200 francs for each article published.[7] With the premiere of his first two *Nocturnes* in December 1900, Debussy became one of the most prominent French musicians of the time, but that did not resolve his financial difficulties. His works from *La Damoiselle élue* to the *Nocturnes* were from this point forward closely associated with the new French music, and *Pelléas* was about to revolutionise French opera. Undoubtedly aware of Debussy's standing, the journal's editors seized the opportunity to strengthen its standing with the avant-garde.[8] Corneau's music criticism tended to concentrate on realist opera, such as works by Charpentier and Bruneau, and the operettas of Claude Terrasse (1867–1923).[9] Debussy thus found himself surrounded by such progressive luminaries as Mallarmé, Heredia, Louÿs, Jammes, Gide, Régnier, Klingsor, Ghéon, and Claudel, which enhanced his reputation as one of the leading figures of this avant-garde milieu in a journal that reflected his fundamental belief in artistic individuality.[10]

Interlude: *La Renaissance Latine*

In 1902, Debussy was approached to write for *La Renaissance latine*, a journal edited by Louis Odéro and sub-editor Gustave Binet-Valmer. Captioned 'Literary, artistic and political monthly journal', it came out monthly from May 1902 to June 1905. *La Renaissance latine* published poems, literary essays, reviews, and performing-arts reports, while reporting on the literary and artistic activity in so-called Latin countries. It came to represent the Pan-Latinism movement, which supported the idea of a strong Latin culture to counter the domination of the Germanic and

---

[6] *Debussy on Music*, ed. François Lesure, trans. Richard Langham Smith (New York: Alfred A. Knopf, 1977), p. 4.
[7] Denis Herlin, 'An Artist High and Low, or Debussy and Money', in Elliott Antokoletz and Marianne Wheeldon (eds.), *Rethinking Debussy* (Oxford: Oxford University Press, 2011), pp. 157–8.
[8] Paul-Henri Bourrelier, *La Revue blanche: Une génération dans l'engagement, 1890–1905* (Paris: Fayard, 2007), p. 806.
[9] Ibid., pp. 802–5.   [10] *Debussy on Music*, p. 10.

Anglo-Saxon worlds.[11] *La Renaissance latine* brought many leading figures together, including authors (Marcel Proust as translator of John Ruskin, Henri de Régnier, Remy de Gourmont), historians (Gabriel Hanotaux, Gabriel Tarde), scholars and politicians (Maurice Barrès), and composers (Déodat de Séverac). At the time, Michel-Dimitri Calvocoressi was music critic for the journal, so Debussy was engaged to write articles on music mostly unconnected to events. Thus it was Calvocoressi who announced Debussy's new column to readers: 'I have good news to announce today to our readers: starting from next month, *La Renaissance latine* will offer, on a regular basis, the very original and endearing musical chronicles of Mr Claude Debussy.'[12] Publishing Debussy's writings so soon after the premiere of *Pelléas* was an excellent thing for the new literary journal, as it reinforced the idea of an artistic community sensitive to new developments in art and in music in particular. Debussy thus became the voice of a 'Latin' music, advantageously positioned against the Germanic musical world dominated by Wagner. This is confirmed in the words of Calvocoressi, who in his announcement of Debussy's participation pointed out that 'The work of Wagner . . . is only accessible to Germans or to those whose spirit is susceptible to the German state of mind; there is nothing, absolutely nothing, German or Germanic in Mr Debussy's work.'[13] However, although *La Renaissance latine*'s offer came just before that of *Gil Blas*, Debussy accepted the latter without completely withdrawing from *La Renaissance latine*. On the basis of a letter Debussy wrote to Calvocoressi in December 1902, we understand that an agreement had been reached to allow him to write for both journals.[14] According to Calvocoressi, Debussy actually submitted an article to *La Renaissance latine* entitled 'Considerations on Outdoor Music'. Branded 'idiotic' by the new director Constantin de Brancovan and consequently declined, the article was withdrawn by Debussy and subsequently published in *Gil Blas* the following month (13 January 1903).[15] Debussy's contribution to *La Renaissance latine* thus ended before it had begun.

Gil Blas

Gil Blas was founded in 1879 by Auguste Dumont (1816–85). For the title of his journal, the publisher was inspired by the eponymous novel by Alain-René Lesage: 'It seemed simple and logical to us to make his hero the title of

---

[11] On this subject, see A. Giladi, 'Origins and Characteristics of Macro-Nationalism: A Reflection on Pan-Latinism's Emergence at the Turn of the Nineteenth Century', *History* 365 (2020), pp. 252–67.
[12] Michel-Dimitri Calcovoressi, 'Claude A. Debussy, critique', *La Renaissance latine* (15 December 1902), p. 774.
[13] Calcovoressi, 'Claude A. Debussy, critique', pp. 776–7.   [14] *Correspondance*, pp. 705–6.
[15] Michel-Dimitri Calcovoressi, *Music and Ballet* (London: Faber and Faber, 1934), p. 119.

a newspaper that strived to be cheerful without triviality, genuine without cynicism, rebellious without malice, human . . . French in variety and taste'.[16] *Gil Blas* differed considerably from both *La Revue blanche* and *La Renaissance latine*. It was a daily newspaper intended for a bourgeois readership that might discover in its pages novels by Émile Zola[17] and short stories and chronicles by Guy de Maupassant.[18] Its editorial policy favoured a certain suggestiveness and gossip, which ensured the newspaper success in the last decades of the nineteenth century, a success enhanced by the attraction of its supplemental illustrated monthly journal. By 1902, however, it was in decline. It was then bought by journalist Antonin Périvier (1847–1924) and publisher Paul Ollendorff (1851–1920). Debussy's arrival coincided with the attempted revival of the paper by its new owners. In the 11 January 1903 issue we read: '*Gil Blas* is pleased to announce to its readers that Mr Abel Hermant has kindly taken on the role of theatre critic and Mr Claude Debussy that of music critic. . . . As for Mr Claude Debussy, we have not forgotten how much interest there was in the music criticism of the distinguished composer of *Pelléas et Mélisande*.'[19] The appointment of Debussy did not prevent the newspaper from enlisting the critic Willy at the same time, under the famous nom de plume of Claudine. Henry Gauthier Villars described how Willy set about his column, his tone fully in harmony with the paper's editorial line: 'Rest assured, I will speak to you very little about music each week, firstly, because it would annoy me; also because Debussy with his ebony curls seems to me altogether more authoritative than me (better Claude than Claudine).'[20] By choosing to write for *Gil Blas*, Debussy seems to have been moving away from avant-garde literary and artistic circle, for although literature always had its place in *Gil Blas*, the approach is more journalistic and oriented to topical events. Thus, despite himself, Debussy was obliged to follow musical news more closely. To discuss concerts 'at length', he had to attend the rehearsals, because the newspaper's production schedule did not give him sufficient time between the concert and the required deadline to compose his weekly (or more) reviews.[21] However, he definitely appreciated the benefits of working for a daily newspaper, in so far as it not only paid him for the articles but paid his travel expenses when necessary. Therefore, in

---

[16] *Gil Blas* (19 November 1879), p. 1.
[17] *Au bonheur des dames* was published in instalments between 1882 and 1883, just like *Germinal* in 1884.
[18] See, for example, É. Reverzy, 'Guy de Maupassant (1850–1893)', in Dominique Kalifa, Philippe Régnier, Marie-Ève Thérenty, and Alain Vaillant (eds.), *La Civilisation du journal* (Paris: Nouveau Monde, 2011), pp. 1267–70.
[19] *Gil Blas* (11 January 1903), p. 1.   [20] *Gil Blas* (12 January 1903), p. 3.
[21] *Correspondance*, p. 720.

a letter to Antonin Périvier, Debussy requested financial assistance in order to attend the premiere of Vincent d'Indy's *L'Étranger* in Brussels.[22] The relationship between the paper and Debussy was not perfect, as was evident from a letter to writer Régine Dansaert; 'I don't know what's going on at *Gil Blas*. These people regard me as a sophisticated fraudster with no intelligence. . . . It doesn't stop me making my request. Alas! we do not choose our working environment; we are not responsible for it!'[23] Debussy wrote to Georges Jean-Aubry in 1908: 'My literary activity for *Gil Blas* continued throughout 1903 . . . It was an adventure that brought me into contact with very strange people and I endured gloomy hours, forced as I was to cover all kinds of music.'[24] Debussy's experience as a music critic at *Gil Blas* lasted only six months.

In 1906, Debussy was asked to contribute to the *Le Mercure musical* by its editor-in-chief Louis Laloy, but he declined the invitation despite the musicologist's insistence.[25] Between 1906 and 1912, the composer wrote several articles variously distributed among the illustrated journal *Musica*, *Le Figaro*, and *Le Matin*, but no new regular collaboration marked this period.

Revue musicale S.I.M.

Debussy agreed to write for the musical monthly *Revue musicale S.I.M* in October 1912: 'My dear Écorcheville, the gods are willing to protect us in this adventure! As for me, I can only assure you of my dedication, imploring you in advance to excuse any possible wrong notes, and to believe in my reasonable disposition.'[26] Jules Écorcheville had managed the journal since 1907 and sought to make it wide-ranging, bringing together musicologists as well as scholars, visual artists, and composers. Concerned about the financial success of the journal, Écorcheville strove to diversify its content in favour of news reported by celebrated contributors (musicians and literary figures), sometimes to the detriment of the musicological content – he knew that authors' reputations benefitted the review. He had already urged Debussy to contribute to a musical celebration in honour of Haydn.[27] Building on the success of his journal in the musical world, Écorcheville brought Debussy around by emphasising the importance of his thoughts on musical taste in the pages of

---

[22] *Correspondance*, pp. 70–8.   [23] *Correspondance*, p. 747.   [24] *Correspondance*, pp. 1048–9.
[25] See Denis Herlin, 'Les Mésaventures de *Monsieur Croche Antidilettante*', in Michel Duchesneau, Valérie Dufour, and Marie-Hélène Benoit-Otis (eds.), *Écrits de compositeurs: Une autorité en questions* (Paris: Vrin, 2013), pp. 232–3; republished in Herlin, *Claude Debussy: Portraits et études* (Hildesheim: Olms, 2021).
[26] *Correspondance*, p. 1552.
[27] Debussy wrote a short piece for piano for the occasion, *Hommage à Haydn*.

22 Music Criticism and Related Writing in Paris

a review intended for a large audience of music lovers. Debussy wrote to Robert Godet in January 1913:

> You may be aware that I have begun to review for the journal *S.I.M* again... You will tell me, with good reason, that this is not one of those things that changes anything out of the ordinary! – it would be fairer to say: organised chaos – However, it is necessary to try to put things back in their proper place; to try to recover values that arbitrary judgements and capricious interpretations have distorted, like no longer knowing how to distinguish a fugue by Bach from the *Marche lorraine*.[28]

Debussy was not diverted from his preferences; the column was but a pretext for his reflections on music, and in some cases the actual concert review was limited to just a few sentences. It will be noted that Émile Vuillermoz, editor-in-chief, brought together the words of Debussy and those of d'Indy or his disciple Auguste Sérieyx, which were bound to draw the attention of readers. It is therefore not surprising that in November 1913 *La Nouvelle Revue française* (*NRF*), through the intervention of André Gide, appealed to Debussy to publish an article on *Parsifal*. Debussy wrote:

> My dear Gide, *La Nouvelle Revue francaise*; its amiable secretary, Mr Jacques Rivière; your kind insistence is too thoughtful for me to let it go without some justification... You know that I wrote music reviews for the journal *S.I.M.* So far, they have been sufficient to occupy the time that I can devote to the singular, as well as useless, task of giving my opinion.
> Wouldn't it be necessary to find something new enough to justify this double chatter?[29]

With the exception of a short article published in *L'Intransigeant* in 1915, Debussy's 'gossip' ceased with the end of *S.I.M*, which did not survive the war. The fact that Debussy agreed to publish a certain number of his columns in a collection (*Monsieur Croche*) leads one to believe that these writings were evidently more than 'gossip'. This is testimony to his unique outlook, which, as Calvocoressi recalled, perhaps says more about the musician and his music than about the music of others.[30] The editorial policies Debussy had to follow at *La Revue blanche* or *La Renaissance latine*, and even those significantly more divergent from his aspirations at *Gil Blas*, offer interesting perspectives on what nourished Debussy intellectually and what appealed to him artistically. Financial gain was a motivation, but the idea of sharing media pages with some of the most noteworthy artists and thinkers at the heart of the evolving artistic practices of his time undoubtedly appealed to Debussy.

---

[28] *Correspondance*, p. 1580. [29] *Correspondance*, p. 1701.
[30] Calvocoressi, 'Claude Debussy, critique', p. 778.

Author's Recommendation
Rapsodie, for orchestra and saxophone.

The *Rapsodie* for orchestra and saxophone is not one of Debussy's most outstanding works, but its history makes it possible to underline the character traits of the composer. who, while not necessarily appreciating certain activities, such as that of criticism, was of a disposition that lent itself to risky ventures, if only for the income derived from it. The *Rapsodie* was commissioned by the American Elise Hall, president of the Orchestral Club of Boston, who decided to learn the saxophone on the advice of her doctor. The request came to Debussy at the beginning of 1903 through Georges Longy, then principal oboe of the Boston Symphony Orchestra and musical director of the Orchestral Club. But he was in no hurry to honour the order, even if it had already been 'paid for [and] dined upon for more than a year'.[31] He started writing in June 1903 when the sponsor and Longy, who were in Paris, put pressure on him. Debussy wrote to Lilly on May 31: 'So I'm trying to finish this blessed piece as quickly as possible. Naturally, the musical ideas take particular care to escape me, like ironic butterflies, and I spend hours in indescribable irritation.'[32] He confided shortly afterwards to Messager: 'I don't know if you have a taste for this instrument, I for my part have forgotten the instrument's distinctive sound to such an extent that I have forgotten "this order" at the same time ... here I am desperately looking for the most original mixtures, the most suitable to bring out this aquatic instrument.'[33]

Debussy adopted the idea of a work with an oriental character, where coloured woodwinds dominate over a rhythmic pulsation maintained by the tensions of two beats against three. The saxophone part, not very virtuosic, exploits the velvety and 'aquatic' timbre of the instrument. But the work remained unfinished. In a letter to Longy, Debussy talks about fifty bars still to be found. The *Rapsodie* was completed by Roger Ducasse in 1919 and premiered the same year at the Société nationale de musique. The work bears witness to the impossibility for Debussy to write under duress, even less to pursue novelty for its own sake, but inspiration is nonetheless there in the first saxophone bars, and the small appoggiatura of the arabesque anticipates *Syrinx*.

---

[31] Letter to Pierre Louÿs, August 1903, *Correspondance*, p. 758.   [32] *Correspondance*, p. 736.
[33] Letter to André Messager, 8 June 1903, *Correspondance*, p. 742.

PART V

The Music of Debussy's Time

CHAPTER 23

Composing for Opera and Theatre outside Established Genres

Hervé Lacombe

Context, Assimilation, and Opposition

The musical context in which a composer finds himself cannot be reduced to new musical trends and works; it also comprises works established in the repertoire and more traditional but still active musical trends. Debussy's era and, more specifically, his personal musical culture are characterised by great eclecticism and diversity of styles. Thus, François de Médicis notes that between 1885 and 1890 'his writing reacts ... to multiple influences': those of Wagner, Franckism, and the Russians;[1] overall, Debussy exhibits a 'strong reactivity to the musical activity of his time'.[2] This chapter can therefore only focus on certain key points.

Debussy's operatic aesthetic is defined as much in relation to the traditional genres of French opera as in relation to Wagner or naturalism. His style is built by both assimilation and opposition – the two processes can be simultaneous. The assimilation process, considered as a more or less visible and conscious form of appropriation, is the most commented on in the case of *Pelléas et Mélisande*: what Wagnerian processes does Debussy retain in his score? How does he integrate earlier styles into his writing? What elements of Russian music may have influenced him? And so on. The opposition process is less often analysed, for it is not confined to the rejection of a work, but hinges on this work by responding negatively to its musical concepts. With Debussy, negation becomes a powerful creative operation. I remarked upon this in Chapter 19: the music he condemns helps him better define and assert his aesthetic position and operatic projects. One of the peculiarities of his personality is radicalism, amplified by the search for an ideal and uniqueness. To write is to gradually eliminate

---

[1] François de Médicis, *La maturation artistique de Debussy dans son contexte historique, 1884–1902* (Turnhout: Brepols, 2020).
[2] Ibid., p. xvii.

the easy solutions, the surplus, the conventions. Composing for the opera becomes for him composing *against* the operatic genre.

Reinventing Operatic Composition

Part of Debussy's modernity lies in deconstructing the traditional way of thinking and writing opera (this goes for his approach to music in general). It all starts with the choice of subject and the form of the libretto. Like Wagner, several composers wrote their own librettos, including d'Indy, who wrote those for *Fervaal* and *L'Étranger*, Magnard for *Yolande* then *Guercœur*, Augusta Holmès for *La Montagne noire*, Chausson for *Le Roi Arthus*, and Gustave Charpentier for *Louise*. Debussy also tried to write his own librettos after *Pelléas*, notably for his unfinished operas after Poe, *Le Diable dans le beffroi*, and *La Chute de la maison Usher*. Around this time, the validity of traditional verse was questioned. For Massenet's *Thaïs*, Gallet wrote free verse.[3] Chausson mixed regular verse, free verse, and rhythmic prose. After writing *Le Rêve* and then *L'Attaque du moulin* for Bruneau, Zola decided to switch to 'rhythmic prose'. In 1897, Bruneau's *Messidor* brought sung prose to the Paris Opéra. Three years later, for his naturalistic subject evoking working-class life in Montmartre, *Louise*, Charpentier chose prose for the stage of the Opéra-Comique. Debussy also questioned verse forms, writing: 'With rhythmic prose, one is more at ease, one can better turn around in all directions.'[4] With *Pelléas*, he essayed a double experiment: combining poetic prose with the setting to music of a piece already written, and so not conceived for opera. This came to be called 'literary opera'.[5]

The music of *Pelléas* occupies a similar iconoclastic position. The great critic of *Le Temps*, Pierre Lalo, observed in 1902 'that *Pelléas et Mélisande* appears at first glance to be different from all ... operas, that it cannot be defined by any of the formulas nor classified under any of the labels in use'. This opera, he explains, differs from both Wagner and Massenet, the two figures whose influence was most striking in French operatic theatre from the turn of the nineteenth to the twentieth century.[6] Lalo describes by negation a music 'free from all romanticism, free from all grandiloquence, hostile to all

---

[3] Louis Gallet, 'À propos de *Thaïs*, poésie mélique', *Le Ménestrel* (11 March 1894).
[4] *Monsieur Croche*, p. 207.
[5] Carl Dahlhaus, *Vom Musikdrama zur Literaturoper* (Munich: Katzbichler, 1983).
[6] Steven Huebner, 'Between Massenet and Wagner', in François de Médicis and Steven Huebner (eds.), *Debussy's Resonance* (Rochester, NY: University of Rochester Press, 2018), pp. 225–53.

emphasis, to any search for effect'.[7] Debussy is like the sculptor who realises an ideal form by removing material from the block of marble placed in front of him. But this still understates the opera's achievement, because the sculptor's creative gesture is often conditioned, the result of culture and learning. The negation must therefore be applied to the creative gesture itself, to free it from all automatism and return it to its quest for truth and only 'inner necessity', a concept we borrow from the painter Kandinsky.[8] The composition is consequently no longer based on received forms. During his career, counter-models – that is to say, music of heterogeneous natures but all removed from the dominant French culture – allowed him to confirm his intuition in various fields. These included Mussorgsky, works of French classicism, music from the Far East discovered during the Exposition Universelle of 1889, and even Old Masters. For example, listening to Palestrina makes him realise that music had been distorted over the centuries and that opera as performed at the Palais Garnier represented the ultimate point of this decadence: 'the very essence [of musical art] has been transformed, and it is a prodigious astonishment that it was able to end up at the Opéra'.[9] This condemnation was uttered in 1893, in a statement of artistic intent, which came at the end of the famous conversations between the musician and his teacher, Ernest Guiraud, a few years earlier.[10]

The moment when Debussy became aware of the compositional work required of a new style that had yet to be accomplished – by subtraction and unlearning – is discoverable. It occurred in 1893, when Debussy re-read a scene from *Pelléas* that he had just composed: 'It looked like the duet of *monsieur un tel*, or anyone, and, above all, the ghost of old Klingsor, alias R. Wagner, appeared at the turn of a bar, so I tore everything up and went back in search of a little chemistry of more personal utterances.'[11] The opposition is clear: on the one hand, the 'personal', which remains to be found; on the other, the unconscious models that were revealed: the form (a duet), the formulaic arrangement (*monsieur un tel* or anyone), and the most influential style (Wagner). To achieve truly personal expression meant nothing less than the reinvention of the entire act of composition, which explains

---

[7] Pierre Lalo, 'La Musique', *Le Temps* (20 May 1902).
[8] This principle is expounded in Wassily Kandinsky, *Über das Geistige in der Kunst* [Concerning the spiritual in art] (1911).
[9] Letter to André Poniatowski, February 1893, *Correspondance*, p. 116.
[10] Sylvie Douche, 'Transcription littérale du carnet de notes de Maurice Emmanuel au sujet des échanges Debussy–Guiraud (1889–1890)', in Jean-Christophe Branger, Sylvie Douche, and Denis Herlin (eds.), Pelléas et Mélisande *cent ans après: Études et documents* (Lyon: Symétrie, 2012), pp. 279–87.
[11] Letter to Ernest Chausson, 2 October 1893, *Correspondance*, p. 160.

this shattering declaration in 1909: 'Since [the Prix de Rome], I have worked to gradually eliminate everything that I have been taught.'[12] To do this, Debussy wanted to change the writing paradigm: no more counterpoint, no more harmony, no longer form in the agreed sense, etc., but 'a little compositional chemistry'. This subtle revolution experienced its Bastille in the Parisian operatic institutions[13] – prisons where the clichés are concentrated, symbols of established musical power, temples of luxury and noise and not of music.[14] *Pelléas* is the storming of the Bastille of French opera!

Three Operatic Models to Deconstruct

The Debussyan project may be defined as a reaction to three major edifices: nineteenth-century French opera and its heirs, Wagnerian music drama and its admirers, and naturalist and realist (verismo) opera. When Debussy described the ideal poem to Guiraud, he mentioned '2 associated dreams', then continued in the negating vein: 'No country, no date. No scene to do. No pressure on the musician, who freely fulfils the vision of the poet.'[15]

He describes the anti-grand opera: dream and no longer realism and local colour, timeless and no longer historical. The 'half-spoken' drama he hopes to find must escape the expected formulas (Scribe's 'to-dos'). Debussy denounces the perpetuation of the genre, dominated as it was by the works of Meyerbeer (particularly *Les Huguenots* and *Le Prophète*), in a musician as fine as Saint-Saëns. After the production of *Les Barbares* at the Opéra he laments the latter's persistence in choosing librettists committed to 'making theatre'.[16] When *Henry VIII* was revived at the start of the twentieth century, he exclaimed: 'It is perhaps the last historical opera to pass! At least it is to be hoped so, and yet it seems hard to achieve greater success there than did Meyerbeer' Fortunately, Saint-Saëns lacked 'that grandiloquence in bad taste, characteristic of the genius of Meyerbeer'.[17] In 1901, Debussy summarised the operatic firmament with three names: Reyer (who was regarded as the poor man's Wagner at the time[18]), Saint-Saëns, and Massenet. Massenet had also tried to revive grand opera with *Le Cid* (1885), but what Debussy – and the vast majority of commentators of the

---

[12] Response to an enquiry, *Comœdia* (4 November 1909), in *Monsieur Croche*, p. 295.
[13] André Boucourechliev, *Debussy: La révolution subtile* (Paris: Fayard, 1998).
[14] Cf. *La Revue blanche* (15 May 1901), in *Monsieur Croche*, pp. 38–9.
[15] Douche, 'Transcription littérale', p. 282.
[16] Debussy, *La Revue blanche* (15 November 1901), in *Monsieur Croche*, p. 57.
[17] Debussy, *Gil Blas* (19 May 1903), p. 3, in *Monsieur Croche*, p. 173.
[18] See, for example, Camille Bellaigue's reviews of theatre music and chamber music, *Revue des Deux Mondes* 52 (1919), p. 207.

time – valued in Massenet was above all the composer of the feminine soul,[19] as embodied in *Marie-Magdeleine* (1873), *Ève* (1875), *Manon* (1884), *Esclarmonde* (1889), Charlotte in *Werther* (1892), *Thaïs* (1894), *La Navarraise* (1894), *Sapho* (1897), *Cendrillon* (1899), and *Grisélidis* (1901). Debussy nevertheless compares him unfavourably with César Franck;[20] he reproaches him for pandering to his listeners, taking the easy way, transforming sensitivity into sentimentality, for capturing the superficiality of emotions rather than their mysterious movement, insisting instead of touching, and forcing pathos instead of avoiding it. These compromises were prerequisites for success; in contrast, Debussy extols a sort of aristocracy of spirit and priesthood of art, but his encomiums do not prevent some meeting points between their two aesthetics: the 'clear tints', the 'whispering melodies' of Massenet, his concern to create, following Gounod, a poetic atmosphere, prefigure certain innovations of Debussy.[21] However, Massenet remains dependent on the most unnatural conventions, particularly that of singing in all circumstances, even when dying! Unlike Werther, Mélisande dies during an entire act without an aria, without crying out, and without sobs amplified by the 'operatic voice'.

Debussy was among the many French people who made the trip to Bayreuth. He went there in 1888 and 1889. Wagner had infiltrated the salons; large excerpts from his scores were heard in concerts; and *Lohengrin* went on a grand tour of France in the years 1887–91.[22] The reception of Wagner in France and his influence on French composers of the second half of the nineteenth century are particularly difficult to analyse. He was so much the theorist and the critic, the poet and the musician, the artist and thinker that the debates around him and his music were passionate, sometimes virulent, and often interlaced with nationalist questions. After the years that saw French Wagnerism emerge, there followed a period of triumphant *wagnérisme*, with d'Indy, Chausson, Bruneau, Magnard, and others, who all reinterpreted or based their ideas on different dramatic levels, the libretto and its themes, compositional technique, vocality, and so on.[23] Debussy admired *Tristan* and *Parsifal* (*Pelléas* is in many ways

[19] Debussy, 'D'*Ève* à *Grisélidis*', *La Revue blanche* (1 December 1901), in *Monsieur Croche*, pp. 59–61.
[20] Letter to Ernest Chausson, 2 October 1893, *Correspondance*, p. 161.
[21] Hervé Lacombe, 'Poetic Expression and Musical Expression', in Lacombe, *The Keys to French Opera in the Nineteenth Century*, trans. Edward Schneider (Berkeley, CA: University of California Press, 2001), pp. 144–79.
[22] Yanick Simon, *Lohengrin: Un tour de France, 1887–1891* (Rennes: Presses universitaires de Rennes, 2015).
[23] Hervé Lacombe, 'L'Émergence du wagnérisme dans l'opéra français', in Lacombe (ed.), *Histoire de l'opéra français*, vol. 2: *Du Consulat aux débuts de la IIIe République* (Paris: Fayard, 2020), pp. 519–27.

a French answer to *Tristan*). He knew Wagner's scores very well, and even played them on the piano, which inevitably amplified his assimilation of them. This was a fundamental problem for French composers: certain procedures, certain musical expressions, became inscribed in their deep memory and hence revealed themselves in the creative act. One can find dramaturgical parallels between Gurnemanz and Arkel, Klingsor and Golaud. The interludes that allow the changes of scenery in *Pelléas* almost quote *Parsifal*. The principle of the leitmotif permeates Debussy's score, even though he distances himself from certain elements of Wagnerian technique, such as the excessively systematic repetition of motifs that makes the *Ring* tetralogy a 'musical directory'; the insertion of motifs whose symphonic development determines the unfolding of the scenic action; the very large orchestra, a monstrous exaggeration of the classical orchestra; the assignment of identifying motifs to individual characters for them sometimes to sing (a sort of musico-dramatic pleonasm); and the deployment of powerful voices, quite the opposite of the nuanced Debussyan voice. As in traditional opera, the voice assumes too much independent importance in the music and becomes an end in itself: 'it sings too much'.[24] Finally, the principle of the musical drama is too subordinate to the text, to the meaning and power of the Wagnerian sonic gesture; according to Debussy, the aim should be not to state the obvious but to allow what cannot be stated to emerge, so that 'music begins where speech ends'. Music represents the inexpressible: 'It should come out of the shadows, be discreet.'[25]

French opera at the end of the nineteenth century and beginning of the twentieth saw the emergence of two trends: French operatic naturalism around Bruneau, Camille Erlanger, and Charpentier; and its Italian counterpart, verismo, which arrived very early on the stage of the Opéra-Comique with, among others, Pietro Mascagni's *Cavalleria rusticana* in 1892 (100 performances by 1895), Giacomo Puccini's *La Bohème* in 1898 (100 performances by 1903) and *Tosca* in 1903 (100 performances by 1910).[26] Their success precipitated a crisis among French composers and a significant part of the press around 1910. Debussy found the naturalistic and verismo tendencies, which projected a 'slice of life' on stage, overwhelmingly prosaic; he sought to reveal existence in all its mystery.[27] However, he evinced interest in some scores by Bruneau, of which *Le Rêve* in 1891 was an event of note.[28] In his review of Bruneau's *L'Ouragan*,

---

[24] Douche, 'Transcription littérale', p. 281.   [25] Ibid., p. 281.
[26] Stéphane Wolff, *Un demi-siècle d'Opéra-Comique, 1900–1950* (Paris: A. Bonne, 1953).
[27] Letter to Georges Hartmann, 4 February 1900, *Correspondance*, p. 538.
[28] Cf. de Médicis, *La maturation artistique*, pp. 586–7.

premiered in 1901 at the Opéra-Comique, Debussy regrets the Wagnerian influence and the weaknesses of Zola's libretto; on the other hand, he recognises Bruneau's imagination, his contempt for formulas, his sometimes non-functional harmony, and his melodic freedom.[29] Premiered in 1900, *Louise* by Gustave Charpentier achieved considerable success, but for Debussy it had the stamp of '*basse beauté*' of an '*art imbécile*'.[30] While his remarks about Charpentier must be put into perspective – he was perhaps motivated by resentment or jealousy – the fact remains that their aesthetics were incompatible.[31] The banal and everyday, which had become the core of French opera's display of materialism, was opposed to Symbolism. To those who dreamt of mystery and the ideal, verismo was a 'factory of nothingness'.[32] But if we overemphasise the Symbolist origins of *Pelléas*, we risk overlooking a component of its music: the violence, which erupts in several places around the character of Golaud, like a naturalistic explosion revealing the power of human urges.

Stage Music outside the Opera House

In November 1895, Debussy took part in a meeting organised by Lugné-Poe, who wanted to reflect on an 'artistic development in which Music would play a certain role'.[33] Even though *Pelléas* was evoked during this meeting, it seems they were looking beyond the limitations of opera in general. Nothing was to be too rigid; invention was king. Avant-garde theatre, to which this meeting aspired, sought to encourage artistic expression outside established genres. Stage music offered a very flexible basis for this through its combination of theatre and periodic musical numbers, mostly just instrumental. It had enjoyed an extraordinary flowering since the 1870s, from which time Bizet and Daudet's *L'Arlésienne* stands out as the first masterpiece.[34] The period was characterised by a desire for renewal, which affected all the performing arts and sometimes produced unclassifiable works. The beginning of the twentieth century was still under the influence of the dream of the *Gesamtkunstwerk*, the total work of art, but revitalised. From 1909, the Ballets Russes, led by Sergei Diaghilev, dazzled the Parisian scene and offered

---

[29] Debussy, *La Revue blanche* (15 May 1901), in *Monsieur Croche*, pp. 41–3.
[30] Letter to Pierre Louÿs, 6 February 1900, *Correspondance*, p. 539.
[31] Cf. de Médicis, *La maturation artistique*, p. 593.
[32] Debussy, *Gil Blas* (16 February 1903), p. 2, in *Monsieur Croche*, p. 99.
[33] Letter to Hartmann, 26 November 1895, *Correspondance*, p. 288.
[34] Sylvain Caron, François de Médicis, and Michel Duchesneau (eds.), *Musique et modernité en France* (Montreal: Presses de l'Université de Montréal, 2006), pp. 135–50.

a new alliance of the arts. Stravinsky brought enchanting Slavic tales and the wild breath of pagan Russia to the French capital, with three ballets, *L'Oiseau de feu* (1910), *Petrushka* (1911), and *Le Sacre du printemps* (1913). Ida Rubinstein worked alongside Nijinsky on Mikhail Fokine's choreography for Rimsky-Korsakov's *Scheherazade* in 1910. She had already triumphed in Florent Schmitt's *Cleopatra* in 1909. Influenced by D'Annunzio, she advocated a religion of art, an art of revelation, communion, deliverance, and truth, which would allow people to escape the mediocrity of their condition. This is how she came to bring together the different artistic worlds of theatre, music, and dance, through collaboration between artists. She sponsored various productions and distinguished herself as a dancer, narrator, and actress. *Le Martyre de saint Sébastien*, premiered at the Châtelet in 1911, brought together around D'Annunzio's play the choreographer Fokine, the set and costume designer Léon Bakst, Ida Rubinstein as the central performer, and Debussy.[35] The difficult understanding between Bakst and Debussy during rehearsals testifies to the gap that often existed between a project of synthesis between the arts and its realisation.

Debussy may have perceived in this commission the means of achieving a poetics of dance (according to Mallarmé, dance could be regarded as the ideal form of the poem).[36] As early as 1900, Paul Valéry wrote to Debussy about a project based on an echo-play between dancers and mimes, accompanied by music; he put forward the myth of Orpheus as a possible subject.[37] In 1903, Debussy dreamt of rediscovering the theatrical formula of the ancient Greeks: tragedy, musical decor enhanced by the modern orchestra, choir, pantomime and dance, and the play of light.[38] Updating the medieval form of the mystery, *Le Martyre* finds itself at the confluence of many ideas and attempts to establish a world outside established genres. Before dying, Debussy thought of making an opera out of it, perhaps even a film; he also planned to compose stage music for a play by Shakespeare.[39]

---

[35] Carlo Santoli, *Le Théâtre français de Gabriele D'Annunzio et l'art décoratif de Léon Bakst: La mise en scène du* Martyre de saint Sébastien, *de* La Pisanelle *et de* Phèdre *à travers* Cabiria (Paris: Presses de l'Université Paris-Sorbonne, 2009); Lesure (Rolf), pp. 273–9.
[36] Stéphane Mallarmé, 'Ballets', in Crayonné au théâtre, repr. in *Œuvres complètes* (Paris: Gallimard, 1945), p. 304.
[37] Letter from Paul Valéry to Debussy, 15 January 1901, *Correspondance*, pp. 579–80.
[38] Debussy, *Gil Blas* (2 March 1903), p. 2, in *Monsieur Croche*, p. 110.
[39] Letter to Jacques Durand, 1 November 1917, *Correspondance*, p. 2160.

Author's Recommendation
Pelléas et Mélisande (1893–1902).

Debussy composed a kind of anti-opera, opposed to the French traditions of the nineteenth century and to the model of Wagnerian musical theatre. There is no libretto, but instead a play written independently of the music; no spoken dialogue (as in the *opéra comique*), but a singing voice that tries to follow the subtle fluctuations of spoken French; no traditional melody, except for Mélisande's brief *chansons*; no ensemble singing (duos, trios, etc.), instead perpetual dialogue and letter-reading. There is singing that is often closer to a murmur than bel canto! The orchestra, which is responsible for setting the mood and evoking the characters and important elements of the drama (notably with recurring motifs), can be considered the central musical protagonist. It manifests life, its mysteries, and its silences, in which human beings are lost and try to act.

CHAPTER 24

Ballet and Dance

David J. Code

'There is a woman at each crossroads of Debussy's life', declared Marcel Dietschy early in his centenary biography *La Passion de Claude Debussy*.[1] Years later, William Ashbrook and Margaret Cobb chose to omit many of Dietschy's 'effusive personal comments' about the composer's love life from their updated, more 'objective' 1990 translation.[2] No doubt the pervasive emphasis on intimate, romantic passions rendered the 1962 original a distinctly antiquated framing of Debussy's creative context. But in trying to navigate the avenues by which myriad ideas and cultures of dance intersect with that context, a slight reframing of Dietschy's romantic conceit suggests a useful guiding thread. At a time when musicologists seek to complicate individualistic focus on 'great men' with attention to the countless Others who aided their practice, it is intriguing to note the central role various foreign women played, directly and indirectly, in the dance worlds that impinged upon this compositional *œuvre*.[3]

For a preliminary mapping of these adventures with foreign females, it helps to frame the *œuvre* against the historical evolution of several overlapping worlds of dance. We begin with both feet firmly planted – *en pointe* – in the nineteenth century. Debussy's first publication, in Moscow in 1880, was a four-hand arrangement of three characteristic dances from Pyotr Ilyich Tchaikovsky's first ballet, *Le Lac des cygnes* (1875–6) – a direct emergence from his youthful sojourns at the piano with Tchaikovksy's patron Nadezhda von Meck.[4] A few short decades after these 'classical' beginnings, a last work written expressly for dance, the (unfinished)

---

[1] Marcel Dietschy, *La Passion de Claude Debussy* (Neuchâtel: La Baconnière, 1962).
[2] Marcel Dietschy, *A Portrait of Claude Debussy*, trans. William Ashbrook and Margaret G. Cobb (Oxford: Clarendon Press, 1990), pp. v, 7.
[3] For a partial list of the many dancers who rendered Belle Époque Paris 'an international mecca for female soloists', see Lynn Garafola, 'Soloists Abroad: The Pre-War Careers of Natalia Trouhanova and Ida Rubinstein', *Experiment* 2 (1996), p. 10.
[4] 'Danse russe', 'Danse espagnole', and 'Danse napolitaine' from Act III, printed by Tchaikovsky's publisher Jurgenson.

220

children's ballet *La Boîte à joujoux* of 1913 might serve as a suggestive exemplar of the new possibilities that had by then emerged for the art form.[5] But perhaps a more telling late bookend for a quick survey can be found in a work written by an erstwhile friend just before the end of Debussy's life. Erik Satie's *Parade*, produced in 1917 during the darkest days of the war, brings into view not only the epochally influential Ballets Russes of Sergei Diaghilev – one key driver of radical changes – but also the new cinematic and pop-cultural inflections of the 'Petite fille américaine' and 'Rag-time du paquebot' that, along with the costumes and sets by Pablo Picasso, most starkly illustrate the new century's leap into realms far removed from Tchaikovskyan tutus and *grands jetés*.

Of course, this was no straightforward linear evolution. Beyond the decorous settings on- and offstage at the Opéra (so memorably portrayed by Edgar Degas), different paths into the stylised populism of *Parade* also ran through iconic Belle Époque haunts like the Moulin Rouge and Chat Noir – fixed indelibly in the new poster art of Henri de Toulouse-Lautrec – as well as the Bouffes-Parisiens (home of Offenbach's cancans) and the recently established Folies-Bergère, memorialised in one of Édouard Manet's greatest late paintings. (From his exile in Rome, Debussy wrote longingly: 'I want to see some Manet! And hear some Offenbach!'[6]) Meanwhile, all manner of other people danced, whether informally – think of Auguste Renoir's social dancers *en plein air* – or more decorously, in the *bals* of the aristocracy and *haute bourgeoisie*, as recorded by lesser-known Impressionist Jean-Louis Forain. Further afield, the same years saw a marked upswell of interest, associated with the decline of a by then mythicised rural France, in all manner of *danses folkloriques*, which tripped into many musical imaginations hand in hand with the *danses exotiques* that also slid seductively through Paris from far-flung origins.

Clearly, this was an unencompassable cornucopia, even before we try to gather in all literary responses – from realists and Symbolists, poets and novelists, critics and fantasists – to the whole whirling array. And yet another story might be told about the stylised or imaginary dance rhythms that swirl through countless works never conceived for real-life choreography (for one towering precursor, think of the 'Un bal' movement in

---

[5] *La Boîte à joujoux* was published as a piano score in 1913. André Caplet completed the orchestration after Debussy's death for a first performance with choreography by Robert Quinault in December 1919. See Simon Morrison, 'Debussy's Toy Stories', *The Journal of Musicology* 30 (2013), pp. 424–59.

[6] Letter to Émile Baron, c. September 1886. *Correspondance*, p. 51.

Berlioz's *Symphonie fantastique*).[7] But maybe it is better, here, to focus on actual dancing bodies. So, for a selective stumble through Debussy's 'dance' contexts, let us accept as guides just a few of the women who, when passing through Paris to and from various 'elsewheres', left the clearest traces in the music and its sustaining milieux.

Some Background Presences

Debussy's early arrangements from *Le Lac des cygnes* emerged from a quintessentially 'French' tradition. Tchaikovsky keenly admired and studied the canonical 'classical' ballet scores of Adolphe Adam and Léo Delibes; his own three ballets would also all draw scenarios from Western European literature. Suggestive early variants on the 'foreign woman' theme occur in Adam's *Giselle* (1841), for which the choreographers Jean Coralli and Jules Perrot created the title role for Italian ballerina Carlotta Grisi, who claimed sole ownership of the part at the Paris Opéra for many years.[8] Decades later, in 1870, Arthur Saint-Léon tried the same sort of thing in staging Delibes's *Coppélia* as a star vehicle for the sixteen-year-old Giuseppina Bozzacchi; her hopes of similar tenure were sadly cut short in the first, war-interrupted season by her terminal illness during the siege of Paris.[9]

Although the tradition of Italian *danseuses étoiles* – as they were later called – continued well into Debussy's time, the classical traditions they embodied seem, with one exception, to have left him unmoved.[10] A disdainful 1901 critique of current productions at the Opéra mentions the art form only once. 'Amidst too many stupid ballets', Debussy opines, 'we find a kind of masterpiece: *Namouna* by Ed. Lalo. Who knows what deaf barbarity has buried it so deeply that nobody hears of it anymore . . . it is sad for music'.[11] He dimly echoes, here, the expressions of raucous enthusiasm back at this ballet's 1882 première (with another Italian, Rita Sangalli, as the titular slave girl) that had seen him thrown out of the Opéra and led to a temporary ban on composition students in the Conservatoire

---

[7] See my 'Debussy and the Dance', forthcoming in David J. Code and Barbara L. Kelly (eds.), *Debussy Studies 2* (Cambridge University Press).
[8] See Ivor Guest, *The Romantic Ballet in Paris* (London: Sir Isaac Pitman and Sons, 1966), p. 215.
[9] George Buckley Laird Wilson, *A Dictionary of Ballet*, 3rd ed. (London: Adam and Charles Black, 1974), p. 82.
[10] See Spire Pitou, *The Paris Opéra: An Encyclopedia of Operas, Ballets, Composers, and Performers*, 3 vols. (Westport, CT: Greenwood Press, 1983–90).
[11] *Monsieur Croche*, pp. 39–40.

loge.[12] A slightly earlier recollection in a 1900 letter to the critic Pierre Lalo (son of Édouard) offers nothing about dance or dancers amidst the paeans to the 'marvellous harmonies' of that 'luminous' work.[13] But greater interest emerges from Debussy's passing celebration of an orchestral suite from *Namouna*, in a 1903 omnibus review, as a 'masterpiece of rhythm and colour' – suggestively foreshadowing, and rooting in ballet music, his famous 1907 definition of music as 'de couleurs et de temps rythmés'.[14]

While most classical *danseuses étoiles* have left little clearer imprint on the historical record than their near-anonymous companions in the *corps de ballet*, the opposite holds true for some of the many influential solo female dancers who swept through Paris across the threshold between two centuries. A substantial literature has sprung up around the American Loie Fuller ('La Loïe' to her French fans), whose spectacular deployment of billowing veils and extravagant lighting inspired erudite literary-critical responses, from Stéphane Mallarmé (writing about her first Parisian appearances in 1892) to Jacques Rancière (theorising the 'aesthetic regime' in 2013); her rich cross-disciplinary resonances, meanwhile, have fed reflections on Art Nouveau, the aesthetics of cinema, technology in artistic modernity, and much else.[15] But inspiring as she proved to writers and artists – Toulouse-Lautrec, for one, produced several fine lithographs – there remains some question about just how much Fuller transformed her principal domain of dance. By all accounts, the music she chose, including Debussy's *Nocturnes* and Wagner's 'Ride of the Valkyries', bore little relationship to her movements; the stage effects that captivated Mallarmé struck others (including Louis Laloy) as kitschy artifice.[16] Debussy's one recorded response gives an inkling of his opinion: in a 1913 letter he drily invites André Caplet, then collaborating on the score of *La Boîte à joujoux*, to come to the Théâtre des Champs-Élysées to see 'your old friend Loïe Fuller in her exercises'.[17] Just as tellingly, when Fuller sought to add this very *ballet pour enfants* to her extravaganzas a year later, the (ultimately fruitless) correspondence unfolded solely with Debussy's wife Emma.[18]

---

[12] As reported by Ramond Bonheur in 'Souvenirs et impressions d'un compagnon de jeunesse', *La Revue musicale* 7 (1 May 1926), p. 101.
[13] Letter to Pierre Lalo, c. 27 August 1900, *Correspondance*, p. 567.
[14] Debussy, 'À la "Schola Cantorum"', *Gil Blas* (2 February 1903), in *Monsieur Croche*, p. 93.
[15] See Stéphane Mallarmé, 'Autre étude de danse: Les fonds dans le ballet', in his *Œuvres complètes*, ed. Georges Jean-Aubry and Henri Mondor (Paris: Gallimard, 1945), pp. 307–9.
[16] Louis Laloy, 'To Dance or Not to Dance', *Revue musicale S.I.M.* (1 June 1914), p. 57.
[17] Letter to André Caplet, 5 May 1913, *Correspondance*, p. 1601.
[18] See the letters from Emma to Fuller, c. 24 March and c. 1 May 1914, *Correspondance*, pp. 1791, 1806.

From Background to Foreground

Debussy's first direct contacts with such dancing *voyageuses* had taken place only a couple of years earlier. In late 1910, he contracted to write a ballet (first entitled *Isis* and then *Khamma*) for the Canadian performer Maud Allan, still enjoying the brief fame she had won for her scantily clad mime-cum-improvisation *The Vision of Salome*.[19] But though Debussy thought he did well even to complete a short score on the paltry story Allan provided, he left it to Charles Koechlin to complete the orchestration; the ballet was never performed in his lifetime.[20] The appearance soon after of another commission from Russian actor, dancer, and impresario Ida Rubinstein, for a far grander collaboration with Italian poet Gabriele D'Annunzio initially left Debussy cold. Remarking to Emma on the unfortunate impression that he now had a 'speciality for *danseuses*', he recalled those recent travails with a Nietzschean quip: 'we must not forget Maud Allan ... *Khamma* (thustra!)'.[21] But he soon accepted the new project, and the five-act (and five-hour) 'mystery play' *Le Martyre de saint Sébastien* was first sung, danced, and declaimed, with about an hour of incidental music, on 22 May 1911. Debussy, who had struggled to complete *Le Martyre* as quickly as required, deemed it a genuinely moving accomplishment.[22]

As wildly different as the substance and fate of Debussy's Allan and Rubinstein collaborations proved, both are best understood against the background of epochal developments in modern dance. A key point of reference was the 1899 arrival in Europe of Isadora Duncan, who brought with her from America a new, improvisatory, and 'natural' approach to dance, for which she was able to draw further inspiration from the ancient Greek art in the British Museum and the Louvre. As Duncan put it in her 1903 manifesto 'The Dancer of the Future', published shortly before she opened a school for young female dancers near Berlin:

> The Greeks in all their painting, sculpture, architecture, literature, dance and tragedy evolved their movements from the movement of nature, as we plainly see expressed in all representations of Greek gods, who, being no

---

[19] Allan had first presented *The Vision of Salome* in Vienna in 1906, with music by Belgian musician and journalist Marcel Rémy. See Felix Cherniavsky, *The Salome Dancer: Life and Times of Maud Allan* (Toronto: McLelland & Stewart, 1991); Maud Allan, *My Life and Dancing* (London: Everett & Co., 1909).

[20] See the letter to Jacques Durand, 12 September 1912, *Correspondance*, p. 1545.

[21] Letter written from Budapest, 3 December 1910, *Correspondance*, p. 1344.

[22] See Robert Orledge, *Debussy and the Theatre* (Cambridge: Cambridge University Press, 1982), pp. 217–36.

other than the representatives of natural forces, are always designed in a pose expressing the concentration and evolution of these forces.[23]

In pursuit of a latter-day equivalent of this 'Greek' vision, Duncan danced barefoot in a loose tunic that allowed her to move freely, like one of those 'dancers of the future' whose body and soul, as she put it, 'have grown so harmoniously together that the natural language of that soul will have become the movement of the body'.[24]

Allan, who had first come to Europe as a piano student and undertook no dance training before turning to 'musically impressionistic mood settings' (i.e. interpretive dance, to such works as Mendelssohn's 'Spring Song' and Chopin's funeral march), always resented the inevitable comparisons with Duncan, and even claimed priority in choosing to dance barefoot.[25] But the work that won her greatest notoriety, and two years of nightly performances at the Palace Theatre in London, perfectly exemplifies the collision of high-minded ideals with frank sensationalism that now came to feature repeatedly in this dance context. Duncan may have mystically claimed that 'dancing naked upon the earth I naturally fall into Greek positions', but in the real world a dancing near-naked woman inevitably courts less idealistic responses.[26] Titillation and scandal rippled through critical reactions to Allan's *Salome* alongside more earnest assessments (pro and con) of her talents as a dancer. The same prurient fascination had served Rubinstein, too, when, in her own offering to the era's widespread 'Salomania' (as *The New York Times* called it), she stripped to a 'wisp of green chiffon' during the 'dance of seven veils' in a self-produced 1908 St Petersburg staging of Oscar Wilde's play.[27] The notoriety of this production caught the attention of Diaghilev, who – no doubt with one eye also to her considerable wealth – included her in his first two *saisons russes* in Paris. Despite her negligible training as a dancer, Rubinstein soon found herself dancing alongside the great Vaslav Nijinsky in two

---

[23] Isadora Duncan, 'The Dancer of the Future', in Sheldon Cheney (ed.), *The Art of the Dance* (New York: Theatre Arts, 1928), p. 58.
[24] Ibid., p. 62.
[25] In a 1907 interview Allan complains: 'It was reported in French newspapers that I had attended Duncan's school. This is not true. It was in 1902 that Duncan first danced barefoot and I already did so in 1890 at Cornelius Vanderbilt's.' See Felix Cherniavsky, 'Maud Allan, Part II: First Steps to a Dancing Career, 1904–1907', *Dance Chronicle* 6 (1982), p. 212.
[26] Duncan, 'The Dancer of the Future', p. 58.
[27] 'The Call of Salome: Rumours that Salomania Will Have a Free Hand This Season', *New York Times* (16 August 1908); Michael de Cossart, *Ida Rubinstein (1885–1960): A Theatrical Life* (Liverpool: Liverpool University Press, 1987), p. 14.

productions choreographed by Mikhail Fokine: *Cléopâtre* (1909) and *Schéhérazade* (1910).

The Ballets Russes phenomenon has long claimed monumental status as the twentieth century's most spectacular early answer to the Wagnerian *Gesamtkunstwerk*. But if those two Nijinsky–Rubinstein productions later largely faded from view, that is no doubt because, though they postdate the grandiose 1908 claims for ballet of Russian 'World of Art' theorist Alexandre Benois, their subject and style hardly depart radically from the orientalist–sensualist tradition Debussy had long ago savoured in Lalo's *Namouna* (which had been drawn, like Bizet's opera *Djamileh*, from Alfred de Musset's Romantic variations on *The Arabian Nights*). More decisive breakthroughs came with the first ballets – *L'Oiseau de feu* (1910), *Petrushka* (1911), and *Le Sacre du printemps* (1913) – danced to the incrementally spikier 'neonationalist' scores of the young Igor Stravinsky. But Debussy's first venture with the Russian troupe, much celebrated in dance historiography, remains a more ambiguous affair.

With a canny eye to box-office receipts, Diaghilev chose a well-known work never conceived for dancing, Debussy's *Prélude à l'après-midi d'un faune* of some twenty years before, as music for the first ballet created by his consort Nijinsky in 1912.[28] The 'dissonance' between this fluid music and the 'angular' choreography Nijinsky drew from ancient Greek vase painting divided critical opinion and became central to the mythology of modern dance.[29] A broader view recognises the kinship of this latest 'Greek' vision – its seven barefoot, white-frocked 'nymphs' gliding quite decorously (if somewhat stiffly) around the more carnal male star – with the ideals propounded by Duncan and emulated by many others. Nijinsky's *Faune*, which offered its own blatant sensationalism in a shockingly 'bestial' final action, now stands as an iconic instance in the construction of modernist aesthetic mythologies, through musical, choreographic, and scenic brilliance, but also the publicity of the consummate master Diaghilev.

The Two Ballet Scores

'I composed this ballet on the subject of lust', claimed Nijinsky about *Jeux*, some years after being temporarily dismissed from the Ballets Russes

---

[28] For details and many reprinted primary sources, see Jean-Michel Nectoux (ed.), *Nijinsky: Prélude à l'après-midi d'un faune* (Paris: Adam Biro, 1989).

[29] 'Dissonance' is Debussy's word; see François Lesure, 'Une interview romaine de Debussy (février 1914)', *Cahiers Debussy* 11 (1987), p. 5.

following his marriage to Romola de Pulszky in late 1913. More precisely – he went on in the 1919 diary that poignantly records his encroaching schizophrenia – he conceived the scenario for Debussy's only completed ballet score 'under the influence of my life with Diaghilev': 'Diaghilev wanted to make love to two boys at the same time and wanted these boys to make love to him. The two boys are two young girls, and Diaghilev is the young man. I camouflaged these personalities on purpose because I wanted people to feel disgust.'[30] But whatever 'disgust' anyone felt about homosexual subtexts in this flirtatious *ménage à trois* in tennis clothes was soon to be overshadowed by the other flavours of aesthetic outrage that greeted Nijinsky's contemporaneous choreography for Stravinsky's *Le Sacre*. That work's riotous premiere two weeks after *Jeux*, on 29 May 1913, now towers over all other mythologised monuments in this era of modernist breakthroughs.

Debussy, at any rate, found in the typical 'nothing at all' of a ballet poem Nijinsky provided for *Jeux* 'everything necessary to give birth to rhythm in a musical atmosphere', and it inspired one of his most quicksilver orchestral scores. Any disgust he felt for the ballet had little to do with 'lust' (of any gender configuration) but rather with what he saw as 'arithmetical' traces, in the choreography, of the then fashionable eurhythmics (roughly: rhythmic gymnastics) of Swiss educator Émile Jaques-Dalcroze – for Debussy 'one of the worst enemies of music' – whose school in Hellerau Nijinsky visited more than once.[31] Even so, his admiration for the other two participants in this sporty *ménage* inspired him to poetic praise for yet two more foreign women: 'for someone who admires her as I do, is it not charming to have Tamar Karsavina, that gently inflected flower, as interpreter, and to see her with the exquisite Ludmila Schollar playing artlessly under the shadow of night?'[32]

Given the childlike stance of Debussy's last ballet project, it is unsurprising to find the love triangle in *La Boîte à joujoux* – between a soldier, a doll, and a mischievous *Polichinelle* – both more conventionally gendered and more conservatively resolved. At the same time, this brilliant *summa* of the composer's lifelong fascination with dance rhythms taps into a last few contemporary contexts. The 'ragtime' rhythms that had reached Europe with nineteenth-century African American entertainers and inspired such works as 'Golliwogg's Cake Walk' and *Le petit nègre* (cause of latter-day

---

[30] Joan Acocella (ed.), *The Diary of Vaslav Nijinsky*, trans. Kyril Fitzlyon (New York: Farrar, Strauss, and Giroux, 1999), p. 207.
[31] Letter to Robert Godet, 9 June 1913, *Correspondance*, p. 1619.
[32] Note on *Jeux* for *Le Matin*, 15 May 1913, in *Monsieur Croche*, p. 243.

discomfort about racist caricature) now return, with more subversive irony, to convey the pompous pretensions of a marching toy soldier. And with the Pierrot, Arlequin, and Polichinelle of André Hellé's 'toybox' scenario, this whimsical children's ballet dips a toe, at least, into the widespread, pan-European revival of *commedia dell'arte* tradition – as in works as varied as Stravinsky's *Petrushka*, Arnold Schoenberg's *Pierrot lunaire*, Richard Strauss's *Ariadne auf Naxos*, and Ferrucio Busoni's *Arlecchino*.

Debussy may not have followed Satie as far as the *surréalisme* Guillaume Apollinaire hailed in his programme note for the first, May 1917, production of *Parade*, with its riffs on circus and cinema, 'synthetic Cubist' costumes, and noise-making machines (thanks to Jean Cocteau).[33] And if *Jeux*, with its orchestra 'without feet' and musical atmosphere 'lit from behind' (as Debussy put it), would later find a place in the most esoteric canons of twentieth-century avant-garde composition, the simpler (but no less inventive) musical pleasures in *La Boîte à joujoux* have remained, by comparison, relatively neglected.[34] Perhaps it is worth another listen, now, as the last work in a chain going all the way back to those student arrangements of Tchaikovsky – and a playfully entertaining contribution to the genre Debussy once celebrated, in terms refreshingly free of publicists' puffery, for its captivating 'rhythm and colour'.

Author's Recommendation

La Boîte à joujoux, 'ballet pour enfants', orig. piano solo (1913), orch. André Caplet (1914–19).

Soon after writing *Jeux* (1913) for Nijinsky's scenario about a risqué *ménage à trois* in tennis clothes, Debussy took on a much different dance project with a scenario by children's author André Hellé (1871–1945). *La Boîte à joujoux* (The toy box) features a more conventional love triangle between a doll, a toy solider, and a mischievous Pulcinella. Unlike the climactic 'triple kiss' and dusky evaporation at the close of *Jeux*, Hellé's scenario resolves more conventionally: Pulcinella defeated, we leave the blissfully married couple raising their burgeoning family on a farm.

---

[33] See the translation in Vassiliki Kolocotroni, Jane Goldman, and Olga Taxidou (eds.), *Modernism: An Anthology of Sources and Documents* (Edinburgh: Edinburgh University Press, 1998), pp. 212–13.
[34] Letter to André Caplet, 25 August 1912, *Correspondance*, p. 1540. For an extensive theoretical bibliography, see Mark McFarland, 'The Games of *Jeux*', in François de Médicis and Steven Huebner (eds.), *Debussy's Resonance* (Rochester, NY: University of Rochester Press, 2018), pp. 476–510.

Now, after the fading of modernist 'master narratives' (in which *Jeux* gained iconic status), it is perhaps time to recognise *La Boîte* as a brilliant, playful summation of Debussy's main musical interests, including exoticism, pastoral idyll, popular parody, and vivid pictorialism – all refracted through the myriad dance rhythms he had been exploring since his student days. The published piano score – richly illustrated by Hellé – exemplifies the variety of character and dramatic effect he could achieve with the sparest means; Caplet's orchestration adds many wonderful colours. Over a century after the posthumous premiere (1919), the work might now be taken as an open invitation: to draw ever new colouristic possibilities from the finely etched piano writing; to find fresh, contemporary games to play in the musical toy box.

CHAPTER 25

Orchestral Music and Symphonic Traditions
Andrew Deruchie

Debussy came of age during a golden era for the orchestral concert in France. Paris alone could claim the accessible and popular *Grands concerts* of Colonne and Lamoureux, the more exclusive Société des concerts du Conservatoire, and a bevy of shorter-lived concertising organisations.[1] Regular coverage in the dailies and the specialised musical press stimulated interest and educated audiences, especially about the canonised repertoire by luminaries of the past – Mozart, Haydn, Beethoven, Schumann, Mendelssohn, Weber, Berlioz, and Wagner – which accounted for the bulk of the programming. As Saint-Saëns, Franck, d'Indy, and others had demonstrated, concert hall success could bring considerable prestige.

Music historiography since the mid-twentieth century has positioned Debussy as the leading French modernist of his day. Working within intellectual and disciplinary traditions prizing 'progress' and radical originality, writers have habitually emphasised the boldly new characteristics of his music. Nonetheless, the material realities of concert culture necessitated continuity with the past. Conductor-entrepreneurs, unavoidably concerned with ticket sales, acted as gatekeepers, and success with critics and especially bourgeois audiences meant speaking musical languages they understood. Therefore, in the public sphere of orchestral music, the array of genres, forms, musical topics, narrative designs, rhetorical devices, and so on that Debussy inherited represented his inevitable starting point. This chapter offers an overview of some of the ways the received symphonic traditions factored in Debussy's orchestral music – and some of the key ways he transformed them – by way of three major works: *Prélude à l'après-midi d'un faune*, *Nocturnes*, and *La Mer*.

---

[1] For a survey of short-lived late nineteenth-century Parisian orchestras, see Michael Strasser, 'Ars Gallica: The Société Nationale de Musique and Its Role in French Musical Life, 1871–1891', PhD thesis, University of Illinois (1998), pp. 246–76.

The 'Beginning of Modern Music' through the Ears of Concertgoers: *Prélude à l'après-Midi d'un Faune*

Critics have long viewed the *Prélude à l'après-midi d'un faune* (1894), based on Stéphane Mallarmé's eponymous poem esoterically relating a flute-playing faun's erotic daydream about a pair of elusive nymphs, as both Debussy's first 'mature' work and a landmark of twentieth-century music.[2] No less a paragon of Modernism than Pierre Boulez famously declared 'modern music began with *l'après-midi d'un faune*'.[3] Much ink has been dispensed on the audacious newness Boulez celebrated. Yet the work quickly became popular and clearly did not unduly alienate early audiences. The question, then, arises: how might contemporary concertgoers have reconciled the *Faune*'s basic materials — its genre, large-scale formal processes, and harmonic language — with the nineteenth-century traditions they understood?

As a single-movement, programmatic orchestral composition making use of colouristic harmony and orchestration, the piece sits comfortably within the genre of the symphonic poem as Debussy's French contemporaries conceptualised it. Their benchmark was not the monumental scale, dramatic cast, and bombast of the genre's inventor Franz Liszt, whose symphonic poems they scarcely knew (prior to 1894, Colonne and Lamoureux performed only *Les Préludes*, *Mazeppa*, and *Tasso* a combined total of five times).[4] This was one genre where native composers prevailed in the French repertoire: Holmès's *Irlande*, Franck's *Les Djinns* and *Le Chasseur maudit*, and d'Indy's *Wallenstein* trilogy were all more prominent than Liszt. Best known by far were the four symphonic poems of Saint-Saëns, which received over eighty *Grand concert* performances during the same period. Although Debussy's *Faune* differs greatly in style, its near miniature scope (relative to Liszt) matches that of Saint-Saens's seven-to-ten-minute works. Its fundamentally lyrical disposition (expressing in the composer's words 'what remains of the dream at the tip of the faun's flute') also parallels Saint-Saëns, whose symphonic poems tend towards scene painting, in contrast with the Beethovenian, struggle-and-victory narratives favoured

---

[2] Many critics take at face value the composer's claim to have rendered 'a very general impression'; others argue that Debussy's work tracks the poem closely. The latter include David J. Code, 'Hearing Debussy Reading Mallarmé: Music *après* Wagner in the *Prélude à l'après-midi d'un faune*', *Journal of the American Musicological Society* 54 (2001), pp. 493–554. Quote in letter to Henri Gauthier-Villars, 10 October 1895, *Correspondance*, pp. 278–9.

[3] Pierre Boulez, 'Entries for a Musical Encyclopaedia: Claude Debussy', in *Stocktakings from an Apprenticeship*, ed. Paule Thévenin, trans. Stephen Walsh (Oxford: Clarendon Press, 1991), p. 267.

[4] This figure is based on transcriptions of *Grand concert* programmes in Élizabeth Bernard, 'Le Concert symphonique à Paris entre 1861 et 1914: Pasdeloup, Colonne, Lamoureux', PhD thesis, Paris-Sorbonne University (1976), vol. 2.

by Liszt.[5] In *Le Rouet d'Omphale*, for example, the captive Hercules strains and fails to escape Omphale's bondage. As in Debussy's *Prélude*, no dramatic action takes place; the scene remains unchanged. Saint-Saëns's programme, which describes the 'triumph' of 'feminine seduction' over helpless masculinity, even reverberates in the *Faune*.

Boulez celebrated Debussy's 'liberation' of form 'from the impersonal constraints of the textbook'.[6] The *Faune*'s large-scale design indeed resists assimilation to the nineteenth century's familiar symphonic patterns such as 'sonata form' or 'ternary form'. Nonetheless, its most readily apparent formal process would have seemed familiar to turn-of-the-century French concertgoers from well-known variation sets, such as the slow movements of Beethoven's Fifth and Ninth and the finale of the Ninth: the piece unfurls varied repetitions of its unmistakable main theme, embedded in ever-changing harmonies and orchestral textures, with contrasting episodes interspersed. And such concertgoers, expecting of symphonic poems novel forms unbeholden to received patterns, would not have found it difficult to hear in all this the 'successive scenes through which pass the desires and dreams of the faun in the heat of this afternoon', as Debussy once articulated the programme.[7]

No aspect of the *Faune* has struck commentators as more radical than its harmony. As is well known, Debussy's successions of chords frequently cast aside received 'functional' syntax. Conventionally dissonant harmonies (such as the half-diminished seventh following the opening flute solo) do not resolve in the usual ways – or even promise resolution – lending them a character Paul Dukas described as 'more harmonious in their complexity than consonances'.[8] With dissonance sapped of the tension and instability that underwrite the ineluctably forward-surging quality of 'common-practice' harmony, Debussy's music floats through time in a manner often likened to the hazy syntax and dreamy, mirage-like subject (were the nymphs even there?) of Mallarmé's poem.[9]

Yet this quality would hardly have struck Debussy's earliest audiences as extraordinary. Relative harmonic stasis had since Haydn's day served as a hallmark of the pastoral mode – a natural domain for fauns and their

---

[5] Letter to Henri Gauthier-Villars, 10 October 1895, *Correspondance*, p. 278.
[6] Boulez, 'Entries', p. 267.
[7] Quoted in Léon Vallas, *Claude Debussy et son temps* (Paris: Alcan, 1932), p. 181.
[8] Paul Dukas, *Chroniques musicales sur deux siècles* (Paris: Stock, 1948), pp. 142–3.
[9] See, for example, John Crotty, 'Symbolist Influences in Debussy's "Prelude to the Afternoon of a Faun"', *In Theory Only* 6 (1982), pp. 17–30; David J. Code, *Claude Debussy* (London: Reaktion Books, 2010), p. 7.

flutes – and is no more radical in Debussy's *Prelude* than in the 'Forest Murmurs' episode in Wagner's *Siegfried*, a symphonic poem embedded in the opera (and sometimes a Parisian concert item). Nineteenth-century composers also frequently immobilised harmony to evoke the timelessness of the 'exotic' and the 'primitive' – both, small steps from the pastoral, and both, categories overlapping the antique world of fauns and nymphs.

Harmony in the *Faune* does not *sound* especially like the established pastoral or exotic styles. As Alexandra Kieffer has recently shown, Debussy's syntax intensifies the harmonic language of 'musique de rêve', a now largely forgotten tradition initiated in an 1870s vogue for dreamy *rêveries* and *méditations* for the salon.[10] Fashionable modern composers, including Prix de Rome winners Georges Marty, Georges Hüe, Xavier Leroux, and Paul Vidal, developed the style in the 1880s and 1890s. In their settings of Symbolist poetry by Baudelaire and Verlaine, they sometimes cultivated somnolent sound worlds with the very harmonic conceits – 'colouristic' usage of seventh, ninth, and added-sixth chords; non-functional oscillations between pairs of harmonies; and even the temporary suspension of tonal centricity that Debussy employed so extensively in the *Faune*.

For all the work's undeniable newness, much of its basic material – generic, formal, harmonic – emerges from traditions familiar to its earliest audiences. The *Faune*'s originality is of the same order as Mozart's style: a fresh and compelling synthesis and adaptation of existing compositional resources.

The Symphonic and the Sensuous: *Nocturnes*

It has become a truism that Debussy's music emphasises the sensuous aspects of harmony, melody, and timbre – this being one way it stands apart from the German Romantic lineage extending through Beethoven's dramatic symphonies to Wagner and the metaphysical connotations of his music dramas. A Parisian in an age when sound shaped the urban environment in new ways, Debussy sometimes made the sensory experience of listening a focal point.[11] *Nocturnes* (1897–9) offers an especially rich

---

[10] Alexandra Kieffer, 'Reverie, Schmaltz, and the Modernist Imagination', *Journal of the American Musicological Society* 74 (2021), pp. 289–363.

[11] On the wide-ranging impacts of noise on nineteenth-century Parisian culture, see Aimée Boutin, *City of Noise: Sound and Nineteenth-Century Paris* (Urbana, IL: University of Illinois Press, 2015); Ross Chambers, *An Atmospherics of the City: Baudelaire and the Poetics of Noise* (New York: Fordham University Press, 2015). On the roles of listening in Debussyan discourses, see Alexandra Kieffer, *Debussy's Critics: Sound, Affect, and the Experience of Modernism* (New York: Oxford University Press,

example. The three movements adapt well-known nineteenth-century symphonic topics or expressive strategies to explore nuances of listening to diverse sounds in various environments.

According to Debussy's early biographer Léon Vallas, 'Nuages', the opening movement, was inspired by late-night cloud-gazing on a bridge over the Seine, punctuated by the 'siren' (*sirène*) of a passing boat.[12] This account has Debussy relocate to the noisy city the nineteenth-century symphonic-pastoral tradition, whereby music portrays a psychological response to nature (as Beethoven famously explained of his Sixth Symphony). Debussy's music evokes Vallas's urban-pastoral scenario. The series of floating – morphing but directionless – chords heard at the outset and at points throughout suggests clouds. Cloud-gazing (naturally) engenders reverie: this motive produces lyrical spans of increasing length and intensity, culminating in the movement's enraptured central episode (rehearsal 7), tinged with exotic and archaic hues redolent of the cultic fantasies favoured by the Symbolists, a *fin-de-siècle* cognate to the pulsating waves of ecstasy nature stimulates in swaths of Beethoven's Sixth.

The boat's siren – the recurring signal always played by the English horn – draws upon the same convention. As an environmental sound encountered while contemplating nature, it registers as an urban descendant of the nature sounds characteristic of nineteenth-century symphonic-pastoral works, such as the famous birds in Beethoven's Sixth and the *ranz des vaches* in Berlioz's *Symphonie fantastique*. But unlike these sounds, which play decorative and symbolic roles, Debussy's 'signal' functions as one of the movement's key motives, and its effect is woven into the piece's expressive fabric. Piercing the stillness with its sounding-from-elsewhere quality, the signal, unpredictable and seemingly random, places listeners on the bridge beneath the clouds. Following Vallas's scenario, it fragments the reverie and sends it in a new direction each time it intrudes upon it. 'Nuages', then, remakes as a recurring motive what in the pastoral tradition had previously been an occasional special effect. The movement thematises the disruptive effects of urban noise upon mental life – a quotidian commonplace for Debussy's Parisian audiences – as much as it does cloud-inspired fantasy.

'Fêtes', the central scherzo, similarly brings the pastoral into the city. Debussy based the movement on 'impressions ... of a festival in the Bois

---

2019); Kieffer, 'The Debussyist Ear: Listening, Representation, and French Musical Modernism', *19th Century Music* 39 (2015), pp. 56–79.

[12] Vallas, *Debussy*, pp. 162–3.

de Boulogne', adding 'a procession passes through the scene and becomes merged with it. But the background remains persistently the same: the festival.'[13] This programme alludes to the scherzo of Beethoven's 'Pastoral' Symphony, which depicts peasant festivities, including (in the middle section) music: Debussy transfers the rural revelry of Beethoven's scherzo to the Bois de Boulogne – a natural space within urban Paris – and the clumsy village orchestra in Beethoven's trio becomes the marching band in Debussy's corresponding section.

Beethoven's band injects rustic local colour in the tradition of Haydn's pastoral trios.[14] Debussy treats his equivalent as 'diegetic' music (music heard as such within the fictional scene). The procession episode begins with a sophisticated act of listening. The opening scherzo section, depicting the festivities, arrives at no formal closure, but vanishes, practically mid-phrase, an effect enhanced by the stark contrast from *ff* to *ppp* and the changes in metre and key signature. It is as though the auditory attention of the listener, through whose ears we experience the party, seizes suddenly and completely upon the distant sound of the cortege when it first comes within earshot, while (as Debussy has it) the scherzo 'persists' in the 'background', no longer heard. The moment captures the esoteric experience of 'segregating' barely audible music from the surrounding din.[15] The usual pleasures of music, however, are not the objective here. A broad *crescendo* depicts the procession's approach. When it arrives on the scene, the episode ends, as abruptly as it began, with a *subito* cut from *ff* to *pp* and the generically conventional return of the scherzo section: the listener now filters out the noisy band to seize upon the party sounds it obscures. Debussy's remaking of Beethoven's pastoral festivities aestheticises the rarefied experience – familiar to turn-of-the-century city dwellers – of listening in a complex *plein air* ecology comprising sounds that are distant, mobile, and occluded by other sounds.

Environmental noise in 'Nuages' becomes music in 'Fêtes'; in 'Sirènes', the last of the set, music becomes singing: Debussy conjures the mythological sirens with a wordless female chorus. By incorporating voices into the finale of a symphonic work, Debussy evoked the legacy of Beethoven's

---

[13] Letter to Paul Dukas, 11 February 1901, *Correspondance*, p. 585; Vallas, *Debussy*, p. 163.
[14] See, for example, the third movement of Haydn's Symphony No. 88 in G.
[15] As cognitive science explains, 'auditory stream segregation' is the perceptual process, often highly developed in musicians, which differentiates various sound sources within an 'auditory scene', allowing us to hold conversation in noisy spaces, focus on an instrument in the orchestra, or isolate a line in a contrapuntal composition. See Albert Bregman, *Auditory Scene Analysis: The Perceptual Organization of Sound* (Cambridge, MA: MIT Press, 1990).

Ninth Symphony. The French reception of this grandest of orchestral masterworks was entangled in Wagner's historicist polemics scarcely less than in Germany. Wagner's enormous influence in France reached its apex in the early 1890s, and his interpretation of the Ninth's marriage of symphony and song as the harbinger of the music drama was well known among Debussy's contemporaries.

Debussy undermined Wagner's aesthetics. In assigning the chorus nothing but wordless vocalises, he upended the new union of music and words foundational to the *Gesamtkunstwerk*. The sirens' music also largely eschews the desire-and-death chromaticism Wagner deployed in *Tristan*, a default language for the erotic and an obvious idiom for the mythological sirens, whose seductive singing lures sailors to fatal shipwreck. Indeed, in their brevity, rudimentary shapes, compressed ranges, and vulgar, fragmentary character, the sirens' melodies seem remarkably banal and bereft of aphrodisiac allure. Why have the sirens sing this way? By forgoing words and music-stylistic conventions signifying desire, Debussy directs attention to the *sound* of the singing voice, in the materiality of which Roland Barthes famously theorised the traces of the singing body he called the 'grain'.[16] Like Barthes, Debussy's sirens seem to discern an erotic quality in the carnality of the grain, capable of swaying listeners to *jouissance*. The sirens seduce, not with enchanting songs, but with the caress of their voices.

In Wagner's epochal account of the Ninth Symphony, Beethoven's incorporation of words into the symphonic style resulted in a quantum leap for musical meaning. In Debussy's reinterpretation, meaning takes an end run around the referential systems of language and musical style to derive from the sensory experience of listening. In 'Sirènes', the sensuous shades into the sensual.

Symphony Deconstructed: *La Mer (Trois Esquisses Symphoniques)*

The symphony was easily turn-of-the-century French concert culture's most prestigious genre. Most programmes of the *Grands concerts* and the Société des concerts du Conservatoire included a symphony. Like their counterparts throughout Europe, these orchestras heavily favoured the canonised classics by Haydn, Mozart, Schumann, Mendelssohn, Berlioz,

---

[16] Roland Barthes, 'The Grain of the Voice', in *Image – Music – Text*, trans. Stephen Heath (London: Fontana, 1977), pp. 179–89.

and especially Beethoven.[17] But herein lay opportunity: a new symphony that could join the permanent collection of masterworks could send a composer's stock soaring, as Saint-Saëns, d'Indy, and Franck had demonstrated.

Debussy took a notoriously dim view of the genre, irreverently dismissing it as formulaic, obsolete, and preoccupied with profound ideas ('metaphysics, but not music', as he once put it).[18] Nonetheless, he could scarcely ignore its cultural capital. *La Mer* stands as his most thoroughgoing reckoning with the genre. As Brian Hart, Simon Trezise, and others have observed, the tripartite cast of 'De l'aube à midi sur la mer' (an allegro with a slow introduction), 'Jeux de vagues' (a scherzo), and 'Dialogue du vent et de la mer' (a weighty, summative finale) follows the French tradition of three-movement symphonies established by d'Indy, Franck, Chausson, and Dukas.[19] Like most contemporary French symphonies, *La Mer* extensively deploys thematic cyclicism (themes from earlier movements return in later ones) and characteristic expressive devices, such as the grand, chorale-style apotheoses in the first and last movements, which 'monumentalise' a mysterious call from the slow introduction. 'Dialogue du vent et de la mer' in places evokes dance, a stalwart topic of eighteenth-century finales. 'De l'aube à midi' even appeals to familiar ('academic' for Boulez) sonata-form conceits. The slow introduction segues via an *accelerando* (as in Schumann's Fourth Symphony) into an engaging melody with simple accompaniment resembling a main theme (b. 33); the entirely new material before rehearsal 9, less rhythmically active, slower in tempo, and following a general pause, suggests a 'second theme'. The list of 'symphonisms' could go on.

Nonetheless, at virtually every turn, *La Mer* resists the formal and expressive conventions that defined the symphony in Debussy's day: the opening movement ultimately pursues a through-composed form which foregoes the usual fragmentation and recapitulation of its themes; the (cyclic) themes do not assume the dramatic agency of their counterparts in Beethoven, Franck, d'Indy, and Saint-Saëns; motivic development – the

---

[17] On the ascendency of the canonised classics, see William Weber, 'Mass Culture and the Reshaping of European Musical Taste, 1770–1870', *International Journal of the Aesthetics and Sociology of Music* 8 (1977), pp. 5–21.

[18] Claude Debussy, 'La musique d'aujourd'hui et celle de demain', *Comœdia* (4 November 1909), in *Monsieur Croche*, p. 296. On Debussy's views of the symphony, see Brian Hart, 'The Symphony in Debussy's World', in Jane F. Fulcher (ed.), *Debussy and His World* (Princeton, NJ: Princeton University Press, 2001), pp. 187–91.

[19] Hart, 'The Symphony in Debussy's World', pp. 192–6; Simon Trezise, *Debussy: La Mer* (Cambridge: Cambridge University Press, 1995), pp. 46–8.

genre's technical bedrock – scarcely figures. The work gives the impression of a nineteenth-century symphony which has been dismantled and some of its parts brilliantly reassembled and adapted to serve purposes other than those for which they were originally intended.

Those original purposes were bound up in what Debussy rejected as 'metaphysics'. In turn-of-the-century France, Beethoven's symphonies continued to serve as the benchmark for value. Listeners and critics celebrated their characteristic struggle-and-victory narratives, which resonate with the nineteenth century's liberal-bourgeois values of subjectivity and becoming. Most French symphonists responded to this aspect of Beethoven. Franck's Symphony and Saint-Saëns's Third begin darkly in the minor mode and conclude triumphantly in the major. Critics often glossed such trajectories as suffering leading to transcendence, faith vanquishing doubt, or in other terms emphasising the development of a dynamic subject.[20]

La Mer traffics in human experiences of a very different order – one related to the modes of listening explored in *Nocturnes* and aligned with the priorities of the Impressionist painters to whom Debussy is frequently compared. There is no battle against the sublime forces of nature. Debussy's music expresses nuanced impressions of a multitude of subtly delineated maritime sensations – sounds, sights, physical feelings – such as waves lapping, splashing, or crashing; gentle breezes, stiff winds, and gales; the mysterious tricks of wind and distance on the timbre and pitch of sound carrying across water; the play of sunlight; and so on.

Debussy's adaptations of the symphonic conventions he inherited serve such ends. For example, the non-recursive form of 'De l'aube à midi sur la mer' (From dawn till noon on the sea), in which themes and motives continually recirculate in endlessly varied musical contexts, produces not the teleological trajectory from crisis to resolution of a Beethovenian sonata form, but suggests instead the open-ended temporal span of the day's early phases and the continually shifting impressions on the sensorium of evolving light and environmental conditions. The form does not seem to be produced by the travails of some acting subject, but provides instead an objective framework for the shifting experiences of a perceiving subject. For another example, the apotheosis since Beethoven's day had served to

---

[20] Andrew Deruchie, *The French Symphony at the Fin de Siècle: Style, Culture, and the Symphonic Tradition* (Rochester, NY: University of Rochester Press, 2013); Brian Hart, 'Wagner and the Franckiste "Message Symphony" in Early Twentieth-Century France', in Annegret Fauser and Manuela Schwartz (eds.), *Von Wagner zum Wagnérisme: Musik, Literatur, Kunst, Politik* (Leipzig: Leipziger Universitätsverlag, 1999), pp. 315–38.

mark the culmination of a work's narrative (the victory earned through struggle or the redemption born from suffering), as do the grandiose chorales crowning the finales of Franck's Symphony, Saint-Saëns's Third, and d'Indy's Second. Debussy's apotheoses, on the other hand, do not come across as achievements. In 'De l'aube à midi', the apotheosis results from no human action – no summoning of will (as in the transition to the finale of Beethoven's Fifth) or act of defiance (the grinding parallel fifths that launch the first-movement coda in the 'Eroica'). The chorale emerges from the calm with a sense of inevitability suggestive of a revelation, an objective phenomenon experienced, like the cathedral of Ys rising from the sea (as in Debussy's piano prelude 'La Cathédrale engloutie') or midday sunrays piercing clouds to bathe the scene in fantastic light.

Debussy's epoch-making orchestral music drew an extensive and sophisticated network of roots from the symphonic repertoire that dominated contemporary concert culture. As exemplified by the *Faune*, *Nocturnes*, and *La Mer*, the composer appealed to a wide range of eminently familiar generic, formal, topical, and rhetorical devices, synthesising, recombining, recontextualising, and reimagining them to suit his own aesthetic priorities.

Author's Recommendation
Images for orchestra (1905–12).

Debussy occupied himself intermittently with *Images* for orchestra from 1905 to 1912. Like *Nocturnes* and *La Mer*, the work could be considered a triptych of symphonic poems ('Gigues', 'Ibéria', and 'Rondes de printemps'), with the added wrinkle that 'Ibéria', the central item, itself contains three movements, thus embedding a triptych within the set. *Images* evinces many of the same priorities as the works discussed in this chapter. In the transition between the final two movements of 'Ibéria', for instance, the sound of distant bells dissipates a nocturnal meditation stimulated by a sensory – in this case olfactory – experience ('Les Parfums de la nuit'). Nonetheless, the work pursues its own distinctive direction. Where the *Faune* prelude, *Nocturnes*, and *La Mer* in their own ways expand upon the nineteenth-century pastoral tradition, the scherzo is the principal symphonic mode in *Images*. The work explores its own set of imaginary places (especially Spanish scenes), and it incorporates folk-like materials and dance *topoi* extensively. Debussy cultivates an idiosyncratic orchestral sound-world in part by way of a percussion section expanded to include xylophone, castanets, pitched bells, tambourine, and more.

CHAPTER 26

Chamber Music

Matthew Brown

Debussy may be best known for composing songs, piano pieces, and orchestral scores, but he also wrote several chamber works that performers and audiences still find engaging. Diverse in nature, these range from student efforts and occasional pieces, such as the Piano Trio (1880) and the *Rapsodie* (1909) and *Petite pièce* (1910) for clarinet, to mature multimovement compositions, such as the String Quartet (1892–3) and sonatas for cello and piano (1915), flute, viola, and harp (1915), and violin and piano (1916–17). The list also includes two theatre pieces – *Musique de scène pour les Chansons de Bilitis* (1900–1) for two flutes, two harps, and celesta; and the solo flute piece *Syrinx* (1913) for Gabriel Mourey's three-act play *Psyché* (1909) – and a couple of transcriptions – *La plus que lente* (1912) for flute, clarinet, piano, cimbalom, and strings; and 'Minstrels' (*Préludes*, book 1) for violin and piano (1914).

No one knows for sure why Debussy wrote so few chamber works, but the socio-economic context for composing such music clearly changed in *fin-de-siècle* Paris.[1] Earlier in the nineteenth century, chamber works were cultivated by amateur musicians; quartet societies were common, sponsoring house concerts and even setting up score libraries. But the rise of the superstar virtuoso and the explosion of symphonic music shifted attention from the salon to the concert hall; chamber works were increasingly performed by professional groups. After France's defeat in the Franco-Prussian War (1870), organisations such as the Société nationale de musique promoted chamber music as part of its mission 'to spread the gospel of French music'.[2] César Franck's early Trio Op. 1 No. 2 in B flat (1839–42) was even performed at the Société's inaugural concert on 17 November 1871. With the proliferation of professional ensembles, such as the Ysaÿe Quartet (founded in 1886) and

---

[1] See Siglind Bruhn, *Debussy's Instrumental Music in Its Cultural Context* (Hillsdale, NY: Pendragon Press, 2019).
[2] Léon Vallas, *César Franck*, trans. Hubert J. Foss (London: George Harrap, 1951), p. 135.

Caput Quartet (founded in 1893), chamber music played an increasingly prominent role in the training of French musicians; students were encouraged to perform famous chamber works of the past, as well as newly minted scores.

Although most major composers of the period had already written chamber works prior to 1870, their output in this area increased after the Société nationale de musique was founded. César Franck (1822–90), for example, completed a piano quintet in F minor (1879), a sonata for violin and piano in A major (1886), and a string quartet in D major (1889–90). These later works are especially important, because their four movements are not only complex thematically but are also interrelated cyclically. Meanwhile, Édouard Lalo (1823–92) completed three piano trios (c. 1850 and 1852, 1880), sonatas for violin (1853) and cello (1856), a string quartet (c. 1859, rev. 1880), and a piano quintet (n.d.); Camille Saint-Saëns (1835–1921) wrote sonatas for violin (1885, 1896), cello (1872, 1905), oboe (1921), clarinet (1921), and bassoon (1921), two piano trios (1864, 1892), string quartets (1899, 1918), piano quartets (1853, 1875), a piano quintet (c. 1855), a septet (1880), and *Le Carnaval des animaux* (1887); and Gabriel Fauré (1845–1924) composed pairs of sonatas for violin (1877, 1917) and cello (1917, 1921), a string quartet (1924), a piano trio (1922), two piano quartets (1879, 1886), and two piano quintets (1895, 1921). Vincent d'Indy (1851–1931) wrote his share, including a piano quartet (1888), two piano trios (1887, 1929), string quartets (1890, 1897, 1929), a violin sonata (1904), *Sarabande et menuet* for wind quintet and piano (1918), a piano quintet (1924), a cello sonata (1925), a suite for flute, string trio, and harp (1927), a string sextet (1927), and *Le Forgeron* for three voices and string quartet (1931).

It was near the end of chamber music's migration from private salons to public concert halls that Debussy wrote his earliest examples of the genre. The Piano Trio in G minor (1880), the *Nocturne et scherzo* (1882), and *Intermezzo* (1882?) for cello and piano are pure salon music. Of these, the trio was completed while Debussy was touring Europe with Nadezhda von Meck, and he even performed it at a soirée in Florence with Pachulsky (violin) and Danilchenko (cello). Meanwhile, his next chamber work – the String Quartet in G minor (1892–3) – is a work of much greater substance and was premiered by the Ysaÿe Quartet at the Société nationale de musique on 29 December 1893. Influenced by the Russian school and Grieg's Quartet in G minor, the piece is cast in the Franckian mould: it is unified by means 'of motivic cells, of sequences, of cyclic repetitions – a few motives incessantly expanded, modified, carried over from one movement to another'.[3]

---

[3] Elliott Carter, 'The Three Late Sonatas of Debussy', in *Elliott Carter: Collected Essays and Lectures, 1937–1995*, ed. Jonathan W. Bernard (Rochester, NY: University of Rochester Press, 1997), p. 127.

Not surprisingly, perhaps, Debussy had trouble completing this complex score: a small sketchbook shows just how much effort he put into the first, second, and fourth movements.[4]

Reaction to Debussy's string quartet was, however, mixed: admired by some, it was criticised by others, notably his old friend Ernest Chausson. On 5 February 1894, Debussy wrote to him, promising to write another quartet whose formal structure would be 'ennobled'.[5] To add insult to injury, Debussy received meagre recompense from Durand for the score: 'I've sold your *Quatuor* to the Barbarians of the place de la Madeleine for 250 francs!'[6] This fee was, in fact, about the same as the ones Debussy received for his four-hand transcription of Saint-Saëns's Second Symphony (1889) and the *Deux arabesques* (1891)![7] Debussy's disappointment only became intensified after he signed an exclusive contract with Durand on 17 July 1905: since Durand encouraged him to focus on lucrative genres, such as stage and piano works, he only wrote chamber music for special reasons. In the case of the *Rapsodie* and *Petite pièce* for clarinet, that reason was his appointment to the Conseil supérieur of the Paris Conservatoire. In the case of the three late sonatas, it was the outbreak of World War I and the lack of opportunity to write large-scale symphonic and stage works. As it happens, Debussy performed the cello and violin sonatas for charity events, the former with Jacques Salmon on 24 March 1917 at a concert for *Le Vêtement du blessé*, and the latter with Gaston Poulet on 5 May and 11 and 14 September 1917 at events for *Le Foyer du soldat aveugle* and the *Œuvre de la Somme dévastée*. Ironically, the Cello Sonata actually became a best seller.[8]

Except for Paul Dukas, who never finished a projected violin sonata, many of his associates also composed significant chamber works around the time of Debussy's mature works. Most famously, perhaps, Ravel wrote a string quartet (1902–3); two violin sonatas (1897, 1922–7); a cello sonata (1920–2); a piano trio (1914); and his *Introduction and Allegro* for flute, harp, clarinet, and string quartet (1905). Of these, Ravel's string quartet

---

[4] Denis Herlin, 'Les Esquisses du Quatuor', *Cahiers Debussy* 14 (1990), pp. 23–54; Peter Bloom, 'Foreword', in *Claude Debussy: Œuvres complètes*, ser. III, vol. 1, pp. xxxi–xlvi.

[5] Letter to Ernest Chausson, 5 February 1894, *Correspondance*, p. 192.

[6] Letter to Chausson, 23 October 1893, *Correspondance*, p. 168; Robert Orledge, 'Debussy, Durand et Cie: A French Composer and His Publishers (1884–1917)', in Michael Talbot (ed.), *The Business of Music* (Liverpool: Liverpool University Press, 2002), p. 127. For the contract with Durand, see *Correspondance*, p. 166.

[7] Denis Herlin, 'An Artist High and Low, or Debussy and Money', in Elliot Antokoletz and Marianne Wheeldon (eds.), *Rethinking Debussy* (New York: Oxford University Press, 2011), p. 153.

[8] Orledge, 'Debussy, Durand et Cie', p. 150.

immediately begged comparison with Debussy's: Jean Marnold and others praised Ravel's score as forward-looking, but Pierre Lalo dismissed it as purely derivative. Certainly, there are some striking similarities: Mark DeVoto has pointed to 'the intervallic relationships and cyclic treatment of the first-movement themes in both works; the frenzied use of pizzicato in the second movement of both works; the slow movement in both works beginning in the key of the second movement and then modulating to a remote flat key'.[9] And yet, each piece has its own distinct flavour; the differences go well beyond Ravel's suggestion that his quartet 'was conceived in terms of four-part counterpoint', whereas Debussy's was 'purely harmonic in conception'.[10]

Regarded by some as the most complete musician of the period, Gabriel Pierné (1863–1937) had known Debussy since his student days at the Paris Conservatoire and won a Prix de Rome two years before him in 1882. He would later conduct the premiere of Debussy's 'Ibéria' (*Images* for orchestra) at the Concerts Colonne on 20 February 1910 and the first concert performance of *Jeux* on 29 February 1914. During the course of his outstanding career, Pierné completed a string of chamber works, including a delightful violin sonata (Op. 36); a sonata da camera for flute, cello, and piano (Op. 48); a piano quintet (Op. 41); a piano trio (Op. 45); a cello sonata (Op. 46); a large group of duos for piano and string or wind instruments (Opp. 4, 5, 7, 8, 16, 19, 21, 35, 53); and a work for saxophone quartet entitled *Introduction et variations sur une ronde populaire*.

Another composer in Debussy's orbit who wrote a substantial body of chamber music was Charles Koechlin (1867–1950). Though not much younger than Debussy, Koechlin did not enter the Paris Conservatoire until 1890 and, after studying composition with Jules Massenet, took lessons with Fauré alongside Ravel and Jean Roger-Ducasse (1873–1954). Famous as an orchestrator, Koechlin was picked by Debussy to finish scoring his ballet *Khamma* (1913). He was also a prolific composer and wrote many chamber works, such as a piano quintet (Op. 80); three string quartets (Opp. 51, 57, 72); sonatas for flute and piano (Op. 52), viola and piano (Op. 53), oboe and piano (Op. 58), violin and piano (Op. 64), cello and piano (Op. 66), horn and piano (Op. 70), bassoon and piano (Op. 70), and clarinet and piano (Opp. 85, 86); and countless other works for diverse instrumental combinations. Incidentally, Roger-Ducasse, who succeeded

---

[9] Mark DeVoto, *Debussy and the Veil of Tonality: Essays on His Music* (Hillsdale, NY: Pendragon Press, 2004), pp. 191–200.
[10] See Arbie Orenstein (ed.), *A Ravel Reader: Correspondence, Articles, Interviews* (New York: Columbia University Press, 1990), p. 473.

Koechlin as professor of orchestration at the Paris Conservatoire, also wrote some significant chamber music, including a piano quartet, a *Romance* for cello and piano, and two string quartets.

Guy Ropartz (1864–1955), Alfred Roussel (1869–1937), and Florent Schmitt (1870–1958) were likewise inspired by Debussy, especially early in their careers. A graduate of the Paris Conservatoire, Ropartz wrote six string quartets, two cello sonatas, three violin sonatas, a piano trio, and several other pieces. Meanwhile, Roussel studied with d'Indy at the Schola Cantorum and completed a piano trio (Op. 2); a *Divertissement* for wind quintet and piano (Op. 6); two sonatas for violin and piano (Opp. 11, 28); *Segovia* for guitar (Op. 29); a *Sérénade* for flute, string trio, and harp (Op. 30); a trio for flute, viola, and cello (Op. 40); a string quartet (Op. 45); a string trio (Op. 58); and a *Poème radiophonique* for flute and string quartet (Op. 59). A member of Les Apaches, Schmitt studied with Fauré and Massenet at the Paris Conservatoire and, after winning a Prix de Rome in 1900, composed numerous chamber pieces, including a piano quintet (Op. 51); a string quartet (Op. 112); a saxophone quartet (Op. 102); a violin sonata (Op. 68); a string trio (Op. 105); duos for piano and violin (Opp. 7. 19, 25, 110), flute (Op. 17, 129), cello (Opp. 24, 77), clarinet (Op. 30), and trumpet (Op. 133); and several works for larger ensembles.

Mention should also be made of one of Debussy's closest friends, André Caplet (1878–1925). A student at the Paris Conservatoire and winner of the Prix de Rome in 1901 ahead of Ravel, Caplet met Debussy in October 1907 to organise a concert at Le Havre. It was the beginning of a beautiful friendship that would last until the end of Debussy's life, with Caplet orchestrating and transcribing many of Debussy's scores (e.g. *Children's Corner*, 'Pagodes', 'Clair de lune', *Le Martyre de saint Sébastien*), as well as *Images* (for orchestra) and *La Mer* (for piano). Caplet attended Debussy's private funeral along with Dukas, Ravel, Pierné, Schmitt, and Roger-Ducasse. He was also a prolific composer, completing a number of interesting chamber works: a wind quintet (1898); *Suite persane* for two flutes, two oboes, two clarinets, and two horns (1900); a septet for string quartet and three voices (1909); a sonata for piano, voice, and cello (1919); *Conte fantastique* for pedal harp and string quartet (1924); *Le Miroir de Jésus* for four voices, harp, and string quartet (1923); and a sonata for violin and organ (1924).

Debussy's chamber music did not simply influence musicians within his own immediate circle: seen in the wider context of twentieth- and twenty-first-century developments, it has also had a profound impact on countless composers of very different stripes. Echoes of his string quartet can, for example, be heard in Béla Bartók's first string quartet (1909), as well as in chamber works by Zoltán Kodály and Karol Szymanowski. Igor Stravinsky and the members of Les Six may have rejected Debussy's Impressionist idioms, but they were clearly influenced by the innovative forms and timbres of his three late sonatas. So, too, were Olivier Messiaen (e.g. *Quatuor pour la fin du temps*, 1941), Elliott Carter (e.g. Cello Sonata, 1948), Pierre Boulez (e.g. *Le Marteau sans maître*, 1955), and Henri Dutilleux (*Ainsi la nuit*, 1973–6). Meanwhile, other composers have quoted Debussy's music in their own chamber works. Edgard Varèse and George Crumb, for example, have been inspired by *Syrinx*: Varèse quotes the opening motif in *Density 21.5* (1935), as does Crumb in *An Idyll for the Misbegotten* (1985) for flute or horn and percussion. Similarly, the third movement of Benjamin Britten's Cello Suite No. 1 (1964) explicitly refers to Debussy's cello sonata, a work Britten recorded with Mstislav Rostropovich in July 1961. Besides sharing the title 'Serenade' and requiring the cello to play pizzicato much or all of the time, both movements centre on D minor and feature similar pitch and intervallic material. In the same vein, Witold Lutosławski frames his *Grave: Metamorphoses for Cello and Piano* (1981) with quotations of the opening motive from *Pelléas et Mélisande*. And Tōru Takemitsu alludes to Debussy's Sonata for flute, viola, and harp in *And Then I Knew 'Twas Wind* (1992), a piece inspired by Emily Dickinson's poem 'Like Rain it sounded till it curved'. To draw parallels between the wind, which blows through the natural world, and the soul, which wafts through human consciousness, Takemitsu not only borrows Debussy's exquisite instrumentation but even quotes the opening of Debussy's piece in bar 22 of his own score.

Many composers have likewise followed Debussy's lead in making chamber versions of his piano and orchestral works. An interesting early example is Henri Mouton's highly abridged *Pelléas et Mélisande* for piano trio with optional clarinet and double bass. Others include Eugène Bozza's transcription of *The Little Nigar* for wind quintet and Benno Sachs's chamber version of the *Prélude à l'après-midi d'un faune* for Schoenberg's Verein für musikalische Privataufführungen. In 2008 Stephen McNeff performed a version of *Pelléas et Mélisande* with the vocal parts and a stripped-down ensemble of just thirty-five players, and in 2012 TableTopOpera performed a chamber version of the opera that replaced the sets and the singers with projections of panels from P. Craig Russell's comic book version of the story.[11] In 2016 the group created chamber versions of *Berceuse héroïque*, the second movement of *En blanc et noir*, and

---

[11] See Stephen Neff, 'Shrinked to Fit', *The Guardian* (18 November 2008), www.theguardian.com/music/2008/nov/18/opera-debussy-pelleas-melisande.

Élégie for their production *Scarred by the Somme*. Once again, these transcriptions underscore the extraordinary scope and richness of Debussy's chamber music and its continued relevance to musicians today.

Lastly, some composers have tried to write some of the 'missing' chamber works that Debussy intended to compose. It is well known that Debussy's three late sonatas for cello, for flute, harp, and viola, and for violin were originally conceived as part of a set of six sonatas: the other three would have been scored for oboe, horn, and harpsichord, for trumpet, bassoon, and clarinet, and for all of the instruments used in the other five sonatas along with a double bass. To indicate how these missing sonatas might have sounded, Kenneth Cooper recently published a hypothetical version of Debussy's sonata for oboe, horn, and harpsichord.[12] This 'reconstruction' actually rescores three existing pieces by Debussy: the Prelude from *La Boîte à joujoux*; 'Pour les notes répétées' (*Douze études*); and 'Mouvement' (*Images*, series 1). A decade earlier, Minako Tokuyama, Theo Loevendie, and Jacques Hétu took a very different tack, writing their own versions of the three projected sonatas – Tokuyama's *Sonata Japanesque* for oboe, horn, and harpsichord (1998); Loevendie's *Golliwog's Other Dances* for trumpet, bassoon, and clarinet (1998); and Hétu's Sonata for Thirteen Instruments (1996) – which were eventually performed alongside Debussy's companion sonatas at music festivals in Canada, Japan, and Holland. Most recently, Robert Orledge wrote his fourth projected sonata for oboe, horn, and harpsichord in homage to Debussy. It premiered on 21 March 2018.[13]

Author's Recommendation
String Quartet Op. 10 (1892–3).

A perennial favourite with performers and audiences alike, Debussy's String Quartet Op. 10 received its premiere in 1893 and was dedicated to Ernest Chausson. The work has four movements, each of which relies in different ways on a single motto theme. This gesture, which recalls a similar motive from Edvard Grieg's Quartet in G minor Op. 27, is introduced in the first bars of the opening movement. Although this movement has a clearly marked exposition, development, and recapitulation, it is perhaps best regarded as a monothematic sonata form in G minor in which the main

---

[12] Kenneth Cooper (arranger), Debussy's Sonata 'No. 4' for Oboe, Horn, and Harpsichord (New York: International Music, 2011).
[13] www.robertorledge.co.uk/performances.

contrasting theme serves as closing material rather than a traditional second group. The second movement is a lively scherzo in G major and treats the motto theme in various ways, most notably as an ostinato. Remarkably, Debussy alluded to this latter version of the motto theme at the start of his opera *La Chute de la maison Usher* (1908–17). The slow movement strikes a different mood entirely: set in the distantly related key of D♭ major, its music is both intimate and ethereal and includes a radical transformation of the motto theme just before the climax. After a brief transition, the lively finale re-establishes the key of G major through another version of the motto theme and ends with brilliant recollections of the original theme from the start of the first movement.

CHAPTER 27

Song and Choral Music
David J. Code

Everybody sings. At some time or other, frequently or infrequently, at children's parties or church services, in the football stadium or the shower, giving voice or just grooving inwardly (with pleasure or exasperation) to the latest catchy earworm – in its broadest definition, song has always offered everyone the simplest, most personal musical pleasure. However rarefied a place in the history of song Debussy might claim for other reasons, he too shared this simple enjoyment.

Consider an amusing vignette from early in the 1931 Debussy biography by his young writer friend René Peter. It begins with some pianistic tomfoolery: the composer plays Chopin's funeral march in the guise of a cancan, transforms the Boulanger-era satirical song 'En revenant de la revue' into a dirge, then he breaks into song:

> 'If those aren't enough for you', [he said], 'here's another: the march of the *Garçons bouchers!* [Butcher boys]' – which is what he called the [patriotic song] *Marche lorraine*, by Ganne – and he started to holler [*hurlait*] at the top of his voice:
>
> > 'Nous sommes les garçons bouchers
> > çons bouchers
> > çons bouchers'
>
> At which he burst out laughing like a fool.[1]

The picture could not contrast more starkly with the more elevated seductions experienced by Scottish soprano Mary Garden, the first Mélisande, during Debussy's first sing-through of *Pelléas* at the piano before the assembled cast:

> When Debussy got to the fourth act I could no longer look at my score for the tears. It was all very strange and unbearable. I closed my book and just

---

[1] René Peter, *Claude Debussy*, rev. ed. (Paris: Gallimard, 1944 [orig. 1931]), p. 47.

27 Song and Choral Music

listened to him, and as he played the death of Mélisande, I burst into the most awful sobbing . . . Before anyone could say or do anything, he faced us all and said:

'*Mesdames et messieurs*, that is my *Pelléas et Mélisande*. Everyone must forget that he is a singer before he can sing the music of Debussy. *Oubliez, je vous prie, que vous êtes chanteurs!*'[2]

'Forget, I pray you, that you are singers!' Whatever all the other highly trained vocalists thought of this faintly mystical (and perhaps slightly insulting) demand, it is no surprise that it struck a chord with Garden. For beyond often characterising herself as a 'singing actress', she offered her own mystical variant of the same idea when insisting that, while 'most of the others' who took the stage in the various characters she sung were 'singers who never lost their identities', in her own case, as she put it bluntly, 'I lived my rôles; I *was* the person.'[3]

Whatever diva-esque self-indulgence we might generously allow in Garden's case, she and Debussy both suggestively complicate the simple notion that everyone – or indeed anyone – really knows what it means to sing. And the sense of ambiguity or contestation around this supposedly natural wellspring of all music soon deepens if we widen the lens to include other singers of the time, flourishing on other stages than the Opéra or Opéra-Comique. The very years of Debussy's protracted struggles with his opera, for instance, also saw the rise to prominence – in venues from the Montmartre cabarets out through the wider world – of the great popular entertainer Yvette Guilbert, forever memorialised (in her signature long black gloves) in the paintings and posters of Henri de Toulouse-Lautrec.[4] In her case, some candid praise from Debussy's second Mélisande, the English soprano Maggie Teyte, brings into view another hybrid creature to place alongside Garden's 'singing actress': 'a supreme artist like Yvette Guilbert could make the world believe she was a singer. She never possessed a voice . . . but she produced her words so beautifully that we always thought of her as a "singing diseuse".'[5]

---

[2] Mary Garden and Louis Biancolli, *Mary Garden's Story* (London: Michael Joseph, 1922), pp. 63–4. This book has been criticised for numerous inaccuracies; however unreliable it remains in documentary detail, it valuably records Garden's suggestive language and musical intelligence.

[3] Garden and Biancolli, *Mary Garden's Story*, pp. 232, 271

[4] There is a substantial literature on Guilbert; for an efficient orientation with rich iconography and useful chronologies, see, for example, the Toulouse-Lautrec Museum exhibition catalogue: Jean Favier et Françoise Cachin, *Yvette Guilbert: Diseuse fin de siècle* (Paris: Bibliothèque nationale de France, 1994).

[5] Maggie Teyte, *Star on the Door* (London: Putnam, 1958), p. 86.

Singing, acting, speaking; 'singing actress' or 'singing diseuse'; no 'voice' but beautiful 'words' – a glance into Guilbert's 1928 entertaining, richly illustrated method book *L'Art de chanter une chanson* finds further grumbles about the whole friable amalgam, attributed (apocryphally or not) to a rather surprising source. Just before the passage in question, she reports Charles Gounod's response to her talents, with praise even more fulsome than Teyte's: 'If it is clear that you have much less than a voice, you also have much more! You have all the voices in your own!' But then, when she goes on to recount a meeting with Giuseppe Verdi – of all imaginable *éminences grises* – Guilbert's claims for her own '*art de chanter*' really take flight:

> Verdi did not hesitate: 'if we could encounter on the great lyric stages a few interpreters who know how to *speak* a text', he confessed to me, 'we could write musical themes appropriate to the words, which we could then take into consideration. But we have only voices, nothing more, voices of greater or lesser beauty, but voices that we are obliged to show off for the good of our works.'[6]

Self-serving as the anecdote may seem, it raises tantalising questions. What, exactly, would a 'musical theme appropriate to the words' sound like – and what would Verdi have written if he had been able to 'take [words] into consideration', rather than (just) writing for all those 'voices'? Did he really never find an ideal *cantatrice-diseuse* embodied to his complete satisfaction?

Of course, with Garden and Teyte and Gounod and Verdi – if not Guilbert – the discussion has so far been overshadowed by opera, whose artifices and extravagances may always render it an extreme case in the world of song. But singers, at least, have always found the boundaries between such vocal realms somewhat fluid. Teyte, also a renowned recitalist (whose recordings of Debussy with Alfred Cortot, she claimed, became 'one of the most profitable albums ever released by [H.M.V.]'), framed her sense of strong and essential continuity against a critique of unnamed others: 'Too often I miss the flexibility of interpretation and thought that I believe comes only from experience in an opera house. Certainly such talent as I myself had in the concert field I owed entirely to my operatic upbringing.'[7] For Debussy, too, the interplay between opera and *mélodie* – the esoteric *salon* genre undergoing constant transformation throughout the era – proved crucial: his expansive settings of *Cinq poèmes de Charles Baudelaire* (1887–9) arguably furthered his fraught negotiations

---

[6] Yvette Guilbert, *L'Art de chanter une chanson* (Paris: Bernard Grasset, 1928), pp. 26–7.
[7] Teyte, *Star on the Door*, pp. 169, 145.

with the creative legacy of Wagnerian music drama at least as much as the unfinished opera *Rodrigue et Chimène* (1892–3) on a libretto by prominent *wagnériste* Catulle Mendès.[8]

Nor, indeed, should we imagine a strong and solid barrier between the hothouse *milieux* of 'art song' and the more popular venues where Guilbert strutted her charms. Debussy's love of clowns and circuses and the like is well known from his instrumental parodies; Peter, with slight distaste, also recalls his enjoyment of the 'pranks' of Jeanne Bloch, an earthier popular singer who 'delighted the public by galumphing towards them, fat-bellied and -bottomed, rogue-voiced, with an infantryman's cap askew on her ear'.[9] And the exchange also flowed the other way. Perhaps Guilbert's invocation of Renaissance poet François Villon as the primordial 'voice of the people' late in her 1945 autobiography *Autre temps, autre chansons* – suggestively recalling Debussy's setting of *Trois ballades* by the same archetypically 'French' poet back in 1910 – seems iconic above all of her ongoing strategic manoeuvres to attain a kind of artistic respectability. But an earlier, passing claim in *L'Art de chanter* about a different Debussy song triptych can serve, coincidentally enough, to bring us back – via yet another conceptual hybrid – to that tangle of deeper questions about 'song'. 'In the *Chansons de Bilitis* Debussy's music is nothing but a spoken song [*chant parlé*]', Guilbert suggests. She adds: 'spoken or sung, Debussy's music remains *littérairement lyrique*' [meaning most simply 'literally lyrical', but also 'literate-ly lyrical'] – a puzzling characterisation that neatly captures the contradiction between 'literary' artifice and 'lyrical' expression threaded all through the multifarious song cultures of her era.

Mélodie, Song Cycle, Triptych

Guilbert's fine distillation of a core contradiction seems a good point at which to step back and sketch some historical outlines of the immediate context for Debussy's 'literate-ly lyrical' song *œuvre*. For any attempt to frame those eighty-plus *mélodies* against the 'mature' *fin-de-siècle* phase of the genre – often said to emerge around 1870 – must navigate an inseparable blend of literary and musical concerns, embracing everything from the

---

[8] The importance of the Baudelaire songs to Debussy's post-Wagnerian struggles has often been noted. For a few suggestive examples of the range of critique now in view, see Katherine Bergeron, 'The Echo, the Cry, the Death of Lovers', *19th-Century Music* 18 (1994), pp. 136–51; Raymond Monelle, 'A Semantic Approach to Debussy's Songs', *Music Review* 51 (1990), pp. 193–207.
[9] Peter, *Claude Debussy*, p. 147.

quality of the poetry selected, through the esoteric refinements of vocal melody and diction, to the harmonic and technical ambition of the piano (and other) accompaniments.[10] A swift overview of the Romantic prehistory in this light readily fastens on such precursors as Hector Berlioz, with his rich settings (for piano and then orchestra) of Théophile Gautier in *Les Nuits d'été* (1841, orch. 1843 and 1856), and various mid-century French responses to the imported models of Schubert and Schumann, including songs by Édouard Lalo and Louis Niedermeyer, for example. Closer to Debussy's time, such leading contemporary opera composers as Gounod, Bizet, and Massenet also wrote songs on the side – including, in the latter case, what has been called the first true French 'song cycle' (*Poème du souvenir*, six settings of Armand Silvestre, c. 1868). The genre also attracted more idiosyncratic figures like the poetically sensitive arch-*wagnériste* Henri Duparc, whose compositional legacy was to consist solely of thirteen *mélodies* (1868–84).

Amidst all other such *points de repère*, the 100-plus *mélodies* of Gabriel Fauré have long stood out for their extraordinary, flexible literary-musical imagination. They would influence everyone from Maurice Ravel (Fauré's composition student) to Lili Boulanger, who, a few years before her tragic early death, dedicated to the older 'Maître' the opening song of her ambitious cycle on bucolic-cum-religious poems by Francis Jammes, *Clairières dans le ciel* (1914). The recent revival of Anglophone academic interest in Fauré – previously somewhat marginalised by the Modernist mythologies around Debussy – has given rise, among other things, to the fine-grained 'cultural musicology' of Katherine Bergeron's *Voice Lessons: French Mélodie in the Belle Époque* (2010), which treats his first two song cycles *La Bonne Chanson* (on Paul Verlaine, 1894) and *La Chanson d'Ève* (on Charles van Lerberghe, 1910) as exemplary emergences from the parallel evolutions of Symbolist literary aesthetics and linguistic cultural politics in the Third Republic.[11] From a more intensively music-critical perspective, on the other hand, Stephen Rumph argues in his recent *The Fauré Song Cycles: Poetry and Music, 1861–1921* (2020) – titled in homage to Joseph Kerman's *The Beethoven Quartets* – for a significant reappraisal of the refined, reflexive, and highly variegated approaches to text-music interaction and multi-part form across all five of Fauré's cycles, from the

---

[10] For the standard account of the evolution of the *mélodie* from roots in the earlier *romance*, see Frits Noske, *French Song from Berlioz to Duparc: The Origin and Development of the Mélodie*, 2nd ed., rev. Rita Benton and Frits Noske, trans. Rita Benton (New York: Dover, 1970).

[11] Katherine Bergeron, *Voice Lessons: French Mélodie in the Belle Époque* (New York: Oxford University Press, 2010).

27 Song and Choral Music

two already named through a second on Van Lerberghe, *Le Jardin clos* (1914), to the later *Mirages* (1919) and *L'Horizon chimérique* (1922).[12]

As for Debussy, whose '*chant parlé*' in the *Chansons de Bilitis* (to recall Guilbert) also earns close consideration from Bergeron in *Voice Lessons*, his thoroughgoing stylistic differences from Fauré render it as hard to pinpoint direct influence (in either direction) for the *mélodie* as for any other genre. Anyone who compares settings of the same poem – say, Verlaine's 'C'est l'extase langoureuse' or 'En sourdine' – by the two composers will likely sense not just two different manners of poetic reading, but two fundamentally different conceptions of the questions and opportunities created by the meeting (or collision) of literature with lyricism. In more practical terms, perhaps Fauré offered distant inspiration, in his one early song triptych (*Poème d'un jour* of 1878, on three linked poems by Charles Grandmougin), for Debussy's pivot around 1890 – after writing dozens of early songs, many under the intimate inspiration of his mistress the amateur soprano Mme Marie-Blanche Vasnier – to publishing his *mélodies* in the triptych form that then became, across fully eight instances, one of his signature compositional genres.[13] But in the absence of any strong evidence for the connection, he may just as well have taken independent inspiration from Massenet or even his eccentric friend Erik Satie, who wrote a song triptych for the singer-pianist Jane Bathori (*Trois mélodies*, on three different poets, 1887) some years before Debussy's *Trois mélodies de Paul Verlaine* (1890).

Possible precedents aside, the first few Debussy triptychs (together with the four *Proses lyriques* on his own texts, 1892–3) further illustrate the importance of the *mélodies* within those grander struggles, first to compose *Pelléas et Mélisande* and then nurse it, year by year, towards its first production. If the Baudelaire songs enact his most direct, 'face to face' engagement with the literary and musical fervours of French *wagnérisme* – then at their apex, with the 1885–8 publication of the *Revue wagnérienne* under largely literary leadership – a subtler and more protracted 'working through' of post-Wagnerian challenges unfolds through what can be heard as a 'triptych of triptychs', extending from the first Verlaine *Fêtes galantes* (1891), through the *faux*-antique prose poetry of Pierre Louÿs's *Chansons de Bilitis* (1897–8), to the second *Fêtes galantes* (1904). Such a hearing

---

[12] Stephen Rumph, *The Fauré Song Cycles: Poetry and Music, 1861–1921* (Oakland, CA: University of California Press, 2020).
[13] See David J. Code, 'The "Song Triptych": Reflections on a Debussyan Genre', in François de Médicis and Steven Huebner (eds.), *Debussy's Resonance* (Rochester, NY: University of Rochester Press, 2018), pp. 127–74.

obviously remains open to debate, and no doubt various other works proved at least as crucial to Debussy's labours in these years to consolidate an aesthetic *après Wagner* (as he famously put it after his opera's 1902 premiere).[14] But the completion of the second *Fêtes galantes* triptych – with its nostalgic last 'panel', 'Colloque sentimental', explicitly mourning 'Les beaux jours de bonheur indicible' (the happy days of inexpressible happiness) – clearly bids farewell to a key phase in his *mélodie* composition, for it overlaps with work on the first of the late triptychs that put aside *symboliste* and *wagnériste* writers in favour of the older, 'classical' poetry of Charles d'Orléans, Tristan L'Hermite, and Villon.

Debussy's creative trajectory, however, was never straightforwardly linear: he would ultimately round off his corpus of *mélodies* – save for a last, propagandistic song *Noël des enfants qui n'ont plus de maison*, whose wartime success gave him some embarrassment – with a return to a key interlocutor from his post-*wagnériste* travails. The publication in 1913 of a last triptych on poems by Stéphane Mallarmé occasioned a wry comment from Ravel about the 'remarkable coincidence' that had seen him also produce a Mallarmé triptych – even featuring two of the same poems – in the same year; in his case, the setting with voice and chamber ensemble also offers one of many early responses to Schoenberg's *Pierrot lunaire* (1912).[15] Whatever the explanation for the synchronicity, a wider view reveals that, of all Debussy's younger contemporaries, Ravel was most drawn to the 'song triptych' as formal model: he first wrote the orchestral triptych *Shéhérazade* (1903) on poems by Tristan Klingsor, then (after the 1913 coincidence) two more: *Chansons madécasses* (1926) on texts by eighteenth-century colonial writer Évariste de Parny, also with chamber ensemble; and finally the orchestral *Don Quichotte à Dulcinée* (1932–3) on poems by Paul Morand. Unlike Debussy, he also continued to explore song in sets or cycles of other configurations, including the five *Histoires naturelles* (1906) on the plainer, more 'modern' texts of Jules Renard, and several folk-like collections – for example, *Cinq mélodies populaires grecques* (1906) and *Deux mélodies hébraïques* (1914), which are of a more quasi-ethnographic cast than the extravagant musical orientalism he had draped around Klingsor's poetic riffs on *The Arabian Nights* in the three songs of *Shéhérazade*.

---

[14] The phrase 'it was necessary to seek ways of being *après Wagner* and not *d'après Wagner*' comes from the 1902 article 'Pourquoi j'ai écrit *Pelléas*', *Monsieur Croche*, pp. 63–4.

[15] Along similar lines, Stravinsky's *Trois poésies de la lyrique japonaise* (1912–13) seems a similar hybrid of Debussyan triptych with Schoenbergian ensemble.

Further comparison of the song *œuvres* of Ravel and Debussy uncovers another coincidence. Ravel, as it happens, also turned early on from *symboliste* settings – for example, Verlaine's 'Un grand sommeil noir' (1895) and Mallarmé's 'Sainte' (1896) – to Renaissance poetry, to set two 'epigrams' by Clément Marot, renowned poetic observer of various political upheavals in the fifteenth-century French court. Indeed, this 'classical' venture, in 1895–9, preceded Debussy's turn to Charles d'Orléans and Tristan L'Hermite for his *Trois chansons de France* of 1904. But, in truth, Debussy had first ventured into Renaissance poetry about the same time as Ravel, in 1898, to begin his only significant a cappella choral work, the *Trois chansons de Charles d'Orléans*, completed only years later. Again, any question about precedence or influence seems to dissipate into vague 'trends' or 'atmospheres' once we widen the lens to include other, similar ventures as well. Teyte brings into view another key figure, for instance, when she recalls 'those charming, intimate concerts in the great houses of Paris and London, and always in the centre of the picture I see (and hear) Reynaldo Hahn, sitting at the piano and accompanying himself in his own songs'.[16] The very year Debussy first started setting Charles d'Orléans, Hahn – whose Verlaine cycle *Chansons grises* (1890) had been well received by Verlaine and Mallarmé, and who later became lover and friend of Marcel Proust – included the same poet, alongside the more recent Théodore de Banville and Mendès, in a cycle of *Rondels* (1898–9). The fortuitous parallel becomes all the more striking when we find Hahn returning to Charles d'Orléans, now alongside other Renaissance poets, for his *Chansons et madrigaux* in 1907, just a year before Debussy belatedly finished his own choral triptych on Charles d'Orléans.

To seek some commonplace explanation for the double synchronicity – say, in documented exchanges within one of the bars or taverns frequented by both composers – comes up short against Peter's recollection that Hahn and Debussy, both inexplicably convinced of a sense of 'disdain' coming from the other, never enjoyed the slightest fruitful exchange.[17] Beyond such personal minutiae, then, perhaps this brief glimpse of the haphazardly shared 'antiquarian' leanings that represent but one of many attractions for 'literate-ly lyrical' composers of the era can best serve reflections along more general lines – say, about the scope and limits of so-called neoclassicism in French music, often assumed to be both clearer in musical outline and plainer in ideological resonance than was ever really the case. More narrowly, Hahn's 1899 *Rondels* can encourage concluding reflection of

[16] Teyte, *Star on the Door*, p. 61.   [17] See Peter, *Claude Debussy*, p. 92.

a different sort — about the ways a history of genre, in privileging some notionally 'normative' creative lineage (like that behind the 'mature' Belle Époque *mélodie*), might fail to account for the more loosely related, less easily categorisable, inventions that always crop up alongside.

Debussy kept his choral and solo settings of Charles d'Orléans separate. Hahn, whose dedication affirms his attempt 'to test the mysterious affinities existing between the voice's natural inflection and harmony', not only weaves Renaissance and contemporary *Rondels* together, but also includes works for SATB and SAT choirs alongside the more conventional settings for voice and piano. He thus opens this world of French song beyond any presumptively homogeneous, ideal-typical form. To extend this generically open approach to the song contexts of Debussy's era might offer, among other things, a place in the story for sacred song (from the Abbey of Solesmes to the Schola Cantorum via much else) that has gone unmentioned here, though perhaps that lineage really requires a chapter of its own. But again, the sacred/secular boundary could well prove as fluid as many others already discussed, within a historical narrative that also sought room, say, for the extraordinarily imaginative, hybrid solo-choral-orchestral/instrumental *Psalmes* the young Boulanger produced during her few fecund years of creativity.[18] And it might thus also suggest, as an appropriately personal and pious, idiosyncratic, and hybrid valedictory 'song' for this chapter, the *Pie Jesu* for soprano, string quartet, harp and organ she wrote for her sister Nadia just prior to her death, ten days before Debussy's, in March 1918.

Author's Recommendation
Chansons de Bilitis, on texts by Pierre Louÿs (1899).

Tempting as it is to hail a lesser-known song triptych like the *Trois ballades de François Villon* (1910) — the only one Debussy published both in piano and orchestral versions — the Louÿs settings undoubtedly stand as a pivotal accomplishment in Debussy's favoured form of the short song cycle. A new, quasi-narrative progression carved from a much larger collection by his close friend Louÿs (first published as 'translations' of a fictive ancient Greek poetess), these three subtly linked, delicately dramatic *mélodies* raise fascinating questions, separately and together, about voice, persona, and setting. Their surface-level evolution from naïve evocation through

---

[18] Debussy admired Boulanger's Prix de Rome cantata *Faust et Hélène*. See his review 'Concerts Colonne', *Revue musicale S.I.M.* (1 December 1913), in *Monsieur Croche*, p. 253.

overripe sensuality to a cold and mournful close arguably carries allegorical resonances with Debussy's strenuous attempts, throughout the 1890s, to find a musical path *'après Wagner'* (as he later put it). Countless fine recordings are available, for example by an early Mélisande, Maggie Teyte, accompanied by Alfred Cortot. A comparison of this with several others is the best way to catch the range of inflections possible for Bilitis's deceptively simple utterances – notably including her last words in the second of the three songs, 'La Chevelure', one of Debussy's finest: 'Il me regarda d'un regard si tendre, que je baissai mes yeux avec un frisson' (He looked at me with a look so tender, that I lowered my eyes with a shudder).

CHAPTER 28

The Piano

Gurminder Kaur Bhogal

It is difficult to reconcile Debussy's rather literal view of the piano as 'a box of hammers and strings' with his dreamy compositions for the instrument, which are today renowned for their subtle nuances, colouristic harmonies, timbral variety, and fluid sense of temporality.[1] This chapter demarcates two eras of piano composition – pre-Debussy and post-Debussy – by taking as its focal point a comment made by the pianist Marguerite Long: 'Since Debussy, no one has heard or played the piano in the same way as it was played before.'[2] As crude as these delineations are, my goal is to emphasise the truly transformative nature of his approach to thinking about the piano in its entirety – as a technological machine, a source of unlimited and variegated sonority, and a catalyst for freeing the human imagination.

While taking into consideration the pianistic tradition that Debussy was born into and the one that he was propelled towards – spurred on by the marvellous innovations of his contemporaries at the piano including Gabriel Fauré, Emmanuel Chabrier, and Maurice Ravel – this chapter highlights Debussy's uniquely refined sense of how the piano might be made to sound anew. By the turn of the twentieth century he was beginning to establish his status as a trailblazer at the keyboard. It would be up to his immediate successors, particularly the French composers Olivier Messiaen and Pierre Boulez, to extend the expressive potential of his engagement with 'the sensual, dramatic, and formal potentials of sound', into a dimension that exploited aspects of acoustics and resonance, as recently explored by Marilyn Nonken.[3] It is worth noting that Debussy's

---

[1] This much-cited phrase does not have a source, though Léon Vallas used a similar version to describe Debussy's playing: *Claude Debussy: His Life and Works*, trans. Maire and Grace O' Brien (New York: Dover Publications, 1973), p. 108.
[2] Marguerite Long, *At the Piano with Debussy*, trans. Olive Senior-Ellis (London: Dent, 1972), p. 19.
[3] Marilyn Nonken, *The Spectral Piano: From Liszt, Scriabin, and Debussy to the Digital Age* (Cambridge: Cambridge University Press, 2014), p. 22.

first compositions for the piano were styled very much within the 'salon' tradition of the nineteenth century in that they were short, tuneful, and not especially demanding to play. He seemed somewhat self-conscious of his technical limitations in writing them. For instance, when Madame Gérard de Romilly attempted to play *Deux arabesques* (1888–91) for the composer during the late 1890s, he threw the score to one side, saying 'not those, they're dreadful'.[4] Similarly, when Debussy finally decided to publish *Suite bergamasque* due to financial constraints in 1905, he ensured that the publisher added '1890' under the heading of the first movement so as to mark this work as a product of his youth. It was only when he returned to writing for the piano after the success of his opera, *Pelléas et Mélisande* (1902), that Debussy was able to hone an idiosyncratic approach to composing for this instrument.

The compositions that began to flow from his pen from 1903 onwards were striking for their stylistic clarity and technical assurance. Even Debussy knew he had earned his place in the pianistic canon by this time; soon after completing his first set of *Images* (1904–5), he wrote to his publisher, Jacques Durand, on 11 September 1905: 'without false vanity, I think these three pieces work well and will take their place in piano literature . . . to the left of Schumann or to the right of Chopin . . . as you like it'.[5] By this time, Debussy felt satisfied in knowing he had found a place on the bookshelf between the two composers to whom his writing for the piano was indebted. Who knows how Debussy would have felt if he had known that those early piano works (which were a source of embarrassment to the composer) would come to be identified with his trademark sound and style while being cherished by audiences and pianists alike?

Early Years

On the basis of Debussy's early encounters at the piano, one would not have predicted that he was destined for greatness, particularly as a performer; the critic Camille Bellaigue reminisced: 'Nothing about the young Debussy, neither his looks, nor his comments, nor his playing, suggested an artist, present or future.'[6] Debussy's first piano teacher, Antoinette Mauté de Fleurville, who claimed to be a student of Chopin's, took charge of his early education such that in the space of

---

[4] See Roger Nichols, *Debussy Remembered* (London: Faber and Faber, 1992), p. 53.
[5] Letter to Jacques Durand, 11 September 1905, *Debussy Letters*, p. 158.
[6] Nichols, *Debussy Remembered*, p. 13.

one year he was able to compete successfully for a place at the Paris Conservatoire in 1872 at the age of ten. There, he studied piano until 1879 with Antoine Marmontel, who did experience Chopin's playing first hand and likely shared anecdotes about Chopin's playing with Debussy and his classmates (who, in addition to Bellaigue, included the composer and conductor Paul Vidal and the composer Gabriel Pierné).[7] Although Debussy did win second prize playing Schumann's Sonata in G minor (Op. 22) in Marmontel's class, his later years were geared more towards composition lessons, with the highlight of his career at the Conservatoire being marked by his receipt of the Prix de Rome in 1884 for his cantata *L'Enfant prodigue*. It was in Rome that he heard Franz Liszt play and whose pedalling Debussy still described as a 'kind of *breathing*' towards the end of his life.[8] This conception of pedalling was likely shaped by Mauté, who, in attempting to trace her lineage back to Chopin, emphasised a similar 'respiratory' approach, which was probably inspired by contemporaneous vocal practices of bel canto opera.

We can hear Debussy treat the piano as a living, breathing organism in an early piece like *Rêverie* (1890). In the opening bars, the undulating left-hand accompaniment, with the sustained B♭ pedal, supports a legato, lilting melody where a regular change of pedal on the downbeat of every bar establishes a periodic pattern akin to breathing; Nonken observes: 'Throughout the piano's history, its practitioners were encouraged to mimic vocal phrasing. Pianists were encouraged to breathe, or phrase, as a singer might'.[9] In *Rêverie*, Debussy positions himself very clearly within the Romantic tradition of piano playing which, in addition to the sustained melody and accompaniment texture and regular pedalling, is also reflected in the titles and genres of his early piano pieces from the 1890s. These include the *Mazurka* (published in 1904), *Tarentelle styrienne* (published in 1903), *Ballade* (published in 1903), *Valse romantique* (1890), and *Nocturne* (1892). Despite the care with which he notated his scores, Debussy was loathe to specify pedal markings for the simple reason that, as he remarked to the pianist Maurice Dumesnil during a lesson, 'pedalling cannot be written down … it varies from one instrument to another, from one room, or one hall, to another … faites confiance à votre oreille

---

[7] For an examination of Debussy's studies at the Conservatoire, see John R. Clevenger, 'Debussy's Paris Conservatoire Training', in Jane F. Fulcher (ed.), *Debussy and His World* (Princeton, NJ: Princeton University Press, 2001), pp. 299–361.
[8] Letter to Jacques Durand, 1 September 1915, *Debussy Letters*, p. 301.
[9] Nonken, *The Spectral Piano*, p. 53.

28 The Piano

[trust your ear]'.[10] Ultimately, it was this inclination – to experience sound in all its vibrating richness – that allowed Debussy to move beyond the predominantly Romantic notion of the pedal as a primary means to sustain sound and slow down acoustical decay, so as to focus on the peculiar properties of resonance itself.

Before I delve into a discussion of Debussy's innovations with pianistic sound, it is worth stating that he was very much against the mushy sonorities that emerge from over-pedalling; Debussy explained to Durand that 'abusing the pedal is only a means of covering up a lack of technique, and that making a lot of noise is a way to drown the music you're slaughtering! In theory we should be able to find a graphic means of representing this "breathing" pedal'.[11] Whether composing for the orchestra or for the piano, Debussy imagined a sound that was defined by qualities of *flou* (haziness, as seen in his verbal exchanges with the conductor Camille Chevillard during a rehearsal of *Nocturnes*); *brume* (mist, as indicated at the opening of 'La Cathédrale engloutie', *Préludes* (Book 1, 1909–10)); and *vibrer* (to vibrate/resonate, as seen in a frequently occurring direction in his piano scores, *laissez vibrer*).[12] These qualities may be attributed to his pursuit of an atmospheric sound as inspired by Impressionist art – particularly Claude Monet's notion of the *enveloppe* – as well as the paintings of J. M. W. Turner and J. M. Whistler. Debussy was particularly harsh on performers who were not able to convey the veiled, gauzy timbres he was after. For example, the Catalan virtuoso, Ricardo Viñes, was criticised by the composer for his dry playing.[13] To his credit, Viñes premiered the piano compositions of both Debussy and Ravel, and given the subtle differences between their compositional styles, it is entirely feasible that the type of sonority that was suitable for Ravel in a piece such as *Jeux d'eau* (1901) was not appropriate for Debussy's 'Poissons d'or', for instance (*Images*, series 2, 1907–8). With regard to *Jeux d'eau*, Viñes remembered Ravel asking him to use sustaining pedal for the upper register in order to emphasise 'the hazy impression

---

[10] Maurice Dumesnil, 'Coaching with Debussy', *The Piano Teacher* 5 (1962), p. 13.
[11] Letter to Jacques Durand, 1 September 1915, *Debussy Letters*, p. 302. Although Debussy mentions a work by Marie Jaëll in this letter, Roy Howat suggests he was probably referring to Georges Falkenberg's treatise on pedalling. See Howat, *The Art of French Piano Music: Debussy, Ravel, Fauré, Chabrier* (New Haven, CT: Yale University Press, 2009), p. 290.
[12] The exchange between Chevillard and Debussy is undocumented and based on a remark made by Louis Laloy, which is mentioned in Edward Lockspeiser, *Debussy: His Life and Mind*, vol. 2 (New York: The Macmillan Company, 1965), p. 44.
[13] See Howat, *The Art of French Piano Music*, p. 279; *Debussy Letters*, p. 222 n. 2, p. 274.

[*l'impression floue*] of vibrations in the air'.[14] This kind of technique was insufficient for Debussy, who sought a broad, resonant swathe of textured sound, as recalled by Dumesnil with regard to 'Clair de lune' (begun in 1890), where Debussy asked for the middle section at bar 27 to be 'drowned in pedal'. He gave a similar instruction for a later piece, 'Reflets dans l'eau' (*Images*, series 1), where Dumesnil recalled learning from Debussy about how to use the pedal 'in long harmonic strokes, without breaks or confusion'. Dumesnil explained that: 'Occasionally he allowed the pedal to encroach a tiny fraction from one harmony into the next … In any case, the blur should be used only for special effects, and with utmost discretion.'[15]

Whereas Ravel preferred the bright tone, light touch, and sharp distinction between registers on Érard pianos, Debussy was drawn to the homogeneous, mellow tone of the Bechstein upright that he owned and the Blüthner grand that he acquired from England in 1905. This preference may also account for his unusual technique – Dumesnil described how Debussy used flat fingers and a caressing, oblique downward motion to elicit from his Blüthner a tone that was 'the loveliest, the most elusive and ethereal'.[16] Several of Debussy's contemporaries noted how his fingers used to penetrate the keyboard; Léon-Paul Fargue described this sensation as being akin to sinking 'into velvet', while Louise Liebich praised Debussy's 'soft, deep touch'.[17] Many pianists who studied with Debussy noted his preference to play with the lid down on the Blüthner, in order to 'noyer le ton' (drown the tone), as described by Dumesnil.[18] Long ascribed the composer's desire to cultivate a muted tone as belonging to the Chopin school of playing half-tint.[19] Debussy worked towards repurposing the sustained subtlety of Chopin's soundscape by moving away from a vocal conception of melody as heard in his early pieces. Instead, he preferred to privilege short motives and fragmented figuration which, when coupled with Debussy's sophisticated conception of pedalling, contributed towards the evocation of an indistinct blur, as we hear at the beginning of one of his most virtuosic pieces for piano, 'Poissons d'or'. Whereas Debussy described Viñes's overly articulate rendition of tremolo figuration in a two-piano arrangement of 'Ibéria' as resembling 'the rumble of so many dead

---

[14] Viñes's remark has also proved difficult to track down except through anecdotal evidence, as provided by his student Vlado Perlemuter. See Vlado Perlemuter and Hélène Jourdan-Morhange, *Ravel According to Ravel*, trans. Frances Tanner (London: Kahn & Averill, 2005), pp. 6–7.
[15] Dumesnil, 'Coaching with Debussy', pp. 11–12.   [16] Ibid., p. 11.
[17] Nichols, *Debussy Remembered*, pp. 50, 202.   [18] Dumesnil, 'Coaching with Debussy', p. 13.
[19] Long, *At the Piano with Debussy*, p. 19.

pebbles', he had imagined the shimmering demisemiquavers of 'Poissons d'or' as conveying a quality of lightness that was 'almost immaterial' – that is, a fluid and mellow sound that evoked '"two clarinets" up above'.[20]

In one respect, the ground for Debussy's engagement with figuration-based keyboard patterning had been laid down by the French performer-composers François Couperin and Jean-Philippe Rameau. Debussy spoke openly of their influence throughout his life, and we can also sense their presence both in the titles of movements from *Suite bergamasque* and the suite *Pour le piano* (1894–1901), as well as in Debussy's cultivation of Baroque-like textures, ornamental gestures, and rhythmic figures in these pieces and in the later *Douze études* (1915).

Another influence that oriented his focus towards patterns of figuration came from Javanese gamelan, whose unique sonorities, layered melodic motifs, and repeating rhythmic patterns stimulated Debussy's imagination after he experienced this music at the Paris World's Fair that ran from May to the end of September in 1889. If the poetry of Paul Verlaine served as the primary stimulus for Debussy's initial efforts to evoke atmospheric intensity at the piano in 'Clair de lune', then the unfamiliar sounds and structures of the gamelan may have been the motivating factor behind Debussy's subsequent conceptualisation of sound as encompassing the notes themselves, as well as their reverberation through overtones.

Debussy, it seems, got to work soon after hearing the gamelan at the fair, and started to compose as early as October a *Fantaisie* for piano and orchestra, which, as Richard Mueller has shown, was a first attempt at alluding to Javanese music. Mueller claims that Debussy withdrew the work 'because he was not content with its assimilation of Javanese influences'.[21] Debussy's dissatisfaction seemed less tied to his approximation of slendro and pelog modes than to his evocation of sonority. Nowadays, scholars regard 'Pagodes', the opening movement from *Estampes* (1903), as the piece in which Debussy achieved his perfectly stylised conception of gamelan, one that acknowledged the timbres and textures of Javanese gamelan while using new techniques to transform the percussive piano into an instrument that is fully resonant and reverberating. The success of this piece was hard won: between 1889 and 1903, Debussy tried his hand at evoking the resonating timbres of the gamelan in several other pieces.

---

[20] See letter to André Caplet, 23 June 1913, *Debussy Letters* p. 274; Dumesnil, 'Coaching with Debussy', p. 12.
[21] Richard Mueller, 'Javanese Influence on Debussy's "Fantaisie" and Beyond', *19th-Century Music* 10 (1986), p. 158.

In the 'Prélude' from *Pour le piano*, for instance, Debussy juxtaposes eighteenth-century keyboard patterning, as heard through the toccata-like figuration of the opening, with gestures that suggest resounding 'gongs' in the low octave pedal A beginning at bar 6. Madame de Romilly, the dedicatee of this piece, also heard the final movement, 'Toccata', as evoking 'the gongs and Javanese music' that Debussy heard at the fair.[22] *D'un cahier d'esquisses*, a contemporaneous piece that paved his way towards 'Pagodes', shows Debussy thinking about the gamelan in various ways: through his multilayered organisation of motivic material across three staves, the use of recurring rhythmic motives, the appearance of whole-tone scales, and his attention to deep 'gong' gestures in the lower registers of the left hand.

Low pitches did not only have a harmonic function for Debussy, as they might have had with Chopin or Liszt. The pianist Robert Schmitz recalled how Debussy was pedantic with regard to how notes are played on the piano: the note 'must be struck in a peculiar way ... otherwise the sympathetic vibrations of the other notes will not be heard quivering distantly in the air'. In the next sentence, Schmitz revealed the source that stimulated Debussy's interest in overtones:

> Debussy regarded the piano as the Balinese musicians regard their gamelan orchestras. He was interested not so much in the single tone that was obviously heard when a note was struck, as in the patterns of resonance which that tone set up around itself. Many of his pieces are built entirely on this acoustical sense of the piano. Played badly, without a consciousness of the fine, almost inaudible, background of overtones, they are mere skeletons. The warm, indefinable, sensitive, inner beauty – the real quality of Debussy – is totally lacking.
>
> One cannot make up for this bareness by thick, gushy pedalling. One cannot substitute for this exquisite and evocative charm, double tempos, hasty phrases, or erratic interpretations. *One must learn to play Debussy's music as he played it himself*, striking each note as though it were a bell, listening always for the hovering clusters of vibrating overtones above and below it.[23]

A keen ear, along with a refined pedalling technique, are essential to privileging overtones in Debussy's piano pieces. With regard to 'Clair de lune', Dumesnil said Debussy asked him to 'depress the two pedals before starting, so that the overtones would vibrate immediately upon contact'.[24]

---

[22] See Howat, *The Art of French Piano Music*, p. 115.
[23] E. Robert Schmitz, 'A Plea for the Real Debussy', *The Etude* 55 (1937), p. 782.
[24] Dumesnil, 'Coaching with Debussy', p. 11.

Furthermore, Debussy's precise notational markings (such as the predominant *laissez vibrer*) reveal his interest in sustaining sonorities and their overtones in permitting the natural decay of these sounds to convey a process of timbral transformation rather than one of sonic decline.

Debussy's steadfast commitment to the pursuit of finely shaded tone colours is seen in his desire to custom-fit his Blüthner piano with an additional set of Aliquot strings in the upper three octaves. Figure 28.1 shows what the interior of his piano might have been looked like with this additional mechanism; the fourth string was attached slightly above the remaining three strings so that the hammer was unable to strike it. The goal of this additional string, then, was to catch the overtones and to enrich the sonority through sympathetic vibration. Cecila Dunoyer reminds us that this mechanism likely produced an effect 'similar to, and even richer than, that of depressing the pedal before starting to play, which Debussy recommended'.[25] These kinds of efforts must be behind the remarks of French pianist Yvonne Lefébure, who maintained that 'after Debussy it became necessary to pedal differently, because from him we learned that the piano could make new sounds'.[26]

While Debussy's first compositions for the piano sit comfortably in relation to the inherited practices of Chopin, Schumann, Liszt, Saint-Saëns, and

Figure 28.1 Photograph showing Aliquot stringing in a Blüthner grand piano. Courtesy of Hampstead Pianos.

---

[25] Cecilia Dunoyer, 'Debussy and Early Debussystes at the Piano', in James Briscoe (ed.), *Debussy in Performance* (New Haven, CT: Yale University Press, 1999), p. 101.
[26] Charles Timbrell, *French Pianism: A Historical Perspective* (Portland, OR: Amadeus Press, 1999), p. 107.

Massenet, his mature pieces reveal the composer's desire to rethink the instrument's sonic capabilities. In one respect, we can see this shift in Debussy's orchestral conception of his piano music – an approach that has roots in Liszt's transcriptions of orchestral music for the piano.[27] It is, however, Debussy's view of the piano as a machine capable of harnessing a tremendous vibrational energy that reveals the distance between him and the composers who fostered his initial learning at the piano; hence Lefébure's sense that Debussy facilitated some radical changes, not only in terms of playing the piano but also in terms of composing for it. Interestingly, while Debussy was to some extent aware of having altered the course of piano composition, he never lost his reverence for Chopin, whose Études he had the pleasure of editing at the same time as he was composing his own set of *Douze études* towards the end of his life. Rather than emphasise rupture with eighteenth-century clavecinists and pianist-composers of the past, Debussy, in his *Douze études*, invoked historical titles, textures, figurations, ornaments, and rhythms in paying tribute to those who continued to nourish his imagination during his final, vulnerable years.

***

For those who studied directly with him, or with someone else who had, Debussy's unique pianism was ultimately tied to his ability to invoke atmosphere. This was the expressive end to which his musical experiments with sonority, form, harmony, and metre were directed – a point also made by the pianist Alfred Cortot: 'The new element he [Debussy] adds to music is not simply a particular use of the harmonic system, but above all a particular quality, a characteristic atmosphere in which his music is steeped.'[28] Verlaine's subtle poetry, particularly his wistful musings on *fête galante* paintings by Jean-Antoine Watteau, played an important role in ushering Debussy towards an atmospheric approach to composition, where meaning is merely hinted at through suggestive rather than prescriptive means. The way that Debussy combined the influence of Verlaine with creative energy that came from his encounters with painting, sculpture, dance, popular music, and the artistic products of other cultural traditions show the workings of a true cultural polyglot, whose curiosity led him to explore and innovate.

At the height of Debussy's career as a composer for piano, the richness of his musical imagination is seen in the highly evocative titles of his pieces

---

[27] Howat explores Debussy's orchestral approach to composing and performing in *The Art of French Piano Music*, pp. 216–19.
[28] *Alfred Cortot's Studies in Musical Interpretation*, ed. Jeanne Thieffry, trans. Robert Jaques (New York: Da Capo Press, 1989), p. 54.

(as reflected in both books of *Préludes* and *Images*), which seem to stand a world apart from the titles that were given to his early and late piano works. When seen from a broader perspective, Debussy's sustained reverence for the classical past, coupled with an awareness of his Romantic inheritance and willingness to experiment, reveals a multifaceted role for this instrument: for Debussy, the piano belonged to the bourgeois salon as much as it did to his piano studio and the various performance venues (both small and large) of Paris. To his mind, the piano was not only a source of solo music; it was also a companion for song and chamber music. Moreover, the piano could just as readily conjure up an orchestra – indeed an entire ballet, as Debussy had attempted with Igor Stravinsky when they read through a four-hand arrangement of *Le Sacre du printemps* in June 1912); not to mention an entire opera, as seen in his performance of Mussorgsky's *Boris Godunov* at the piano for Ernest Chausson and his family in Luzancy during August 1893 (see Fig. 28.2).

Figure 28.2 Debussy playing Mussorgsky's *Boris Godunov*.

Perhaps the most striking aspect of his pianistic innovations resides in his treatment of sound as an acoustical phenomenon that has the potential to touch and envelop the audience, urging the listener to forget 'their petty, mundane troubles' in order to go 'into the depth of oneself, setting one's whole being in motion and seeking for new and hidden treasures'.[29] The piano's sonic vibrations were not just intended for the purposes of salon entertainment; they were also, as Debussy indicated, a catalyst for introspection and the contemplation of a sense of beauty that is immaterial and unfathomable.

Author's Recommendation
Douze études (1915).

Whereas Debussy sometimes agonised over the completion of his piano music, the late set of piano pieces, *Douze études*, was completed over a period of just six weeks in 1915. Dedicated to the memory of Chopin, these studies in piano technique show Debussy's continued commitment to making piano-playing fun, above all. In a letter to his publisher, Jacques Durand, he wrote: 'there's no need to make technical exercises over-sombre just to appear more serious; a little charm never spoilt anything. Chopin proved it'.[30] Playfulness resides at the core of this work even as he tackles 'serious' matters of piano technique such as five-finger exercises in no. 1 (a parody of nineteenth-century technical studies by Carl Czerny); legato playing in thirds, fourths, and sixths in nos. 2, 3, and 4; and a virtuosic treatment of octaves in no. 5, which culminates in a vigorous exploration of finger dexterity 'for the eight fingers' (*pour les huits doigts*) in no. 6.

The second half of the work is devoted to compositional topics that are tied to piano technique: speedy chromatic figuration in no. 7; ornamentation in no. 8 (a homage to a much-loved eighteenth-century composer, François Couperin); staccato, repeated notes in no. 9; the juxtaposition of unusual sonorities in no. 10; a delicate interweaving of arpeggios in no. 11; and, finally, an energetic display of synchronised chord agility in no. 12. Despite the personal challenges that he faced during this time of war and ill health, Debussy gave his all to this final collection of solo piano pieces.

---

[29] Letter to Paul Dukas, 11 February 1901, *Debussy Letters*, p. 118; *Monsieur Croche*, p. 586.
[30] Letter to Jacques Durand, 28 August 1915, *Debussy Letters*, p. 300.

PART VI

Performers, Reception, and Posterity

CHAPTER 29

Performers and Performance

Simon Trezise

In exile in Switzerland, a long way from home, Wagner followed the 1850 Weimar premiere of *Lohengrin* in his imagination. He soon discovered its duration from Liszt, conductor of the performance, which was over an hour longer than he had envisaged. Willing to concede that Liszt had not misconceived the work, he concluded that the extra length was due to singers dragging the tempo in recitatives, the passages where the conductor had least power to influence pulse, a fault he was familiar with.[1]

It seems natural that composers should be concerned about how their creations sounded, but it was only in the nineteenth century that changes in the status and perception of the composer made likely such incidents as this between Liszt and Wagner. Wagner had alighted upon a specific technical issue that adversely affected his conception of the work; he felt entitled to assert his authorship, with the text as his property, subject to his control. By the time of Debussy and his contemporaries, such conflict was unexceptional, as witnessed in the notorious Ravel–Toscanini incident, the gist of which is that the Italian conductor at a Paris Opéra concert with the New York Philharmonic (1930) conducted *Boléro* much faster than the score's metronome marking, provoking Ravel to fury and his refusal to acknowledge the performance when invited to by Toscanini. They had it out backstage, but Ravel would not budge; he did not want his music interpreted.[2] Defending Marguerite Long's performance of the Concerto in G against negative criticism, he asserted his right to 'affirm that this interpretation conforms . . . to my own thoughts, and that it should form the basis of a tradition for future performances'.[3]

Although Debussy's fond recollection of the piano-playing of his first piano teacher, Antoinette Mauté, may seem removed from the above

---

[1] Ernest Newman, *The Life of Wagner: 1848–1860*, vol. 2 (New York: Alfred A. Knopf, 1937), pp. 231–2.
[2] Benjamin Ivry, *Maurice Ravel: A Life* (New York: Welcome Rain Publishers, 2000), p. 160.
[3] Ronald Woodley, 'Performing Ravel: Style and Practice in the Early Recordings', in Deborah Mawer (ed.), *The Cambridge Companion to Ravel* (Cambridge: Cambridge University Press, 2000), p. 235.

stories, his recollection that she played Bach like 'no one does nowadays, bringing it to life' reveals a view of performance that throughout his criticism acknowledges the vital role of the musician's mediation in the communication of the text.[4] Unlike Wagner, who could provide an optimum timing of eight minutes for the Prelude to *Die Meistersinger von Nürnberg* plus a substantial critical apparatus for its tempo modification, and Ravel, who simply pointed the conductor to a score's metronome marking, Debussy often held back, shuffling off authority to the really good performer, like his piano teacher in Bach (though he would, when prompted, give direction on points of detail, as shown below).

For many composers, the challenge of achieving 'authentic' performances of their music, in so far as it was even recognised as an issue, was ameliorated by the circumstance of their having a hand in the realisation of their creations. Most of the creative musicians Debussy studied with at the Paris Conservatoire were as versatile as Haydn and Mozart. Composition was only one aspect of their musical economy. An illuminating close parallel to Debussy is Gabriel Pierné (1863–1937), who shared the distinction of winning the Prix de Rome (1882). His years at the Conservatoire included first prizes in performance, piano, and organ, as well as solfège, counterpoint, and fugue. Pierné enjoyed a career as an organist, succeeding Franck at the Sainte-Clotilde Basilica in 1890, one of the nation's top positions. He became chief conductor of the Concerts Colonne in 1910, giving the world premiere in that year of the then very demanding ballet *The Firebird* by Stravinsky. This was alongside his prolific compositional production. Pierné's range may appear extraordinary to us, but he was more typical of his time than Debussy, whose activities outside composition included very little teaching, piano performance, and conducting, but none entered into with any enthusiasm. His record at the Conservatoire indicates that he was not one of the best pianists, though it is not clear if this was due to lack of application or ability. Certainly, those who heard him play thought his command of the instrument remarkable, especially his touch, and not only in his own music, but Debussy later claimed that he could not play all of his own music; his fingers were simply not nimble enough. As a conductor, he seems to have been limited and worked best when a more experienced (and able) conductor prepared the orchestra for him. There is little doubt that Debussy would have avoided public performance had he not been desperately in need of the money, especially in

---

[4] Lesure (Rolf), p. 10.

the later years, or motivated to make a contribution to charity events in the war.

Unable or unwilling to perform his music, Debussy suffered greatly from performances that failed to meet his often ill-defined standards. No work caused him more agony than his only completed opera, *Pelléas et Mélisande*. What makes it especially interesting for us is that, against the odds, for a short run of performances, including the premiere, Debussy's aspirations were fulfilled. Of great concern was the role of Mélisande, but miraculously he found in the Scottish singer Mary Garden his ideal (see below). He struggled with unsympathetic or poorly equipped conductors throughout his career, but not with the opera's first, André Messager (1853–1929). However, though a benchmark was evidently established in 1902 for both the performance and staging of *Pelléas*, it is impossible for performers today to extrapolate from the available documentation a suitably informed or 'authentic' performance. Such has been the goal of musicians working in the historically informed performance movement, who seek to recreate works in a manner that their creators might recognise and whose attention has lately been directed to Debussy (see Chapter 31). Debussy's appreciative letter to Messager reveals the crux of the problem:

> you knew how to awaken the sonorous life of *Pelléas* with a tender delicacy that no longer must be sought, because it is quite certain that the internal rhythm of all music depends on the one who evokes it, as a word depends on the mouth that pronounces it ... Thus, such an impression of *Pelléas* was deepened by what your personal emotion had sensed in it, and from this came the marvellous effect of 'everything in its place'.[5]

He admires Messager's 'tender delicacy' and the rest seems to stem from the conductor's individual musical intelligence. These sentiments are recalled in a letter written a few days later, after Messager had left the production: 'I have the impression since you are no longer here that there is something rotten in the kingdom of Allemonde! So true is it that no one in the Opéra-Comique has for *Pelléas* the anxious tenderness that you felt for it.'[6] Although Debussy notated his music with great care, no form of prescription could substitute for the right intuition, the instinctive grasp of the music born of delicacy, goodwill, and, contradictory though it sounds, fidelity to the text.

---

[5] Letter to André Messager, 9 May 1902, *Correspondance*, p. 656.
[6] Letter to André Messager, 13 May 1902, *Correspondance*, p. 658.

Debussy's positive embrace of sensitive performers is borne out by George Copeland, a pianist who played for the composer. After playing 'Reflets dans l'eau', he recounts that Debussy

> got up from his chair in apparent excitement and ... exclaimed: 'Why did you play the last two bars as you did?'
> 'I don't know –' I was puzzled. 'Perhaps because that is the way I feel them.'
> 'It's funny,' he said reflectively, 'that's not the way I feel them.' But when I said, 'Then I will interpret them as you intended,' his reply was a definite 'No, no! Go on playing them just as you do.'[7]

Even Debussy's sporadically supplied metronome markings – a form of notation that promises greater certainty – come with heavy qualification, as illustrated in a letter to the organist Désiré Walter. Debussy states:

> I am only a simple composer of music, by no means a virtuoso, who seeks to draw from the piano as much from the sound point of view as from the mechanical point of view, as it is possible to draw from it. So I do not feel obliged to leave written lessons which, moreover, would run the risk of being misunderstood. – ... I think I will be able to send you a copy tomorrow, bearing the metronomic indications, which will only be valid as a starting point.[8]

He apparently did not expect a strict pulse to be maintained, but neither did he (usually) indicate how the performer might modify it. Rather than addressing technical matters pertaining to the interpretation of *L'Isle joyeuse*, Debussy tantalisingly draws Walter's attention to François Couperin's 'Les Barricades mystérieuses' (1717), the work's title, and to Watteau's painting *L'Embarquement pour Cythère* (1717), where one meets 'young women singing and dancing; all ending in the glory of the setting sun'.[9] Thus he writes of the image rather than the musical text.

One more extract from Debussy's letters will help to round out his performance aesthetic. This stance appears many times in his writings and can hardly be overstated if one seeks an 'authentic' or 'informed' performance style for Debussy. In response to a query from the English critic Edwin Evans, he wrote:

> I tried to prove that people who sing could remain human and natural, without ever having to sound like madmen or rebuses! This initially

---

[7] Roger Nichols (ed.), *Debussy Remembered* (Portland OR: Amadeus Press, 1992), pp. 164–5.
[8] Letter dated 13 July 1914, *Correspondance*, pp. 1834–5.
[9] Letter to Désiré Walter, 13 July 1914, *Correspondance*, pp. 1834–5.

bothered the 'professionals' and also the simple public who, accustomed to being moved by means as false as they were grandiloquent, did not understand immediately that all that was required of them was a little goodwill. – It matters very little that one penetrates into the secrecy of the means employed. It is a curiosity as blameworthy as it is ridiculous, and to be honest, completely useless.[10]

In the same vein, in a BBC interview Garden recalled him saying that there 'is much too much singing in grand opera; my singers in opera sing like real people'. The composer evidently rejected the rhetorical infrastructure of practising musicians, some may say 'tricks of the trade'. It seems that unthinking gestures were at the heart of his disaffection from the profession. This is supported by Garden's singing style around the time of the premiere, which is documented in a tiny excerpt from *Pelléas* and three of the *Ariettes oubliées*, accompanied by the composer (1904, in execrable sound, due more to a malfunctioning lathe than the primitive technology – other recordings of the period are much clearer). The voice we hear is naive, innocent even, lacking some of the more cultivated stylistic qualities of contemporaries. One understands her appeal to Debussy.

Debussy associated with many performers, some of whom came to him for advice. For all that his criticism and negativity could be devastating, he enjoyed congenial relations with several and did not stint in his admiration of those who understood his music. Of the string players who came into his orbit, Eugène Ysaÿe (1858–1931) was among the most important figures of his first maturity. As befits the early years, Debussy looked to him for the promotion of his music as much as for model performances. So it was that the Ysaÿe Quartet gave the premiere of the String Quartet in 1893. Debussy spent several years ruminating on a concerted work for him, but none appeared. As a critic for *La Revue blanche*, he praised Ysaÿe's Bach playing, writing of his 'freedom of expression and a spontaneous, natural beauty of tone – essential gifts for the interpretation of this music'.[11] In stark contrast is his response to the cellist Louis Rosoor, a professor at the Bordeaux Conservatoire, who visited Debussy and presumably played his Cello Sonata to him. Debussy was sorry he had composed a sonata and wondered if his writing was at fault; 'bad musicians are everywhere!' he concluded. He blamed such musicians for the failure of the public to understand his music.[12]

Several pianists came to Debussy for advice and, as Copeland proves, some went away reassured. Maurice Dumesnil (1886–1974) provides some

---

[10] Letter to Edwin Evans, 18 April 1909, *Correspondance*, pp. 1170–1.   [11] *Monsieur Croche*, p. 33.
[12] Letter to Jacques Durand, 12 October 1916, *Correspondance*, p. 2036.

of the most precise details of Debussy's coaching, though they may sow confusion. For example, he kept challenging Dumesnil's triplets, sometimes finding them too free but other times demanding more flexibility, even though the pianist was unable to detect a difference. Octaves should not be played flat but with one note emphasised. The *crescendo* should be strictly controlled, with more of it at lower dynamic levels, not attaining a full *forte*. Rubato should be within the entire phrase, never on a single beat. The pedal could be used to create washes of sound, as in 'Clair de lune', so long as it did not blur harmonic areas. He used orchestral analogies for such effects, sometimes citing specific instruments in order to guide the pianist towards the extensive variety of touch he sought. Clarity and simplicity were also goals for such works as *Pour le piano*.[13]

Varied and gruelling though his dealings with instrumentalists sometimes were, he suffered even more from conductors. In fact, some of his complaints might be drawn directly from Wagner on conducting, who deplored the tendency of some in the profession to maintain a rigid, insensitive beat, regardless of affect. Lack of sensibility clearly blighted some conductors and their orchestras, which must have been exacerbated by the novelty and difficulty of the music. Just as pianists were frequently told to reduce dynamic levels and do more between *pp* and *f*, so conductors had to persuade orchestras to moderate their tone, which is hard to do. His criticism of Arthur Nikisch (1855–1922) and his 'marvellously disciplined' Berlin Philharmonic perfectly encapsulates Debussy's performance priorities. Nikisch is named 'an incomparable virtuoso', but this is not a compliment in Debussy's vocabulary, because 'his virtuosity makes him forget that one also needs good taste'. He cites trombone portamentos in the *Tannhäuser* Overture 'more suited to that lady in charge of the sentimental songs at the Casino de Suresnes'. Such '"effects" without appreciable justification' are condemned.[14] Pierné's direction of Beethoven's 'Pastoral', in contrast, draws praise for being unencumbered with commentaries but just allowed to 'speak for itself'.[15] How much Debussy meant this cannot be known, but in 1911 the same Pierné is berated in a letter to André Caplet: 'For my sins I heard *La Mer* conducted by G. P.; it was awful and embarrassing. The same *Mer* by C. Ch. [Camille Chevillard] much better.'[16] Young, diligent, sympathetic conductors such

---

[13] Roger Nichols, *Debussy Remembered* (London: Faber and Faber, 1992), pp. 158–63.
[14] 'The Nikisch Concerts', *La Revue blanche* (1 June 1901), in *Debussy on Music*, ed. François Lesure, trans. Richard Langham Smith (New York: Alfred A. Knopf, 1977), pp. 39–40.
[15] 'Notes on the Concerts', *S.I.M.* (November 1912), in *Debussy on Music*, p. 266.
[16] Letter to André Caplet, 22 December 1911, *Debussy Letters*, p. 222.

as Désiré-Émile Inghelbrecht (1880–1965) and Vittorio Gui (1885–1975) drew praise. In a rare evocation of the deity, he wrote to Gui: 'I'm still prepared to swear before God, and even before men, that you are a conductor of the very first rank. Really, I don't see the necessity of putting one's grey cells into orbit in order to become a *debussyste*. I feel it's just a question of having a modicum of taste!'[17]

However much instrumentalists and conductors impinged upon Debussy, none played such a central role as his singers. It was a soprano who inspired some of Debussy's earliest works: a series of songs for the soprano voice that bear many hallmarks of his mature style. As his muse and mistress, Marie-Blanche Vasnier was one of the most important figures in Debussy's life. Other than her possession of a beautiful, high, flexible singing voice, we know nothing more of her performances. Along the way there was the precipitous and soon abandoned engagement to the soprano Thérèse Roger in 1894 while he was cohabiting with Gabrielle Dupont. Debussy's second wife, Emma, née Moyse, another talented singer, was the muse for Fauré's *La Bonne Chanson*. She performed a similar role in Debussy's music; he dedicated his *Trois chansons de France* to her, for example. In her autobiography, Garden claims that Debussy was in love with her, Mary Garden, but there is little evidence to support this. What is beyond doubt is that she represented the perfect path from conception to realisation that Debussy so rarely experienced. In *Musica*, in 1908, he wrote:

> I had tried to convey [Mélisande's] fragility and distant charm in the music, but there were still her gestures to be decided. ... Even the most beautiful voice in the world could have been quite antipathetic to the special feelings her character requires. ... I hardly had to speak a word to her as the character of Mélisande took shape. ...
>
> At last came the fifth act – Mélisande's death – a breathtaking event whose emotions cannot be rendered in words. There I heard the voice I had secretly imagined – full of sinking tenderness, and sung with such artistry as I would never have believed possible.[18]

It is of great interest that the three composers most often associated with the emergence of Modernism in music – Debussy, Schoenberg, and Stravinsky – all left traces of their performance style. While one might reasonably expect Modernism to penetrate their performances, only Stravinsky hoed a path of transparency, strict adherence to notation, uniformity of tempo, and so on – the tenets of Modernist (sometimes called

[17] Letter to Vittorio Gui, 25 February 1912, *Debussy Letters*, p. 225.   [18] *Debussy on Music*, p. 227.

'geometric') performance and features beloved of the early historical performance movement and many other twentieth- and twenty-first-century performers. It is often found in modern performances of Debussy's music. Stravinsky was therefore a Modernist in both the conception and the realisation of his music, in which case he was paralleled by Ravel, as intimated above. Debussy and Schoenberg are much more readily situated in the music-making they grew up with, which we summarise as 'Romantic' (also referred to as 'vitalist').

In addition to the four murky gramophone and typewriter recordings made in 1904 with Garden, Debussy participated in a Welte-Mignon session for reproducing piano in the summer of 1912. Together with the gramophone recordings, this yields around fifty minutes of Debussy as a piano soloist and accompanist.[19] The Welte-Mignon rolls, while fascinating and engrossing, have to be listened to with caveats, for the choice of piano and other factors greatly affect playback. One cannot assume all one hears was characteristic of Debussy's piano-playing.[20] Nevertheless, Jocelyn Ho concludes: 'The piano rolls reveal unequivocally that Debussy invoked a rich array of performing styles rooted in late romantic performing practices otherwise indiscernible in his notation, others contradict it altogether.'[21] These practices include Debussy's frequent dislocation of the hands when music aligned in notation is played apart, as in *La plus que lente*; unnotated arpeggiation, as in 'La Soirée dans Grenade'; metrical rubato and rhythmic alteration, where the accompaniment in in strict time but the melody wanders off; tempo modification, where both hands speed up or slow down together, including the large-scale modification heard in 'La Cathédrale engloutie'.[22]

Some of Debussy's performances differ significantly from the published texts. In 'La Cathédrale engloutie' (*Préludes*, book 1) pianists have often attempted to maintain a constant tempo based on the 6/4 = 3/2 time signature (often unsuccessfully). Debussy, however, from bar 7 and

---

[19] All the Welte rolls and the gramophone recordings with Garden are included in *Claude Debussy: The Complete Works* (33 CDs, Warner Classics 0190295 736750). These realisations were originally issued on Pierian PIR0001.

[20] For extensive discussion of the Welte rolls, see Roy Howat, 'Between and Beyond the Perforations in Debussy's Welte Rolls' and 'Debussy's Welte Roll of *La plus que lente*', in Tihomir Popović and Peter Mutter (eds.), *Claude Debussy: Die Klavieraufnahmen* (Hofheim: Wolke Verlag, 2023), pp. 62–91, 356–72.

[21] Jocelyn Ho, 'Debussy and Late-Romantic Performing Practices: The Piano Rolls of 1912', in François de Médicis and Steven Huebner (eds.), *Debussy's Resonance* (Rochester NY: University of Rochester Press, 2018), p. 557.

[22] I have followed Ho's categories and adopted her examples from 'Debussy and Late-Romantic Performing Practices', pp. 519–58.

elsewhere, plays the 3/2 minims at the pace of the preceding crotchets, effectively doubling the tempo. This and other variations helpfully correct or clarify the original publication and are consequently reflected in the *Œuvres complètes* volumes of the solo piano music by publisher Durand.

In Garden's singing, one is aware that this is a singer in the late Romantic tradition. In particular, her use of portamento in support of legato singing and expression is quite different to the approach of more recent singers. One recalls eighteenth-century theorists who placed so much emphasis on the correct use of portamento of varying degrees to bind notes together and thereby produce a true legato. This need not always result in a slow, deliberate glissando between notes, so much as it involves a way of creating the sensation of leaning into the next note before it sounds. This is especially telling in Garden's performance of 'L'Ombre des arbres'; and she does indeed use full portamento between the last two syllables of 'noy-é-es' as the melodic lines drops a minor seventh. In this song one hears, too, the composer 'grafting the "expressive" performance practices common in his time on to his detailed, prescriptive-looking scores' as he penetrates 'des sentiments de l'âme'.[23] String players from Debussy's time also used far more prominent portamento than violinists today. What more attractive illustration of this than the performance of the violin solo in Saint-Saëns's Prelude to *Le Déluge* by members of the Conservatoire orchestra, conducted by Messager, no less (the hero of the *Pelléas* premiere), recorded in the last year of Debussy's life (Columbia Col 6087).

Taking these examples, along with the views on the role of the performer outlined above, it is clear that Debussy's attitude to performance was born of a nineteenth-century, late-Romantic sensibility, traceable to Beethoven as much as to Wagner. Just as his music challenges music theory in its apparent freedom from systematic organisation, so too is the performance of his music shrouded in a sort of Impressionist haze. The diligent, accurate style of so much historically informed performance and many other performers might seem best suited to a composer regarded as a harbinger of Modernism, but the musicians around Debussy, in so far as we can know them, and the composer himself, performed in a freer, more expressive, more spontaneous way than is usual today.

---

[23] Richard Langham Smith, 'Debussy on Performance: Sound and Unsound Ideas', in James R. Briscoe (ed.), *Debussy in Performance* (New Haven, CT: Yale University Press, 1999), p. 12. Smith discusses Garden's portamento in detail.

Author's Recommendation

Debussy: Ses premiers interprètes (10 CDs, Warner Classics 0190295 665425).

The centenary of Debussy's death brought several events and publications, including two substantial sets of recordings from Warner Classics. The larger set was the most ambitious attempt yet to cover all his music in one box set, including arrangements and unfinished works;[24] the other was a wide-ranging compilation of historical material that covers many of the major works and even provides alternate versions of a few, notably three versions of *Prélude à l'après-midi d'un faune*. The earliest of these dates from 1922 and is conducted by Camille Chevillard, who premiered the first two movements of *Nocturnes* and *La Mer*. It is an extremely brisk performance (7:07), raising suspicions that the conductor was trying to fit the work onto two sides of a record, but Debussy's suggested metronome markings for the *Prélude* are remarkably close to Chevillard's tempos.[25] The others are conducted by Walther Staram (1930, 9:04) and Gabriel Pierné (1930, 8:52). Also in the set are Mary Garden's three *Ariettes oublieés* (second version) recordings with the composer, but not the snippet she recorded from *Pelléas*. One of Debussy's Welte-Mignon piano rolls is given, 'La Soirée dans Grenade', which some consider the finest of them. *Pelléas* is exceptionally well represented, with the whole of the famous 1941 Roger Désormière Paris recording and earlier extracts with Piero Coppola (1927) and Georges Truc (1928). On the ten well-filled CDs there is a great deal of piano, chamber, vocal, and orchestral music to flesh out an excellent survey of early Debussy performance on record.

---

[24] *Debussy: The Complete Works*.
[25] See the preface to Debussy, *Prélude à l'après-midi d'un faune, pour orchestre*, ed. Douglas Woodfull-Harris, Bärenreiter Urtext (Kassel: Bärenreiter, 2012), p. ix.

CHAPTER 30

Early Music

Catrina Flint de Médicis

Writing several months after the premiere of *Pelléas*, Debussy declared the well-known early music advocate Charles Bordes to be 'universally known, and for the best reasons in the world'.[1] In 1903, he further described a scene at the Parisian Schola Cantorum that would later become frozen in many an historical imagination, one indelibly marked by an earnest, selfless atmosphere that hovered over its performances: 'I don't know if it is because of the smallness of the room, or because of some mysterious influence of the divine, but there is a real communion between those who play and those who listen.'[2] Debussy's praise for this particular performance (two acts from Rameau's *Castor et Pollux*) and his solid defence of the composer ring with a degree of sincerity. And this is probably because woven into the complex cultural texture that is Debussy's context are several distinct strands of experience, spun from his own connections to early music.

During the late nineteenth and early twentieth centuries in France, a multiplatformed staging ground took shape for a wide variety of undertakings in music composed prior to 1750. Churches, schools, universities, private salons, select societies, major concert halls, and even opera houses became sites for performances of music dating from the Middle Ages to the Baroque. Sometimes, the repertoire of centuries past served as a point of focus for discussions about religion; at other times, it provided a vehicle for unabashedly secular, virtuosic performances. Choral performances, in particular, could as easily allow talented socialites to exert cultural influence as facilitate bonding among male workers. Through it all, the revival of early music provided the nation with a sense of artistic ancestry that could be summoned to shape notions of a collective musical identity, or even difference.

---

[1] Debussy, 'At the Schola Cantorum', *Gil Blas* (2 February 1903), in Richard Langham Smith (ed.), *Debussy on Music: The Critical Writings of the Great French Composer* (New York: Cornell University Press, 1977), p. 110.
[2] Debussy, 'At the Schola Cantorum', p. 111.

Concerts and Large Amateur Choral Societies

Freshly redirected from studies in piano performance to composition at the Paris Conservatoire, a teenaged Debussy appears to have had little interest in the music-history classes that Louis Bourgault-Ducoudray gave there after 1878.[3] But this history teacher's outside performance activities were likely difficult to ignore. With mainstream concert organisers Jules Pasdeloup and Charles Lamoureux, Bourgault-Ducoudray was part of a trend in the 1870s to perform large-scale choral works by Bach and Handel. These events also sometimes involved integrating local *orphéon* choirs, made up of working-class men, for performances that reached audiences numbering in the thousands.[4] Programmes for the Société Bourgault-Ducoudray also featured individual works of Renaissance vocal polyphony by composers such as Lassus, Palestrina, Josquin, Arcadelt, and Victoria, to name a few. As a composer who had previously captured the Prix de Rome in 1862, and as a man of some means, Bourgault-Ducoudray enjoyed an extensive network of social connections. He was an honorary member of the close-knit Concordia society, established in 1879 by the wealthy Edmond Fuchs and his wife, Henriette, a much-appreciated amateur singer. The society often programmed a mix of modern and historical music, but is probably best remembered for its performances of large-scale works by Bach and Handel, notably the Saint Matthew Passion in 1888.[5] Other amateur choral societies organised along similar lines were to emerge later, such as the Société des grandes auditions musicales (headed by the Countess Élisabeth Greffulhe) and L'Euterpe (directed by Abel Duteil d'Ozanne). These groups mainly followed the precedent set by the Concordia society. During the 1880s, the mighty Société des concerts du Conservatoire performed only a limited range of excerpts from this type of repertoire (Bach's Mass in B Minor, Handel's *Saul, Israel in Egypt, Judas Maccabeus,* and *Messiah*). This changed in 1891 with the Société's first performance of the Mass in B Minor, which they gave on three further occasions during the 1890s. This same mass was later performed during Holy Week of 1900 at the Église Saint-Eustache, along with Handel's *Messiah*.

Performances of early choral works by larger organisations do not appear to have resonated with Debussy's musical sensibilities. He traded places

---

[3] Lesure (Rolf), p. 34.
[4] Katharine Ellis, *Interpreting the Musical Past* (Oxford: Oxford University Press, 2005), pp. 67–9, 226–30.
[5] Ellis, *Interpreting the Musical Past*, pp. 98–9.

with his fellow student, Paul Vidal, as accompanist for the Concordia society, very briefly, between 1883 and 1884, but it is unlikely he derived much musical inspiration or stimulation from the experience. Judging by Vidal's correspondence, the arrangement also appears to have rankled Henriette Fuchs. Vidal bent over backwards, in several apologies to Fuchs, writing in July of 1884, 'For a moment last year, I believed that art had put him [Debussy] back on the right track. Wanting to ease his path to victory, I introduced him to you and heartily recommended him to Concordia. But his current behaviour gives me remorse.'[6] If rubbing shoulders with a bevy of countesses and trudging through monumental choral works proved a heartily unsuccessful undertaking for Debussy, his short stint with Concordia came with an advantage. It probably brought him into closer contact with the writer and poet Maurice Bouchor, someone well liked by Debussy's fellow students and whose poems he set to music in the early 1880s ('Chanson triste' and 'Les Baisers d'amour'). Bouchor had a genuine love of music; he collaborated with musicians on various projects up until the First World War and was close to the circle of Wagnerites in the 1870s and 1880s. In 1882, he joined a large contingent of musicians, high-society individuals, and literary figures who made the well-documented pilgrimage to Bayreuth to hear *Parsifal*.[7] This is the kind of person a younger Debussy would have been attracted to. We also know that he later attended performances of Bouchor's works at the intimate, 250-seat Petit-Théâtre de la Marionnette in the Galerie Vivienne. With music by Paul Vidal, Ernest Chausson, and Casimir Baille, the first of these productions in 1888 was attended by Stéphane Mallarmé, and hailed in the press as 'théâtre symboliste'.[8]

The Palestrinian

During the early decades of the Third Republic, the Palestrinian referred to almost any type of sacred Renaissance vocal polyphony. Performances of this music often provided a far different experience for music lovers than they might have experienced at events featuring large-scale, Baroque choral works. Sacred works might be performed in the midst of a church service or at smaller, more exclusive venues. During the 1890s, this kind of exclusivity

---

[6] François Lesure and Paul Vidal, 'Debussy de 1883 à 1885 d'après la correspondance de Paul Vidal à Henriette Fuchs', *Revue de musicologie* 48 (1962), p. 100.
[7] Jean Gallois, *Camille Saint-Saëns* (Sprimont: Mardaga, 2004), p. 234.
[8] U. Saint-Vel, 'Le Théâtre symboliste: Shakespeare et les marionnettes', *Revue d'art dramatique*, 12 (1888), pp. 288–90.

began to widen out and become more accessible to the public with the work of Charles Bordes at the Église Saint-Gervais, and also with the Schola Cantorum that he helped to form after 1894. For Maundy Thursday of 1891, he turned to the folk music specialist Julien Tiersot for help in preparing his choir for performances of Gregorio Allegri's *Miserere* and Palestrina's *Stabat Mater*. This celebrated event has gone down in history for having been so well attended that critics were obliged to sit through the service in the church's confessional booths. This service also featured a sermon by the well-known theologian, speaker, and writer Abbé Ferdinand Brettes, whose presence may have helped to swell the crowds. Bordes probably learned a great deal from this happy coincidence; later efforts included collaborations with the Société d'ethnographie, establishing a link with those interested in regional folk music. He also joined forces with literary figures, like the long-time director of the *Revue des deux mondes* Ferdinand Brunetière, or virtuosos, like the pianist Francis Planté. Between 1893 and 1895, he led a number of performances given by the Chanteurs as part of Eugène d'Harcourt's newly established series of 'eclectic' concerts for the general public. These included a series of twelve historical concerts that featured a survey of over three hundred years of music (1893–4), and two short series of Bach cantata concerts in the winters of 1894 and 1895, both underwritten by the Princesse de Polignac (Winnaretta Singer). And Bordes was even willing to go beyond traditional concerts. In April of 1896, he joined with the Société Saint-Jean for a magic-lantern show of paintings on the life of Christ. These kinds of collaborations greatly expanded awareness of the repertoire and became integral to Bordes and the Schola's activities. At Saint-Gervais, he quickly expanded his early music performances for the Easter season, and with the help of Vincent d'Indy treated Parisians to sacred Renaissance music from Wednesday to Saturday during Holy Week of 1892 and throughout the 1890s. He introduced the practice of performing responsory settings by Victoria and Ingegneri (then attributed to Palestrina), which became the most stable repertoire for these events, along with a limited number of motets. Enthusiasm ran high for Bordes's Holy Week performances in the early 1890s; they attracted the fashionable and literary alike, and also generated considerable revenue for the church through the reservation of seats. It is also possible that Debussy encountered Stéphane Mallarmé there in the winter of 1893.[9]

---

[9] *Correspondance*, p. 116 n. 5.

Prior to the acceleration of Bordes's activities after 1892, Palestrinian music was often confined to closed, specialist, sometimes elite venues. This is one of the reasons that Bordes's revival was often touted as new and innovative. But those in the know prior to 1892 could access Palestrinian music at the annual concerts of the École Niedermeyer – a school that provided a fairly well-rounded education for future church musicians. Its affiliate, the Société des concerts de musique vocale classique, also gave concerts of this repertoire twice a year.[10] Niedermeyer came by his connection to early music honestly. In the 1840s, he worked as an assistant for the Prince de la Moskowa (Napoléon Joseph Ney), who brought together a group of aristocrats over a period of three years to give performances of sixteenth- and seventeenth-century music.[11] Moskowa also published editions of his concert repertoire that survived well into Bordes's time, and may still be found in a number of libraries today. Pre-Bordes, Palestrinian music could also be heard at a limited number of churches, including the Église Notre-Dame-des-Blancs-Manteaux in Paris. There, Louis-Lazare Perruchot put the training in Palestrinian repertoire he had received at the cathedral in Langres (one of the few with an actual choir school) to good use.[12] Like the events held at the Niedermeyer school, Perruchot's performances did not get much exposure in the press. Yet they were later acknowledged as the inspiration for Bordes's work at Saint-Gervais.[13]

Some performances of Palestrinian music were more visible, but also more exclusive. Shortly before Bordes's first major set of performances for Holy Week, in March of 1892, Joséphin or Sâr Péladan inaugurated his Salon de la Rose+Croix and with it a series of concerts at the Galerie Durand-Ruel. This was the same 'smaller' gallery that in 1876 had welcomed Impressionist painters anxious to be free of the commercial, overblown nature of official salons in favour of a space that could offer a more purely artistic experience.[14] Sixteen years later, the choice of venue was probably not lost on many. The music for the occasion was limited to works by composers who had 'the most characteristic, most irreproachably beautiful works of masters who only ever conformed to ideas ... that is to say, Palestrina, Sébastien [sic] Bach, Beethoven, Wagner and César

---

[10] Ellis, *Interpreting the Musical Past*, p. 109.
[11] Clair Rowden, 'Choral Music and Music Making in France', in Donna Di Grazia (ed.), *Nineteenth-Century Choral Music* (New York: Routledge, 2013), p. 206.
[12] Ellis, *Interpreting the Musical Past*, p. 72; Catrina Flint, 'The Schola Cantorum, Early Music and French Political Culture, from 1894 to 1914', PhD thesis, McGill University (2006), p. 12.
[13] Amédée Gastoué, 'Charles Bordes', *La Tribune de Saint-Gervais* 15 (1909), p. 5.
[14] Martha Ward, 'Impressionist Installations and Private Exhibitions', *The Art Bulletin* 73 (1991), p. 604.

Franck', with a choir of sixty-four singers (sixteen to a part) from the Opéra for the Missa Papae Marcelli. The audience was limited to three hundred, paying twenty francs each.[15] Vincent d'Indy and members of the Société nationale programmed a similarly exclusive event in January of the same year, featuring Palestrinian music alongside modern works.[16] Although the Société nationale gave a limited number of public concerts, many of its events were reserved for members only. Like the performances at the Salon de la Rose+Croix, there was a certain exclusivity associated with these events, which was absent from the more open, accessible performances given by Bordes and the Chanteurs de Saint-Gervais. Also rather select were performances of early music (both Palestrinian and Baroque) at the private salons of various *mondaines*, such as the Princesse de Polignac.[17]

Debussy's early documented experiences with the Palestrinian revival fall more in line with these kinds of less mainstream performances. He first came into contact with the repertoire far from Paris, in Italy, shortly after his success in the Prix de Rome, and years before Bordes's performances began to gather steam. Unhappy and uninspired as a resident of the Villa Medici, he confessed to his former benefactor, Henri Vasnier, that the time he spent listening to Palestrina and Lassus at the church of Maria dell'Anima were the only hours that had awakened the musician in him that month.[18] Debussy did experience at least one performance of Palestrinian music at Saint-Gervais, but not during Holy Week as most Parisians did. The comments he made in a letter to André Poniatowski shortly thereafter have gone down in history: 'It's wonderfully beautiful; this music, which is nevertheless in a very severe style, seems quite white, and the emotion is not translated (as it has since become) by cries, but by arabesques.'[19] Debussy also referred to the arabesque in his discussions of works by Bach and Gregorian chant.[20] It was an aesthetic desideratum that prevailed among the many Symbolists with whom Debussy associated, and as a result a number of scholars have explored this idea both in the composer's writings and as manifested in his own music.[21] The latter

---

[15] 'Nouvelles Diverses – Paris et Départements', *Le Ménéstrel* (13 March 1892), p. 87.
[16] Michel Duchesneau, *L'Avant-garde musicale à Paris de 1871 à 1939* (Sprimont: Mardaga,1997), p. 252.
[17] Myriam Chimènes, *Mécènes et musiciens: Du salon au concert à Paris sous la IIIe République* (Paris: Fayard, 2004), p. 100.
[18] Letter to Henri Vasnier, end of November 1885, *Correspondance*, p. 45.
[19] Letter to André Poniatowski, February 1893, *Correspondance*, p. 116.
[20] Langham Smith (ed.), *Debussy on Music*, pp. 27, 84.
[21] See, among many others, Gurminder Kaur Bhogal, *Details of Consequence: Ornament, Music, and Art in Paris* (New York: Oxford University Press, 2013); Barbara L. Kelly, 'Debussy's Parisian

include not only the *Deux arabesques* of 1891, but many other works that have no reference to the term, or even early music, such as the *Prélude à l'après-midi d'un faune*. The relationship between the free rhythms of chant *à la Solesmes* and Debussy's musical style was not lost on *fin-de-siècle* observers. The music critics Louis Laloy and Jules Écorcheville made this fairly explicit some five years after the premiere of *Pelléas*. Laloy underscored what he perceived as a positive influence and drew comparisons between chant and some of Debussy's works.[22] Jules Écorcheville condemned the flattening of metrical accent in both chant and the composer's music:

> We know that for a long time there has been an effort to level [*uniformiser*] the dynamism of speech, and the declamation in *Pelléas* is, in the theatre, the final victory of this national tendency. They have involuntarily conformed to this taste for unified rhythms that allowed our medieval forefathers to transform Gregorian song, oriental vocalise, into flat syllabics, in equal note values.[23]

There is a wider context that illuminates Écorcheville's disapproval here. When he alludes to efforts 'to level the dynamism of speech', he may also be voicing the discontent of many who championed regionalism at the turn of the century – a group that deeply resented attempts to stamp out local accents and expressions through nationalist political policies.

The French Baroque in Print and Performance

Debussy's 1908 edition of Jean-Philippe Rameau's *Les Fêtes de Polymnie* has been interpreted as part of that movement to establish a uniform, nationalised vision of Frenchness in music (i.e. ethnic-linguistic nationalism). And so have other figures associated with Auguste Durand's edition of the 'complete' works of Rameau that began in 1895.[24] It included contributions

---

Affiliations', in Simon Trezise (ed.), *The Cambridge Companion to Debussy* (Cambridge: Cambridge University Press), pp. 25–42; Caroline Potter, 'Debussy and Nature', in *The Cambridge Companion to Debussy*, pp. 137–52. For a concise review of literature on Debussy and the arabesque, see Carolyn Rose Rynex, 'Arabesque and the Early Music Influence in Debussy's *Trois Chansons de Charles d'Orléans*', PhD thesis, Arizona State University (2016), pp. 6–19.

[22] Bhogal, *Details of Consequence*, pp. 168–74.
[23] 'La Schola Cantorum et le style de Bach', *Revue musicale S.I.M.* (15 April 1907), pp. 399–406.
[24] Anya Suschitzky, 'The Nation on Stage: Wagner and French Opera at the End of the Nineteenth Century', PhD thesis, University of California at Berkeley (1999); see also Suschitzky, 'Rameau, d'Indy, and French Nationalism', *The Musical Quarterly* 86 (2002), pp. 398–448. More particularly directed at Vincent d'Indy: Charles B. Paul, 'Rameau, d'Indy, and French Nationalism', *The Musical Quarterly* 58 (1972), pp. 46–56; Graham Sadler, 'Vincent d'Indy and the Rameau *Œuvres Complètes*: A Case of Forgery?' *Early Music*, 21 (1993), pp. 415–21.

by its general editor, Camille Saint-Saëns, as well as Vincent d'Indy, Alexandre Guilmant, and Paul Dukas, among others. Prior to the 1890s, Parisian audiences had been primed for performances enabled by this major Rameau edition through the occasional hearings of short excerpts given by the Bourgault-Ducoudray and Concordia societies. Closer to the turn of the century, audiences for the Société des concerts and the Concerts Colonne might expect to experience the odd choral number or orchestrated dance from one of the operas. Excerpts from Rameau's vocal works could also be heard at daytime lecture recitals, directed mainly at society women and retired military men; Arthur Pougin gave a number of these during the 1890s.

It is significant that Saint-Saëns launched Durand's collection with a volume of harpsichord pieces, because this repertoire was quite well known to music lovers of the 1890s. A number of the pieces he included had appeared earlier: in the *Trésor des pianistes* by Aristide and Louise Farrenc in 1861 or *Les Clavecinistes de 1637 à 1790* by Amédée Méreaux after 1864, or even closer to Debussy's time in the virtuoso Louis Diémer's *Les Clavecinistes français du XVIIIe siècle*. Performances and reviews of this repertoire dated back to at least the 1850s, including concerts at the 1889 Paris World's Fair.[25] In the decade prior to Debussy's 1903 review of Rameau's *Castor et Pollux* noted at the outset of this chapter, Diémer performed a number of short pieces from the clavecinist repertoire, joining Louis van Waefelghem and others for periodic concerts of similar music with the Société des instruments anciens. These kinds of events offered a pleasurable, nostalgic, refined retreat from the seriousness of regular 1890s concerts. They were identity-forming, perhaps, but only for the privileged few.[26] Some of the music critics who responded to Rameau performances in the 1890s came down hard on what they perceived as uncritical listeners swayed only by a prevailing fashion for the composer's music. Adolphe Jullien mocked audiences who came to hear the Société des instruments anciens at the Salle Érard in 1896, pigeonholing them as, 'amateurs who wagged their heads to and fro and never once appeared to sleep, for they did not let a single work pass without a burst of applause. Which at least

---

[25] For mid-century performances of Rameau and other French Baroque composers' keyboard music, see Katharine Ellis, *Interpreting the Musical Past*, pp. 56–7; for performances by Louis Diémer and what would become the Société des instruments anciens, see Annegret Fauser, *Musical Encounters at the 1889 Paris World's Fair* (Rochester, NY: University of Rochester Press, 2005), pp. 27–42.

[26] Ellis, *Interpreting the Musical Past.*, pp. 94–6; Catrina Flint de Médicis, 'Nationalism and Early Music at the French *Fin de Siècle*: Three Case Studies', *Nineteenth-Century Music Review* 1 (2004), pp. 47–54.

proves that Bach and Rameau, however old they may be, are now all the rage.'[27] Responding to the same event for *Le Ménestrel*, Arthur Pougin noted that the composer's music had become cheapened at the hands of some performers.[28] Facile public enthusiasm for Rameau's music also irked the Opéra's archivist-librarian Charles Malherbe – someone who would later have a major hand in annotating many volumes of Durand's Rameau edition.[29]

Debussy does not appear to connect with either the fashionable, nostalgic renditions of keyboard and instrumental music written for the *Ancien Régime* or the individual arias or choir pieces given by larger concert societies. Much like his appreciation of Palestrina's music, his connection to Rameau appears highly particular and very personal. It coincides with an increase in performances of single-act works or longer excerpts from Rameau's operas. The warmth that Debussy cast on Charles Bordes and the Schola in his review from the autumn of 1903 likely carried with it the remnants of a sunny afternoon in June of that same year, when he heard the entirety of *La Guirlande* given outdoors in the Schola's grounds. In the years leading up to the state Opéra's revival of *Hippolyte et Aricie* in 1908, the Schola Cantorum continued to offer both a sonic window on Rameau's music and a space for artistic communing between those who played and the small audience, sometimes including Debussy, that listened.

Author's Recommendation
Trois chansons de Charles d'Orléans (1898/1908).

Claude Debussy's *Trois chansons de Charles d'Orléans* (1898/1908) came into being during a relatively difficult period in the composer's life. The first two songs (later repositioned as the first and third songs) were composed in 1898 for an amateur family choir organised by Lucien and Arthur Fontaine, who were very close to Debussy in the mid-1890s and whose extended family included Henry Lerolle and Ernest Chausson. The public premiere of 1909 featured revised versions of the first and third songs, with a completely new song placed between them. Some contemporary critics reacted negatively to what they perceived as pastiche – composing in an historical style. Pierre Lalo defended the composer against such accusations, asserting that for all its reference to archaic styles, there remained

---

[27] Adolphe Jullien, *Le Journal des débats* (24 May 1896).
[28] Arthur Pougin, *Le Ménestrel* (24 May 1896).
[29] Charles Malherbe, *Le Monde musical* (30 October 1899).

a piece of Debussy in its bars (*Le Temps*, 13 April 1909). In our own time, scholars such as Marielle Cafafa and Harry Halbreich have tended to agree. Indeed, these songs exhibit a number of Debussy tells: tremendous rhythmic flexibility that sometimes leads to metric ambiguity; calculated use of range to create high points and structural markers; reservation of expressive, disjunct melodies for climactic moments; harmonic ambiguities sometimes infused with modal pitch languages. Even though Debussy set a few short passages in imitative counterpoint, it could be argued that this texture is used for expressive purposes, to create tension and underscore the meaning of the text (see the end of the third song). Each of the three poems consists of three octosyllabic quatrains, with an added refrain at the end of the final verse. This structure lends itself well to quasi-ternary forms, clearest in the final song. The second song divides more easily into two main parts at 'Jeunes gens', or two-thirds of the way through the poem. The first song may be best described as through-composed with a recurring refrain.

CHAPTER 31

Performance Today: Hearing Debussy Anew on Period Instruments

Brian Hart

Debussy is well represented in concert and recital halls today. Most of his compositions are firmly ensconced in the repertory, and many lesser-known pieces such as the *Fantaisie* for piano and orchestra and *Khamma* enjoy occasional hearings. In addition, the centenary of his death produced complete or near-complete recorded anthologies of his total output. Debussy's music also figures prominently outside mainstream 'classical' traditions. 'Duke' Ellington, Bix Beiderbecke, Bill Evans, Jacques Loussier, Chick Corea, Fred Hersch, and Branford Marsalis have all attested to his impact in jazz.[1] Further – and fittingly enough for one so attracted to the popular music of his day – his music has been featured throughout various strands of contemporary popular culture, including rock albums and scores for films, television programmes, and video games. His most influential works in this realm have proved to be the 'salon' piano pieces from 1890–1, especially *Rêverie*, the first Arabesque, and above all 'Clair de lune', although his more revolutionary compositions, most notably *Prélude à l'après-midi d'un faune*, are by no means absent.[2]

Not all innovative aspects of present-day Debussy performance and reception relate to non-classical contexts, however; there have also been significant developments looking 'backwards', so to speak. In recent decades the interest in 'period performance' has moved beyond the Classical and early Romantic periods to embrace early twentieth-century composers, including Debussy. Beginning in the 1990s with recordings on pianos with which he would have been familiar, the movement has extended to his

---

[1] For a recent study of intersections of Debussy and jazz, see Deborah Mawer, *French Music and Jazz in Conversation: From Debussy to Brubeck* (Cambridge: Cambridge University Press, 2014).
[2] See Matthew Brown, *Debussy Redux: The Impact of His Music on Popular Culture* (Bloomington, IN: Indiana University Press, 2012); Gurminder Kaur Bhogal, *Claude Debussy's* Clair de Lune (New York: Oxford University Press, 2018). The IMDb website lists the use of his music in film and TV, documentaries, video shorts, and selected video games (www.imdb.com/name/nm0006033/?ref_=fn_nm_nm_1); it does not include commercials.

works in other genres. The purpose of this chapter will be to look briefly at some of the major developments in period recordings of the composer's piano music, *mélodies*, and orchestral works; the best of these recordings show that in hearing these pieces on the instruments of his day, we can gain new insights into his compositional and scoring choices as well as his own performance practice.

Piano Music and *Mélodies*

Musicians who heard Debussy play Debussy marvelled that 'at the keyboard [he could] give his scores the colour of the orchestra, with the most perfect balance, even in the instrumental nuances!'[3] The composer himself described his pianistic effects in terms of orchestral sonorities: for example, the left-hand arpeggios in the second section of 'Clair de lune' should sound 'as if played by a harp on a background of strings'; the right-hand figures that open 'Poissons d'or' should give the impression of 'two clarinets'; and the *Tristan* parody in 'Golliwogg's Cake Walk' 'has the suggestion of the trombone'.[4]

How did Debussy achieve this? As the fortepiano transitioned into the modern concert grand, the instrument acquired several features that give a distinctive sound to the music of Chopin, Liszt, Schumann, and other composers from the first half of the nineteenth century. These include a lighter action that facilitates quick passagework and, very significantly, clear timbral contrasts between the registers from a bright treble to a clear middle and a resonant bass.[5] These differences in tone colour illuminate compositional choices such as sweeping motions from one end of the keyboard to the other (as in Chopin's Étude in A Minor, Op. 25 No. 11, or Prelude No. 24 in D Minor) and precise pedalling instructions – whether to sustain the more brittle upper registers, avoid muddying the bass, or, conversely, to hold the pedal in the bass precisely in order to create a sonic blur. Although such features are much less prominent in instruments from the end of the century, they still exist to a degree in pianos that Debussy favoured. German instruments especially appealed to him: in his

---

[3] Gustave Doret, quoted in Jürg Stenzl, 'In Search of the Lost Sound in Debussy's Piano Music', trans. J. Bradford Robinson, liner notes to Alexei Lubimov, *Debussy: Préludes* (ECM New Series 2241/42), p. 15.

[4] Maurice Dumesnil, 'Coaching with Debussy', in Roger Nichols (ed.), *Debussy Remembered* (London: Faber and Faber, 1992), pp. 160, 162.

[5] For a cogent discussion of the sound of the early Romantic piano, see Robert S. Winter, 'Orthodoxies, Paradoxes, and Contradictions: Performance Practice in Nineteenth-Century Piano Music', in R. Larry Todd (ed.), *Nineteenth-Century Piano Music* (New York: Schirmer Books, 1990), pp. 16–54.

31 Hearing Debussy Anew on Period Instruments

studio he kept an upright Bechstein as well as an upright Pleyel, and his parlour housed a 1904 Blüthner *Aliquotflügel* baby grand. The treble notes of the *Aliquotflügel* featured an extra unstruck fourth string that vibrated sympathetically and enhanced the resonance.[6] By listening to Debussy's music on the types of pianos he employed or might have heard, we can newly reimagine some of the timbral richness that he strove to evoke in his music and which others heard in his own playing.

Among period recordings, Alexei Lubimov's 2012 presentation of the *Préludes* (ECM New Series 2241/42) stands out both for the beauty of the chosen instruments – a 1925 Bechstein for book 1 and a 1913 Steinway for book 2 – and the sensitivity of his interpretations. The distinct timbral changes between registers plainly manifest themselves in runs – whether the gentle traceries of 'La Terrasse des audiences du clair de lune' or the violent surges of 'Ce qu'a vu le vent d'ouest' – and in passages contrasting high and low as in 'Danseuses de Delphes' and 'Feux d'artifice'. The registral changes enhance the imagery of 'La Cathédrale engloutie' as it emerges from the water and sinks back down, and they provide colour contrast to the 'Tierces alternées' as the intervals migrate from one end of the keyboard to another; they also demarcate inner lines to such a degree that in three-stave pieces like 'Feuilles mortes' one has the sense of hearing the separate voices distinctly, since each is in a unique register. Furthermore, in works like 'La Terrasse des audiences' or 'La Fille aux cheveux de lin', which feature harmonic parallelism, subtle timbral shadings can differentiate the various chordal iterations. Finally, the lighter touches and colour changes – and of course the performances – reinforce the moods hinted at in Debussy's titles: 'Voiles' appears more shadowy, 'General Lavine – eccentric' more eccentric (because so bass-heavy), 'La Puerta del vino' more exotic, and Puck's dance more whimsical; and 'Feux d'artifice' takes on the varied hues of Stravinsky's orchestral fantasy.

Other period recordings of the *Préludes* are somewhat more uneven: the 1897 Bechstein in Alain Planès's traversal (Harmonia Mundi HMC901695, 1999) sounds clangy by comparison with Lubimov's instruments, and the top of Jos van Immerseel's 1897 Érard in his presentation of book 1 and the *Images oubliées* can be piercing, most notably in 'Les Collines d'Anacapri' (Channel Classics CCS4892, 1993). Alexander Melnikov surveys book 2 on an 1885 Érard; while his instrument lacks the clarity of the 1913 Steinway, it

---

[6] Charles Timbrell, 'Debussy in Performance', in Simon Trezise (ed.), *The Cambridge Companion to Debussy* (Cambridge: Cambridge University Press, 2003), p. 260. He purchased the Blüthner in either 1904 or 1905, and he acquired the Pleyel around 1907 and the Bechstein by 1913.

still possesses much colour, and his performances are very nuanced, especially in dynamic shadings (Harmonia Mundi HMM902302DI, 2018). Planès's 2006 recording of assorted early and mature pieces (Harmonia Mundi HMC901893) commands attention because it offers pieces not represented elsewhere on period pianos – *Suite bergamasque*, *Deux arabesques*, *Children's Corner*, and both series of *Images* – and it employs a Blüthner, dating from 1902.

Immerseel's Érard is heard to much better effect in his recording with Sandrine Piau of various Debussy *mélodies* (Naïve V4932, 2003). In this recital, the varied hues of the accompaniment lend a special colouring to the vocal lines, and its 'orchestral' qualities are particularly evident in numbers such as 'De rêve' and 'De grêve' from *Proses lyriques*. Even more striking is a 2014 recording of the complete *mélodies*, with Jean-Louis Haguenauer supporting five vocalists on Debussy's own Blüthner piano, housed at the Labenche Museum in Brive-la-Gaillarde (Ligia LIDI 0201285-14); again, the colours of the accompaniments come through, if perhaps with less immediacy.[7]

Orchestral Music

In the years since Roger Norrington's pioneering recordings of Beethoven's symphonies in the late 1980s, the interest in period performances of symphonic music has extended beyond the Classical and early Romantic periods to embrace compositions of the post-Wagnerian and *fin de siècle* generations: today, one can find recordings of 'historically informed' renditions of Verdi and Brahms (Orchestre Révolutionnaire et Romantique), Mahler's symphonies and song cycles (Orchestra of the Age of Enlightenment), orchestral works of Ravel (Anima Eterna Brugge and Les Siècles), and Stravinsky's early ballets (Les Siècles). Since 2010, the interest in period performances has extended to Debussy's orchestral output, and much of it, including all of the most significant works, has been recorded by Anima Eterna Brugge and Les Siècles.

To attempt 'historically informed' renditions of orchestral works presents various challenges. Does the ensemble consist exclusively of instruments of genuinely antique vintage, or does it mix them with modern copies? Do the chosen instruments differ from those that the composer would have chosen (Debussy's *Rapsodie* for clarinet played on a Viennese

---

[7] On YouTube (www.youtube.com/watch?v=9LZZ81sUu7k) one can view a lecture-recital of assorted *Préludes* and other pieces on Debussy's Blüthner. The colours are very clear, though both the performances and the recorded sound are variable ('La Terrasse des audiences' loses a full page due to a memory lapse).

clarinet, for example)? Does the size of the ensemble match that of the original, especially with the proper balance of winds and strings? And is the instrumental sound paired with equally 'authentic' interpretive details such as the treatment of vibrato, tempo fluctuations, and vocal and instrumental slides? The questions differ somewhat with Debussy and other early twentieth-century figures, because here we possess recordings, by the composer as well as contemporaries (including people intimately close), which can provide concrete hints, however technologically limited, of how the music sounded when it was new. Granting the impossibility of achieving a fully accurate reproduction of *Nocturnes* or *La Mer* as performed in Debussy's lifetime, employing period instruments within an appropriately sized ensemble can, as with the piano music, provide suggestions about the sounds and textures Debussy envisioned and his reasons for selecting them. As François-Xavier Roth, the director of Les Siècles, has said:

> When we not only restored these instruments ... but started to rehearse Stravinsky and Ravel for the first time, I can't describe the shock. You understand why Stravinsky chose this combination of instruments and not another. ... [W]hen you start the beginning of 'The Firebird', the double basses with gut string pizzicato, and then suddenly the chorale of the [Parisian] trombones, with these tiny trombones – my God![8]

How did Debussy's orchestra differ from that of today? The winds he would have heard had an overtly 'reedy' sound and were more individually characterised. In the words of Richard Langham Smith, the family produced a '*décor orchestral* less homogenized than the sonorities of modern-day wind sections. Here the bassoon, clarinet, English horn and oboe blended perfectly yet somehow retained more noticeably their individual characters.'[9] For their part, the narrow-bored brass could be 'guttural': horns in particular took on an almost trombone-like sonority. Both families penetrated with greater ease through the smaller body of strings (which continued to play on gut), with the result that, as on the piano, the varied strands and layers of colour could more easily be distinguished.

Three recordings by Les Siècles have proved particularly successful in demonstrating the virtues of a period performance while presenting musically sensitive renditions. Their first recording (Musicales Actes Sud ASM 10D,

---

[8] David Allen, 'The Conductor Transforming Period Performance', *New York Times* (1 July 2021).
[9] See his approving comments on a performance of *Pelléas et Mélisande* by John Eliot Gardiner and the Orchestre Révolutionnaire et Romantique at the 2012 Proms: 'Debussy Fifty Years Later: Has the Barrel Run Dry?', in François de Médicis and Steven Huebner (eds.), *Debussy's Resonance* (Rochester, NY: University of Rochester Press, 2018), pp. 22–3.

2013) features *La Mer* coupled with the recently rediscovered *Première suite d'orchestre* of 1883–4; the second includes 'Ibéria' on a programme of French evocations of Spain (Musicales Actes Sud ASM 17D, 2015); and the third, part of a series commemorating the centenary of Debussy's death, presents *Prélude à l'après-midi d'un faune*, *Nocturnes*, and *Jeux* (Harmonia Mundi HMM905291DI, 2018).

The mellow flute, the 'brassier' horns, and the clearly distinguished layers of the gamelan-like climax – all are highpoints of their rendition of *Prélude à l'après-midi d'un faune*. On the same recording, *Nocturnes* proves equally revealing: the *divisi* gut strings and the shadowy English horn enhance the subdued mystery of 'Nuages', while in 'Fêtes' the pointed brass, the wind tuttis (in which one clearly perceives the subtle differences between timbres), and the luminous texture at the climax of the march all heighten its celebratory affect. As in the discs of *mélodies*, we hear 'Sirènes' in a new way when the vocal lines are set against the shifting layers and colours of the period instruments. Similar virtues appear in *La Mer*: most impressive is 'Jeux de vagues', where the increased timbral distinctions enhance the gossamer changes as well as the fleeting passages of heterophony. As for 'Ibéria', the 'raw' brass and percussion augment the Spanish aura of the outer movements and nocturnal atmosphere of the central movement, especially in *divisi* passages and moments of cross-family blending; Rehearsal No. 48, for example, combines flute and trumpet *divisi*, two solo violins, and two solo cellos, and the period sound highlights the individual timbral distinctions while still blending them effectively. Similar textures are highlighted in *Jeux*: as in *La Mer*, the heterophonic passages come through clearly, as do the special effects in the strings.

The sound in Anima Eterna Brugge's 2012 recordings of *Prélude à l'après-midi d'un faune* and *La Mer* (led by Jos van Immerseel on Zig-Zag Territories ZZT 313) is quite transparent, but the performances luxuriate in individual textures to such an extent that each piece arguably sounds more like a sequence of discrete moments than an organic whole. (The palpably slower tempos – over two minutes in the *Prélude* – reinforce this impression.) The principal virtue of this recording is the inclusion of the complete orchestral *Images*. While the same problems beset 'Ibéria' and 'Rondes des printemps', 'Gigues' is a revelation: the period oboe d'amore sounds all the more plaintive and all the more 'sweet and melancholy' (Debussy's indication), especially when in play with the other instruments.

While in no way denying the virtues of listening to Debussy on modern-day instruments, the best 'historical' performances have provided new ways of hearing his sound-world. The lighter action and timbral changes of the pianos give a special colouring to runs, inner voices, and juxtapositions of registers (not to mention the passages of sustained pedalling); one can understand more readily contemporaries' comments about Debussy's 'orchestral' handling of the keyboard as well as his own remarks about the instrumental timbres the piano evokes in his compositions. In orchestral music, the distinctive sounds of the flute in *Prélude à l'après-midi d'un faune*, the English horn in 'Nuages', and the oboe d'amore in 'Gigues' deepen the respective senses of sensuality, ethereality, and wistfulness. The more pronounced timbral contrasts allow us to hear layers of heterophony in *La Mer* and *Jeux* more clearly and to detect individual differences within blended textures more sharply. In short, hearing performances on these instruments allows us new insights into the composer's sound-world and also throws potential light on reasons behind some of his compositional choices in particular works.

Author's Recommendations

Recordings with period instruments:

Mélodies, Complete

Various soloists with Jean-Louis Haguenauer on Claude Debussy's personal Blüthner piano (Ligia LIDI 0201285-14, 2014).

Mélodies, selected. Sandrine Piau, soprano, with Jos van Immerseel, 1897 Érard piano (Naïve V4932, 2003).

Orchestral Music

'Ibéria' and other compositions. Les Siècles, conducted by François-Xavier Roth (Musicales Actes Sud ASM 17D, 2015).

La Mer and *Première suite d'orchestre*. Les Siècles, conducted by François-Xavier Roth (Musicales Actes Sud ASM 10D, 2013).

Prélude à l'après-midi d'un faune, Nocturnes, and *Jeux*. Les Siècles, conducted by François-Xavier Roth (Harmonia Mundi HMM90529IDI, 2018).

Prélude à l'après-midi d'un faune and *La Mer*. Anima Eterna Brugge, conducted by Jos van Immerseel (Zig-Zag Territories ZZT 313, 2012).

Piano Music

Préludes, books 1 and 2. Alexei Lubimov and Alexei Zuev, pianos (ECM New Series 2241-42, 2012).

Préludes, books 1 and 2. Alain Planès, 1897 Bechstein piano (Harmonia Mundi HMC901695, 1999).

Préludes, book 1, and *Images oubliées*. Jos van Immerseel, 1897 Érard piano (Channel Classics CS4892, 1993).

Préludes, book 2, and *La Mer*. Alexander Melnikov, 1885 Érard, joined by Olga Paschenko in *La Mer* (Harmonia Mundi HMM902302DI, 2018).

Various piano pieces. Alain Planès, 1902 Blüthner piano (Harmonia Mundi HMC901893, 2006).

CHAPTER 32

Debussy Today

Matthew Brown

In the decades since his death, Debussy has become a cultural icon – a symbol of music's modernity. He has been immortalised by a monument in the Bois de Boulogne in Paris, a museum in his hometown of Saint-Germain-en-Laye, and a bust in the Théâtre national de l'Opéra-Comique. His portrait even appeared on a twenty-franc banknote![1] Over the past few years, Debussy's stock has only risen. In 2011, *New York Times* critic Anthony Tommasini ranked him the fifth greatest composer of all time, behind Bach, Beethoven, Mozart, and Schubert, and ahead of Stravinsky, Brahms, Verdi, Wagner, and Bartók. Tommasini credited him with challenging the hegemony of German music and showing that 'there could be tension in timelessness'. Debussy, so the story goes, was responsible for pushing music into the twentieth century through his 'pioneering harmonic language, the sensual beauty of his sound, and his uncanny, Freudian instincts for tapping the unconscious'.[2] Writing for *The Guardian* in 2012, Tom Service echoed these views, proclaiming Debussy 'the father of musical Modernism', a 'visionary', a 'sonic explorer', and the 'creator of new worlds of feeling'. Citing the final climax of 'Jeux de vagues' (second movement of *La Mer*), Service notes that Debussy created musical images so intense and precise that 'it's the rest of the world that seems like an impression of music, rather than the other way round'.[3]

Given such accolades, it is hardly surprising that Debussy's works have had a massive impact on twentieth- and twenty-first-century music. That influence has been especially strong on fellow composers – Igor Stravinsky, Béla Bartók, Edgard Varèse, Olivier Messiaen, Pierre Boulez, Witold Lutosławski, George Crumb, and Tōru Takemitsu immediately spring to mind. His works have also inspired some of the period's greatest

---

[1] For the history of Debussy's reputation, see Marianne Wheeldon, *Debussy's Legacy and the Construction of Reputation* (New York: Oxford University Press, 2017).
[2] Anthony Tommasini, 'The Greatest', *New York Times* (21 January 2011).
[3] Tom Service, 'We Should Celebrate Debussy by Assessing His Real Legacy', *The Guardian* (29 March 2012).

performers, from Mary Garden, Maggie Teyte, and Alfred Cortot, to Walter Gieseking, Pierre Monteux, and Claudio Abbado, as well as countless novelists, painters, sculptors, film-makers, choreographers, video-game creators, and even comic-book artists. At the same time, Debussy's impact on the scholarly community has been no less profound.[4] Leading the charge has been French musicologist Lesure (1923–2001). Lesure's contributions have been enormous. He helped found the Centre de documentation Claude Debussy in 1972 and *Cahiers Debussy* in 1974, and compiled the *Catalogue de l'œuvre de Claude Debussy* in 1977.[5] Lesure also became the first editor-in-chief of the *Œuvres complètes de Claude Debussy* and, with help from Denis Herlin, Georges Liébert, Roger Nichols, and Richard Langham Smith, prepared reliable editions and English translations of Debussy's letters, interviews, and essays. In 1994, he even completed a definitive biography of Debussy, which has recently been updated and translated into English.[6]

While Debussy's reputation is currently as high as ever, it is by no means obvious why his music sounds so prescient and continues to inspire musicians and audiences alike. In an effort to address these issues, let us follow Service's advice and briefly consider one of Debussy's most evocative compositions: the final climax of 'Jeux de vagues' (bars 163ff.).[7] Perhaps the most striking features of the passage are its gorgeous melodic writing and glittering orchestration. It begins in bar 163 with a reprise of the movement's main theme first in the flutes and then in the oboes. In bar 171 another theme appears in the cellos and second violins accompanied by triplet diminutions in the first violins. As Debussy develops this new gesture, he allows it to soar up into ever higher registers and combine with ideas, such as a rising scale, and even augmentations of itself. After an enharmonic shift from G♯ to A♭, the passage culminates in a spectacular B♭^{9} sonority that Debussy accompanies with a dotted figure in the trumpets and four-note figure C–B♮–(B♭)–D in the violins. The music eventually dissipates, hinting at the main theme over a whole-tone dominant (F–G–A–B–C♯) in bars 237–44 and again over the tonic (D♯–E–F♯–G♯) in bars 245–61.

Besides illustrating Debussy's extraordinary gifts as a melodist and orchestrator, the climax of 'Jeux de vagues' confirms many of the other points made by Tommasini and Service. Take, for example, their claims

---

[4] See *Debussy Revealed* (Paris: Durand Salabert Eschig, 2011).
[5] François Lesure, *Catalogue de l'œuvre de Claude Debussy* (Geneva: Minkoff, 1977).
[6] Lesure (Rolf).
[7] See Simon Trezise, *Debussy: La Mer* (Cambridge: Cambridge University Press, 1994), pp. 67–8.

32 Debussy Today

about his pioneering harmonic language. The elements of this language are extensions of traditional procedures. Bars 163–261 begin and end in E major, but the tonic chord is overlaid with the non-harmonic tones F♯ and D♯. Similarly, bars 171–214 project a long G♯/A♭ pedal – a device that is not only unusual in the context of E major, but that creates the 'tension in timelessness' mentioned by Tommasini. The climactic B♭^{9} sonority in bars 215–18 is even more difficult to explain from a tonal perspective. Although the whole-tone sonority B–C♯–D♯–F♮–G♮–A♮ in bars 237–44 serves as a V^9 chord in E major, with D♯ resolving to E and A to G♯, its sense of functionality is eroded considerably by lowering the fifth from F♯ to F♮. Rather than conceive of the passage in purely harmonic terms, Figure 32.1 suggests that it might be more profitably treated contrapuntally as a long G♯/A♭ pedal supporting strings of ascending lines. Such an interpretation resonates with the following comment by Debussy: 'Counterpoint is not given to us for nothing. As the parts go forward we come across some splendid chords.'[8]

The final climax of 'Jeux de vagues' also highlights the beauty and sonic power of Debussy's writing, just as Tommasini and Service observe. Indeed, few melodies are more enchanting than the one presented in bar 171. The elegant profile, supple triple metre, and four-bar hypermeter are,

Figure 32.1 Contrapuntal plan of Debussy, 'Jeux de vagues', *La Mer*, bb. 171–215.

---

[8] Edward Lockspeiser, *Debussy: His Life and Mind*, vol. 1: *1862–1902*, 2nd corrected edition (Cambridge: Cambridge University Press, 1978), appendix B, p. 208.

in fact, typical of waltz tunes. The waltz, by far the most popular dance of the nineteenth century, was a particular favourite of Debussy's: he not only composed a string of them for piano, such as *Valse romantique*, *Hommage à Haydn*, 'Les Sons et les parfums tournent dans l'air du soir', the first book of *Préludes*, *La plus que lente*, *La Boîte à joujoux*, *Page d'album*, and 'Pour les octaves' in *Douze études*, but he alluded to them in other large-scale works, such as *L'Isle joyeuse*, a work dating from around the same time as *La Mer*, and the ballet *Jeux*.[9] Debussy's allusion to the waltz near the end of 'Jeux de vagues' seems entirely consonant with the ebullient mood and dynamic quality of the music. As Service explains, 'it's not the sea, the water, or the waves, that's the real element of this piece, but what the piece does with different kinds of musical motion'.[10] As the waltz theme is tossed from one register to another, the music conjures up the image and sensation of couples dancing round a room. Perhaps at the ball in Flaubert's *Madame Bovary*? Service is once again right on target: 'The final climax ... isn't "about" tides or breakers or surfers; instead, it creates an energy that you can't help but be swept away by. That's the real connection between *La Mer* and the sea: the music traps you in its own undertow of sheer sonic power.'[11]

While the final climax of 'Jeux de vagues' encapsulates the novelty and allure of Debussy's music, it does not completely address all of the issues mentioned at the outset. As regards the modernity of Debussy's musical language, the passage certainly deviates from normal tonal practices, but it is still a lot more conventional than some of Debussy's other works, especially with respect to their use of extreme chromaticism, modal and exotic inflections, parallel voice-leading, unusual dissonances, and innovative forms. Furthermore, while Debussy's mature scores are generally more radical than his earlier works, he always wrote experimental pieces alongside more conventional ones. In the late 1880s, for example, he composed radical songs, such as 'L'Ombre des arbres' and 'Spleen' (*Ariettes oubliées*), at the same time as traditional salon pieces, such as *Rêverie* and *Petite suite*; and in 1915 he began the revolutionary second movement of the cello sonata just after finishing a simple waltz for piano entitled *Page d'album*. Such stylistic diversity is, of course, hard to account for theoretically; as Douglass M. Green noted in 1992, there is currently no comprehensive

---

[9] On Debussy's penchant for the waltz, see Matthew Brown, *Debussy Redux: The Impact of His Music on Popular Culture* (Bloomington, IN: Indiana University Press, 2012), pp. 80–98.
[10] Service, 'We Should Celebrate'.   [11] Ibid.

32 Debussy Today

framework for explaining what makes Debussy's musical language sound so coherent.[12] Thirty years on, there is still no such framework.

What this stylistic diversity does, however, is suggest that Debussy was ultimately an eclectic; he used different compositional voices at different times for different purposes. As various scholars have noted, those voices range from parallel organum, as in 'Danse sacrée' (*Danse sacrée et danse profane*) and 'Canope' (*Préludes*, Book 2); pastoral genres, as in 'La Fille aux cheveux de lin' (*Préludes*, book 1) and 'Bruyères' (*Préludes*, book 2); and folksongs as in 'La Belle au bois dormant', 'Quelques aspects de "Nous n'irons plus au bois"' (*Images oubliées*), and 'Rondes de printemps' (*Images* (for orchestra)); to Spanish works, as in 'La Sérénade interrompue' (*Préludes*, book 1), 'La Puerta del vino' (*Préludes*, book 2), and 'Ibéria' (*Images* (for orchestra)); piano rags, as in 'Golliwogg's Cake Walk' (*Children's Corner*) and 'Minstrels' (*Préludes*, book 1); and non-Western music, as in 'Pagodes' (*Estampes*) and 'Poissons d'or' (*Images*, series 2). Depending on one's personal tastes and aesthetic agenda, there is something here for everyone; this is something that surely contributes to his popularity.

And yet, it is hard to deny Debussy's radical tendencies; after all, they foreshadow nearly all the major trends in twentieth- and twenty-first-century music. Modernists, such as Bartók, Messiaen, Stravinsky, and Varèse, praised him for challenging tonal norms, experimenting with cellular composition and stratification, and revolutionising musical form. His music even inspired Schoenberg, whose student Benno Sachs created a chamber version of the *Prélude à l'après-midi d'un faune* in 1920–1 for the Verein für musikalische Privataufführungen in Vienna.[13] George Perle went so far as to suggest that Debussy's 'Voiles' (*Préludes*, book 1) is a progenitor of 'non-dodecaphonic serialism' through its horizontal and vertical projections of a whole-tone collection.[14] More recently, Christian von Borries produced *Replay Debussy* (Universal: 472 801–2, 2003), a CD of radical 'rehearings' of Debussy's music by Mangurekan/Elaine Bouchez, Terre Thaemlitz, Alvin Lucier, Jamie Lidell, Paul Paulen, Ryuichi Sakamoto, Pierre Henry, and Panasonic SV-38000.

---

[12] Observation made in his review of Richard S. Parks, The Music of Claude Debussy (New Haven, CT: Yale University Press, 1989), in *Music Theory Spectrum* 14 (1992), p. 214.
[13] Richard S. Parks, 'A Viennese Arrangement of Debussy's "Prélude à l'après-midi d'un faune": Orchestration and Musical Structure', *Music and Letters* 80 (1999), pp. 50–73.
[14] George Perle, *Serial Composition and Atonality*, 3rd ed. (Berkeley, CA: University of California Press, 1972), pp. 40–5.

Many composers have also adopted Debussy's revolutionary approach to sound, form, and musical time. Most obviously, perhaps, Pierre Boulez, Karlheinz Stockhausen, Herbert Eimert, and other Darmstadt composers credit Debussy with anticipating so-called moment form.[15] At the same time, Elliott Carter has pointed to Debussy's use of specific sonorities 'as an item of musical thought'; Witold Lutosławski has highlighted his 'sensitivity to vertical aggregations, and the ways they appear in our music'; Joan Tower has lauded his 'profile of sound, [a] kind of sensual, colourful, harmonic language that is so profound'; John Harbison has mentioned his treatment of '*chords as objects*' and his 'sense of *chordal sonority*'; and George Crumb has singled out his use of sonorities as 'the primary conveyor of the image'.[16] In the late 1970s, Hughes Dufourt, Gérard Grisey, and Tristan Murail heralded Debussy as a harbinger of spectralism. Debussy's remarkable ear for texture and instrumental colour has even prompted composers to orchestrate his songs and piano music: notable examples include Robin Holloway's orchestration of *En blanc et noir* (2002) and ten early songs in 'C'est l'extase' (2012), and John Adams's orchestration of the first four of Debussy's *Cinq poèmes de Charles Baudelaire* in *Le Livre de Charles Baudelaire* (1994).

At the same time, Adams's score also demonstrates some of the diverse ways in which minimalist composers have been drawn to Debussy's music. Steve Reich, for example, has admitted that the recurring cycle of harmonies in *Music for 18 Musicians* (1976) recalls procedures employed by Debussy in his Sonata for flute, viola, and harp.[17] Philip Glass has applauded Debussy for his multiculturalism: 'And then, here's this jackass listening to something that no one else was hearing, Asian music at that [1889] Paris World's Fair – those sounds are still in my music to this day.'[18] Significantly, Debussy's forays into multicultural music have inspired composers from every corner of the globe: Manuel de Falla was clearly impressed by Debussy's Spanish music and Tōru Takemitsu, Bright Sheng, Minako Tokuyama, and Tan Dun have been equally attracted to his non-Western compositions. In short, Debussy wrote music that speaks to people across time.

His impact has not, however, been confined to twentieth- and twenty-first-century art music; it has also been felt on musicians working in the

---

[15] See Marianne Wheeldon, 'Interpreting Discontinuity in the Late Works of Debussy', *Current Musicology* 77 (2004), pp. 97–115.
[16] See James Briscoe, 'The Resonance of Debussy for United States Post-Modernists', *Revue musicale OICRM* 2 (2014), pp. 123–5.
[17] Ibid., p. 128.   [18] Ibid., p. 121.

32 Debussy Today

popular domain. Jazz musicians are a good case in point. Much has, of course, been made of Debussy's debts to ragtime in works such as 'Minstrels' (*Préludes*, book 1) and 'Golliwogg's Cake Walk' (*Children's Corner*). Nevertheless, works such as Bix Beiderbecke's piano piece 'In a Mist' show just how much jazz musicians have absorbed from Debussy's style in general. To quote pianist Stephen Hough:

> Although his taste for popular styles found expression in ragtime take-offs such as 'Minstrels' and the 'Golliwogg's Cake Walk', it was his more serious music that later had an immense influence on jazz composers like Gershwin, Bill Evans, Keith Jarrett, and Fred Hersch. And not just because of a shared sense of improvisation: The repeated patterns, the piling up of sonorities, and the way Debussy would crack open a chord, finding creativity in the very color of its vibrations, found its way into their very DNA.[19]

Perhaps because of his skill at evoking images and emotions, his penchant for multimedia projects, and his personal connections with writers and painters, Debussy has had an equally powerful impact on movie music. Beginning with *Limite* (1931) and *Death Takes a Holiday* (1934), his own music has appeared in countless movie soundtracks – everything from period romances, such as *Frenchman's Creek* (1944), and romantic fantasies, such as *Portrait of Jennie* (1948), to action flicks, such as *Escape from New York* (1981), horror films, such as *The Birds* (1963), and even animations, such as *Allegro non Troppo* (1976).[20] By far the most popular choice is 'Clair de lune' (*Suite bergamasque*): starting with *Boléro* (1934), the piece can be heard in numerous films, including *Frenchman's Creek* (1944), *Giant* (1956), *Frankie and Johnny* (1991), *Ocean's Eleven* (2001), *Man on Fire* (2004), *Atonement* (2007), *Ocean's Thirteen* (2007), *Twilight* (2008), and *The Purge* (2013). Walt Disney even completed an animation of 'Clair de lune' entitled 'Blue Bayou' for inclusion in *Fantasia* (1940). After that plan fell through, the sequence was slated for *Make Mine Music* (1946), but Debussy's music was replaced by the song 'Blue Bayou' performed by the Ken Darby Singers. It was not until 1998 that the segment was finally shown with Debussy's original music at the London Film Festival, thanks to a restoration by Scott MacQueen.

Debussy has likewise inspired film composers to write music of their own. Bernard Herrmann is a good example. Trained in music at NYU and Juilliard, Herrmann was an ardent devotee of Debussy and even recorded

---

[19] Steven Hough, '100 Years After Debussy's Death, He Remains the First "Modern" Composer', *New York Times* (2 March 2018).
[20] See 'Claude Debussy' IMDb website: www.imdb.com/name/nm0006033/.

'Clair de lune' and *La plus que lente* on his album *The Impressionists* (Decca, 1970). A few years after making the record, Herrmann paid homage to Debussy in his score for Brian De Palma's thriller *Obsession* (1976). This score specifically recalls *La Mer*, 'Sirènes' (*Nocturnes*), and *La plus que lente* through its distinctive use of the harp, a wordless women's chorus, and a haunting waltz theme.[21] In the first kidnapping scene, Herrmann evokes Act 4, scene 4 of *Pelléas et Mélisande*: like Debussy before him, he uses short motivic cells to mirror the moment-to-moment emotions of the characters, as well as the scene's overall change in mood from ecstasy to horror to despair. Herrmann even ends with a short motive, just like one from the start of 'Dialogue du vent et de la mer' (*La Mer*).[22]

Jazz and film composition are not, however, the only genres of popular music that have been influenced by Debussy: he has inspired musicians working in other domains. In the years around WWII, two of his most famous piano works appeared as hit tunes: Larry Clinton rewrote *Rêverie* as 'My Reverie' (1938) and Domenico Savino recast 'Clair de lune' as 'Moonlight Love' (1956). Both tunes became mainstays of easy listening and lounge music; among the most interesting are the versions of 'My Reverie' by Juan Garcia Esquivel (*Infinity in Sound*, 1960) and Martin Denny (*Romantica*, 1961), and 'Clair de lune' by Denny (*A Taste of Honey*, 1962) and Arthur Lyman (*Ilikai*, 1967). Decades later, Debussy's music has influenced musicians who specialise in ambient music and electronica. The most famous is surely Isao Tomita's *Snowflakes Are Dancing* (1974), an album of Debussy's music arranged for Moog synthesiser and Mellotron. In 1999, Art of Noise subsequently released *The Seduction of Claude Debussy* (1999), a concept album intended as 'a soundtrack to Debussy's life'. More recently still, the Australian electronica duo Flight Facilities produced a version of 'Clair de lune' featuring vocals by Christine Hoberg. This track reached number seventeen on the Triple J Hottest 100 for 2012.

So far, we have seen some ways in which Debussy's music has shaped the development of music during the past hundred years. But this tells only part of the story. Audiences and academics have been just as intrigued by his personal life and career path. Such interest has been so strong that he has even been a character in biopics, such as *The Debussy Film* (BBC, 1965) and *Camille Claudel* (Gaumont, 1988). One reason for this is that Debussy epitomises what it means to be a contemporary composer. Debussy's Paris

---

[21] Christopher Palmer, *The Composer in Hollywood* (London: Marion Boyars, 1990), pp. 271, 286, 293.
[22] Herrmann described the cinematic and melodramatic qualities of *Pelléas et Mélisande* in a talk reprinted in Evan William Cameron (ed.), *Sound and Cinema: The Coming of Sound to American Film* (Pleasantville, NY: Redgrave, 1980), pp. 117–35.

looked much the same as it does today: the Eiffel Tower was completed in 1889, the Paris Métro was opened in 1900, electric street lights were introduced in 1878, and telephones in 1879. Debussy was not averse to embracing modern technologies artistically. In 1904, for example, he recorded four tracks with Mary Garden for the Compagnie française du gramophone and in 1912 he made piano rolls of thirteen pieces for Welte-Mignon. After watching Louis Feuillade's film *L'Agonie de Byzance* in 1913, Debussy implored opera composers to start thinking cinematically and even toyed with the idea of creating a film version of *Le Martyre de saint Sébastien*![23]

It is no less important to point out that Debussy's career path followed a thoroughly modern trajectory. It began with twelve years of professional training at the Paris Conservatoire (1872–84) and three years as a winner of the Prix de Rome (1885–7).[24] On returning to Paris, Debussy set about earning a living as a freelance composer: instead of finding a permanent position as a choral director, conductor, or pedagogue, he received support from his publishers, first by Georges Hartmann, who supported him by regular advances between 1895 and 1900, and then by Durand, with whom he signed an exclusive contract in July 1905. Debussy supplemented his income with commissions, appearances as a conductor, and occasional private students. In the meantime, he earned a name for himself as a critic, writing for *La Revue blanche* in 1901, *Gil Blas* and other papers in 1903, *Musica* and other sources in 1908–12, and *S.I.M.* and other journals in 1912–17. Under the guise of his alter ego Monsieur Croche, Debussy used his essays to denounce the musical establishment, promote French music, and endorse his Modernist agenda. Above all, he insisted that the processes of composition are ultimately ineffable and urged composers to be spontaneous and original.

Although Debussy was capable of conveying the excitement and beauty of the world around him – something he did so effectively in the climax of 'Jeux de vagues' – he nonetheless recognised the stress that modern life inevitably produced. Such stresses were apparent to astute listeners, such as Wassily Kandinsky: 'in [Debussy's] music one hears the suffering and tortured nerves of the present time'.[25] The same tensions were described in great detail many

---

[23] See Richard Langham Smith, 'Debussy and the Art of the Cinema', *Music and Letters* 54 (1973), pp. 61–70; Robert Orledge, *Debussy and the Theatre* (Cambridge: Cambridge University Press, 1982), p. 233.
[24] John R. Clevenger, 'Debussy's Paris Conservatoire Training', in Jane F. Fulcher (ed.), *Debussy and His World* (Princeton, NJ: Princeton University Press, 2001), pp. 299–361.
[25] Wassily Kandinsky, *Concerning the Spiritual in Art*, trans. M. T. H. Sadleir (New York: Dover, 1977), p. 16.

years earlier by Charles Baudelaire in his seminal essay 'The Painter of Modern Life'.[26] Baudelaire, who was one of Debussy's literary idols, was a relentless commentator on modern life and its adverse effects on the human psyche. On the one hand, he drew attention to the ephemeral nature of urban life: 'Modernity is the transient, the fleeting, the contingent; it is one half of art, the other being the – eternal and the immovable.'[27] On the other, he associated modernity with idea of the *flâneur*: '[The *flâneur*] was a figure of the modern artist-poet, a figure keenly aware of the bustle of modern life, an amateur detective and investigator of the city, but also a sign of the alienation of the city and of capitalism.'[28]

The analysis of modernity offered by Baudelaire contributes to our understanding of Debussy and his music in several ways. His concept of the *flâneur* certainly helps to explain Debussy's eclecticism, especially his fondness for vernacular and non-Western music.[29] While the significance of his interests in such music should not be underestimated, it is important to remember that Debussy was no expert in these areas and did not aspire to authenticity per se: on the contrary, he was an armchair observer, who projected as much of himself onto such repertories as he borrowed from them. In many cases, Debussy drew on vernacular and non-Western music precisely because they included pedal tones, ostinato, pentatonic scales, whole-tone collections, and other devices that he had already incorporated into his musical language.[30]

Living in the modern world also meant that Debussy was acutely aware of how he appeared in the press and with potential audiences. Much as he enjoyed the upsurge in his reputation nationally and internationally following the successful premiere of *Pelléas et Mélisande*, Debussy also had to cope with pushback from gossip columnists and hostile critics. The worst scandal erupted in the autumn of 1904, after his affair with his future second wife Emma Bardac and the unsuccessful suicide attempt of his first wife Lilly Texier. The popular press had a field day and the sordid details of what transpired were even parodied in Henry Bataille's play *La*

---

[26] Charles Baudelaire, 'La Peintre de la vie modern', in *Charles Baudelaire: Œuvres Complètes*, vol. II, ed. Claude Pichois, Bibliothèque de la Pléiade (Paris: Gallimard, 1976), pp. 683–724; Baudelaire, 'The Painter of Modern Life', in *The Painter of Modern Life and Other Essays*, trans. Jonathan Mayne, 2nd ed. (London: Phaidon, 1995), pp. 1–41.

[27] Baudelaire, 'The Painter of Modern Life', p. 12.

[28] Gregory Shaya, 'The *Flâneur*, the *Badaud*, and the Making of a Mass Public in France, circa 1860–1910', *The American Historical Review* 109 (2004), p. 47.

[29] Langham Smith, '*Pelléas* and *Gil Blas*: Claudine and Monsieur Croche', in *Debussy on Music*, ed. François Lesure, trans. Richard Langham Smith (New York: Alfred A. Knopf, 1977), pp. 70–3.

[30] See Matthew Brown, *Debussy's 'Ibéria'* (Oxford: Oxford University Press, 2003), pp. 61–4.

32 Debussy Today

Femme nue (1908). Many of Debussy's old friends deserted him, including Gustave Doret, Henry Lerolle, Eugène Ysaÿe, and Pierre Louÿs. His mistrust of the press only became more intense later in his career, after he was diagnosed with cancer in 1909.

The ephemeral nature of the modern world, described in such detail by Baudelaire, likewise challenged Debussy's sense of creativity and self-worth. As audience's tastes changed, so his tastes changed as well. So much so that he found it hard to keep producing new works, as he explained in a letter to Robert Godet (11 December 1916):

> I'm terrified of planning any sort of work whatsoever – that in itself is enough to condemn it to the waste-paper basket, the cemetery of bad dreams. What an existence! I'm exhausted by chasing phantoms but not tired enough to sleep. So I wait for the morrow, for better or for worse; and it starts all over again.[31]

Nevertheless, Debussy's precarious financial situation meant that he was under constant pressure from his publisher to compose works that would do well in the marketplace. Recent research has shown that, starting in July 1905, Debussy was contracted to write 'a minimum of four works a year' and that Durand encouraged him to focus on composing in more lucrative genres, such as piano pieces and stage works, rather than art songs.[32]

Baudelaire's image of the artist as *flâneur* helps to explain Debussy's fears about remaining relevant as an artist. Those fears became especially acute during WWI, as Debussy made clear in a letter to Durand dating from five days after war was declared:

> As you know, I'm quite devoid of sang-froid and even more so of the military mentality, never having had the occasion to handle a gun. Then there are my memories of 1870 which prevent me reaching a pitch of enthusiasm, as well as the anxiety of my wife who has a son and a son-in-law both in the army! As a result, my life is one of intensity and disquiet. I'm nothing more than a wretched atom hurled around by this terrible cataclysm, and what I'm doing seems to me so miserably petty![33]

Remarkably, however, Debussy did find a way to keep his music relevant during these catastrophic times: he wrote and performed pieces in support of

---

[31] *Correspondance*, p. 2058; *Debussy Letters*, pp. 321–2.
[32] Robert Orledge, 'Debussy, Durand et Cie: A French Composer and His Publishers (1884–1917)', in Michael Talbot (ed.), *The Business of Music* (Liverpool: Liverpool University Press, 2002), pp. 137, 146–50.
[33] Letter to Jacques Durand, 8 August 1914, Debussy, *Correspondance*, pp. 1842–3; *Debussy Letters*, p. 291.

fundraisers for wounded soldiers, orphans, and even for rebuilding devastated communities.[34] The violin sonata was just such a piece; it tried to show 'what an invalid can write in time of war'.[35] Completed between October 1916 and April 1917, during one of the bleakest times in French history, Debussy still found ways to inject his piece with a sense of optimism: 'By one of those very human contradictions it's full of happiness and uproar.'[36] It is precisely this capacity to show us how to face the challenges of the world with a sense of humanity and hope that makes Debussy and his music as relevant today as it was a century ago. Since there are no signs that such challenges are diminishing, we have every reason to suppose that he and his music will be inspiring audiences a century from now.

Author's Recommendation
La Mer (1903–5).

One of the truly great orchestral works, *La Mer* was composed by Debussy at a time when his personal life was in a state of upheaval. Though still married to Lilly, he met Emma Bardac in 1903 and set up house with her in 1904. Lilly became distraught and attempted to commit suicide, prompting many of Debussy's friends to desert him. And yet Debussy managed to complete his score, giving each movement an evocative title and a distinct mood. 'De l'aube à midi sur la mer' (first movement) begins mysteriously with a rising motive that recalls a Javanese gamelan, and ends with a sombre brass chorale. Meanwhile, 'Jeux de vagues' (second movement) shows Debussy at his most exuberant and climaxes with a glorious waltz. Finally, 'Dialogue du vent et de la mer' (third movement) conveys the sheer power of the sea and culminates in a restatement of the chorale from the first movement. Besides alluding to Hokusai's famous print *Kanagawa oki nami ura*, part of which Durand reproduced on the work's cover, Debussy's subtitle 'Three Symphonic Sketches' has several implications. For one thing, it highlights the work's departure from traditional large-scale forms; in the same vein, Debussy had complimented Chopin for replacing conventional sonata forms with 'finely wrought sketches'. For another, Debussy used some of the work's motivic material in *D'un cahier d'esquisses*, a short piano piece that he finished in 1904.

---

[34] See Marianne Wheeldon, *Debussy's Late Style* (Bloomington, IN: Indiana University Press, 2009), pp. 14–18.
[35] Letter to Robert Godet, 7 June 1917, Debussy, *Correspondance*, p. 2117; *Debussy Letters*, p. 327.
[36] Letter to Robert Godet, 7 May 1917, Debussy, *Correspondance*, p. 2106; *Debussy Letters*, p. 324.

Recommendations for Further Reading and Research

Chapter 1

Berton, Claude and Alexandre Ossadzow, *Fulgence Bienvenüe et la construction du métropolitain de Paris* (Paris: Presses de l'école nationale des ponts et chaussées, 1998).

Fourcaut, Annie and Florence Bourillon (eds.), *Agrandir Paris: 1860–1970* (Paris: Éditions de la Sorbonne, 2012).

Kalifa, Dominique, *La Culture de masse en France, 1: 1860–1930* (Paris: La Découverte, 2001).

López-Galviz, Carlos, *Cities, Railways, Modernities: London, Paris, and the Nineteenth Century* (London: Routledge, 2019).

Prochasson, Christophe, *Paris 1900: Essai d'histoire culturelle* (Paris: Calmann-Lévy, 1999).

Rearick, Charles, *Paris Dreams, Paris Memories: The City and Its Mystique* (Stanford, CA: Stanford University Press, 2011).

Whiting, Steven Moore, *Satie the Bohemian: From Cabaret to Concert Hall* (New York: Oxford University Press, 1999).

Yon, Jean-Claude, *Une histoire du théâtre à Paris: De la Révolution à la Grande Guerre* (Paris: Aubier, 2012).

Chapter 2

Agulhon, Maurice, *The French Republic, 1879–1992* (Oxford: Blackwell, 1993).

Cahm, Eric, *The Dreyfus Affair in French Society and Politics* (London: Longman, 1996).

Charle, Christophe, 'Debussy in Fin-de-Siècle Paris', in Jane F. Fulcher (ed.), *Debussy and His World* (Princeton, NJ: Princeton University Press, 2001), pp. 271–95.

Fortescue, William, *The Third Republic in France, 1870–1940: Conflicts and Continuities* (London: Routledge, 2000).

Fulcher, Jane F., *French Cultural Politics and Music: From the Dreyfus Affair to the First World War* (New York: Oxford University Press, 1999).

Kelly, Barbara L., 'Debussy and the Making of a *musicien français*: Pelléas, the Press, and World War I', in Barbara L. Kelly (ed.), *French Music, Culture, and*

National Identity, 1870–1939 (Rochester, NY: University of Rochester Press, 2008), pp. 58–76.

Larkin, Maurice, *Church and State after the Dreyfus Affair: The Separation Issue in France* (London: Palgrave Macmillan, 2014).

McAuliffe, Mary, *Dawn of the Belle Époque: The Paris of Monet, Zola, Bernhardt, Eiffel, Debussy, Clemenceau, and Their Friends* (Lanham, MD: Rowman & Littlefield, 2014).

Moore, Rachel, *Performing Propaganda: Musical Life and Culture in Paris during the First World War* (Woodbridge: The Boydell Press, 2018).

Pasler, Jann, '*Pelléas* and Power: Forces behind the Reception of Debussy's Opera', *19th-Century Music* 10 (1983), pp. 243–64.

Wheeldon, Marianne, *Debussy's Late Style* (Bloomington, IN: Indiana University Press, 2009).

Chapter 3

Brown, Matthew, *Debussy's 'Ibéria'* (New York: Oxford University Press, 2003).

Howat, Roy, 'Russian Imprints in Debussy's Piano Music', in Elliott Antokoletz and Marianne Wheeldon (eds.), *Rethinking Debussy* (New York: Oxford University Press, 2011), pp. 31–51.

Kelly, Barbara L., (ed.), *French Music, Culture, and National Identity, 1870–1939* (Rochester, NY: University of Rochester Press, 2008).

Médicis, François de, *La maturation artistique de Debussy dans son contexte historique, 1884–1902* (Turnhout: Brepols, 2020).

Smith, Richard Langham (ed.), *Debussy Studies* (Cambridge: Cambridge University Press, 1997).

Wheeldon, Marianne, *Debussy's Late Style* (Bloomington, IN: Indiana University Press, 2009).

Chapter 4

Abbott, Helen, 'Baudelaire's "Le jet d'eau" and the Politics of Performance', *Dix-Neuf* 17 (2013), pp. 37–56.

Fauser, Annegret, '*La Guerre en dentelles*: Women and the *Prix de Rome* in French Cultural Politics', *Journal of the American Musicological Society* 51 (1998), pp. 83–129.

Holmes, Diana and Carrie Tarr (eds.), *A 'Belle Époque'?: Women and Feminism in French Society and Culture, 1890–1914* (New York: Berghahn Books, 2006).

Kelly, Barbara L. and Christopher Moore (eds.), *Music Criticism in France, 1918–1939: Authority, Advocacy, Legacy* (Woodbridge: The Boydell Press, 2018).

Kieffer, Alexandra, *Debussy's Critics: Sound, Affect, and the Experience of Modernism* (New York: Oxford University Press, 2019).

Pasler, Jann, '*Pelléas* and Power: Forces behind the Reception of Debussy's Opera', *19th-Century Music* 10 (1987), pp. 243–64.

Roberts, Mary Louise, *Disruptive Acts: The New Woman in Fin-de-Siècle France* (Chicago, IL: Chicago University Press, 2002).

Chapter 5

Blake, Jody, *Le Tumulte noir: Modernist Art and Popular Entertainment in Jazz-Age Paris, 1900–1930* (University Park, PA: Pennsylvania State University Press, 1999).
Jensen, Eric Frederick, *Debussy* (Oxford: Oxford University Press, 2014).
Sumarsam, *Javanese Gamelan and the West* (Rochester, NY: University of Rochester Press, 2013).
Tamagawa, Kiyoshi, *Echoes from the East: The Javanese Gamelan and Its Influence on the Music of Claude Debussy* (Lanham, MA: Lexington Press, 2019).

Chapter 6

Ashworth, Amanda, 'Associations with the Visual Arts in the Music of Debussy', PhD thesis, Open University (2021).
Bhogal, Gurminder Kaur, *Details of Consequence: Ornament, Music, and Art in Paris* (New York: Oxford University Press, 2013).
Byrnside, Ronald L., 'Musical Impressionism: The Early History of the Term', *The Musical Quarterly* 66 (1980), pp. 522–37.
Lethève, Jacques, 'La Connaissance des peintres préraphaélites anglaise en France (1855–1900)', *Gazette des beaux-arts* (1959), pp. 315–28.
Mauclair, Camille, 'La Peinture musicienne et la fusion des arts', *La Revue bleue* 6 (1902), pp. 297–303.
Schaeffner, André, 'Debussy et ses rapports avec la peinture', in Edith Weber (ed.), *Debussy et l'évolution de la musique au XXe siècle* (Paris: CNRS, 1965), pp. 151–62.
Venturi, Lionello, *Les Archives de l'impressionnisme* (Paris: Durand-Ruel, 1939).

Chapter 7

Bergeron, Katherine, *Voice Lessons: French Mélodie in the Belle Epoque* (Oxford: Oxford University Press, 2010).
Bhogal, Gurminder Kaur, *Details of Consequence: Ornament, Music, and Art in Paris* (Oxford: Oxford University Press, 2013).
Code, David J., 'The "Song Triptych": Reflections on a Debussyan Genre', in François de Médicis and Steven Huebner (eds.), *Debussy's Resonance* (Rochester, NY: University of Rochester Press, 2018), pp. 127–74.
Lesure, François, *Claude Debussy: A Critical Biography*, rev. and trans. Marie Rolf (Rochester, NY: University of Rochester Press, 2019).
Nectoux, Jean-Michel, *Harmonie en bleu et or: Debussy, la musique et les arts* (Paris: Fayard, 2005).

Nichols, Roger and Richard Langham Smith, *Claude Debussy:* Pelléas et Mélisande, Cambridge Opera Handbooks (Cambridge: Cambridge University Press, 1989).
Rolf, Marie, 'Semantic and Structural Issues in Debussy's Mallarmé Songs', in Richard Langham Smith (ed.), *Debussy Studies* (Cambridge: Cambridge University Press, 1997), pp. 179–200.

Chapter 8

Charle, Christophe, 'Debussy in Fin-de-Siècle Paris', in Jane F. Fulcher (ed.), *Debussy and His World* (Princeton, NJ: Princeton University Press, 2001), pp. 271–95.
Compagnon, Antoine, *Cinq paradoxes de la modernité* (Paris: Éditions du Seuil, 1990).
Kieffer, Alexandra, *Debussy's Critics: Sound, Affect, and the Experience of Modernism* (Oxford: Oxford University Press, 2019).
Médicis, François de, *La maturation artistique de Debussy dans son contexte historique, 1884–1902* (Turnhout: Brepols, 2020).
Nectoux, Jean-Michel, *Harmonie en bleu et or: Debussy, la musique et les arts* (Paris: Fayard, 2005).

Chapter 9

Chimènes, Myriam, 'Élites sociales et pratiques wagnériennes', in Annegret Fauser and Manuela Schwartz (eds.), *Von Wagner zum Wagnérisme: Musik, Literatur, Kunst, Politik* (Leipzig: Leipziger Universitätsverlag, 1999), pp. 155–97.
Huebner, Steven, *French Opera at the* Fin de Siècle: *Wagnerism, Nationalism, and Style* (Oxford: Oxford University Press, 1999).
Leblanc, Cécile and Danièle Pistone (eds.), *Le Wagnérisme dans tous ses états, 1913–2013* (Paris: Presses Sorbonne Nouvelle, 2016).
Maynard, Kelly, 'Strange Bedfellows at the *Revue Wagnérienne*: Wagnerism at the Fin de Siècle', *French Historical Studies* 38 (2015), 633–59.
Schwarz, Manuela, *Wagner-Rezeption und französische Oper des Fin de siècle: Untersuchungen zu Vincent d'Indys 'Fervaal'* (Sinzig: Studio, 1999).

Chapter 10

Duchesneau, Michel, 'Debussy and Japanese Prints', in François de Médicis and Steven Huebner (eds.), *Debussy's Resonance* (Rochester, NY: University of Rochester Press, 2018), pp. 301–25.
Hartman, Elwood, '*Japonisme* and Nineteenth-Century French Literature', *Comparative Literature Studies* 18 (1981) (East-West Issue), pp. 141–66.
Howat, Roy, 'Debussy and the Orient', in Andrew Gerstle and Anthony Milner (eds.), *Recovering the Orient: Artists, Scholars, Appropriations* (Reading: Harwood, 1994), pp. 45–81.

Miner, Earl, *The Japanese Tradition in British and American Literature* (Princeton, NJ: Princeton University Press, 1958).
Mueller, Richard, 'Javanese Influence on Debussy's "Fantaisie" and Beyond', *19th-Century Music* 10 (1986), pp. 157–86.
Nichols, Roger (ed.), *Debussy Remembered* (London: Faber and Faber, 1992).
Pasler, Jann, 'Revisiting Debussy's Relationships with Otherness: Difference, Vibrations, and the Occult', *Music and Letters* 101 (2020), pp. 321–42.
Weisberg, Gabriel P. (ed.), *Japonisme: Japanese Influence on French Art 1854–1910* (Kent, OH: Kent State University Press, 1975).

Chapter 11

Dorf, Samuel N., *Performing Antiquity: Ancient Greek Music and Dance from Paris to Delphi, 1890–1930* (New York: Oxford University Press, 2019).
Howat, Roy, *The Art of French Piano Music: Debussy, Ravel, Fauré, Chabrier* (New Haven, CT: Yale University Press, 2009).
Howat, Roy, *Debussy in Proportion* (Cambridge: Cambridge University Press, 1983).
Lesure, François, *Claude Debussy: A Critical Biography*, rev. and trans. Marie Rolf (Rochester, NY: University of Rochester Press, 2019).
Pasler, Jann, 'Revisiting Debussy's Relationship with Otherness: Difference, Vibrations, and the Occult', *Music and Letters* 101 (2020), pp. 321–42.
Wheeldon, Marianne, *Debussy's Late Style* (Bloomington, IN: Indiana University Press, 2009).

Chapter 12

Berenson, Edward, Vincent Duclert, and Christophe Prochasson, *The French Republic: History, Values, Debates* (Ithaca, NY: Cornell University Press, 2011).
Kertzer, David I. and Marzio Barbagli, *The History of the European Family* (New Haven, CT: Yale University Press, 2001).
Mainardi, Patricia, *Husbands, Wives, and Lovers: Marriage and Its Discontents in Nineteenth-Century France* (New Haven, CT: Yale University Press, 2003).
Offen, Karen M., *European Feminisms, 1700–1950: A Political History* (Stanford, CA: Stanford University Press, 2000).

Chapter 13

Debussy, Claude, *Correspondance 1872-1918*, ed. François Lesure and Denis Herlin (Paris: Gallimard, 2005).
Goblot, Edmond, *La Barrière et le niveau: Étude sociologique sur la bourgeoisie française moderne* (Paris: Félix Alcan, 1925).

Herlin, Denis, 'Un cercle amical franco-belge de Debussy: Les Dansaert, les Loewenstein et les Peter', in Herlin, *Claude Debussy: Portraits et études* (Hildesheim: Olms, 2021), pp. 131–46.

Holt, Richard, 'Social History and Bourgeois Culture in Nineteenth-Century France: A Review Article', *Comparative Studies in Society and History* 27 (1985), pp. 713–26.

Lallement, Michel, 'Social Trajectory and Sociological Theory: Edmond Goblot, the Bourgeoisie, and Social Distinction', *Social Epistemology* 30 (2016), pp. 692–709.

Lesure, François. *Claude Debussy: A Critical Biography*, rev. and trans. Marie Rolf (Rochester, NY: University of Rochester Press, 2019).

Perrot, Michelle (ed.), *A History of Private Life: From the Fires of Revolution to the Great War*, trans. Arthur Goldhammer (Cambridge, MA: Harvard University Press, 1990).

Plott, Michèle, 'The Rules of the Game: Respectability, Sexuality, and the *Femme Mondaine* in Late-Nineteenth-Century Paris', *French Historical Studies* 25 (2002), pp. 531–56.

Chapter 14

Joly-Segalen, Annie, *Segalen et Debussy* (Monaco: Éditions du Rocher, 1962).

Lloyd, Rosemary, *Mallarmé: The Poet and His Circle* (Ithaca, NY: Cornell University Press, 1999).

Pasler, Jann, 'Revisiting Debussy's Relationships with Otherness: Difference, Vibrations, and the Occult', *Music and Letters* 101 (May 2020).

Shattuck, Roger, *The Banquet Years: The Origins of the Avant-Garde in France, 1885 to World War I*, rev. ed. (London: Jonathan Cape, 1969).

Wenk, Arthur B., *Claude Debussy and the Poets* (Berkeley, CA: University of California Press, 1976).

Chapter 15

Durand, Jacques, *Quelques souvenirs d'un éditeur de musique*, 2 vols. (Paris: Durand, 1924–5).

Herlin, Denis, 'An Artist High and Low, or Debussy and Money', in Elliott Antokoletz and Marianne Wheeldon (eds.), *Rethinking Debussy* (New York: Oxford University Press, 2011), pp. 149–202; French revised version: Herlin, 'Grandeur et servitude d'un artiste ou Debussy et l'argent', in Herlin, *Claude Debussy: Portraits et études* (Hildesheim: Olms, 2021), pp. 147–96.

Macdonald, Hugh, 'Georges Hartmann, "éditeur idéal"', in Damien Colas, Florence Gétreau, and Malou Haine (eds.), *Musique, esthétique et société au XIXe siècle* (Sprimont: Mardaga, 2007), pp. 285–98.

Nectoux, Jean-Michael, 'Un début dans la vie d'artiste: Gabriel Fauré et ses premiers éditeurs', in Cécile Reynaud and Herbert Schneider (eds.), *Noter, annoter, éditer la musique* (Genève: Droz, 2012), pp. 565–77.

Orledge, Robert, 'Debussy, Durand et Cie: A French Composer and His Publishers (1884–1917)', in Michael Talbot (ed.), *The Business of Music* (Liverpool: Liverpool University Press, 2002), pp. 121–51.

Chapter 16

Goubault, Christian, 'Chausson et Debussy à la croisée des chemins', *Ostinato rigore: Revue internationale d'études musicales*, 14 (2000), pp. 29–79.

Orledge, Robert, 'Debussy, Satie, and the Summer of 1913', *Cahiers Debussy* 26 (2002), pp. 31–44.

Orledge, Robert, 'Satie's Personal and Musical Logic', in Caroline Potter (ed.), *Erik Satie: Music, Art and Literature* (Aldershot: Ashgate, 2013), pp. 1–17.

Perret, Simon-Pierre, 'Debussy et Dukas: Une amitié méconnue', *Cahiers Debussy* 34 (2010), pp. 5–52.

Southon, Nicolas, 'Paul Dukas and Gabriel Fauré: Portrait of a Friendship', in Helen Julia Minors and Laura Watson (eds.), *Paul Dukas: Legacies of a French Musician* (Abingdon: Routledge, 2019), pp. 53–68.

Watson, Laura, 'Dukas, Critical Conversations, and Intellectual Legacies', in Helen Julia Minors and Watson (eds.), *Paul Dukas*, pp. 17–37.

Weilbaecher, Daniel, 'Ernest Guiraud: A Biography and Catalogue of Works', DMA thesis, Louisiana State University (1990).

Wheeldon, Marianne, *Debussy's Late Style* (Bloomington, IN: Indiana University Press, 2009).

Woldu, Gail Hilson, 'Debussy, Fauré, d'Indy and Conceptions of the Artist: The Institutions, the Dialogues, the Conflicts', in Jane F. Fulcher (ed.), *Debussy and His World* (Princeton, NJ: Princeton University Press, 2001), pp. 235–53.

Chapter 17

Andrieux, Françoise (ed.), *Gustave Charpentier: Lettres inédites à ses parents* (Paris: Presses universitaires de France, 1984).

Bongers, Cyril (ed.), *Gabriel Pierné: Correspondance romaine* (Lyon: Symétrie, 2005).

Bongrain, Anne and Alain Poirier (eds.), *Le Conservatoire de Paris, 1795–1995: Deux cents ans de pédagogie* (Paris: Buchet-Chastel, 1999).

Fulcher, Jane F. (ed.), *Debussy and His World* (Princeton, NJ: Princeton University Press, 2001).

Hondré, Emmanuel (ed.), *Le Conservatoire de musique de Paris: Regards sur une institution et son histoire* (Paris: Association du bureau des étudiants du Conservatoire national supérieur de musique de Paris, 1995).

Lu, Julia, 'The Prix de Rome in the Age of Romanticism', PhD thesis, Royal Holloway, University of London (2010).

Lu, Julia and Alexandre Dratwicki (eds.), *Le Concours du Prix de Rome de musique, 1803–1968* (Lyon: Symétrie, 2011).

Chapter 18

Herlin, Denis, 'An Artist High and Low, or Debussy and Money', in Elliott Antokoletz and Marianne Wheeldon (eds.), *Rethinking Debussy* (New York: Oxford University Press, 2011), pp. 149–202; French revised version: Herlin, 'Grandeur et servitude d'un artiste ou Debussy et l'argent', in Herlin, *Claude Debussy: Portraits et études* (Hildesheim: Olms, 2021), pp. 147–96.

Herlin, Denis, 'Un cercle amical franco-belge de Debussy: Les Dansaert, les Loewenstein et les Peter', in Herlin, *Claude Debussy: Portraits et études* (Hildesheim: Olms, 2021), pp. 131–46.

Orledge, Robert, 'Debussy, Durand et Cie: A French Composer and His Publishers (1884–1917)', in Michael Talbot (ed.), *The Business of Music* (Liverpool: Liverpool University Press, 2002), pp. 121–51.

Chapter 19

Lacombe, Hervé (ed.), *Histoire de l'opéra français*, vol. 2: *Du Consulat aux débuts de la IIIe République* (Paris: Fayard, 2020); vol. 3: *De la Belle Époque au monde globalisé* (Paris: Fayard, 2022).

Lesure, François, *Claude Debussy: A Critical Biography*, rev and trans. Marie Rolf (Rochester, NY: University of Rochester Press, 2019).

Médicis, François de, *La maturation artistique de Debussy dans son contexte historique, 1884–1902* (Turnhout: Brepols, 2020).

Orledge, Robert, *Debussy and the Theatre* (Cambridge: Cambridge University Press, 1982).

Chapter 20

Cooper, Jeffrey, *The Rise of Instrumental Music and Concert Series in Paris, 1828–1871* (Ann Arbor, MI: UMI Research Press, 1983).

Deruchie, Andrew, *The French Symphony at the Fin de Siècle: Style, Culture, and the Symphonic Tradition* (Rochester, NY: University of Rochester Press, 2013).

Duchesneau, Michel, *L'Avant-garde musicale et ses sociétés à Paris de 1871 à 1939* (Sprimont: Mardaga, 1997).

Hart, Brian, 'The Symphony and National Identity in Early Twentieth-Century France', in Barbara L. Kelly (ed.), *French Music, Culture, and National Identity, 1870–1939* (Rochester, NY: University of Rochester Press, 2008), pp. 131–48.

Holoman, D. Kern, *The Société des Concerts du Conservatoire, 1828–1967* (Berkeley, CA: University of California Press, 2004).
Pasler, Jann, *Composing the Citizen: Music as Public Utility in Third Republic France* (Berkeley, CA: University of California Press, 2009).
Strasser, Michel, 'Ars Gallica: The Société Nationale de Musique and Its Role in French Musical Life, 1871–1891', PhD thesis, University of Illinois (1997).
Strasser, Michel, 'Grieg, the Société Nationale, and the Origins of Debussy's String Quartet', in Barbara L. Kelly and Kerry Murphy (eds.), *Berlioz and Debussy: Sources, Contexts and Legacies* (Aldershot: Ashgate, 2007), pp. 103–15.
Strasser, Michael, 'The Société Nationale and Its Adversaries: The Musical Politics of *L'Invasion germanique* in the 1870s', *19th-Century Music* 24 (2001), pp. 225–51.

Chapter 21

Caddy, Davinia, 'Parisian Cake Walks', *19th-Century Music* 30 (2007), pp. 288–317.
Gutsche-Miller, Sarah, *Parisian Music-Hall Ballet, 1871–1913* (Rochester, NY: University of Rochester Press, 2015).
Mawer, Deborah, *French Music and Jazz in Conversation: From Debussy to Brubeck* (Cambridge: Cambridge University Press, 2014).
Orledge, Robert, *Debussy and the Theatre* (Cambridge: Cambridge University Press, 1982).
Whiting, Steven Moore, *Satie the Bohemian: From Cabaret to Concert Hall* (Oxford: Oxford University Press, 1999).

Chapter 22

Debussy, Claude, *Debussy on Music*, ed. François Lesure, trans. Richard Langham Smith (New York: Alfred A. Knopf, 1977).
Donnellon, Deirdre, 'Debussy as Musician and Critic', in Simon Trezise (ed.), *The Cambridge Companion to Debussy* (Cambridge: Cambridge University Press, 2007), pp. 43–58.
Goubault, Christian, *La Critique musicale en France de 1870 à 1914* (Geneva: Slatkine, 1984).
Herlin, Denis, 'Les Mésaventures de *Monsieur Croche Antidilettante*', in Michel Duchesneau, Valérie Dufour, and Marie-Hélène Benoit-Otis (eds.), *Écrits de compositeurs: Une autorité en questions* (Paris: Vrin, 2013), pp. 231–57, republished in Herlin, *Claude Debussy: Portraits et études* (Hildesheim: Olms, 2021), pp. 366–90.
Picard, Timothée (ed.), *La Critique musicale au XXe siècle* (Rennes: Presses universitaire de Rennes, 2020).

Chapter 23

Branger, Jean-Christophe, Sylvie Douche, and Denis Herlin (eds.), Pelléas et Mélisande *cent ans après: Études et documents* (Lyon: Symétrie, 2012).
Depaulis, Jacques, *Ida Rubinstein : Une inconnue jadis célèbre* (Paris : H. Champion, 1995).
Huebner, Steven, *French Opera at the* Fin de Siècle*: Wagnerism, Nationalism, and Style* (Oxford: Oxford University Press, 2004).
Lacombe, Hervé (ed.), *Histoire de l'opéra français*, vol. 2: *Du Consulat aux débuts de la IIIe République* (Paris: Fayard, 2020); vol. 3: *De la Belle Époque au monde globalisé* (Paris: Fayard, 2022).
Lécroart, Pascal (ed.), *Ida Rubinstein: Une utopie de la synthèse des arts à l'épreuve de la scène* (Besançon: Presses universitaires de Franche-Comté, 2008).
Médicis, François de, *La maturation artistique de Debussy dans son contexte historique, 1884–1902* (Turnhout: Brepols, 2020).

Chapter 24

Debussy, Claude, *Monsieur Croche et autres écrits*, rev. ed. François Lesure (Paris: Gallimard, 1987).
Guest, Ivor, *The Romantic Ballet in Paris* (London: Sir Isaac Pitman and Sons, 1966).
Médicis, François de and Steven Huebner (eds.), *Debussy's Resonance* (Rochester, NY: University of Rochester Press, 2018).
Morrison, Simon, 'Debussy's Toy Stories', *The Journal of Musicology* 30 (2013), pp. 424–59.
Nectoux, Jean-Michel (ed.), *Nijinsky: Prélude à l'après-midi d'un faune* (Paris: Adam Biro, 1989).
Orledge, Robert, *Debussy and the Theatre* (Cambridge: Cambridge University Press, 1982).

Chapter 25

Code, David J., *Claude Debussy* (London: Reaktion Books, 2010).
Code, David J., 'Hearing Debussy Reading Mallarmé: Music *après Wagner* in the *Prélude à l'après-midi d'un faune*', *Journal of the American Musicological Society* 54 (2001), pp. 493–554.
Crotty, John, 'Symbolist Influences in Debussy's "Prelude to the Afternoon of a Faun"', *In Theory Only* 6 (1982), pp. 17–30.
Deruchie, Andrew, *The French Symphony at the Fin de Siècle: Style, Culture, and the Symphonic Tradition* (Rochester, NY: University of Rochester Press, 2013).
Hart, Brian, 'Wagner and the Franckiste "Message Symphony" in Early Twentieth-Century France', in Annegret Fauser and Manuela Schwartz (eds.), *Von Wagner*

zum *Wagnérisme: Musik, Literatur, Kunst, Politik* (Leipzig: Leipziger Universitätsverlag, 1999), pp. 315–38.

Hart, Brian, 'The Symphony in Debussy's World', in Jane F. Fulcher (ed.), *Debussy and His World* (Princeton, NJ: Princeton University Press, 2001), pp. 187–91.

Trezise, Simon, *Debussy: La Mer* (Cambridge: Cambridge University Press, 1995).

Chapter 26

Bruhn, Siglind, *Debussy's Instrumental Music in Its Cultural Context* (Hillsdale, NY: Pendragon Press, 2019).

Code, David J., 'Debussy's String Quartet in the Brussels Salon of the "La Libre Esthétique"', *19th-Century Music* 30 (2007), pp. 257–87.

Debussy, Claude, String Quartet, ed. Peter Bloom, *Œuvres complètes de Claude Debussy*, series III: *Musique de chambre*, vol. 1 (Paris: Durand, 2015).

DeVoto, Mark, *Debussy and the Veil of Tonality: Essays on His Music* (Hillsdale, NY: Pendragon Press, 2004).

Herlin, Denis, 'Les Esquisses du Quatuor', *Cahiers Debussy* 14 (1990), pp. 23–54.

Wheeldon, Marianne, 'Debussy and *La Sonate cyclique*', *The Journal of Musicology* 22 (2005), pp. 644–79.

Chapter 27

Bergeron, Katherine, 'The Echo, the Cry, the Death of Lovers', *19th-Century Music* 18 (1994), pp. 136–51.

Bergeron, Katherine, *Voice Lessons: French Mélodie in the Belle Époque* (New York: Oxford University Press, 2010).

Code, David J., 'The "Song Triptych": Reflections on a Debussyan Genre', in François de Médicis and Steven Huebner (eds.), *Debussy's Resonance* (Rochester, NY: University of Rochester Press, 2018), pp. 127–74.

Guilbert, Yvette, *L'Art de chanter une chanson* (Paris: Bernard Grasset, 1928).

Monelle, Raymond, 'A Semantic Approach to Debussy's Songs', *Music Review* 51 (1990), pp. 193–207.

Rumph, Stephen, *The French Song Cycle: Poetry and Music, 1861–1921* (Oakland, CA: University of California Press, 2020).

Chapter 28

Bhogal, Gurminder Kaur, *Claude Debussy's Clair de Lune* (New York: Oxford University Press, 2018).

Debussy, Claude, *Debussy Letters*, ed. François Lesure and Roger Nichols, trans. Nichols (Cambridge, MA: Harvard University Press, 1987).

Debussy, Claude, *Debussy on Music*, ed. François Lesure, trans. Richard Langham Smith (New York: Alfred A. Knopf, 1977).

Dumesnil, Maurice, 'Coaching with Debussy', *The Piano Teacher* 5 (1962), pp. 10–13.
Howat, Roy, *The Art of French Piano Music: Debussy, Ravel, Fauré, Chabrier* (New Haven, CT: Yale University Press, 2009).
Long, Marguerite, *At the Piano with Debussy*, trans. Olive Senior-Ellis (London: Dent, 1972).
Nichols, Roger, *Debussy Remembered* (London: Faber and Faber, 1992).
Nonken, Marilyn, *The Spectral Piano: From Liszt, Scriabin, and Debussy to the Digital Age* (Cambridge: Cambridge University Press, 2014).
Roberts, Paul, *Images: The Piano Music of Claude Debussy* (Portland, OR: Amadeus, 1996).

Chapter 29

Briscoe, James R. (ed.), *Debussy in Performance* (New Haven, CT: Yale University Press, 1999).
Debussy, Claude, *Correspondance (1872–1918)*, ed. François Lesure and Denis Herlin (Paris: Gallimard, 2005).
Debussy, Claude, *Debussy on Music*, ed. François Lesure, trans. Richard Langham Smith (New York: Alfred A. Knopf, 1977).
Ho, Jocelyn, 'Debussy and Late-Romantic Performing Practices: The Piano Rolls of 1912', in François de Médicis and Steven Huebner (eds.), *Debussy's Resonance* (Rochester NY: University of Rochester Press, 2018), pp. 513–61.
Howat, Roy, 'Between and Beyond the Perforations in Debussy's Welte Rolls', in Tihomir Popović and Peter Mutter (eds.), *Claude Debussy: Die Klavieraufnahmen* (Hofheim: Wolke Verlag, 2023), pp. 62–91.
Howat, Roy, 'Debussy's Welte Roll of *La plus que lente*', in Tihomir Popović and Peter Mutter (eds.), *Claude Debussy: Die Klavieraufnahmen* (Hofheim: Wolke Verlag, 2023), pp. 356–72.

Chapter 30

Bhogal, Gurminder Kaur, *Details of Consequence: Ornament, Music, and Art in Paris* (New York: Oxford University Press, 2013).
Cafafa, Marielle, *La Chanson polyphonique française au temps de Debussy, Ravel et Poulenc* (Paris: L'Harmattan, 2017).
Ellis, Katharine, *Interpreting the Musical Past* (Oxford: Oxford University Press, 2005).
Lockspeiser, Edward and Harry Halbreich, *Debussy: Sa vie et sa pensée* (Paris: Fayard, 1980).
Suschitzky, Anya, 'Rameau, d'Indy, and French Nationalism', *The Musical Quarterly* 86 (2002), pp. 398–448.
Vendrix, Philippe (ed.), *La Renaissance et sa musique au XIXe siècle* (Paris: Klincksieck, 2000).

Chapter 31

Bhogal, Gurminder Kaur, *Claude Debussy's* Clair de Lune (New York: Oxford University Press, 2018).
Brown, Matthew, *Debussy Redux: The Impact of His Music on Popular Culture* (Bloomington, IN: Indiana University Press, 2012).
Mawer, Deborah, *French Music and Jazz in Conversation: From Debussy to Brubeck* (New York: Cambridge University Press, 2014).
Nichols, Roger (ed.), *Debussy Remembered* (London: Faber and Faber, 1992).
Smith, Richard Langham, 'Debussy Fifty Years Later: Has the Barrel Run Dry?', in François de Médicis and Steven Huebner (eds.), *Debussy's Resonance* (Rochester, NY: University of Rochester Press, 2018), pp. 19–37.
Timbrell, Charles, 'Debussy in Performance', in Simon Trezise (ed.), *The Cambridge Companion to Debussy* (Cambridge: Cambridge University Press, 2003), pp. 259–77.

Chapter 32

Brown, Matthew, *Debussy's 'Ibéria'* (Oxford: Oxford University Press, 2003).
Brown, Matthew, *Debussy Redux: The Impact of His Music on Popular Culture* (Bloomington, IN: Indiana University Press, 2012).
Cox, David, *Debussy: Orchestral Music* (London: British Broadcasting Corporation, 1974).
Debussy, Claude, *La Mer*, ed. Marie Rolf, *Œuvres complètes de Claude Debussy*, series V: *Œuvres pour orchestre*, vol. 5 (Paris: Durand, 1997).
Trezise, Simon, *Debussy: La Mer* (Cambridge: Cambridge University Press, 1994).

Index

Abbado, Claudio, 300
Abbey of Solesmes, 256
Académie des beaux-arts, 170
Académie française in Rome. *See* Villa Medici
Acanthus Column, 11
Adam, Adolphe, 222
   Giselle, 222
Adam, Paul and Jean Moréas
   Thé chez Miranda, Le, 71
Adams, John, 304
Albéniz, Isaac, 32
   Iberia, 32
Albert I, 22, 23
Alcazar, 195
Alençon, Émilienne d', 196
Alhambra, 9
Allais, Alphonse, 136
Allan, Maud, 30, 36, 175, 176, 200, 224, 225–6
Allegri, Gregorio
   Miserere, 284
Allegro non Troppo, 305
Ambassadeurs, 195
Andersen, Hans Christian, 55
Âne Rouge, L', 7
Anély, Max. *See* Cras, Jean
Anglophilia, 9, 53
Anima Eterna Brugge, 294, 296
Annunzio, Gabriele D'. *See* D'Annunzio, Gabriele
Antoine, André, 7
Apollinaire, Guillaume, 83, 228
   Bestiaire ou le Cortège d'Orphée, Le, 83
   Orphée-roi, 83
Arcadelt, Jacques, 282
Art Nouveau, 6, 12, 28, 66, 67, 80, 223
Art of Noise
   Seduction of Claude Debussy, The, 306
Association syndicale professionnelle et mutuelle de la critique dramatique et musicale, 38
Astruc, Gabriel, 176
Atonement, 305

Auber, Daniel, 150, 178, 182
   Domino noir, Le, 151
   Muette de Portici, La, 178
Auberge du Clou, 7, 198, 199

Bach, Johann Sebastian, 185, 207, 272, 282, 285, 289, 299
   cantata concerts, 284
   Mass in B Minor, 282
   St Matthew Passion, 41, 282
Bach, Johann Sebastian (ed. Debussy)
   chamber music, 172
Baille, Casimir, 283
Bailly, Edmond, 7, 12, 73, 102, 108, 137, 140, 145, 148
Bakst, Léon, 218
Ballets Russes, 30, 31, 155, 157, 158, 200, 217, 221, 226–7
bande à Franck, 152, 237
Banville, Théodore de, 62, 68, 70, 71, 255
   Diane au bois, 82
Bardac, Dolly, 48
Bardac, Emma, 19, 48, 49, 53, 123–4, 126, 134, 140, 149, 154, 157, 173, 176, 223, 224, 277, 308, 310
Bardac, Raoul, 60, 172
Bardac, Sigismond, 19, 123, 132
Barnum and Bailey Circus, 12, 199
Baron, Émile, 71, 79
Barrault, Jean-Louis, 135
Barrès, Maurice, 26, 204
   Déracinés, Les, 26
Barthes, Roland, 236
Bartók, Béla, 54, 299, 303
   String Quartet No.1, 244
Baschet, Marcel, 62
   'Printemps, Le', 62
Bataille, Henri
   Femme nue, La, 309
Baudelaire, Charles, 69, 71, 73–4, 77, 96, 99, 100, 101, 104, 138, 233, 307–8, 309

Index

Correspondances, 93
flâneur, 119
Fleurs du mal, Les, 43, 70
Poe translations, 139
Bayreuth Festival, 29, 52, 88, 92, 151, 215, 283
Bechstein, 262, 293
Beethoven, Ludwig van, 22, 95, 185, 187, 230, 237, 238, 279, 285, 299
  sonata form, 238
  symphonies, 186, 233, 237, 238, 294
  Symphony No.3, 24, 232, 239
  Symphony No.5, 232, 239
  Symphony No.6, 234, 235, 276
  Symphony No.9, 151, 232, 236
Beiderbecke, Bix, 291
  'In a Mist', 305
Bellaigue, Camille, 260
Belle Époque, 3, 8, 9, 11, 193, 195, 221, 256
Benois, Alexandre, 226
Benson & Co., 80
Béraud, Jean
  Pâtisserie Gloppe, La, 50
  Sortie des ouvrières de la maison Paquin, rue de la Paix, 50
Berger, Rodolphe
  Joyeux Nègres, Les, 15
Berlin Philharmonic, 276
Berlioz, Hector, 164, 180, 189, 190, 230, 236
  Damnation de Faust, La, 190
  Enfance du Christ, L', 150, 190
  Nuits d'été, Les, 252
  Requiem, 190
  Symphonie fantastique, 222, 234
Bernstein, Leonard, 176
Besnard, Paul-Albert, 66
Bibliothèque-musée de l'Opéra, 66
Bibliothèque nationale de France, 65
Bienvenüe, Fulgence, 5
Binet-Valmer, Gustave, 203
Bing, Siegfried, 12, 28, 51, 80, 99
Birds, The, 305
Bismarck, Otto von, 90
Bizet, Georges, 146, 162, 164, 178, 183, 184
  Arlésienne, L', 217
  Carmen, 28, 31, 183
  Djamileh, 226
  songs, 252
Bizet, Georges (arr. Guiraud)
  Carmen, 150
Bloch, Jeanne, 251
Blum, Léon, 202
Blüthner, 262, 265, 293, 294
Bois, Jules, 107, 137
  Noces de Sathan, Les, 107, 138
Boléro, 305

Bonaparte, Napoleon, 28
Bonheur, Raymond, 59
  'Bien loin d'ici', 73
  'Mort des pauvres, La', 73
Bonnard, Pierre, 82, 100, 101, 202
Bordes, Charles, 281, 283–6
Borodin, Alexander, 44
Borries, Christian von
  Replay Debussy, 303
Boston, Orchestral Club of, 208
Boston Symphony Orchestra, 208
Bouchor, Maurice, 105, 283
Boulanger, General. *See* Boulanger, Georges Ernest Jean-Marie
Boulanger, Georges Ernest Jean-Marie, 16, 21
Boulanger, Lili, 34, 108
  Clairières dans le ciel, 252
  Pie Jesu, 256
  Psalmes, 256
Boulanger, Nadia, 34
Boulez, Pierre, 104, 135, 176, 231, 232, 237, 258, 299, 304
  Marteau sans maître, Le, 245
Bourgault-Ducoudray, Louis, 282, 288
Bourget, Paul, 136
  Aveux, Les, 136
Bourjat, General Albert, 147
Bozzachi, Giuseppina, 222
Bracquemond, Marie, 99
Brahms, Johannes, 294, 299
Brainerd, Eleanor, 50
Brancovan, Constantin de, 204
Brettes, Abbé Ferdinand, 284
Bréville, Pierre de
  'Cloche fêlée, La', 73
  'Harmonie du soir', 73
British Museum, 224
Britten, Benjamin, 245
  Cello Suite No.1, 245
Bruneau, Alfred, 38, 83, 85, 203, 215, 216
  Attaque du moulin, L', 83, 96, 212
  Messidor, 83, 96, 212
  Ouragan, L', 216
  Rêve, Le, 96, 212, 216
Brunetière, Ferdinand, 70, 284
Buddhism, 102, 140
Bulla (publisher), 143
Burne-Jones, Edward, 59, 67
  Love among the Ruins, 65
Busoni, Ferrucio
  Arlecchino, 228
Bussine, Romain, 187, 188

Cabaret des Quat'z'Arts, 198
Café Pousset, 74

Index

Café Vachette, 73
café chantant, 195
café-concert, 194, 195, 198, 199
Caillé, Renée, 42
Caine, Hall, 22, 23
Calvocoressi, Michel-Dimitri, 204, 207
Camille Claudel (film), 306
Campenhout, François van
    Brabançonne, La, 24
Caplet, André, 44, 67, 117, 176, 223, 244, 276
    chamber works, 244
    Masque de la mort rouge, Le, 87
Caput Quartet, 241
Carnot, President Sadi, 16, 47
Carré, Albert, 112, 146, 183
Carter, Elliott, 304
    Cello Sonata, 245
Carvalho, Léon, 90, 183
Casa de Velázquez, 33
Casino de Paris, 195, 197
Casino de Suresnes, 276
Centre de documentation Claude Debussy, 300
Cernuschi, Enrico, 99
Cézanne, Paul, 61
Chabrier, Emmanuel, 7, 11, 95, 182, 190, 258
    España, 32
    'Invitation au voyage, L'', 73
Champ de Mars, 47
Chansarel, René, 173
Chanteurs de Saint-Gervais, 286
Charles d'Orléans, 254, 255, 256
Charpentier, Alexandre, 82
Charpentier, Gustave, 43, 73, 74, 82, 83, 162, 183, 203, 216, 217
    'Chevaux de bois, Les', 74
    Louise, 74, 83, 96, 183, 212, 217
    Vie du poète, La, 83
Chat Noir, 7, 45, 82, 107, 108, 136, 138, 195, 198, 199, 221
Chausson, Ernest, 46, 63, 66, 80, 83, 92, 108, 121, 129, 144, 150, 157, 161, 169, 172, 215, 242, 246, 267, 283, 289
    'Albatros, L'', 73
    Concert for Violin, Piano, and String Quartet, 145
    Roi Arthus, Le, 67, 95, 152, 153, 212
    Symphony, 237
Chavannes, Puvis de, 66
Chemin de fer de Petite Ceinture, 5
Chéret, Jules, 12
Chevillard, Camille, 191, 261, 276, 280
Chopin, Frédéric, 159, 259, 260, 262, 264, 265, 268, 292, 310
    Durand edition, 23
    Étude in A Minor, Op. 25 No.11, 292

Études, 266
Piano Sonata No.2,
    funeral march, 225, 248
Prelude No.24, 292
Chopin, Frédéric (ed. Debussy)
    complete works, 172
Chouchou. *See* Debussy, Claude-Emma
    (Chouchou)
Choudens (publisher), 143, 145, 146, 171
Cirque d'Été, 50
Cirque d'Hiver, 89, 186
Cirque Molier, 8
Cirque Napoléon. *See* Cirque d'Hiver
Claudel, Camille, 80, 102
Claudel, Paul, 7, 73, 145, 203
Clinton, Larry
    'My Reverie', 306
Cocteau, Jean, 157, 228
Collet, Henri, 31
Colonne, Édouard, 47, 89, 90, 146, 169, 189, 190, 191, 231
commedia dell'arte, 71
Compagnie française du gramophone, 14, 307
Concerts Colonne, 169, 191, 230, 243, 272, 288
Concerts d'Harcourt, 192
Concerts de danse, 155
Concerts du Châtelet, 146
Concerts du Conservatoire. *See* Société des concerts du Conservatoire
Concerts éclectiques et populaires, 189
Concerts Lamoureux, 30, 88, 190, 201, 230
Concerts Pasdeloup, 30
Concerts populaires, 151, 186
Concordia, 171, 282, 283, 288
Congrès international d'automobilisme (1900), 6
Conservatoire (Bordeaux), 275
Conservatoire (Paris), 19, 46, 70, 71, 72, 86, 88, 103, 121–2, 126, 143, 150, 152, 155, 156, 159, 160, 161, 163, 165, 166, 169, 170, 178, 188, 195, 202, 222, 243, 244, 260, 272, 282, 307
    Conseil supérieur, 155, 242
Copeland, George, 274, 275
Coppola, Piero, 280
Coralli, Jean, 222
Corea, Chick, 291
Corneau, André, 202, 203
Coronio, Nicolas, 172
Corot, Jean-Baptiste Camille
    Silène, 63
Cortot, Alfred, 250, 257, 266, 300
Couperin, François, 25, 112, 263, 268
    'Barricades mystérieuses, Les', 274
Crane, Walter, 67
Cras, Jean, 140
Crimean War, 98

Index

Cros, Charles, 136
Crumb, George, 245, 299, 304
   Idyll for the Misbegotten, An, 245
cubism, 80, 83, 84, 86
cyclic form, 166, 237, 241
Czerny, Carl, 268

D'Annunzio, Gabriele, 20, 113, 138, 175, 176, 218, 224
   Martyre de saint Sébastien, Le, 218
   Piacere, Il, 138
Dalayrac, Nicolas, 181
Danilchenko, Peter, 241
Dansaert, Régine, 206
Dargomyjsky, Alexander, 11
Daudet, Alphonse
   Arlésienne, L', 217
de Bussy. *See* Debussy
Death Takes a Holiday, 305
Debay, Victor, 43
Debussy Film, The, 306
Debussy, Adèle, 121
Debussy, Alfred, 121
Debussy, Claude
   piano rolls. *See* Welte-Mignon
Debussy, Claude (arr. Benno Sachs)
   Prélude à l'après-midi d'un faune, 245, 303
Debussy, Claude (arr. Eugène Bozza)
   petit nègre, Le, 245
Debussy, Claude (arr. Henri Mouton)
   Pelléas et Mélisande, 245
Debussy, Claude (arr. Stephen McNeff)
   Pelléas et Mélisande, 245
Debussy, Claude (arr. TableTopOpera)
   Berceuse héroïque, 245
   Élégie, 246
   En blanc et noir
      ii. Lent. Sombre, 245
Debussy, Claude (orch. André Caplet)
   Boîte à joujoux, La, 229
   Children's Corner, 244
   Estampes
      'Pagodes', 244
   Suite bergamasque
      'Clair de lune', 244
Debussy, Claude (orch. John Adams)
   Livre de Baudelaire, Le (Baudelaire songs), 304
Debussy, Claude (orch. Robin Holloway)
   'C'est l'extase' (early songs), 304
   En blanc et noir, 304
Debussy, Claude (reconstruction Kenneth Cooper)
   sonata for oboe, horn, and harpsichord, 246
Debussy, Claude
   'Apparition', 71
   'Archet, L'', 136

'Baisers d'amour, Les', 283
'Beau soir', 144
'Belle au bois dormant, La', 7, 136, 303
'Chanson espagnole', 32
'Chanson triste', 283
'Clair de lune' (1882), 71, 72
'En sourdine' (1882), 71
'Fantoches' (1882), 71, 72
'Fête galante', 71
'Fleur des blés', 144
'Hymnis', 68
'Ibéria'. *See Images* (for orchestra)
'Madrid, princesse des Espagnes', 32
'Mandoline', 71, 144, 171
'Matelot qui tombe à l'eau, Le', 105
'Nuit d'étoiles', 143
'Pantomime', 71
'Pierrot', 71
'Rondel chinois', 102, 103
'Séguidille', 32
'Sérénade', 71
Ariettes oubliées, 21, 71, 72, 74, 144, 147, 188, 275
Ariettes oubliées, 280
   'ombre des arbres, L'', 279, 302
   'Spleen', 302
arrangements by Debussy. *See* original composers
Ballade slave, 145
Berceuse héroïque, 22, **23**, 33
Boîte à joujoux, La, 45, 123, 193, 196, 221, 223, 227–8, **228**, 302
   Prelude, 246
Cello Sonata, 242, 245, 275
chamber sonatas, 77, 86, 112, 240, 242, 246
Chansons de Bilitis, 35, 63, 73, 110, 146, 251, 253, **256**
   'Chevelure, La', 257
   See also Musique de scène pour les Chansons de Bilitis
Children's Corner, 9, 45, 123, 174, 175, 193, 294
   'Golliwogg's Cake Walk', 9, 11, **15**, 227, 292, 303, 305
   'Gradus ad Parnassum', 15
   'Serenade for the Doll', 15
Chute de la maison Usher, La, 139, 175, 176, 212, 247
Cinq poèmes de Charles Baudelaire, 35, 72, 73, **96**, 102, 137, 144, 148, 250, 253
   'Harmonie de soir', 73
   'Jet d'eau, Le', 42, **43**
D'un cahier d'esquisses, 264, 310
Damoiselle élue, La, 12, 22, 66, 82, 83, 93, 137, 145, 148, 188, 203
Danse. *See Tarentelle styrienne*
Danse sacrée et danse profane, 148

Debussy, Claude (cont.)
    'Danse sacrée', 303
Daphnis et Chloé, 109, 141
Deux arabesques, 144, 171, 242, 259, 287, 294
    Arabesque No.1, 291
Diable dans le beffroi, Le, 139, 149, 174, 175, 212
Diane au bois, 62, 63, **68**
Douze études, 22, 77, 112, 174, 263, 266, **268**
    'Pour les notes répétées', 246
    'Pour les octaves', 302
Élégie, 22
En blanc et noir, 22, 77, 154
Enfant prodigue, L', 26, 29, 143, 175, 260
Estampes, 29, 104, 148, 188
    'Pagodes', 11, 103, 263, 303
    'Reflets dans l'eau', 274
    'Soirée dans Grenade, La', 32, 278, 280
Fantaisie for piano and orchestra, 145, **166**, 263, 291
Fêtes galantes, 193
Fêtes galantes, set 1, 71, 147, 253
    'Clair de lune', 72
Fêtes galantes, set 2, 148, 253
    'Colloque sentimental', 254
Hommage à Haydn, 113, 302
Images, 109, 267
Images (for orchestra), 62, 192, 244, 296, 297
    'Ibéria', 32, **33**, **239**, 243, 262, 296, 303
    'Rondes de printemps', 303
Images, series 1, 20, 29, 259
    'Hommage à Rameau', 33, 112
    'Mouvement', 246
    'Reflets dans l'eau', 61, 262
Images, series 2, 29, 98, 104, 294
    'Et la lune descend sur le temple qui fut', 103, 104
    'Poissons d'or', 29, 104, **105**, 261, 262, 263, 292, 303
Images oubliées
    'Quelques aspects de "Nous n'irons plus au bois"', 303
    'Souvenir du Louvre', 11
Intermezzo, 241
Isle joyeuse, L', 35, 63, 148, 174, 188, 274, 302
Jeux, 103, 149, 155, **158**, 176, 192, 193, 196, 226–7, 228, 243, 296, 297, 302
Khamma, 30, 31, 36, 111, 175, 196, **200**, 224, 243, 291
Marche écossaise, 47, 145
Martyre de saint Sébastien, Le, 20, 111, 138, 175, **176**, 218, 224, 244, 307
    Fragments symphoniques, 113
Masques, 148, 174
Mazurka, 145, 147, 260

Mer, La, 31, 53, 60, 98, 103, 109, 148, 149, 192, 230, 244, 276, 280, 295–7, 306, **310**
    'Dialogue du vent et de la mer', 306
    'Jeux de vagues', 226–7, 299, 307
Musique de scène pour les Chansons de Bilitis, 73, 110, 140, 240
Nocturne, 145, 260
Nocturne et Scherzo, 241
Nocturnes, 86, 146, 147, **149**, 175, 191, 192, 201, 203, 223, 230, 238, 239, 261, 280, 295, 296
    'Fêtes', 86
    'Sirènes', 306
Noël des enfants qui n'ont plus de maison, 22, **124**, 254
Nuits blanches, 76
Ode à la France, 23, 33, 137
Page d'album, 302
Pelléas et Mélisande, 21, 31, 35, 67, 70, 77, 112, 139, 146, 155, 175, 178, 180, 203, 212–14, 217, **219**, 245, 306
    Arkel toad ornament, 51
    censorship, 178
    dedication, 147
    early recordings, 280
    genesis, 27, 75, 76, 153, 170, 184, 202, 212, 217, 253
    harmonic language, 39
    influences, 211, 215
    interpretation, 184
    performance, 273, 275, 277
    premiere, 25, 39, 46, 51, 67, 74, 123, 139, 146, 171, 172, 183, 184, 192, 204, 279, 281, 308
    reception, 22, 27, 38, 39, 153, 156, 205, 259, 287
    role of Mélisande, 215, 248, 249
    role of Pelléas, 181
    Satie's reaction, 61
    success, 147, 148, 174, 176
    transfer to Durand, 147, 148, 175
    Wagner's influence, 96
petit nègre, Le, 11, 227
Petite pièce, 240, 242
Petite suite, 144, 302
Piano Trio, 240, 241
Pièce pour l'œuvre du 'Vêtement du blessé', 22
plus que lente, La, 7, 240, 278, 302, 306
Pour le piano, 113, 146, 147, 188, 263, 264, 276
Prélude à l'après-midi d'un faune, 20, 35, 47, 63, 68, 75, 76, 86, 109, 110, 138, 146, 149, 155, 188, 191, **192**, 192, 230, 239, 287, 291, 296–7
Prélude à l'après-midi d'un faune (ballet), 30, 175, 226, 280
Prélude, interludes et paraphrase finale pour l'après-midi d'un faune, 145

Index

Préludes, 193, 267, 293
Préludes, book 1, **55**, 293
   'Cathédrale engloutie, La', 239, 261, 278, 293
   'Ce qu'a vu le vent d'ouest', 61, 293
   'Collines d'Anacapri, Les, 293
   'Danseuses de Delphes', 11, 84, 110, 293
   'Fille aux cheveux de lin, La', 293, 303
   'Minstrels', 9, 240, 303, 305
   'Sérénade interrompue, La', 303
   'Sons et les parfums tournent dans l'air du soir, Les', 302
   'Vent dans la plaine, Le', 11, 61
   'Voiles', 29, 196, 293, 303
Préludes, book 2, **55**, 174, 293
   'Brouillards', 61
   'Bruyères', 303
   'Canope', 111, 303
   'Feuilles mortes', 293
   'Feux d'artifice', 293
   'General Lavine – eccentric', 9, 45, 197, 293
   'Puerta del vino, La', 32, 293, 303
   'Terrasse des audiences du clair de lune, La', 293
   'Tierces alternées', 293
Première suite d'orchestre, 296
Printemps, 149
Promenoir des deux amants, Le, 76
Proses lyriques, 76, 145, 146, 253
   'De grève', 294
   'De rêve', 294
Rapsodie for clarinet, 155, 242, 294
Rapsodie for orchestra and saxophone, **208**
recordings with period instruments, **291–8**
Recueil Vasnier, **133**
Rêverie, 145, 147, 260, 291, 302, 306
Rodrigue et Chimène, 31, 32, 182, **184**, 251
Siddharta, 111
Six Épigraphes antiques, 84, 110, 111, 140
Soirs illuminés par l'ardeur du charbon, Les, 22, 77
Sonata for flute, viola, and harp, **86**, 245, 304
String Quartet, 22, 82, 144, 153, 171, 188, 240, 241, 242, 244, **246**
Suite bergamasque, 145, 147, 193, 259, 263, 294
   'Clair de lune', 262, 263, 264, 276, 291, 292, 305, 306
Symphony, 36
Syrinx, 110, 208, 240, 245
Tarentelle styrienne, 145, 260
Trois ballades de François Villon, 33, 76, 113, 137, 251, 256
Trois chansons de Charles d'Orléans, 33, 76, 113, 255, **289**
Trois chansons de France, 76, 148, 255, 277
Trois mélodies de Paul Verlaine, 145, 253

Trois poèmes de Stéphane Mallarmé, 76, **142**, 188, 254
Valse romantique, 260, 302
Violin Sonata, 157, 242, 310
Debussy, Claude-Emma (Chouchou), 15, 47, 48, 53, 123
Debussy, Clémentine, 159
Debussy, Emma. *See* Bardac, Emma
Debussy, Emmanuel, 121
Debussy, Eugène-Octave, 121
Debussy, la musique et les arts (exhibition), 62
Debussy, Lilly, 148, 149. *See* Texier, Lilly
Debussy, Manuel-Achille, 18, 120, 136
Degas, Edgar, 66, 99, 100, 141, 221
   Foyer de danse, 30
   Henri Rouart et sa fille Hélène, 120
Delage, Maurice, 11
Delarue-Mardrus, Lucie, 36, 37, 39–42
Delibes, Léo, 183, 222
   Lakmé, 28, 183
Delius, Frederick
   Paris: The Song of a Great City, 14
Delmet, Paul, 195
Delville, Jean, 66
Denis, Maurice, 12, 66, 80, 82, 83, 100, 137, 145, 202, 203
Denny, Martin
   Romantica, 306
   Taste of Honey, A, 306
Derain, André, 84
   Baigneuses, 84
Déroulède, Paul, 16
Désormière, Roger, 280
DeSoye, Louise, 99
Diaghilev, Sergei, 30, 31, 176, 200, 217, 221, 226, 227
Dickens, Charles, 55
Dickinson, Emily, 245
Diémer, Louis, 288
Donizetti, Gaetano, 182
Donnay, Auguste, 65
Doret, Gustave, 309
Doudelet, Charles, 64, 66
Dreyfus affair, 16, 17, 21, 26, 202
Dreyfus, Captain Alfred, 21
Droz, Gustave
   Monsieur, madame et bébé, 120
Ducasse, Roger, 208
Duchamp, Marcel, 84
Dufourt, Hughes, 304
Dugazon, Louise-Rosalie, 181
Dujardin, Édouard, 94
Dukas, Paul, 74, 94, 112, 135, 139, 150, 154, 156, 157, 161, 184, 201, 232, 242, 244, 288
   Apprenti sorcier, L', 155, 156

Dukas, Paul (cont.)
   Ariane et Barbe-bleue, 155, 156
   Péri, La, 155, 158
   Symphony, 156, 237
Dumas, Alexandre
   Dame de Monsoreau, La, 194
Dumesnil, Maurice, 260, 262, 264, 275
Dumont, Auguste, 204
Dun, Tan, 304
Duncan, Isadora, 35, 224, 225, 226
Duparc, Henri
   'Invitation au voyage, L'', 73
   'Vie antérieure, La', 73
   songs, 252
Dupont, Gabrielle, 45, 47, 131, 132, 133, 277
Dupont Paul (publisher), 143, 145
Durand (publisher), 104, 105, 143, 144, 146, 148, 149, 171, 172, 174, 175, 242, 279, 287, 288, 310
Durand, Auguste, 143, 144, 149
Durand, Jacques, 37, 54, 98, 124, 143, 144, 148, 173, 174, 175, 242, 259, 261, 268, 307, 309
Durand, Marguerite, 37
Durand-Schoenewerk, 143
Duret, Théodore, 99
Dutilleux, Henri
   Ainsi la nuit, 245

École française d'Athènes, 11
École Niedermeyer, 285
Écorcheville, Jules, 206, 287
Éden-Concert, 195
Éden-Théâtre, 90, 91, 197
Eiffel Tower, 9, 307
Eimert, Herbert, 304
Eldorado, 195
Elgar, Edward, 23
Elks, Mr and Mrs, 197
Ellington, 'Duke', 291
Élysée Montmartre, 198
Emmanuel, Maurice, 88, 109
Ensor, James
   Russian Music, 66, 67
Entr'acte, 157
Érard, 262, 293, 294
Erlanger, Camille, 182, 216
Escape from New York, 305
Escudier, Philippe, 92
Esquivel, Juan Garcia
   Infinity in Sound, 306
Étienne-Marcel, 144
E. Fromont (publisher). *See* Froment
Euterpe, L', 282
Evans, Bill, 291, 305
Evans, Edwin, 274

Exposition Universelle (1867), 99
Exposition Universelle (1878), 9, 51
Exposition Universelle (1889), 9, 10, 11, 29, 102, 213, 263, 288, 304
Exposition Universelle (1900), 5, 6, 9, 11, 22, 29, 30, 45, 49, 50, 99, 102, 197
Expositions Universelles, 11, 12, 52, 81, 99, 106

Falla, Manuel de, 32, 304
   Noches en los jardines de España, 32
Fantasia, 305
Fantin-Latour, Henri, 99, 100
   Autour du piano, 95
Fargue, Léon-Paul, 262
Farrenc, Aristide and Louise, 288
Fauré, Gabriel, 7, 72, 74, 76, 109, 123, 150, 153, 154, 155, 157, 170, 171, 189, 202, 243, 244, 252, 253, 258
   'Chant d'automne', 73
   'Clair de lune', 72
   'Hymne', 73
   'Rançon, La', 73
   Bonne Chanson, La, 72, 252, 277
   chamber works, 241
   Chanson d'Ève, La, 75, 252
   Cinq mélodies 'de Venise', 72
   Horizon chimérique, L', 253
   Hymne à Apollon, 109
   Jardin clos, Le, 75, 253
   Mirages, 253
   Pelléas et Mélisande, 75
   Poème d'un jour, 253
   songs, 252
Fauré, Gabriel and André Messager
   Souvenirs de Bayreuth, 15
Fauvism, 80, 83–4, 86
Fénéon, Félix, 202
Ferroud, Pierre-Octave
   Au parc Monceau, 14
Féval, Paul
   Bossu, Le, 194
Fibonacci series, 108
First World War, 3, 16, 17, 26, 32, 37, 77, 86, 95, 99, 112, 124, 170, 172, 176, 188, 190, 242, 273, 309
Five, The, 11
Flaubert, Gustave
   Madame Bovary, 302
Flaxland, 46
Fleury, Hélène, 34
Flight Facilities, 306
Fokine, Mikhail, 218
Folies-Bergère, 9, 47, 195–6, 197, 221
Folies-Nouvelles, 178
Fontaine, Lucien and Arthur, 289

Index

Foottit et Chocolat, 197
Forain, Jean-Louis, 221
Fort, Paul, 70
Fourrier, Camille, 43
Franck circle. *See bande à Franck*
Franck, César, 95, 146, 169, 188, 190, 191, 211, 215, 230, 237, 241, 286
   Chasseur maudit, Le, 231
   Djinns, Les, 231
   Piano Quintet, 241
   Piano Trio No.2, 240
   String Quartet, 241
   Symphony, 237, 238, 239
   Violin Sonata, 241
Franco-Prussian War, 17, 18, 27, 29, 99, 118, 120, 125, 159, 178, 186, 222, 240
Frankie and Johnny, 305
Frenchman's Creek, 305
Freud, Siegmund, 117
Fromont (publisher), 145, 146, 147
Fuchs, Edmond and Henriette, 282
Fuchs, Henriette, 171, 283
Fuller, Loie, 175, 196, 223
Futurism, 80

Gaîté, 194
Galerie Durand-Ruel, 12, 285
Galerie Vivienne, 283
Gallet, Louis, 180, 212
gamelan, Balinese, 264
gamelan, Javanese, 11, 29, 102, 103, 111, 263, 264, 310
Ganne, Louis
   Marche lorraine, 207, 248
Garden, Mary, 63, 124, 147, 248, 249, 250, 273, 275, 277, 279, 300
   recordings with Debussy, 14, 275, 278, 279, 280, 307
Garibaldi, Giuseppe, 19
Garnier, Charles, 8, 181
Gauguin, Paul, 28, 100
Gaulle, Charles de, 17
Gauthier-Villars, Henry, 38
Gautier, Théophile, 32, 100, 252
   Constantinople, 28
Geisha and the Samurai, The, 102
Gershwin, George, 305
   American in Paris, An, 14
Gervex, Henri
   Cinq heures chez Paquin, 50
   soir de grand prix au pavillon d'Armenonville, Un, 50
Gesamtkunstwerk, 93, 95, 217, 226, 236
Ghéon, Henri, 203
Ghil, René, 70

Ghilbert, René François. *See* Ghil, René
Giant, 305
Gide, André, 7, 73, 141, 145, 203, 207
Gieseking, Walter, 300
Giraud, Albert
   Pierrot lunaire, 76
Glasgow School of Art, 66
Glass, Philip, 304
Glazunov, Alexander, 11, 30
Glinka, Mikhail, 11, 32
Gluck, Christoph Willibald, 95, 112, 178, 185
Godet, Robert, 80, 81, 86, 144, 207, 309
Goethe, Johann Wolfgang von
   Faust, 73
Golden Section, 108
Goncourt, Edmond and Jules de, 100
Goncourt, Edmond de, 99
Goncourt, Jules de, 99
Gounod, Charles, 164, 178, 215, 250
   Roméo et Juliette, 183
   songs, 252
Gourmont, Remy de, 204
   Idéalisme, L', 70
Grand Café, 9
grand opéra, 151, 177, 178, 180, 182
Grand Palais, 9
Grand Prix (Longchamp), 50
Grandmougin, Charles, 253
Greenwich Mean Time, 52
Greffulhe, Countess Élisabeth, 46, 282
Gregorian chant, 95, 106, 111, 113
Grétry, André, 181
Grieg, Edvard, 173
   String Quartet No.1, 241, 246
Grisey, Gérard, 304
Grisi, Carlotta, 222
Gros, Antoine-Jean, 99
Groux, Henry de, 65, 81
Guilbert, Yvette, 195, 249–50, 251, 253
Guilmant, Alexandre, 288
Guimard, Hector
   édicules, 5, 12
Guimet, Émile Étienne, 99
Guiraud, Ernest, 143, 150, 155, 157, 171, 213, 214
   Chasse fantastique, 151
   David, 150
   Suite d'orchestre, 151
   Traité pratique d'instrumentation, 151–2
Guiraud, Ernest (completed Dukas and Saint-Saëns)
   Frédégonde, 151, 152
Guiraud, Jean-Baptiste, 150

Hachette (publisher), 12
Hagenbeck, Carl, 47

Haguenauer, Jean-Louis, 294
Hahn, Reynaldo, 7, 39, 182, 255
   Chansons et madrigaux, 255
   Chansons grises, 255
   Rondels, 255, 256
Halévy, Fromental, 150, 182
   Juive, La, 151
   Reine de Chypre, La, 151
Hall, Elise, 208
Hamelle (publisher), 145, 171
Handel, George Frideric, 185, 282
   Israel in Egypt, 282
   Judas Maccabeus, 282
   Messiah, 282
   Saul, 282
Hanotaux, Gabriel, 204
Harbison, John, 304
Harcourt, Eugène d', 284
Hartmann (publisher), 143, 146
Hartmann, Arthur, 48, 49, 74
Hartmann, Georges, 131, 143, 146, 147, 149, 172, 184
Hartmann, Marie, 48
Haussmann, Georges-Eugène, 4, 5, 7, 8, 45
Haydn, Josef, 206, 230, 232, 235, 236, 272
Hellé, André, 228, 229
Henry, Charles, 108, 137
Henry, Pierre, 303
Heredia, José Maria de, 203
Hermant, Abel, 205
Herrmann, Bernard, 305–6
Hersch, Fred, 291, 305
Hervé, 177, 194
Hervilly, Ernest d'
   Belle Saïnara, La, 100
Hétu, Jacques
   Sonata for Thirteen Instruments, 246
Heugel (publisher), 143, 146
hispanophilie, 32
Hokusai, Katsushika
   Kanagawa oki nami ura, 98, 103, 310
   Thirty-Six Views of Mount Fuji, 101
Holmès, Augusta
   Irlande, 231
   Montagne noire, La, 212
Hough, Stephen, 305
Hüe, Georges, 161
Hugo, Victor
   Orientales, Les, 28
Huysmans, Joris-Karl, 100, 102
   À rebours, 93, 100, 138
   Croquis parisiens, 6
Hydropathes, 136
Hyspa, Vincent, 7, 136

Imbert, Hugues, 38
Immerseel, Jos van, 293, 294, 296
Imperial Academy of Arts, 30
Impressionism, 69, 80, 81, 82, 106, 120, 238, 261, 285
Indy, Vincent d', 75, 83, 95, 112, 152, 166, 188, 189, 212, 215, 230, 237, 244, 284, 286, 288
   chamber works, 241
   Étranger, L', 95, 206, 212
   Fervaal, 66, 95, 179
   Symphonie sur un chant montagnard, 166
   symphonies, 237
   Symphony No.2, 239
   Wallenstein trilogy, 231
Ingegneri, Marc'Antonio, 284
Inghelbrecht, Désiré-Émile, 176, 277
Institut de France, 154, 163, 166
Irish and American Bar, 9
Isle, Leconte de l'
   Elfes, Les, 82
Isle-Adam, Villiers de l', 137
Isola, Émile and Vincent, 179

Jammes, Francis, 203, 252
Janequin, Clément
   vocal music, 112
Japonism, 12, 27, 28
Jaques-Dalcroze, Émile, 227
Jardin d'acclimatation, 46, 47
Jarrett, Keith, 305
Jaurès, Jean, 16
Jauss, Hans Robert, 17
Jean-Aubry, Georges, 31, 206
Jeanne d'Arc, 25
Jhouney, Alber, 107
Josquin des Prez, 282
Jounet, Albert, 79
Jules Ferry Laws, 20, 119, 121
Jullien, Adolphe, 288
Jusseaume, Lucien, 64

Kahn, Gustave, 70
Kandinsky, Wassily, 31, 83, 84, 213, 307
Kant, Immanuel, 70
Karsavina, Tamar, 227
Ken Darby Singers, 305
Khnopff, Fernand, 67
   Listening to Flowers, 67
   Listening to Schumann, 67
King Albert's Book, 23
Kipling, Rudyard
   Jungle Book, The, 54
Klimt, Gustav, 84
Klingsor, Tristan, 203, 254

Index

Kodály, Zoltán
  chamber works, 245
Koechlin, Charles, 30, 175, 189, 201, 224, 243
  chamber works, 243
Koussevitzky, Serge, 173
Krüger, Wilhelm, 160

La Vine, General, 197
Labenche Museum, 294
Lacerda, Francisco de, 112
Laforgue, Jules, 60
Lalo, Édouard
  chamber works, 241
  Namouna, 222, 226
  Namouna Suite, 223
  songs, 252
  Symphonie espagnole, 31
Lalo, Pierre, 38, 190, 212, 223, 243, 289
Laloy, Louis, 20, 43, 61, 206, 223, 287
Lamoureux, Charles, 89, 90, 91, 95, 190, 191, 231, 282
Landormy, Paul, 59
Landowska, Wanda, 112
Lange-Müller, Peter Erasmus
  Lamentation, 23
Laoureux, Denis, 65
Lapin Agile, 198
Lascoux, Antoine, 91, 95
Lassus, Orlande de, 282, 286
Lavignac, Albert, 88, 89, 92
Lavine, Edward, 9
Lecocq, Jacques
  Kosiki, 100
Lefeuve, Mr and Mrs Gabriel, 42
Lejeun, Claude
  vocal music, 112
Lekeu, Guillaume
  Piano Quartet, 173
Leoncavallo, Ruggero, 179
Lerberghe, Charles van, 75, 252, 253
Lerolle, Henry, 63, 80, 83, 128, 172, 289, 309
Leroux, Xavier, 161, 169, 233
Lesage, Alain-René, 204
Lesure, François, 300
Levadé, Marguerite, 36, 37, 42
Liadov, Anatoly, 11
Librairie de l'Art indépendant, 7, 12, 73, 102, 107, 108, 109, 137, 138, 140, 145, 203
Lidell, Jamie, 303
Liebich, Louise, 262
Limite, 305
Liszt, Franz, 154, 159, 177, 231, 260, 264, 265, 271, 292
  Mazeppa, 231
  Préludes, Les, 231

Tasso, 231
  transcriptions, 266
Lockspeiser, Edward, 68
Locle, Camille du, 183
Loevendie, Theo
  Golliwog's Other Dances, 246
Loewenstein family, 172
Loewenstein, Alice. *See* Peter, Alice
Long, Marguerite, 258, 271
Longy, Georges, 208
Lothe, André, 84
Loti, Pierre, 100
Loubet, President, 21
Louis XVIII, 5
Loussier, Jacques, 291
Louvre, 11, 224
Louÿs, Pierre, 6, 11, 16, 73, 80, 83, 107, 109, 130, 137, 139–40, 141, 145, 147, 172, 173, 196, 202, 203, 253, 256, 309
  Aphrodite: Mœurs antiques, 110, 140
  Chansons de Bilitis, 140
Lubimov, Alexei, 293
Lucier, Alvin, 303
Ludwig II, 170
Lugné-Poe, Aurélien-Marie, 63, 64, 75, 180, 217
Lully, Jean-Baptiste, 112
  operas, 112
  Psyché, 151
Lumière, Auguste and Louis, 9
Lutosławski, Witold, 299, 304
  Grave: Metamorphoses for Cello and Piano, 245
Lyman, Arthur
  Ilikai, 306

MacMahon, Patrice de, 120
MacQueen, Scott, 305
Maeterlinck, Maurice, 59, 63–6, 67, 75, 80, 101, 155
  Aveugles, Les, 65
  Intérieur, 66
  Pelléas et Mélisande, 8, 32, 63, 64, 65, 66, 67, 75, 82, 180, 184
  poems, 66
  Princesse Maleine, La, 64, 75
  Serres chaudes, 153
  Trois petits drames pour marionnettes, 65
Magnard, Albéric, 215
  Bérénice, 95
  Guercœur, 95, 212
  Yolande, 212
Mahler, Gustav, 294
Maison de l'Art Nouveau, 12, 80, 99
Make Mine Music, 305
Malherbe, Charles, 289

Mallarmé, Stéphane, 47, 48, 64, 67, 70, 71, 74, 80, 94, 100, 102, 107, 138, 142, 179, 192, 203, 218, 223, 254, 255, 283, 284
   'Hommage à Wagner', 94
   Apparition, 94, 142
   Après-midi d'un faune, L', 68, 74, 82, 94, 109, 110, 142, 231, 232
   Hérodiade, 69
   'Mardis de Mallarmé'. *See* Mallarmé, Stéphane: salon
   salon, 7, 73, 74, 102, 141
Man on Fire, 305
Manet, Édouard, 99, 100, 139
   Bar aux Folies-Bergère, Un, 221
   Déjeuner sur l'herbe, Le, 67
Mangurekan, 303
Manoury, Victorine, 120, 121
Marchetti (publisher), 12
Marmontel, Antoine, 91, 121, 260
Marnold, Jean, 38, 243
Marot, Clément, 255
Marsalis, Branford, 291
Martin, Nicolas-Jean-Blaise, 181
Marty, Georges, 169, 233
Mascagni, Pietro, 179
   Cavalleria rusticana, 216
   Sunt lacrimae rerum!, 23
Massenet, Jules, 40–1, 113, 146, 162, 163, 179, 182, 183, 184, 190, 203, 212, 215, 243, 244, 253, 266
   Cendrillon, 215
   Cid, Le, 214
   Esclarmonde, 96, 215
   Ève, 215
   Grisélidis, 215
   Madame Chrysanthème, 100
   Manon, 41, 183, 215
   Marie-Magdeleine, 215
   Navarraise, La, 215
   Poème du souvenir, 252
   Sapho, 215
   Thaïs, 212, 215
   Werther, 41, 96, 215
Matisse, Henri, 84
   Danse, La, 84
   Jeune Marin II, Le, 84
   Musique, La, 84
Mauclair, Camille, 60
Maupassant, Guy de, 205
Maus, Octave, 82
Mauté de Fleurville, Antoinette-Flore, 19, 72, 135, 159, 161, 259, 260, 271
Max, Cécile, 36, 37, 39
Meck, Nadezhda von, 11, 29, 32, 36, 52, 220, 241
Mellery, Xavier

The Hours: Eternity and Death, 66
Melnikov, Alexander, 293
Mendelssohn, Felix, 185, 230, 236
   'Spring Song', 225
Mendès, Catulle, 7, 32, 80, 92, 145, 173, 182, 251, 255
Méreaux, Amédée, 288
Mérode, Cléo de, 196
Messager, André, 7, 146, 182, 184, 208, 273, 279
   'Pour la patrie', 24
   Madame Chrysanthème, 184
Messiaen, Olivier, 258, 299, 303
   Quatuor pour la fin du temps, 245
Métra, Olivier
   Yedda, 100
metronome markings, 274
Métropolitain. *See* Paris Métro
Meyerbeer, Giacomo, 159, 182, 214
   Huguenots, Les, 214
   Prophète, Le, 214
Michelin, 52
minimalism, 304
Minne, George, 64–5
   Saintes Femmes au tombeau, Les, 64
Mirbeau, Octave, 75
Mirliton, 198
Misme, Jane, 42
Missa, Edmond, 161
Mistinguette, 195
Modernism, 113, 230, 231, 303
Molinari, Bernardino, 86
Monet, Claude, 52, 60, 61, 99, 100, 141, 261
   Lever du soleil, 59
   Rouen Cathedral series, 101
Monsieur Croche, 43, 60, 180, 207, 307
Monte-Carlo Opéra, 179
Montesquiou, Robert de, 72, 100
Monteux, Pierre, 300
Monteverdi, Claudio
   Orfeo, 151
Morand, Paul, 254
Moréas, Jean, 70, 73, 79
   Cantilènes, Les, 71
Moreau, Gustave, 66, 100, 141
Morice, Charles, 79
Mortier, Alfred, 11
Moskowa, Prince de la, 285
Moulin de la Galette, 198
Moulin Rouge, 9, 198, 221
Mourey, Gabriel, 138
Moyse, Emma. *See* Bardac, Emma
Mozart, Wolfgang Amadeus, 22, 178, 230, 233, 236, 272, 299
   Symphony No.31, 151
Murail, Tristan, 304

Index

Musée Carnavalet, 12
Musée Cernuschi, 12
Musée Debussy, 105
Musée des arts décoratifs, 12, 51
Musée Guimet, 12
Musée Gustave Moreau, 12
Musée indochinois, 11
Musset, Alfred de, 32
   Arabian Nights, The, 226
Mussorgsky, Modest, 11, 29, 44, 213
   Boris Godunov, 27, 267

Nabis, 12, 49, 82, 100, 202
Napoleon I, 8
Napoleon III, 4, 7, 8, 17, 19, 25, 181
Natanson, Alexandre, Louis-Alfred, and Thadée, 202
Naturalism, 69, 80, 83, 102, 216–17
Nectoux, Jean-Michel, 62
neoclassicism, 255
Neo-Impressionism, 80, 82
Nerval, Gérard de
   Voyage en orient, 28
Neumann, Angelo, 90
New York Philharmonic, 271
Niedermeyer, Louis
   songs, 252
Nietzsche, Friedrich
   Nietzsche contra Wagner, 29
Nijinsky, Vaslav, 30, 35, 158, 175, 218, 225, 226, 227, 228
Nikisch, Arthur, 276
Norrington, Roger, 294
Nouveau Cirque, 15, 197
Nouveau Théâtre-Lyrique, 8
Nouveau-Théâtre, 195, 197
Nuncques, William Degouve de, 65, 66

Obsession, 306
Ocean's Eleven, 305
Ocean's Thirteen, 305
Ochs, Robert L., 41
Odéro, Louis, 203
Offenbach, Jacques, 89, 178, 194, 221
   cancans, 221
   Contes d'Hoffmann, Les, 183
Offenbach, Jacques (completed Guiraud)
   Contes d'Hoffmann, Les, 150
Ollendorff, Paul, 205
Olympia, 9, 195, 196, 197
opéra comique, 90, 219
Opéra Garnier, 8, 23, 30, 89, 91, 92, 169, 177, 178, 179, 180, 181, 182, 194, 212, 213, 214, 221, 222, 249, 271, 289

Opéra-Comique, 8, 39, 63, 64, 90, 100, 146, 148, 169, 172, 175, 177, 178, 179, 180, 181, 182, 212, 216, 249, 273, 299
Orchestra of the Age of Enlightenment, 294
Orchestre Révolutionnaire et Romantique, 294
Orfer, Kahn and Léo d', 71
Orledge, Robert, 68
   sonata for oboe, horn, and harpsichord, 246
Orphism, 80, 83
Orsini bombing, 181
Ozanne, Abel Duteil d', 282

Pachulsky, Ladislas, 241
Paderewski, Ignacy Jan, 173
Palace Theatre, 225
Palais de Glace, 46
Palais du Trocadéro, 9, 11, 12
Palais Garnier. *See* Opéra Garnier
paléophone, 136
Palestrina, Giovanni Pierluigi da, 11, 95, 112, 213, 282, 284, 286, 289
   counterpoint, 106, 111
   Missa Papae Marcelli, 285
   Stabat Mater, 284
Panasonic SV-38000, 303
Papadhiamandopoulos, Ioannis. *See* Moréas, Jean
Paquin, Jeanne, 50
Paris Commune, 3, 11, 17, 19, 118, 120, 136, 179, 186
Paris Conservatoire. *See* Conservatoire (Paris)
Paris Métro, 5, 6, 45, 307
Paris Opéra. *See* Opéra Garnier
Parisiana, 195
Parnassianism, 68, 69, 70, 71, 81, 82, 102
Parny, Évariste de, 254
Pasdeloup, Jules, 89, 90, 186, 189, 190, 282
Pathé, 14
Paulen, Paul, 303
Pavillon Chinois, 51
Péladan, Joséphin, 108, 137, 138
   Fils des étoiles, Le, 108
Péladan, Sâr, 285
Périvier, Antonin, 205
Perle, George, 303
Perrot, Jules, 222
Perruchot, Louis-Lazare, 285
Perry, Matthew C., 98
Pessard, Émile, 182
Peter, Alice, 133, 134
Peter, Michel, 130
Peter, René, 7, 8, 130, 172, 248, 251, 255
Petipa, Marius, 30
Petit Journal, Le, 9
Petit Palais, 9

Petit-Théâtre de la Marionnette, 283
Pfeiffer, Georges, 160
Piau, Sandrine, 294
Picabia, Francis, 83
Picasso, Pablo, 157, 193, 221
Pierné, Gabriel, 161, 162, 164, 165, 169, 170, 243,
    244, 260, 272, 276
  chamber works, 243
Pissarro, Camille, 60, 62, 82, 100
Planès, Alain, 293, 294
Planté, Francis, 284
Plato, 70
Pleyel, 293
Pleyel, Wolff et Cie, 160
Poe, Edgar Allan, 138, 139, 149, 174, 175, 212
  Fall of the House of Usher, The, 139
  Philosophy of Composition, The, 139
  Raven, The, 139
Poe, Edgar Allan (trans. Baudelaire)
  Histoires extraordinaires, 139
Poe, Edgar Allan (trans. Mallarmé)
  Corbeau, Le, 139
Poincaré, Raymond, 22
Polignac, Princesse de, 46, 284, 286
Poniatowski, André, 51, 286
Popelin, Gustave, 127
portamento, 279
Porte chinoise, La, 99
Porte Saint-Martin, 194
Portrait of Jennie, 305
Pougin, Arthur, 288, 289
Pougy, Liane de, 196
Poulet, Gaston, 242
Pre-Raphaelitism, 9, 66, 81
Primoli, Count Guiseppe, 62
Prix de Rome, 20, 26, 29, 34, 71, 74, 96, 126, 143, 145,
    150, 151, 155, 162, 165, 166, 169, 171, 175, 179,
    180, 214, 233, 243, 244, 260, 272, 282,
    286, 307
Proust, Marcel, 100, 204, 255
  À la recherche du temps perdu, 72
Puccini, Giacomo, 179
  Bohème, La, 216
  Madame Butterfly, 100
  Tosca, 216
Pugno, Raoul, 173
Pulszky, Romola de, 227
Purge, The, 305

Quittard, Henri
  Noces de Sathan, Les, 107

Rachmaninov, Sergei, 30
Rackham, Arthur, 55
Rameau, Jean-Philippe, 25, 109, 112, 154, 263, 288–9

Acanthe et Céphise Overture, 151
Castor et Pollux, 23, 281, 288
complete edition, 112, 287, 289
Fêtes de Polymnie, Les, 112
Guirlande, La, 289
Hippolyte et Aricie, 289
Œuvres complètes, 154
Rameau, Jean-Philippe (ed. Debussy)
  Fêtes de Polymnie, Les, 154, 287
Rancière, Jacques, 223
Raunay, Jeanne, 43
Ravel, Maurice, 7, 11, 35, 76, 139, 142, 170, 189,
    243, 244, 252, 258, 261, 271, 272, 278,
    294, 295
  'Sainte', 76, 255
  'Un grand sommeil noir', 255
  Boléro, 271
  chamber works, 242
  Chansons madécasses, 254
  Cinq mélodies populaires grecques, 254
  Deux épigrammes de Clément Marot, 255
  Deux mélodies hébraïques, 254
  Don Quichotte à Dulcinée, 254
  Histoires naturelles, 254
  Jeux d'eau, 261
  Ma mère l'Oye, 174
  Piano Concerto in G, 271
  Rapsodie espagnole, 32
  Shéhérazade, 254
  String Quartet, 242
  Trois poèmes de Stéphane Mallarmé, 76, 254
  'Soupir', 76
  Valses nobles et sentimentales, 174
realism, 59, 102, 221
Redon, Ernest, 62
Redon, Odilon, 62, 80, 100, 141
Régnier, Henri de, 7, 73, 80, 137, 145, 203, 204
Reich, Steve
  Music for 18 Musicians, 304
Remy, Marcel
  Vision of Salome, The, 224, 225
Renan, Ernest, 187
Renaud, Madeleine, 135
Renoir, Pierre-Auguste, 141, 221
Reyer, Ernest, 214
Rilke, Rainer Maria, 141
Rimsky-Korsakov, Nikolai, 11, 30
  Capriccio espagnol, 173
  Scheherazade, 218, 226
Rivière, Jacques, 207
Robert, Paul, 7
Roberts, Mary Louise, 36
Rodin, Auguste, 141
Roger, Thérèse, 129, 130, 131, 132, 133, 277
Roger-Ducasse, Jean, 170, 243, 244

Index

chamber works, 243
Rollinat, Maurice, 43
Romilly, Madame Gérard de, 259, 264
Romilly, Michèle Worms de, 172
Ropartz, Guy, 244
   chamber works, 244
Rose+Croix, 64, 108, 138, 285, 286
Rosoor, Louis, 275
Rossetti, Dante Gabriel, 67, 82
   Blessed Damozel, The, 66
Rossini, Gioachino, 182
   William Tell, Overture, 151
Rostropovich, Mstislav, 245
Roth, François-Xavier, 295
Rouché, Jacques, 180
Rouquairol, madame, 92
Rousseau, Jean-Jacques
   Confessions, 117
Rousseau, Samuel, 38
Roussel, Alfred
   chamber works, 244
Rubinstein, Ida, 20, 175, 176, 218, 224, 225
Ruskin, John, 204
Russo-Japanese War, 99
Russolo, Luigi
   Art des bruits, L', 85
   Dynamique d'une automobile, 85

Sachs, Benno, 303
Saint-Aubin, Émile de, 92
Saint-Léon, Arthur, 222
Saint-Marceaux, Marguerite de, 7, 46
Saint-Saëns, Camille, 29, 95, 112, 146, 150, 157, 164, 171, 173, 180, 187, 188, 190, 191, 203, 214, 230, 237, 265, 288
   Africa, 28
   Ascanio, 96
   Barbares, Les, 180, 214
   Carnaval des animaux, Le, 241
   chamber works, 241
   Déluge, Le, Prelude, 279
   Henry VIII, 96, 214
   Pallas Athéné, 111
   Phryné, 111
   Princesse jaune, La, 100
   Rouet d'Omphale, Le, 232
   Six études pour la main gauche, 174
   symphonic poems, 231
   symphonies, 237
   Symphony No.3, 238, 239
Saint-Saëns, Camille (arr. Debussy)
   Airs de ballet by Étienne Marcel, 144
   Caprice pour piano sur les airs de ballet d'Alceste de Glück, 144
   Introduction et rondo capriccioso, 144

   Symphony No.2, 144, 171, 242
Saint-Saëns, Camille (arr. Fauré)
   Suite algérienne, La, 171
Saint-Saëns, Camille (arr. Guiraud)
   symphonic poems, 171
Sakamoto, Ryuichi, 303
Salabert (publisher), 12
Salle d'Harcourt, 288
Salle Érard, 187
Salle Favart, 183
Salle Gaveau, 173, 187
Salle Le Peletier, 181
Salle Pleyel, 187
Salmon, Jacques, 242
Salon d'automne, 81, 84
Salon de la libre esthétique, 82
Salon des Beaux Arts, 67
Salon des indépendants, 83
Salon des refusés, 67
Salon des XX, 82
Sangalli, Rita, 222
Sappho, 140
Sardou, Victorien, 180
Satie, Erik, 7, 35, 61, 62, 67, 80, 108, 113, 135, 136, 137, 150, 199, 228
   'Chez le docteur', 136
   'Tendrement', 136
   Entr'acte, 157
   Parade, 136, 157, 221, 228
   Prélude de la porte héroïque du ciel, 138
   Sonneries de la Rose+Croix, 108
   Trois mélodies, 253
   Uspud, 108
Savard, Augustin, 161
Savino, Domenico
   'Moonlight Love', 306
Scala, 195
Schmitt, Florent, 244
   chamber works, 244
   Cleopatra, 218
Schoenberg, Arnold, 254, 277, 278, 303
   Pierrot lunaire, 76, 228
Schola Cantorum, 244, 256, 281, 284, 289
Schopenhauer, Arthur, 70, 73
Schott (publisher), 146
Schubert, Franz, 22, 299
   Lieder, 252
Schumann, Robert, 154, 185, 230, 236, 259, 265, 292
   Lieder, 252
   Piano Sonata No.2, 260
   Symphony No.4, 237
Schumann, Robert (arr. Debussy)
   Six études en forme de canon pour piano ou orgue à pédales, 144, 171

Schwabe, Carlos, 66
  Evening Bells, 66
  Fate, 66
  Hymne, 66
  Mort, 66
  Sadness, 66
Scriabin, Alexander, 30
Scribe, Eugène, 90, 214
secessionism, 66
Second World War, 306
Segalen, Victor, 80, 83, 140
Sérieyx, Auguste, 207
Sérusier, Paul, 82
Seurat, Georges, 61, 100
Séverac, Déodat de, 35, 204
Shakespeare, William, 75, 218
Shelley, Percy Bysshe, 79
Sheng, Bright, 304
Siècles, Les, 294, 295
Signac, Paul, 60, 61, 82, 100
Silvestre, Armand, 252
Singer Manufacturing Company, 46
Sivry, Charles de, 18, 72, 135, 136
Six, Les, 245
Smyth, Ethel
  March of the Women, The, 23
SNM. *See* Société nationale de musique
Société Bourgault-Ducoudray, 282
Société d'ethnographie, 284
Société des auteurs, compositeurs et éditeurs de musique, 146
Société des concerts de musique vocale classique, 285
Société des concerts du Conservatoire, 169, 185, 189, 190, 191, 192, 230, 236, 282, 288
Société des grandes auditions musicales, 282
Société des instruments anciens, 288
Société japonaise du Jinglar de Sèvres, 99
Société nationale de musique, 21, 27, 72, 74, 95, 152, 153, 173, 178, 208, 240, 241, 286
Société Saint-Jean, 284
Solesmes, 111, 287
Soucho, Victor, 146
Sousa, John Philip, 11, 197
spectralism, 304
Spillaert, Léon, 65
Steinway, 293
Stevens, Alfred, 129
Stevens, Catherine, 130, 131, 133, 134
Stockhausen, Karlheinz, 304
Strauss, Richard
  Ariadne auf Naxos, 228
  Heldenleben, Ein, 9
  Till Eulenspiegel, 9

Stravinsky, Igor, 30, 31, 54, 80, 245, 277, 295, 299, 303
  Firebird, The, 30, 200, 218, 226, 272, 295
  Fireworks, 293
  Oiseau de feu, L'. *See Firebird, The*
  Petrushka, 30, 31, 200, 218, 226, 228
  Rite of Spring, The, 76, 218, 226, 227, 267
  Russian ballets, 294
  Sacre du printemps, Le. *See Rite of Spring, The*
  Three Japanese Lyrics, 76, 103
Surrealism, 228
Symbolism, 7, 59, 60, 61, 63, 65, 66, 79, 80, 81, 82, 102, 104, 106, 107, 138, 141, 145, 181, 192, 196, 217, 221, 233, 234, 252, 283
synaesthesia, 93, 96
Szymanowski, Karol
  chamber works, 245

TableTopOpera, 245
  Scarred by the Somme, 246
Taffanel, Paul, 169
Taine, Hippolyte, 187
Takemitsu, Tōru, 245, 299, 304
  And Then I Knew 'Twas Wind, 245
Tarde, Gabriel, 204
Tchaikovsky, Pyotr Ilyich, 11, 29, 221
  Swan Lake, 220, 222
Terrasse, Claude, 203
  Sire de Vergy, Le, 194
Texier, Lilly, 19, 49, 53, 122, 123, 172, 174, 208, 308, 310
Teyte, Maggie, 249, 250, 255, 257, 300
Thaemlitz, Terre, 303
Théâtre Annamite, 102
Théâtre Antoine, 180
Théâtre cinématographe Pathé, 9
Théâtre d'Application, 109
Théâtre d'Orléans, 150, 151
Théâtre de l'art, 107
Théâtre de l'Impératrice, 8
Théâtre de l'œuvre, 64, 180
Théâtre de la Gaîté, 8, 194
Théâtre de la Porte Saint-Martin, 8, 194
Théâtre de la Ville, 8, 183
Théâtre des Arts, 180
Théâtre des Bouffes du Nord, 8
Théâtre des Bouffes-Parisiens, 8, 75, 178, 194, 221
Théâtre des Champs-Élysées, 223
Théâtre des Folies-Concertantes, 178
Théâtre des Folies-Dramatiques, 194
Théâtre des Nouveautés, 194
Théâtre des Variétés, 8, 194, 195
Théâtre du Château-d'Eau, 183
Théâtre du Châtelet, 8, 189, 194, 218

Index

Théâtre du Vaudeville, 8
Théâtre Libre, 7
Théâtre Marigny, 197
Théâtre national de l'Opéra. *See* Opéra Garnier
Théâtre royal de la Monnaie, 67, 179
Théâtre-Français, 8
Théâtre-Italien, 177, 179
Théâtre-Lyrique, 89, 178, 179, 183
Théâtre-Lyrique de la Gaîté, 179
Thiers, Adolphe, 18, 120
Thomas, Ambroise, 179
Tinan, Jean de, 137
Tissot, Victor, 89
Tokuyama, Minako, 304
  Sonata Japanesque for oboe, horn, and harpsichord, 246
Tomita, Isao
  Snowflakes Are Dancing, 306
Toscanini, Arturo, 271
Toulouse-Lautrec, Henri de, 61, 66, 100, 193, 198, 202, 221, 223, 249
  prints, 101
Tout Paris, 50
Toutain, Juliette, 34
Tower, Joan, 304
Tristan L'Hermite, 76, 254
Trochu, Louis-Jules, 17
Trouhanova, Natasha, 155
Truc, Georges, 280
Turner, William, 62, 261
Twilight, 305

Upton, Florence Kate
  Adventures of Two Dutch Dolls and a 'Golliwogg', The, 15

Vaillant, Auguste, 16
Valéry, Paul, 80, 141, 218
Vallin-Pardo, Ninon, 173
Vallotton, Félix, 49, 66, 82, 202
  Bon Marché, Le, 49
  Promenade de la mer à Étretat, La, 53
Van Gogh, Vincent, 100
Vanor, Georges, 70
Varèse, Edgard, 66, 299, 303
  chamber works, 245
  Density 21.5, 245
Vasnier, Henri, 127, 132, 286
Vasnier, Marie-Blanche, 20, 35, 68, 71, 128, 132, 133–4, 142, 253, 277
Vauxcelles, Louis, 83
Verdi, Giuseppe, 159, 182, 250, 294, 299
Verein für musikalische Privataufführungen, 245, 303
verismo, 216

Verlaine, Paul, 67, 70–1, 72–3, 74, 79, 100, 102, 108, 135, 141, 147, 203, 233, 252, 253, 255, 263, 266
  'C'est l'extase langoureuse', 253
  'En sourdine', 253
  Fêtes galantes, 63
  Poèmes saturniens, 71
Victoria, Tomás Luis de, 282, 284
Vidal, Paul, 121, 169, 233, 260, 283
Villa Medici, 6, 29, 33, 50, 74, 79, 127, 134, 163, 164, 165, 169, 286
Villard, Édouard, 202
Villars, Henry Gauthier, 205
Villon, François, 25, 76, 137, 251, 254
Viñes, Ricardo, 7, 32, 105, 108, 261
Vlaminck, Maurice de, 84
  Voiliers, 84
Vuillard, Édouard, 100
Vuillermoz, Émile, 25, 38, 44, 60, 174, 207

Waefelghem, Louis van, 288
Wagner, Richard, 15, 27, 70, 112, 151, 154, 155, 170, 179, 182, 185, 187, 190, 191, 204, 211, 212, 213, 214, 215–16, 217, 230, 236, 271, 279, 285, 299
  aesthetic, 61
  chromaticism, 77
  Götterdämmerung, 90, 151
  Judenthum in der Musik, Das, 89
  Kapitulation, Eine, 89
  leitmotif, 39
  Lohengrin, 90, 91, 215, 271
  Meistersinger von Nürnberg, Die, 52, 91, 93
    Prelude, 272
  music drama, 214, 219, 233
  Parsifal, 52, 66, 93, 97, 172, 207, 215, 216, 283
  Rheingold, Das, 173
  Rienzi, 89
  Ring des Nibelungen, Der, 92, 196, 216
  Siegfried, 92
    'Forest Murmurs', 233
  Tannhäuser, 89, 91, 93
    Overture, 88, 276
  Tristan und Isolde, 9, 15, 27, 52, 66, 88, 96, 97, 172, 215, 216
  Walküre, Die, 91
    Ride of the Valkyries, 223
Wagner, Richard (arr. Debussy)
  fliegende Holländer, Der, Overture, 144, 171
Wagnerism, 15, 27, 29, 76, 91, 92, 95, 151, 152–3, 155, 179, 187, 215, 253, 283
Waldeck-Rousseau Law, 19
Walker, Rudy and Fredy, 15
Walt Disney, 305

Watteau, Jean-Antoine, 63, 71
    Embarquement pour Cythère, L', 63, 274
    Fêtes galantes, 266
Weber, Carl Maria von, 178, 230
Welte-Mignon, 14, 278, 280, 307
Whistler, James Abbott McNeill, 64, 66, 99, 100, 141, 261
    Rose and Silver: The Princess from the Land of Porcelain, 100
Wilde, Oscar, 141
    Salomé, 225
Willette, Adolphe, 198
Willy, 202, 205. *See also* Henry Gauthier-Villars

Wilson, Marguerite, 91, 92
World's Fair. *See* Exposition Universelle
Worth, Charles-Frédéric, 49
Wyzewa, Téodor de, 94

Yakko, Sada, 102
Yeats, W. B., 141
Ysaÿe Quartet, 240, 241, 275
Ysaÿe, Eugène, 109, 275, 309

Ziloti, Alexandre, 173
Zola, Émile, 83, 85, 96, 99, 202, 205, 212, 217
Zweig, Stefan, 6

Printed in the United States
by Baker & Taylor Publisher Services